بِسْمِ ٱللَّهِ ٱلرَّحْمَٰنِ ٱلرَّحِيمِ

In the name of Allah, the Beneficent, the Merciful.

40 HADITH ON MASCULINITY

HOW TO BE A GOOD MAN

Nabeel Azeez
with Wordsmiths

ISBN: 978-1-7349208-9-5

Bonus: Claim Your Free Gift

As a “thank you” for purchasing 40 Hadith on Masculinity: How to Be a Good Man, we'd like to offer you a PDF copy of your book along with other exclusive bonuses, gratis.

To claim your free gift, simply email a copy of your receipt to hello@muslimman.com

Extra credit: We'd also be grateful if you'd post a picture of you holding your copy of the book on social media and tag @beamuslimman.

Acknowledgements

Praise be to Allah who made us Muslims and honored us over many of His creations. May Allah's blessings and peace be on our beloved prophet Muhammad, as many times as the mindful remember him and as many times as the heedless forget.

This book is dedicated to Shaheed Azeez. You were an old-school man who did what you had to do and never complained. You spent your entire life in service to your family, much of it away from us and alone. The last time I saw you alive, I thanked you for being my father and asked you to forgive me for all the times I wronged you and caused you pain. The next time I saw you, you'd gone to meet your Maker. The final time I saw you was when I turned your face to the Qibla after Irshad and I lowered you into your grave with our own hands. You were an excellent father. I was a terrible son. May Allah have mercy on you.

Jazakumullahu khairan and thank you to Dr. Salah Sharief and the entire Wordsmiths team. You went above and beyond in researching, translating, and editing this book. It wouldn't exist without you. Readers should check out your website, wordsmiths.org.uk.

Thank you to Kristin McTiernan, who got this book ready for publishing. You made my life easy. God bless you. Readers should check out your website, nonsensefreeeditor.com.

To non-Muslims who read this work, I invite you to convert to Islam and gain felicity in this life and the next.

Glory be to your Lord, the Lord of Might, beyond anything they describe. And peace be upon the Messengers. And praise be to Allah, the Lord of all the worlds.

Table of Contents

الحمد لله الذي خلق الإنسان وأنعمه بنعمة الرجولة، وزاده بسطة في العلم والقوة، والصلاة والسلام على سيد الأنام صاحب المروءة وأصحابه الذين اتبعوه بأبلغ الفتوة، أما بعد:

Praise belongs to Allah, Who has created man and bestowed upon him the gift of manliness, and has increased his stature in knowledge and strength. Allah's blessings be upon the leader of mankind, the perfect embodiment of manhood, and upon his Companions who followed his example with utmost chivalry. Thereafter:

INTRODUCTION

It is the subject of our age. What is a man and how should he behave? The question itself seems preposterous: why is this even a question? For men have existed as long as humankind has. Indeed, the first of us—the Prophet Adam ﷺ—was himself a man.

For all the many thousand years that mankind has lived and walked on this Earth, the term has never needed defining, nor did man's mode of proper comportment ever come into question. Men were expected to be upright, self-sufficient, interpersonal, and organised. In previous epochs and ages, it was the men who were the scholars, breadwinners, leaders, and warriors in their respective societies. They were confident in themselves and in their role in civilisation, and did not need to be told who and what they were, nor what was expected of them.

For the Western world this all changed in the Twentieth Century, as this was the period of 'liberation'. It brought about 'liberation' from all so-called 'social constructs', the breaking of which became the core value of Western society. In light of these changes epistemic misperceptions emerged, as the lines between men and women began to blur. In the twenty-first century, this has now become a global pandemic.

Masculinity in Crisis

Is manliness still a word of value and meaning? In the modern age, it seems to have lost its lustre. Men themselves are disappearing from the words of our language. We are no longer mankind, but rather humankind; no longer firemen, policemen, or clergymen, but simply 'persons'.

Make no mistake, masculinity in the West is in a state of crisis. For the modern Western man, there is no exclusive domain or space left to call his own. There is no bastion or refuge left in the place of work, on the field of sport, or even in the theatre of war. No longer the sole bread-winner, no longer the leader of his household, no longer even sure of what manhood means.

His mere presence is now considered 'toxic'. The very idea of 'him' is relegated to the aforementioned status of a mere 'social construct'. And consequently, he searches for meaning. He searches for a way to establish a sense of self, for a way to signify or help define who he is, and for a model or standard by which to know the truth of what it means to be a *Man*.

Of course, the Muslim man has long since had such a model and standard available to him: the noble life and sublime character of the Perfect Man ﷺ. Allah ﷻ tells us in the Qur'an:

لَّقَدْ كَانَ لَكُمْ فِى رَسُولِ ٱللَّهِ أُسْوَةٌ حَسَنَةٌ

There is indeed a good model for you in the Messenger of Allah...[1]

And yet, as the Prophet ﷺ told us, 'A man is upon the religion of his close companion, so let each of you carefully consider whom you take as a friend.'[2] Thus, living in an age of confusion amongst the confused, the modern Western Muslim has lost his way and found himself in a state of equal bewilderment, forgetting his heritage and falling prey to all the

---

[1] *Qur'an* 33:21.

[2] *Sunan Abī Dāwūd* 4833; *Jāmiʿ al-Tirmidhī* 2378.

same traps and patterns as others around him. He finds himself also asking what it means to be a man.

A Man Defined

To surmount the confusion and find some ground to make a decisive stand, it is best that we first define our terms to better understand what it means to be a man.

Evidently, being a man is about more than just having the correct anatomy. In the renowned classical lexicon, *Lisān al-ʿArab*, the word '*rajul*' (man) is defined in three ways: firstly, in opposition to femaleness, followed by opposition to adolescence, and then simply as someone born with a male physiognomy. A complete man must then be the triangulation of all three components: outward appearance, inner qualities, and physical nature. Thus, we can say that a man is an adult male who avoids effeminate behaviours and manifestations and sheds all childlike modes of self-centredness and dependency. Now, the question to ask ourselves is when we look at ourselves in the mirror, is there such a man staring back at us?

The man that modern media outlets and the dominant cultural discourse has created is unfortunately the opposite of the abovementioned qualities. He is highly feminised, infantilised, and ultimately neutered, thereby being nothing more than a timid adolescent in an adult body. He is Peter Pan: a man-child obsessed with puerile pursuits and hobbies, being concerned with games, gadgets, and sports.

He is preoccupied with self-gratification through play and entertainment, all the while ever-seeking the affirmation and endorsement of wider society. Tragically, the few men whose minds and souls see this for what it is and reject the role that society wants them to play still find themselves ensnared in yet another trap: the ploy of superficial masculinity.

Such men become obsessed with the aesthetics of manhood. They project a faux machismo and perpetuate another form of self-centred childishness. Rather than actually embodying the principles and qualities of true manhood, they place more importance on merely being *perceived* as manly. Confused Western Muslims are often drawn into this latter category, adopting the subculture, mannerisms, and jargon of the so-called 'manosphere'. They talk of 'taking the Red Pill', blissfully oblivious to the fact that this is just another flavour of 'the *Kool-Aid*', and merely another form of selfish play and self-adoration.

As it stands, a reset is required. Men need to be reminded that there is another and far enhanced course of action. Muslim masculinity is in urgent need of revival, and providentially the elixir that shall revive it has long been within reach. We must simply return to the roots of our religion, to remind ourselves once more of all the knowledge and wisdom possessed therein, and learn again to be men of the Qur'an and Sunnah. The benefits of this shall extend far beyond the pursuit of returning to true masculinity. The Prophet ﷺ said, 'Whoever revives my Sunnah then he has loved me, and whoever loves me shall be with me in Paradise.'[3]

The Prophet ﷺ: A Standard of Perfect Virtue

To be men of the Qur'an and Sunnah, we must render the Prophet Muhammad ﷺ as our paradigm and standard in all that we do. We must look to his character and virtues, his mannerisms and advice, and then exert sincere efforts to internalise them. The path to true masculinity has always been in

[3] *Jāmiʿ al-Tirmidhī* 2678.

plain view and documented in meticulous detail within the *sīrah* (biography) of the Prophet ﷺ; and yet we have looked to others to define it for us, seeking to take inspiration from the lowest of people, namely the movie stars, singers, and so-called influencers. Weak men with weak minds and weak hearts can teach nothing save weakness. This is not the way that a Muslim should follow, for our way is clear. Allah ﷻ addresses His Prophet ﷺ in the Qur'an, declaring:

وَإِنَّكَ لَعَلَىٰ خُلُقٍ عَظِيمٍ

And assuredly you are upon an excellent standard of character.[4]

In his explanation of this verse, Imam Fakhr al-Dīn al-Rāzī[5] ؒ states that man can only be virtuous in two capacities: in his ideals and in his actions. Islam is the perfection of moral ideals and principles, while the exactness of actions is found in good moral character and conduct. The Prophet ﷺ was the perfect epitome of both, and thus the ultimate role model for human existence. As Sufyān ibn 'Uyaynah ؒ would say, 'The Messenger of Allah ﷺ is the greatest measure. His character, life, and guidance are that by which all things are gauged. Whatever matches them is the Truth, and whatever goes against them is Falsehood.'[6]

As for the Prophet ﷺ himself, he declared that:

إِنَّمَا بُعِثْتُ لِأُتَمِّمَ صَالِحَ الْأَخْلَاقِ

I was sent to perfect virtuous character.[7]

It should be noted that the Prophet's statement that he was

---

[4] *Qur'an* 68:4.
[5] *Al-Tafsīr al-Kabīr*, vol. 30: p. 81.
[6] *Al-Jāmiʿ li Akhlāq al-Rāwī wa Ādāb al-Sāmiʿ*, vol. 1: p. 120.
[7] *Al-Adab al-Mufrad* 273.

sent to 'perfect virtuous character' implies that the internal and external virtues were always known by the wise individuals amongst the ancients, and such values simply needed perfecting. A brief glance at mankind's past history emphatically affirms this.

Manliness Across the Ages

In cultures across the globe and throughout the history of our species, from Ancient Greece to feudal Japan, from pre-Islamic Arabia to pre-Colonial America, men have always fulfilled the same role, following codes of conduct and championing the same values of duty and honour. 'Manliness' then is not a nebulous notion, or even one that is hard to pin down and define. Rather, the qualities and characteristics of manliness have been known and understood by individuals across all times, borders, and cultures. It is a universal concept rather than a fungible concept that is shaped by one's temporal and spatial context. It is a set of ideals and virtues that have been a code and way for men in all geographical settings and intervals. Though some cultures have emphasised certain virtues above others, the broad range of them are found everywhere, as we shall soon come to realise.

For the ancient Greeks, the ideal man was one who lived a life of *eudaimonia*, namely an existence in which one flourished by doing and living well. This was achieved through the practice of *aretê*, which translates to 'excellence in virtue'. These cardinal virtues were four: manly courage (*andreia*), prudence or wisdom (*phronesis*), temperance (*sophrosyne*), and justice (*dikaiosyne*). Among these, *andreia* was the most important, for it was needed to counter faint-heartedness, laziness, and over-attachment to pleasure. It allowed a man to realise the full potential of his body, mind, and soul, that is, to fulfil his life's purpose and create a legacy. For the Romans, the word for manliness was *virtus*, which is the root of the English word *virtue*; the latter can be traced back to the Latin word *vir*, which literally means 'man'. *Virtus* at first primarily pertained to valour and martial courage, but later grew to encompass the other cardinal virtues.

In the ancient East, the Samurai lived by a similar code, which was later defined as *bushido*, the embodiment of refined manhood. At its heart were eight virtues: courage (*yū*), temperance (*jisei*), justice (*gi*), integrity (*makoto*), honour (*meiyo*), compassion (*jin*), loyalty (*chu*), and respect (*rei*). For the Samurai, the ultimate aim of all virtues was to live a life of constant preparation for death, such that one would be able to die with honour.

For the ancient Arabs, the epitome of proper manly behaviour lay in the compound virtue of *al-murū'ah*. The word itself literally means 'manliness' and 'manly perfection', but in the figurative sense it represented all qualities and virtues which the Arabs adored and sought within their menfolk. In the world of pre-Islamic Arabia, where war was a socioeconomic necessity and knighthood was not given but earned, it was *al-murū'ah* that was valued above everything else. This was displayed in the form of martial skill on the battlefield, poetic skill in the joust of wits between tribal versifiers, displays of unbound munificence when hosting, and staunch loyalty to familial and ancestral networks. Whoever excelled in these virtues of *al-murū'ah* would earn his place in the knightly ranks.

It was this latter concept of *al-murū'ah* which was prevalent during the time of the Prophet ﷺ and his Companions رضي الله عنهم. It would later form the chivalric code of *futuwwah*, which was perfected by his person ﷺ and can be summarised by the ethical injunctions of the Qur'an and Sunnah. Indeed, the greatest of his Companions رضي الله عنهم were those who excelled above others in this quality:

قِيلَ: 'يَا رَسُولَ اللَّهِ، مَنْ أَكْرَمُ النَّاسِ؟' قَالَ: 'أَتْقَاهُمْ لله.' قَالُوا: 'لَيْسَ عَنْ هَذَا نَسْأَلُكَ.' قَالَ: 'فَيُوسُفُ نَبِيُّ اللَّهِ، ابْنُ نَبِيِّ اللَّهِ، ابْنِ نَبِيِّ اللَّهِ، ابْنِ خَلِيلِ اللَّهِ.' قالوا: 'لَيْسَ عَنْ هَذَا نَسْأَلُكَ.' قَالَ: 'فَعَنْ مَعَادِنِ الْعَرَبِ تَسْأَلُونِي؟ خِيَارُهُمْ فِي الْجَاهِلِيَّةِ خِيَارُهُمْ فِي الإِسْلاَمِ إِذَا فَقُهُوا.'

It was asked, 'O Allah's Messenger, who is most worthy of respect amongst the people?' He ﷺ replied, 'The most God-conscious amongst you.' The Companions رضي الله عنهم said, *'It is not this that we ask about.' Whereupon the Prophet ﷺ then said, 'Then it is Yūsuf, the Apostle of Allah and the son of Allah's Apostle, who was also the son of Allah's Apostle, who was the son of Allah's friend.' They again said, 'This is not what we are asking you about.' He ﷺ said, 'Are you then asking me about the tribes of Arabia? Those who were the best of them in pre-Islamic days are the best of them in Islam, that is, when they gain an understanding of it.'*[8]

Imam al-Nawawī رحمه الله explains this to mean that the best of men are those who exemplified *al-murū'ah* and virtuous character in the Days of Ignorance and then embraced Islam and gained an understanding of it.[9]

Futuwwah

إِنَّهُمْ فِتْيَةٌ ءَامَنُواْ بِرَبِّهِمْ وَزِدْنَـٰهُمْ هُدًى.

They were young men who believed in their Lord and We gave them more guidance.[10]

Futuwwah is taken from the route *fatā*, which literally means

[8] *Ṣaḥīḥ Muslim* 2378.
[9] *Al-Minhāj bi Sharḥ Ṣaḥīḥ Muslim*, vol. 15: p. 194.
[10] *Qur'an* 18:13.

'young man'. The Persian *Javānmardī* code has the same meaning and was likely mutually influential in its codification of masculine virtue, with the title meaning 'young manliness'. The *fatā* is the youth who is chivalrous, brave, inwardly and outwardly handsome, and the one who gives without care for himself – to the point that he would give his life if required. Its association with youthfulness hints toward the promise of the young man's potential. Men are composed of mind, body, and soul, and *futuwwah* espouses the improvement of each of these elements, with a particular focus on inner character. The code emphasises complete reliance on Allah ﷻ exclusively and the appreciation that all events happen through His Divine Will, holding oneself personally accountable, and fulfilling the rights of others.

فَجَعَلَهُمْ جُذَٰذًا إِلَّا كَبِيرًا لَّهُمْ لَعَلَّهُمْ إِلَيْهِ يَرْجِعُونَ. قَالُوا۟ مَن فَعَلَ هَـٰذَا بِـَٔالِهَتِنَآ إِنَّهُۥ لَمِنَ ٱلظَّـٰلِمِينَ.

قَالُوا۟ سَمِعْنَا فَتًى يَذْكُرُهُمْ يُقَالُ لَهُۥٓ إِبْرَٰهِيمُ.

Then, he turned all of them into pieces, except the largest of them, so that they may come back to it. They said, 'Who has done this to our gods? He is one of the wrongdoers indeed.' Some of them said, 'We have heard a youth talking about them. He is called Ibrāhīm.'[11]

Imam Abū al-Qāsim al-Qushayrī ؒ writes in *al-Risālah* that the *fatā* – namely the ideal Muslim man – is the one who breaks idols, as the Prophet Ibrāhīm ؑ did. He further adds that the idol within each man is his ego, which must be broken. Thus, the man who goes against his desires is the chivalrous youth in truth.[12] Ḥārith al-Muḥāsibī ؒ says that *futuwwah* also entails the following precept: 'To be just even when you have been treated

[11] *Qur'an* 21:58-60.
[12] *Al-Risālah al-Qushayriyyah*, p. 391.

unjustly.'[13]

Futuwwah is an umbrella term for a chivalric code comprising several masculine virtues and traits. In this regard, one can mention the values of chivalry, honour, courage, temperance, generosity, altruism, service, hospitality, wisdom, and justice. Sahl ibn ʿAbdullāh ﷺ perfectly defined *futuwwah* when he said, '*Futuwwah* is to follow the Sunnah.'[14]

Codifying Modern Masculine Virtues

Having firmly established the universal basis for the characteristics of masculinity and defined what it is, it should now be clear that masculinity is from the *fiṭrah* (primordial nature) of mankind, that is to say it is natural, intuitive, and intrinsic to being human. In light of these preceding facts, a question naturally arises, however: if the claim that the Prophet ﷺ is the Perfect Man is true, and the universal virtues of manliness and masculinity are from the *fiṭrah*, can this be proven through the Qur'an and Sunnah? The answer is a resounding yes.

This book has been compiled primarily to codify masculine virtues - as established in the blessed life of the noble Prophet ﷺ - for the modern Muslim man. This will be done by following the *arbaʿīn* structure found in the Hadith sciences, whereby a collection of forty Hadiths are carefully selected for highlighting a specific religious objective. The goal of this collection is to teach the men of today how to embody manly virtues by emulating the character, actions, and qualities of the most virtuous of men ﷺ.

The book itself is divided into four sections, every one of them encompassing ten core Hadiths. Each section is defined

---

[13] *Al-Risālah al-Qushayriyyah*, p. 391.

[14] *Al-Risālah al-Qushayriyyah*, p. 391.

with its own subject matter based on the established *fiṭrah* mentioned in the preceding pages through the lens of *al-murū'ah* and *futuwwah.* In each section, related Quranic verses as well as further narrations will be brought under the heading of the main Hadith to shed further light on the topic discussed.

The first section will focus on internal virtues such as faith, education, good character, and morality. These are our spiritual and mental virtues. Internal betterment is essential, and true success in this life and the next can only be achieved through the perfection of these intangible qualities. What good is a house without strong foundations, or a tree without strong roots? What good is a man without strong values or faith? If a man is to stand at all, his base must first be made firm.

With a strong spiritual and mental foundation established, the second section will unpack the realm of personal virtues. These are qualities which address our physical selves and our place in the world, such as self-sufficiency, independence, and discipline. A man is to be relied upon and should not be reliant on others – for he places his trust on Allah ﷻ alone. He is to be resilient, adaptable, and resilient, such that he can subsist without luxury, external aid, or approval.

Section three will build upon its predecessors and expand further outward, looking into interpersonal virtues that teach us how to optimally undertake interactions with other men, as well as with women and children, in our communities. Qualities such as leadership, brotherhood, sexuality, and communication are discussed here. Every person amongst us is, or will soon be, a leader in their own household, and thus every man must know how to lead proactively. The nature of the world is such that not all men can be leaders beyond the walls of their homes, and thus every man must equally know how and when to follow orders.

By extension, each of us must also know how to communicate in our speech, writing, and behaviour.

The final section will go beyond the interpersonal realm and enumerate the virtues that stress exercising awareness for matters from outside the safety of our communities and relationships. Here, we will look into the qualities most often associated with 'manliness', such as fitness, martial prowess, and courage. A man plans, tempers his body, and patiently anticipates challenging situations. A man does not shy away or hide, nor does he act rashly or without control. A man is prepared for anything, and ultimately, must be prepared for death and all that it entails.

1 | THE GOOD MAN

1
His Intentions are Righteous

عَنْ عُمَرَ بْنِ الْخَطَّابِ رَضِيَ اللَّهُ عَنْهُ قَالَ: قَالَ رَسُولُ اللَّهِ صَلَّى اللَّهُ عَلَيْهِ وَسَلَّمَ:
"إِنَّمَا الْأَعْمَالُ بِالنِّيَّاتِ وَإِنَّمَا لِكُلِّ امْرِئٍ مَا نَوَى فَمَنْ كَانَتْ هِجْرَتُهُ إِلَى اللَّهِ وَرَسُولِهِ
فَهِجْرَتُهُ إِلَى اللَّهِ وَرَسُولِهِ وَمَنْ كَانَتْ هِجْرَتُهُ إِلَى دُنْيَا يُصِيبُهَا أَوِ امْرَأَةٍ يَتَزَوَّجُهَا
فَهِجْرَتُهُ إِلَى مَا هَاجَرَ إِلَيْهِ."

ʿUmar ibn al-Khaṭṭāb ﷺ narrated that the Messenger of Allah ﷺ said, 'Deeds are to be judged by intentions, and a man shall have only what he intended. Thus, whoever's emigration was to Allah and His Messenger ﷺ, his emigration was indeed to Allah and His Messenger ﷺ; but whoever's emigration was to attain some worldly gain, or to marry some woman, his emigration is for that which he emigrated for.'[15]

INTENTION

Imam al-Shāfiʿī ﷺ states that this Hadith 'contains half of all knowledge', as acts of worship pertain to either the limbs or to the heart, and the heart's worship is encompassed by exercising

[15] *Ṣaḥīḥ Muslim* 1907.

sincerity of intent.[16] Yet other scholars, including Imam al-Bayhaqī ؒ, state that this Hadith contains one-third of all knowledge or one-third of Islam, because the means by which man earns reward or sin are through the undertakings of the limbs, speech of the tongue, or intent of the heart.[17]

Success in any endeavour is measured by the degree to which an agent executes their plan and achieves their intended target. This ultimately means that if an actor is unsuccessful in undertaking a prescribed religious end, they may still be rewarded if their intentions were sincere and they exerted their best efforts. At an equally important level, in the aforementioned Hadith we infer that the same action carried out with different intentions will vary depending on the thought process and sincerity of the actors. Put in another way, an act's moral significance and value can be magnified or minimised by the intent behind it: taking a bullet intended for someone else can be the most heroic of actions if one throws himself in the line of fire to protect a loved one or an innocent bystander, but the same action carried out because one happened to stumble at the wrong time – though no less tragic – would not be considered manly or heroic. Accordingly, the Messenger of Allah ﷺ said, 'People will be resurrected according to their intentions.'[18] Thus, the intentions of our deeds will dictate how we are judged for them. The Prophet ﷺ also said:

> *The first of people whose matter will be decided on the Day of Resurrection will be a man who had died as a martyr. He shall be brought forth. Allah ﷻ will make him recount His blessings and he will recount them. Allah ﷻ*

---

[16] *Al-Futūḥāt al-Rabbāniyyah ʿalā al-Adhkār al-Nawawiyyah*, vol. 1: p. 41.

[17] *Al-Futūḥāt al-Rabbāniyyah ʿalā al-Adhkār al-Nawawiyyah*, vol. 1: p. 41.

[18] *Sunan Ibn Mājah* 4229.

will then ask, 'What did you do with these blessings?' The man will say, 'I fought for Your cause until I was martyred.' Allah ﷻ will say, 'You lie. You fought so that you might be called a courageous warrior, and you were called such.' Allah ﷻ will then pass the order and he will be dragged face-down and cast into the Fire.

After this, another man will be brought forward who had acquired knowledge, imparted it to others, and had also recited the Qur'an. Allah ﷻ will make him recount His blessings and he will recount them. Allah ﷻ will then ask, 'What did you do with these blessings?' The man will say, 'I acquired knowledge and disseminated it to others, and recited the Qur'an, seeking Your pleasure.' Allah ﷻ will respond, 'You lie. You acquired knowledge so that you might be called a scholar, and recited the Qur'an so that it might be said, "He is a qārī", and such has been said.' Allah ﷻ will then pass the order and he will be dragged face-down and cast into the Fire.

Then a man will be brought forth whom Allah ﷻ had made abundantly rich and granted every kind of wealth. Allah ﷻ will make him recount His blessings and he will recount them. Allah ﷻ will ask, 'What have you done with these blessings?' The man will say, 'I did not leave a cause that You wished for me to support save that I supported it.' Allah ﷻ will say, 'You lie. You did all this to be called a generous man, and so it was said.' Then Allah ﷻ will pass the order and he will be dragged face-down and cast into the Fire.[19]

[19] *Ṣaḥīḥ Muslim* 1905a.

A man's deeds will ultimately be judged by Allah ﷻ, and it is not for any of us to judge what is in someone's heart. However, the essence of the intention can also be derived by the nature of our actions. ʿUmar ibn al-Khaṭṭāb ؓ stated, 'In the time of the Messenger of Allah ﷺ, people were judged by divine revelation. Since now that revelation has ceased, we judge by what is apparent of your outward actions. Whoever shows us good, we shall trust and favour. It is not for us to take account of what he does in secret, for Allah ﷻ will judge him for that. And whosoever presents to us an evil deed, we shall neither trust nor believe him, even if he claims that his intentions were good.'[20]

It is therefore imperative for every man to ensure that his public actions are noble and honourable, for this is how he will be judged by his peers. Likewise, his private actions must be equally noble and honourable, for in this realm it is Allah ﷻ that will judge him. A man's actions are always under scrutiny, and there is no place, be it public, private, or in the depths of his heart, where he is not being judged.

وَلَيْسَ عَلَيْكُمْ جُنَاحٌ فِيمَآ أَخْطَأْتُم بِهِۦ وَلَـٰكِن مَّا تَعَمَّدَتْ قُلُوبُكُمْ ۚ وَكَانَ ٱللَّهُ غَفُورًا رَّحِيمًا.

There is no sin on you in the mistake you make, but in that which you do with intention of your heart; and Allah is Most-Forgiving, Very-Merciful.[21]

DETERMINATION AND CONVICTION

The Prophet ﷺ said, 'When one of you makes a supplication, he should do so with determination, and should not say, "O Allah, confer upon me if You like," for there is none to

[20] *Ṣaḥīḥ al-Bukhārī* 2641.
[21] *Qur'an* 33:5.

coerce Allah.'[22]

A Muslim does what he sets out to do. He does not give up at the first hurdle, nor the last. Determination should be a quality that is imbued within everything we do. When we pray to Allah ﷻ we should pray with determination; when we set out to complete a task, it should be done in an efficient manner. The Messenger of Allah ﷺ said, 'O people, perform deeds you are capable of doing. Allah ﷻ will not give up on you unless you give up. The most beloved deeds to Allah ﷻ are those performed regularly, even if they are small.' The Mother of the Believers, ʿĀ'ishah ﷺ said, 'When the household of Muhammad ﷺ committed to a deed, they would be determined in it.'[23]

Shortly after the Battle of Ḥunayn, Abū Mūsā al-Ashʿarī ؓ was in the company of his uncle Abū ʿĀmir ؓ following a skirmish between the Muslim army at Auṭās and the retreating Jushamite army from the Hawāzin. At this point, Abū ʿĀmir ؓ was fatally wounded by an arrow that struck his knee. Abū Mūsā ؓ asked Abū ʿĀmir ؓ to point out his assailant on the battlefield and when his comrade did so, Abū Mūsā ؓ set out, determined to slay the man. He overtook the assailant and cut him off, and the man turned on his heel and began to flee.

At this point, Abū Mūsā ؓ called out to him, 'Do you not feel ashamed that you flee from me? Are you not an Arab? Why will you not stop and face me?' The man must have indeed felt shame, for he turned to face Abū Mūsā ؓ and they exchanged sword strokes, until Abū Mūsā ؓ struck him down and slew him. Abū Mūsā ؓ returned to Abū ʿĀmir ؓ and said, 'Allah

[22] *Ṣaḥīḥ Muslim* 2678.
[23] *Ṣaḥīḥ Muslim* 782a.

has slain the one who slew you.' He then drew out the arrow from his uncle's knee, which bled profusely and could not be staunched. As he bled out, Abū ʿĀmir ﵁ appointed his nephew as the Chief of his people and his final words were for his greetings to be passed on to the Prophet ﷺ, and that a request be made that he ﷺ pray for Abū ʿĀmir's forgiveness. Abū Mūsā al-Ashʿarī ﵁ did as his noble uncle requested and the Prophet ﷺ prayed for each of them.[24]

Here we see the example of Abū Mūsā al-Ashʿarī ﵁ and his single-minded determination when he set out to achieve his goal. When a goal is set, whether individually, by instruction, or for the good of one's tribe or clan, a man must be single-minded and determined to achieve it; there can be no distraction. Abū Mūsā al-Ashʿarī ﵁ was on the field of battle, and had many other concerns, such as the barrage of arrows and other armed attackers, but he was not once distracted from his objective: to avenge his uncle. His sheer determination cowed his opponent when he caught up to him, and he did not return to his dying uncle's side until he could report that the man that had dealt the fatal blow to Abū ʿĀmir ﵁ was himself now dead. It should be noted here that despite the considerable risk to his own life, his dogged determination, and the achievement of his objective, he did not feel the need to claim the victory for himself. Rather, he attributed the victory to Allah ﷻ alone, thereby exhibiting humility, a theme which will be further assessed later in this book.

The Messenger of Allah ﷺ said, 'The beginning of righteousness in this nation is by conviction and temperance, and

[24] *Ṣaḥīḥ Muslim* 2498.

the beginning of its corruption is by miserliness and vain hopes.'[25] It is not enough to merely be upright in action and intention, for a man must also have conviction. When a man knows he is right, he cannot be cowed from his position. This unwavering resolve in a man's heart is his conviction, and it is a fundamental quality which must be built into each of us. If what one is doing is right, he must hold steadfast to it and continue. If what one deems to be true is challenged, he must stand up for it. No amount of ridicule, pain, or torture should derail one from upholding this truth, since a real man's conviction is unwavering. The *mu'adhdhin* (caller to prayer) of the Messenger ﷺ, Bilāl ibn Rabāḥ رضي الله عنه, was a man of titanic conviction. An Abyssinian slave, with no family or clan to protect him. A man at the mercy of his slavers, tortured and beaten daily for weeks on end. Dragged through hot coals, crushed under great rocks, made to wear chainmail in the Arabian heat, lashed until his torturers grew tired and had to take turns. Bilāl رضي الله عنه was told again and again to denounce his faith, to simply utter a single word of *kufr* (disbelief), and be freed from his seemingly unending torment. Yet, Bilāl's reply each time was the same:

أَحَدٌ أَحَدٌ

'The One. The One.'[26]

When asked later on in life why he chose those words specifically over any other declaration of faith, Bilāl's response was that it was these words that enraged his torturers the most. This is the height of conviction. As William Ernest Henley wrote:

It matters not how strait the gate,

---

[25] *Shuʿab al-Īmān* 10350.
[26] *Sunan Ibn Mājah* 150; *Musnad al-Imam Aḥmad* 3822.

How charged with punishments the scroll,

I am the captain of my fate,

I am the master of my soul.[27]

[27] *Invictus*, William Ernest Henley.

2
He Does What He Says

عَنْ أَبِي هُرَيْرَةَ رَضِيَ اللَّهُ عَنْهُ، عَنِ النَّبِيِّ صَلَّى اللَّهُ عَلَيْهِ وَسَلَّمَ، قَالَ: "آيَةُ الْمُنَافِقِ ثَلاَثٌ، إِذَا حَدَّثَ كَذَبَ، وَإِذَا اؤْتُمِنَ خَانَ، وَإِذَا وَعَدَ أَخْلَفَ."

Abū Hurayrah ﵁ narrated from the Prophet ﷺ that he said, 'The signs of a hypocrite are three: when he speaks, he lies; when he is entrusted, he is dishonest; and when he promises, he breaks it.'[28]

KEEPING YOUR WORD AND OATH-KEEPING

This Hadith highlights three fundamental signs through which a hypocrite can be identified. All three involve the breaking of trust through dishonesty. Hypocrisy in this context refers to a man that claims to be Muslim but belies himself through his actions. From this prophetic description of the hypocrite, we can derive the qualities of a true man: when a man speaks, he tells the truth; whenever he is entrusted, he proves himself honest; and when he makes a promise, he keeps it. The Prophet ﷺ said, 'He who acts dishonestly towards us is not from amongst us.'[29]

A man's word truly is his bond. A man should not make a promise that he is unable to keep - or worse, does not mean to keep - for the word of a man is a powerful thing. If a man says something will happen, it *will* happen. Saʿīd ibn Jubayr ﵀ was once approached by a Jew who asked him which of the two promised periods of labour the Prophet Mūsā ﵇ completed as

[28] *Ṣaḥīḥ al-Bukhārī* 2749.
[29] *Ṣaḥīḥ Muslim* 101, 102; *Jāmiʿ al-Tirmidhī* 1315, 4307; *Sunan Abī Dāwūd* 3452; *Sunan Ibn Mājah* 2309.

an offering for the hand of his wife. Sa'īd ﷺ approached Ibn 'Abbās ﷺ for the answer, with the latter replying, 'He completed the longer and better period. No doubt, a Prophet of Allah ﷺ always does what he says.'[30]

The words of Ibn 'Abbās ﷺ, '...always does what he says,' describe exactly how a man's word should function: once it is said, it is done. Your word must be binding, and you should be prepared to undergo whatever trials may come to ensure your word is fulfilled. A person that says he will do something and then does not support it with concrete actions cannot be truly considered a man.

وَإِن نَّكَثُوٓا۟ أَيْمَـٰنَهُم مِّنۢ بَعْدِ عَهْدِهِمْ وَطَعَنُوا۟ فِى دِينِكُمْ فَقَـٰتِلُوٓا۟ أَئِمَّةَ ٱلْكُفْرِ ۙ إِنَّهُمْ لَآ أَيْمَـٰنَ لَهُمْ لَعَلَّهُمْ يَنتَهُونَ.

And if they break their oaths after they have made a covenant, and speak evil of your faith, then fight the leaders of infidelity, since their oaths are nothing, so that they may desist.[31]

Oaths are still taken in the modern age, although nowadays for many of us such words of assurance have come to mean very little. An oath is often seen as the words one says to complete a legal action. Examples of such oaths are those sworn by police constables during their affirmation, by army recruits prior to their passing out, by medical personnel prior to beginning their practice, or as part of the formal ceremony in the marriage contracts of certain cultures.

We swear oaths to be truthful in court proceedings. These oaths are more than just traditions and process, though many an oath-taker has fallen foul of such false belief. How many soldiers,

[30] *Ṣaḥīḥ al-Bukhārī* 2684.
[31] *Qur'an* 9:12.

doctors, and police officers have we read about who have clearly not understood or meant their oaths? How many men have sworn to be faithful to their wives and then proven themselves to be weak-willed? It should also be noted that there are still people among these groups that understand the importance of oaths and hold firm to them.

The Prophet ﷺ said, 'False oaths lay waste to homelands.'[32] The sanctity of the oath must be maintained by every man, as any failure to ensure they are preserved will lay waste to the societies in which they are regularly broken. But a false oath is not only an oath unkept, but also one made falsely. This is why the Prophet ﷺ made it clear that 'an oath is to be interpreted according to the intention of the one who requests it to be taken'.[33] In this way, there can be no misinterpretation or deception - the requester makes the wording clear, and the oath-taker is left with a clear understanding of what the oath entails.

Though an oath should not be taken for a trivial matter, one should not shy away from issuing such pledges altogether as grave matters can often only be sealed and executed through them. When the Prophet ﷺ asked his Companions ﷺ to take an oath, so many rushed forward to take it that lots had to be drawn to see who would take the first pledge.[34]

That said, an oath should not be taken to carry out something harmful to oneself, one's family, or society. Grammatically, when used with an object as well as a subject, the verb *waʿada* (to take an oath) may have either positive or negative connotations. But when used without an object, as in the Hadith here, it can only

[32] *Arbaʿīn Shāh Walī Allāh* 31.
[33] *Ṣaḥīḥ Muslim* 1653b; *Sunan Ibn Mājah* 2120.
[34] *Ṣaḥīḥ al-Bukhārī* 2674.

refer to something sworn for the sake of good.[35] When confronted with a matter in which the fulfilling of the oath is more harmful than the breaking of it, then the Muslim man should complete the better action and offer some form of expiation in recompense for breaking the oath.[36] But even in these circumstances, the oath maintains its sanctity and its breaking requires recompense.

Here it should also be noted that going against your word is only a sign of hypocrisy when you never had any intention of fulfilling it to begin with. Otherwise, if your intention is pure and you are unable to keep it due to an unforeseen circumstance, then there is no harm in this.[37] This is clear from the Hadith of Zayd ibn Arqam ﷺ, in which it is reported that:

إِذَا وَعَدَ الرَّجُلُ أَخَاهُ – وَمِنْ نِيَّتِهِ أَنْ يَفِيَ لَهُ – فَلَمْ يَفِ وَلَمْ يَجِئْ لِلْمِيعَادِ فَلاَ إِثْمَ عَلَيْهِ

When a man makes a promise to his brother with the intention of fulfilling it, but is unable to do so and ultimately fails to meet the deadline, there is no sin upon him.[38]

FULFILLING TRUSTS, CONTRACTS, AND DEBTS

In the Qur'an, Allah ﷻ states:

وَٱلَّذِينَ هُمْ لِأَمَـٰنَـٰتِهِمْ وَعَهْدِهِمْ رَٰعُونَ.

And success is attained by those who honestly look after their trusts and covenant.[39]

A contract is a covenant between two individuals or groups, and is successfully executed by having both parties satisfy their

---

[35] *Mukhtār al-Ṣiḥāḥ*, p. 728.
[36] *Ṣaḥīḥ al-Bukhārī* 6625; *Jāmiʿ al-Tirmidhī* 1530.
[37] *Kashf al-Bārī*, vol. 2: p. 274.
[38] *Sunan Abī Dāwūd* 4995.
[39] *Qur'an* 23:8.

side of the agreement. It is a relationship of trust, and it is cited here by Allah ﷻ to describe the believer who has attained success, that is, the one who honestly looks after their covenants with others.

وَأَوْفُوا۟ بِٱلْعَهْدِ ۖ إِنَّ ٱلْعَهْدَ كَانَ مَسْـُٔولًا.

And fulfil the covenant. Surely, the covenant shall be asked about (on the Day of Reckoning).[40]

A trust is when something has been left in someone's care for safekeeping. The Prophet ﷺ was given the name 'the Trustworthy' (al-Amīn) in his youth due to his meticulous safekeeping of trusts, whether the entrusted matter was verbal (e.g., secrets) or physical (e.g., items) in nature. Furthermore, the Prophet ﷺ described the Muslim man as 'the one from whose tongue and hand the Muslims are safe' and 'with whom the people trust their blood and their wealth'.[41]

A man can be trusted to look after the things that are delegated to him, be they objects, words, or living things. If asked to watch over a neighbour's house whilst they are out of town, he makes it his duty to ensure no harm comes to their property. If entrusted with information, it does not find its way to the ears of others. If another man gives his daughter's hand in marriage to him, she too is taken as a trust, protected, and provided an optimal level of care.

Just as trusts and contracts must be upheld by a man, so too must their debts be fulfilled. There is nothing unmanly about borrowing from others to fulfil an immediate and unforeseen need. In this day and age, it is nigh impossible to avoid when buying property due to the extortionate prices of housing in the

---

[40] *Qur'an* 17:34.
[41] *Jāmiʿ al-Tirmidhī* 2627.

Western world. Though incurring debt is permissible to fulfil an immediate need, repaying the debt is a man's moral duty.

Furthermore, a man should do his utmost to free himself from debt as soon as possible, as the Prophet ﷺ would often seek Allah's refuge from being in debt. For as one report states, 'A person who is in debt tells lies when he speaks, and breaks his promises when he gives assurances.'[42] The same qualities have been mentioned here as those in the Prophet's description of hypocrisy, and this alone should deter one from falling in the state of debt for any period unless when deemed absolutely necessary. This is not to say that an indebted person will *always* lie when he speaks or renege on his promises, but the nature of his situation is likely to lead to a position where he is forced to do so. These are unmanly qualities, and a true gentleman must avoid such at all costs.

[42] *Ṣaḥīḥ al-Bukhārī* 2397.

3
He Stands Against Evil

عَنْ أَبِي سَعِيدٍ الْخُدْرِيِّ رَضِيَ اللهُ عَنْهُ قَالَ: سَمِعْتُ رَسُولَ اللَّهِ صَلَّى اللهُ عَلَيْهِ وَسَلَّمَ يَقُولُ: "مَنْ رَأَى مِنْكُمْ مُنْكَرًا فَلْيُغَيِّرْهُ بِيَدِهِ، فَإِنْ لَمْ يَسْتَطِعْ فَبِلِسَانِهِ، فَإِنْ لَمْ يَسْتَطِعْ فَبِقَلْبِهِ، وَذَلِكَ أَضْعَفُ الإِيمَانِ."

Abū Saʿīd al-Khudrī ﷺ narrated, 'I heard the Messenger of Allah ﷺ say, "Whosoever amongst you sees an evil, let him change it with his hand; if he is unable to do so, then with his tongue; and if he is unable to do so, then with his heart - and that is the weakest of faith."'[43]

Enjoining Good and Forbidding Evil

In the Qur'an, Allah ﷻ encapsulates the moral duty of every Muslim in a single verse:

كُنتُمْ خَيْرَ أُمَّةٍ أُخْرِجَتْ لِلنَّاسِ تَأْمُرُونَ بِٱلْمَعْرُوفِ وَتَنْهَوْنَ عَنِ ٱلْمُنكَرِ وَتُؤْمِنُونَ بِٱللَّهِ

You are the best ummah ever raised for mankind. You bid the Fair and forbid the Unfair, and you believe in Allah.[44]

The qualities listed here elucidate why Allah ﷻ has named our *ummah* the best of mankind, and further constitute an explanation for what our moral duties are as members of this *ummah*: to enjoin good, to forbid evil, and to believe in Allah ﷻ.

All individuals, including male or female and Muslim or non-Muslim, are measured morally by the level of their adherence to the perpetuation of these three duties. The Muslim man, however, is best placed to do so. He exhorts people towards the

---

[43] *Ṣaḥīḥ Muslim* 49a.
[44] *Qur'an* 3:110.

good, both through his own example, and by teaching and encouraging others to be better. He stands up against evil in whatever form he may find it and does not fear the consequences.[45] He believes in the One True God, Allah ﷻ, and humbles himself before Him and worships Him.

In the aforementioned Hadith, the Prophet ﷺ has categorised the level of a man's faith in accordance with how staunchly he stands against evil. The highest form of this act is to stop evil through physical intervention. This in itself highlights other qualities that a man must have, such as strength, martial prowess, and courage, all of which are seminal features that will be assessed later in this book. His faith is such that he cannot stand to witness an evil being carried out in front of him, and he is driven to promptly stop it. As a Muslim, you must be willing and able to stop the evil act from occurring with your own hands. This could be a sinful act, such as another man engaging with a woman he has no reason or right to engage with, or an act of oppression, such as the torture and abuse of a subjugated people.

The second level is that of the man who sees an evil act being carried out, and again his faith is such that he cannot idly stand by as a passive observer - he has to speak out against it. Perhaps he does not have the strength - be it physical or spiritual - to stop the injustice, but he can still stand in front of the tyrant and announce what is right. The Prophet ﷺ stated, 'The best jihad is a just word spoken to an unjust ruler.'[46]

The third and final level is that of a Muslim that sees the injustice being perpetrated and knows and feels it is wrong. Yet, he can neither stop it himself, nor speak out against it. He can

---

[45] *Qur'an* 5:54.

[46] *Jāmiʿ al-Tirmidhī* 2174; *Sunan Abī Dāwūd* 4344.

only pray to Allah ﷻ to stop the injustice from occurring.[47] The scholars of Hadith mention that changing through the heart does not simply imply that the witnessing person sees the injustice as wrong, but they also make a firm intention that if they ever gain the power or opportunity to intervene physically or to speak out against it, they will do so.[48] Many of us are in this lowest category, and even more fall far below this. May Allah ﷻ forgive and protect us from such an existence. *Āmīn.*

Today, our so-called role models and 'influencers' are falling into the trap of secular liberalism and its sub-categories, and are subsequently unable to perceive evil acts when they occur right in front of them. Even worse, they begin to champion them, and condemn those who speak out against them. There are others that are so engrossed in sin and vice that it is no longer seen as immoral to them, and they in turn *speak out against the believers* for not engaging in these sins and vices as well.

A Muslim man must be upright and stand for what is right, even if society itself stands against him. What is right is governed by the laws of Allah ﷻ, and not the social norms of the age in which he lives. This point is neatly encapsulated in the words of John Stuart Mill:

> *'Let not any one pacify his conscience by the delusion that he can do no harm if he takes no part, and forms no opinion. Bad men need nothing more to compass their ends, than that good men should look on and do nothing.'*[49]

COMPETITIVENESS IN GOOD ACTION

Competition is often considered a good thing, and man is

[47] *Mukammil Ikmāl al-Ikmāl,* vol. 1: p. 154.
[48] *Fatḥ al-Mulhim:* vol. 1: p. 435.
[49] John Stuart Mill, 1867.

naturally inclined towards contending with his fellow man. This is part of our *fiṭrah*, and therefore Islam incorporates it. However, as Muslim men, we are encouraged to compete in things which are of benefit to ourselves and our fellow Muslims, and to refrain from competition for its own sake or for the sake of pride. Competition in itself is not meritorious, but competition in good action is not only permissible, but desirable. Allah ﷻ says:

سَابِقُوٓا۟ إِلَىٰ مَغْفِرَةٍ مِّن رَّبِّكُمْ وَجَنَّةٍ عَرْضُهَا كَعَرْضِ ٱلسَّمَآءِ وَٱلْأَرْضِ

Compete with one other in advancing towards forgiveness from your Lord and to Paradise, the width of which is like the width of the sky and the Earth...[50]

In this verse Allah ﷻ has provided us two goals which we must pursue with our fellow Muslims: forgiveness and Paradise. The former revolves around how often and how much we seek Allah's forgiveness, while the latter entails completing good actions and earning our places in Paradise.

The Companions ﷺ of the Prophet ﷺ would often compete with one another in this regard. There is a famous narration of ʿUmar ibn al-Khaṭṭāb ﷺ which relates how he attempted to compete with and surpass Abū Bakr ﷺ in the giving of charity. He brought half of everything he owned and donated it. When the Prophet ﷺ asked what he had left for his family, he replied, 'The same amount.' When Abū Bakr ﷺ brought his donation, he was asked the same question. He replied, 'I left them with Allah and His Apostle' – he had brought all that he owned. ʿUmar ibn al-Khaṭṭāb ﷺ said to him, 'I shall never

[50] *Qur'an* 57:21.

surpass you in anything!'[51]

Such competition is not carried out to prove one's superiority over another, or to make others feel inferior. Rather, the aim is to exhort others to do what is good and to help each other in earning the pleasure of Allah ﷻ. In the race to Paradise, there are no losers.

However, men are proud creatures, and thus in danger of falling foul of Shayṭān's greatest trap: *pride*. The Prophet ﷺ warned us specifically of people competing with one another in the building of mosques as a sign of the Hour,[52] and we merely need to look out of our windows to see this very competition in full flow within our own communities. The purpose of beautifying a mosque is to help incline the hearts of the believers towards using it for worship, but too often the purpose is lost and we find ourselves competing for pride and social standing. True men are not vain but humble.

SCRUPULOUSNESS

Scrupulousness is the avoidance of doubtful matters and an abhorrence to committing sin. The Prophet ﷺ once explained that between the legal and illegal realms there is a grey area of doubtful matters, and stated: 'Whoever saves himself from these suspicious things saves his religion and his honour.'[53] He ﷺ then gave the analogy of a shepherd grazing his herd near the private pasture of a king, which ultimately made it very likely for him to trespass on the latter's territory (which will no doubt result in punishment). In this analogy the king represents the sovereignty

---

[51] *Sunan Abī Dāwūd* 1678.
[52] *Sunan Ibn Mājah* 739.
[53] *Ṣaḥīḥ al-Bukhārī* 52; *Ṣaḥīḥ Muslim* 1599a.

of Allah ﷻ and the private pasture is the haram realm.[54]

A Muslim should be in control of his desires and this should extend to a level of self-control where he does not feel the need nor the temptation to dabble in the doubtful. Allah ﷻ has rendered clear for us the legal and illegal matters. It is not from among the qualities of the Muslim to seek out grey areas and loop holes. Furthermore, it is not becoming of a man to be underhanded in his dealings, and it is the height of foolishness to employ furtive tactics in his dealings with Allah ﷻ.

For a man, his faith and honour should be incorruptible. Excursions into doubtful matters have an effect on both of these areas, whether the man in question realises these subtle changes or not. In the same Hadith, the Prophet ﷺ warned that if the heart is reformed in a man, it will reform his entire existence, but if it is allowed to be corrupted, it will spoil everything.[55] Sin is a poison that seeps into the veins and spreads throughout the body, corrupting every fibre and vein. Would any of us drink something if we had a doubt that it contained poison? Only a fool would take such a risk, and a Muslim man is never imprudent in such matters.

Nāṣir al-Dīn ibn al-Munayyir relates that his teacher Shaykh Abū al-Qāsim al-Qabbārī, used to say, 'The undesirable action (*makrūh*) is a barrier which stands between a servant and the forbidden (haram). Whoever excessively indulges in undesirable actions ends up broaching forbidden ones. The admissible action (*mubāḥ*) is a barrier between a servant and the undesirable (*makrūh*). Whoever excessively

[54] *Ṣaḥīḥ al-Bukhārī* 52; *Ṣaḥīḥ Muslim* 1599a.
[55] *Ṣaḥīḥ al-Bukhārī* 52; *Ṣaḥīḥ Muslim* 1599a.

indulges in admissible actions ends up broaching undesirable ones.'[56]

[56] *Fatḥ al-Bārī*, vol. 1: pp. 267-268.

4
He Remembers Allah

عَنْ أَبِي هُرَيْرَةَ رَضِيَ اللَّهُ عَنْهُ قَالَ: قَالَ النَّبِيُّ صَلَّى اللَّهُ عَلَيْهِ وَسَلَّمَ: "يَقُولُ اللَّهُ تَعَالَى أَنَا عِنْدَ ظَنِّ عَبْدِي بِي، وَأَنَا مَعَهُ إِذَا ذَكَرَنِي، فَإِنْ ذَكَرَنِي فِي نَفْسِهِ ذَكَرْتُهُ فِي نَفْسِي، وَإِنْ ذَكَرَنِي فِي مَلأٍ ذَكَرْتُهُ فِي مَلأٍ خَيْرٍ مِنْهُمْ، وَإِنْ تَقَرَّبَ إِلَيَّ بِشِبْرٍ تَقَرَّبْتُ إِلَيْهِ ذِرَاعًا، وَإِنْ تَقَرَّبَ إِلَيَّ ذِرَاعًا تَقَرَّبْتُ إِلَيْهِ بَاعًا، وَإِنْ أَتَانِي يَمْشِي أَتَيْتُهُ هَرْوَلَةً."

Abū Hurayrah ﵁ narrated that the Prophet ﷺ said, 'Allah says, "I am just as My slave thinks I am, and I am with him if he remembers Me. If he remembers Me in himself, I too remember him in Myself; and if he remembers Me in a gathering, I remember him in a better gathering; and if he comes a single span nearer to Me, I go one cubit nearer to him; and if he comes one cubit nearer to Me, I go a distance of two outstretched arms nearer to him; and if he comes to Me walking, I go to him running."'[57]

REMEMBRANCE OF ALLAH AND SPIRITUAL GROWTH

This narration is what is known as a Hadith Qudsī, a special category of prophetic narrations in which the meaning of the Hadith has been revealed by Allah ﷻ while the phrasing is formulated by the Messenger of Allah ﷺ. Thus, the Prophet ﷺ narrates from Allah ﷻ Himself in relation to His remembrance. The man that remembers Allah ﷻ has Allah ﷻ with him, so what then can ever cause him fear or harm? Allah ﷻ also extols the virtue of remembering Him in one's heart and aloud separately, and therefore a Muslim should do both.

Furthermore, the scholars of Hadith expound that the phrase

[57] *Ṣaḥīḥ al-Bukhārī* 7405; *Ṣaḥīḥ Muslim* 2675a.

'I am just as My slave thinks I am' means that 'I am as My servant expects Me to be and am fully capable of treating him as he expects to be treated'.[58] Thus, they stress that a person should hold his Lord in good regard and be optimistic of His Mercy.[59]

It is Man and jinn alone who fall short in remembering Allah ﷻ and in having hope in Him. Allah ﷻ asks in the Qur'an:

أَلَمْ تَرَ أَنَّ ٱللَّهَ يَسْجُدُ لَهُۥ مَن فِى ٱلسَّمَـٰوَٰتِ وَمَن فِى ٱلْأَرْضِ وَٱلشَّمْسُ وَٱلْقَمَرُ وَٱلنُّجُومُ
وَٱلْجِبَالُ وَٱلشَّجَرُ وَٱلدَّوَآبُّ وَكَثِيرٌ مِّنَ ٱلنَّاسِ ۖ

Have you not seen that to Allah submit all those in the skies and all those on the Earth, and the Sun, the Moon, the stars, the mountains, the trees, the animals and many from mankind?[60]

The word 'submit' (*yasjud*) here is used in its broader sense, and entails obedience to the Divine Will and Authority of Allah ﷻ, rather than the literal sense of prostration.[61] When all the flora and fauna of the Earth and each animate and inanimate thing – from the tiniest of single-celled organisms to the greatest of celestial bodies – worship Allah ﷻ and are ever-mindful of Him, how is it that man believes himself so privileged and great that he thinks he does not have to do the same? In so many definitions of manliness and masculinity, the idea of faith in Allah ﷻ and His remembrance is often removed from the list of qualities and traits that a man should have.

Yet, this is one of the most fundamental attributes, for man has been given free will and his choice to worship and remember Allah ﷻ is therefore a commendable act that affirms the position

---

[58] *Fatḥ al-Bārī*, vol. 24: p. 285.
[59] *Fatḥ al-Bārī*, vol. 24: p. 285.
[60] *Qur'an* 22:18.
[61] *Ma'ārif al-Qur'an*, vol. 6: pp. 251-252.

he has been given. That a man chooses to remember Allah ﷻ and worship Him makes no difference to Allah ﷻ, but it benefits the man in many ways. A man who is mindful of Allah ﷻ is steadfast and upright at all times, for he is aware that Allah ﷻ watches him; he knows his place in the world and remains humble; he objectively makes the right choice in any dilemma; and above all other benefits he obtains the pleasure of Allah ﷻ and will be rewarded for his remembrance.

The Prophet ﷺ would remember Allah ﷻ at all times and in all of his affairs,and advised us to do the same.[62][63] The Prophet ﷺ said, 'If anyone sits at a place where he does not remember Allah ﷻ, deprivation will descend on him from Allah ﷻ; and if he lies at a place where he does not remember Allah ﷻ, deprivation will descend on him from Allah ﷻ.'[64]

The Prophet ﷺ also said, 'No people sit in a gathering remembering Allah ﷻ except that the Angels surround them, mercy envelops them, tranquillity descends upon them, and Allah ﷻ remembers them before those who are with Him.'[65]

Spiritual growth is the process of bringing oneself closer to Allah ﷻ through self-improvement and self-purification. The self craves fulfilment, which a weak man believes can be satiated by self-indulgence. In truth, this fulfilment can only be attained through purification and complete submission to Allah ﷻ. This is a continuous process called *tazkiyah al-nafs* (self-purification). Allah ﷻ describes this course of spiritual development in the

---

[62] *Ṣaḥīḥ Muslim* 373.
[63] *Jāmiʿ al-Tirmidhī* 3384.
[64] *Sunan Abī Dāwūd* 4856.
[65] *Sunan Ibn Mājah* 3971.

Qur'an:

وَنَفْسٍ وَمَا سَوَّىٰهَا. فَأَلْهَمَهَا فُجُورَهَا وَتَقْوَىٰهَا. قَدْ أَفْلَحَ مَن زَكَّىٰهَا. وَقَدْ خَابَ مَن دَسَّىٰهَا.

And by the soul, and the One Who made it well, then inspired it with its instincts of evil and piety, success is really attained by him who purifies it, and failure is really suffered by him who pollutes it.[66]

Oftentimes, we wrongly assume that the *nafs*, or self, is naturally inclined towards indulgence in sin and that acts of piety are a means to control this in-built desire. From these verses it is clear that the capacity to do both good and evil is developed within us, and our selves have deeply-rooted instincts to commit acts of carnal indulgence or piety. Failure or success are attained by the poisoning or purification of our hearts respectively. The Prophet ﷺ described this beautifully in his warning, 'Beware! There is a piece of flesh in the body. If it becomes good, the whole body becomes good. But if it is spoiled, the whole body is spoiled. It is the heart.'[67]

Ḥāfiẓ Ibn Ḥajar al-ʿAsqalānī ﷺ posits that the reason for why the heart is singled out in this Hadith is that the latter organ is the body's leader: its rectitude means the rectitude of its subjects, and its corruption leads to their corruption.[68] As men, it is up to us to choose the harder and better path, and not to give in to temptation and weakness. A man is measured by his self-control and discipline. Ultimately, contentment cannot be found through the fulfilment of the sensual desires in this world, as pleasure in this world is – by design – a fleeting thing.

Frequently, people complain about an emptiness they feel

[66] *Qur'an* 91:7-10.

[67] *Ṣaḥīḥ al-Bukhārī* 52.

[68] *Fatḥ al-Bārī*, vol. 1: p. 274.

and they feed the wrong instinct to fill this void. The result is only a greater sense of emptiness. It is only through turning to Allah ﷻ, carrying out His commands, and living our lives according to the way of the Prophet ﷺ that this emptiness can be filled and this inner battle will be ultimately won. The Prophet ﷺ said that 'The *mujāhid* (warrior) is the one who strives against his self.'[69]

Two wolves fight in a man's heart. One is Evil and the other is Good.

Which one wins?

The one you feed.[70]

Mindfulness and Self-Improvement

A secular understanding of mindfulness is being present in the moment, as well as the awareness and acceptance of one's thoughts and feelings at that time. However, in Islam, mindfulness, or *murāqabah,* is the state of being aware of oneself in relation to Allah ﷻ, and the knowledge that He is aware of you in your every moment.

In the well-known Hadith of Jibrīl, the Angel Jibrīl ﷺ asked the Prophet ﷺ, 'What is *iḥsān* (perfecting the self)?' He ﷺ replied, 'To worship Allah ﷻ as if you see Him, and if you cannot achieve this state of devotion then understand that He is looking at you.'[71]

The concept of *aretê* in Greek philosophy, which was alluded to in the introduction, echoes this idea of *iḥsān.* Modern thinkers and self-help advisers would have us believe that

---

[69] *Jāmiʿ al-Tirmidhī* 2012.
[70] A Native American proverb.
[71] *Ṣaḥīḥ al-Bukhārī* 50.

accepting one's faults and simply being 'present' in oneself is being mindful and will lead to a better life. In truth, however, mindfulness is to be so aware of the presence of Allah ﷻ that it is as if He is in front of you. For most of us, this highest form of *iḥsān* is unattainable, but the second level - namely the knowledge and understanding that Allah ﷻ is watching us in every moment - is achievable. *Iḥsān* is the ultimate form of the state of mindfulness, and it is through the achievement of this state that *murāqabah* is executed. According to Imam al-Ghazālī ﵀, 'The essence of *murāqabah* is in perceiving al-Raqīb (The Ever Watchful) and devoting your attention to Him...in the knowledge that He is entirely acquainted with what is in our consciences, cognisant of all our secrets, and ever watchful of the actions of His slaves.'[72]

A man should strive to attain this state and remain in it, and time should be set aside to practise *murāqabah.* However, it is not possible for any man to remain in this state at all times. The Prophet ﷺ said, 'There is at times a shadow over my heart, and I seek forgiveness of Allah ﷻ a hundred times a day.'[73] In his commentary on this Hadith, Imam al-Nawawī ﵀ explains that there were moments in the day when he ﷺ did not have complete attentiveness of Allah ﷻ in his heart, which was the Prophet's normal state, and he ﷺ would consider these brief moments sinful and seek forgiveness.[74] For us lower-ranking men, spending time in the day focusing on achieving this state for a set time is a good place to start on the journey to achieving *iḥsān.*

---

[72] *Iḥyā ʿUlūm al-Dīn,* vol. 9: p. 138.
[73] *Ṣaḥīḥ Muslim* 2702a.
[74] *Al-Minhāj bi Sharḥ Ṣaḥīḥ Muslim,* vol. 17: p. 38.

إِنَّ ٱللَّهَ لَا يُغَيِّرُ مَا بِقَوۡمٍ حَتَّىٰ يُغَيِّرُواْ مَا بِأَنفُسِهِمۡۗ

Surely, Allah does not change the condition of a people unless they change themselves.[75]

A man is never content with his life and always seeks to better himself. Some men strive to do this financially or socially, while others attempt to improve themselves physically or mentally. All these parties have merit. The highest form of self-improvement, however, is found in the spiritual plane. The Prophet ﷺ said, 'If any one of you perfects his Islam then his good deeds will be rewarded ten to seven hundred-fold for each good deed, and a bad deed will be recorded as it is.'[76] Perfecting one's Islam has been considered by scholars to mean accepting Islam and its tenets fully and wholeheartedly, remaining firm and steadfast upon it, and working on increasing good deeds and decreasing bad deeds.[77] A man that consistently performs his obligatory prayers should beautify his devotion by increasing his concentration in them, or the time he spends in them; he can add to them the supererogatory (*nafl*) prayers, and ensure he prays each of them in congregation in a *masjid.*

A man that has learned the last ten or twenty *sūrahs* can work towards memorising more of the Qur'an. A man that spends five minutes a day learning his religion can increase this time to an hour. Islam is a broad religion, with many sciences and disciplines to master, and there is always more to learn and improve upon.

Throughout this process, a Muslim man must be conscious that there can be no development without the help and

---

[75] *Qur'an* 13:11.
[76] *Ṣaḥīḥ al-Bukhārī* 42.
[77] *In'ām al-Bārī*, vol. 1: p. 519.

permission of Allah ﷻ. As much as we may want to improve ourselves spiritually, physically, or mentally, without the support of Allah, there can only be failure. Thus, even as one seeks to be a better servant of Allah, he must also seek Allah's help and support to achieve this:

يَـٰمَعْشَرَ ٱلْجِنِّ وَٱلْإِنسِ إِنِ ٱسْتَطَعْتُمْ أَن تَنفُذُوا۟ مِنْ أَقْطَارِ ٱلسَّمَـٰوَٰتِ وَٱلْأَرْضِ فَٱنفُذُوا۟ ۚ لَا تَنفُذُونَ إِلَّا بِسُلْطَـٰنٍ

O genera of jinn and mankind, if you are able to penetrate beyond the realms of the Heavens and the Earth, then penetrate. You cannot penetrate without power.[78]

[78] *Qur'an* 55:33.

5
He Has Mastered the Basics

عَنْ أَبِي هُرَيْرَةَ رَضِيَ اللَّهُ عَنْهُ، أَنَّ رَسُولَ اللَّهِ صَلَّى اللَّهُ عَلَيْهِ وَسَلَّمَ كَانَ يَوْمًا بَارِزًا لِلنَّاسِ إِذْ أَتَاهُ رَجُلٌ يَمْشِي فَقَالَ: "يَا رَسُولَ اللَّهِ، مَا الْإِيمَانُ؟" قَالَ: "الْإِيمَانُ أَنْ تُؤْمِنَ بِاللَّهِ وَمَلاَئِكَتِهِ وَرُسُلِهِ وَلِقَائِهِ وَتُؤْمِنَ بِالْبَعْثِ الآخِرِ." قَالَ: "يَا رَسُولَ اللَّهِ، مَا الْإِسْلاَمُ؟" قَالَ: "الْإِسْلاَمُ أَنْ تَعْبُدَ اللَّهَ وَلاَ تُشْرِكَ بِهِ شَيْئًا، وَتُقِيمَ الصَّلاَةَ، وَتُؤْتِيَ الزَّكَاةَ الْمَفْرُوضَةَ، وَتَصُومَ رَمَضَانَ." قَالَ: "يَا رَسُولَ اللَّهِ، مَا الإِحْسَانُ؟" قَالَ: "الْإِحْسَانُ أَنْ تَعْبُدَ اللَّهَ كَأَنَّكَ تَرَاهُ، فَإِنْ لَمْ تَكُنْ تَرَاهُ فَإِنَّهُ يَرَاكَ." قَالَ: "يَا رَسُولَ اللَّهِ، مَتَى السَّاعَةُ؟ قَالَ: "مَا الْمَسْئُولُ عَنْهَا بِأَعْلَمَ مِنَ السَّائِلِ، وَلَكِنْ سَأُحَدِّثُكَ عَنْ أَشْرَاطِهَا؛ إِذَا وَلَدَتِ الْمَرْأَةُ رَبَّتَهَا، فَذَاكَ مِنْ أَشْرَاطِهَا، وَإِذَا كَانَ الْحُفَاةُ الْعُرَاةُ رُءُوسَ النَّاسِ، فَذَاكَ مِنْ أَشْرَاطِهَا، فِي خَمْسٍ لا يَعْلَمُهُنَّ إِلاَّ اللَّهُ {إِنَّ اللَّهَ عِنْدَهُ عِلْمُ السَّاعَةِ وَيُنَزِّلُ الْغَيْثَ وَيَعْلَمُ مَا فِي الأَرْحَامِ}." ثُمَّ انْصَرَفَ الرَّجُلُ، فَقَالَ: "رُدُّوا عَلَيَّ." فَأَخَذُوا لِيَرُدُّوا فَلَمْ يَرَوْا شَيْئًا. فَقَالَ: "هَذَا جِبْرِيلُ، جَاءَ لِيُعَلِّمَ النَّاسَ دِينَهُمْ."

Abū Hurayrah ؓ narrated, 'One day while the Messenger of Allah ﷺ was sitting with the people, a man came to him walking and said, "O Messenger of Allah, what is īmān (faith)?" The Prophet ﷺ replied, "Īmān is to believe in Allah, His Angels, His Books, His Apostles, the meeting with Him, and to believe in the Resurrection." The man asked, "O Messenger of Allah, what is Islam?" The Prophet ﷺ replied, "Islam is to worship Allah and not worship anything besides Him, to establish the prayers, to pay the compulsory zakāh, and to fast the month of Ramadan." The man again asked, "O Messenger of Allah, what is iḥsān?" The Prophet ﷺ said, "Iḥsān is to worship Allah as if you see Him, and if you do not achieve this state of devotion, then understand that Allah sees you." The man further asked, "O Messenger of Allah, when will the Hour be established?" The Prophet ﷺ replied, "The one being asked does not know more than the one asking, but I will describe to you its portents. When a slave gives birth to her master – that will be one of its portents; when the bare-footed and scantily clad become the Chiefs of the people, that will be of its portents. The Hour is one of five things which nobody knows except Allah. 'Indeed, the knowledge of the Hour is with Allah alone. He sends down the rain, and knows that which is in the wombs.'"[79] Then the man left. The Prophet ﷺ said, "Call him back to me."

They went to call him back but could not find him. The Prophet ﷺ said, "That was Jibrīl. He came to teach the people their religion.""[80]

MASTERING THE FUNDAMENTALS

This Hadith is the clearest explanation of the core tenets of the faith of Islam and its obligations. Entire treatises have been written on this Hadith alone, and therefore we will not re-tread this ground when far more knowledgeable people than us have written expositions more eloquent and worthy than this one could ever muster. That being said, among the qualities and attributes a man is required to develop, a deep understanding and mastery of the fundamentals of *īmān* (faith), Islam the religion, and *iḥsān* (perfecting the self) are chief among them. We have covered *iḥsān* in a previous section, and consequently we will focus here on the former two, following a brief explanation of how the three concepts tie together.

Īmān covers what our *ʿaqā'id* (doctrinal tenets) as Muslims are, such as the Oneness of Allah ﷻ, His omniscience, His infallibility, and so on. Islam is the concrete fulfilment of our duties as Muslims, such as how we worship Allah ﷻ. *Iḥsān* is the perfection of our spiritual selves, as we discussed earlier. Each of

[79] *Qur'an* 31:34.

[80] *Ṣaḥīḥ al-Bukhārī* 4777.

these three aspects work in tandem to allow us to become fully developed Muslims. As such, mastery in these three areas is a goal that every man should have.

Mastery of the basics in any field is key to attaining proficiency in the field itself. The best boxers in the world are not the best because of the speed of their hands or the power of their punches, but their technique, their footwork, their control over the space within which they are fighting, and their perfect execution of the essential skills needed in the ring. Likewise, a *mu'min* (believer) must master his understanding of the fundamentals of his faith. Moreover, he must affirm his conviction in these beliefs daily such that they are fully internalised. Without *īmān*, what good is there in displaying manliness?

ءَامَنَ ٱلرَّسُولُ بِمَآ أُنزِلَ إِلَيْهِ مِن رَّبِّهِۦ وَٱلْمُؤْمِنُونَ ۚ كُلٌّ ءَامَنَ بِٱللَّهِ وَمَلَٰٓئِكَتِهِۦ وَكُتُبِهِۦ وَرُسُلِهِۦ لَا نُفَرِّقُ بَيْنَ أَحَدٍ مِّن رُّسُلِهِۦ ۚ وَقَالُوا۟ سَمِعْنَا وَأَطَعْنَا ۖ غُفْرَانَكَ رَبَّنَا وَإِلَيْكَ ٱلْمَصِيرُ.

The Messenger has believed in what has been revealed to him from his Lord, and the believers as well. All have believed in Allah and His Angels and His Books and His Messengers. 'We make no division between any of His Messengers', and they have said: 'We have listened, and obeyed. Our Lord, we seek Your pardon! And to You is the return.'[81]

Islam is defined as belief in the Oneness of Allah ﷻ, establishing *ṣalāh* (prayer), giving *zakāh*, and fasting in Ramadan. Islam is therefore the external religious dimension of a Muslim's life, and a person cannot be a Muslim in the true sense of the word if he does not act upon Islam. The elements of Islam that deal with acts of worship, and in this context, the obligatory

[81] *Qur'an* 2:285.

aspects of them, must be fulfilled. This is our duty to Allah ﷻ, and if we cannot fulfil our obligation to Him, then is there any responsibility that we can claim to fulfil?

On another occasion, the Prophet ﷺ said, 'Islam is built on five [pillars]: that Allah ﷻ alone should be worshipped and all others beside Him should be categorically denied, establishment of prayer, the payment of *zakāh*, the pilgrimage to the House (Kaʿbah), and fasting Ramadan.'[82]

A man should know how to perform all these acts of worship and the legal rulings around each of them to the point that he can comfortably apply these decrees in most common situations. For example, in terms of *ṣalāh* he should know how to lead a prayer, what to do if he joins a prayer late, what to do if he misses a part of the prayer, when he should or should not pray aloud, and the like.

Too often the very fundamentals of our religion are neglected and left to the *ʿulamā'* (scholars) to the point that the average Muslim cannot even answer the most basic questions regarding their faith. Many Muslims currently are searching for the answers to these simple issues via the internet and accessing websites that even a novice practitioner of the religion would realise are being established and run by hypocrites and non-Muslims. We should be learning our faith through established and learned teachers and ensure that we gain our knowledge from authentic and trustworthy sources.

Knowing one's fundamentals is about being able to function as a Muslim and helping others to do the same, without having to rely on any outside sources. A Muslim should know enough

---

[82] *Ṣaḥīḥ Muslim* 16b.

about his faith and religion to raise his children with the correct beliefs and understanding of their obligations.

6

He Pursues Knowledge

عَنْ كَثِيرِ بْنِ قَيْسٍ، قَالَ: كُنْتُ جَالِسًا عِنْدَ أَبِي الدَّرْدَاءِ رَضِيَ اللَّهُ عَنْهُ فِي مَسْجِدِ دِمَشْقَ، فَأَتَاهُ رَجُلٌ، فَقَالَ: "يَا أَبَا الدَّرْدَاءِ، أَتَيْتُكَ مِنَ الْمَدِينَةِ مَدِينَةِ رَسُولِ اللهِ صَلَّى اللَّهُ عَلَيْهِ وَسَلَّمَ لِحَدِيثٍ بَلَغَنِي أَنَّكَ تُحَدِّثُ بِهِ عَنِ النَّبِيِّ صَلَّى اللَّهُ عَلَيْهِ وَسَلَّمَ." قَالَ: "فَمَا جَاءَ بِكَ تِجَارَةٌ؟" قَالَ: "لَا." قَالَ: "وَلَا جَاءَ بِكَ غَيْرُهُ؟" قَالَ: "لَا." قَالَ: "فَإِنِّي سَمِعْتُ رَسُولَ اللهِ صَلَّى اللَّهُ عَلَيْهِ وَسَلَّمَ يَقُولُ: 'مَنْ سَلَكَ طَرِيقًا يَلْتَمِسُ فِيهِ عِلْمًا سَهَّلَ اللَّهُ لَهُ طَرِيقًا إِلَى الْجَنَّةِ، وَإِنَّ الْمَلَائِكَةَ لَتَضَعُ أَجْنِحَتَهَا رِضًا لِطَالِبِ الْعِلْمِ، وَإِنَّ طَالِبَ الْعِلْمِ يَسْتَغْفِرُ لَهُ مَنْ فِي السَّمَاءِ وَالأَرْضِ، حَتَّى الْحِيتَانِ فِي الْمَاءِ، وَإِنَّ فَضْلَ الْعَالِمِ عَلَى الْعَابِدِ كَفَضْلِ الْقَمَرِ عَلَى سَائِرِ الْكَوَاكِبِ. إِنَّ الْعُلَمَاءَ هُمْ وَرَثَةُ الأَنْبِيَاءِ، إِنَّ الأَنْبِيَاءَ لَمْ يُوَرِّثُوا دِينَارًا وَلاَ دِرْهَمًا، إِنَّمَا وَرَّثُوا الْعِلْمَ، فَمَنْ أَخَذَهُ أَخَذَ بِحَظٍّ وَافِرٍ'."

Kathīr ibn Qays ﷺ said, 'I was sitting with Abū al-Dardā' ﷺ in the masjid of Damascus when a man came to him and said, "O Abū al-Dardā', I have come to you from al-Medina, the city of the Messenger of Allah ﷺ, for a Hadith which I have heard that you narrate [directly from the Prophet ﷺ]." Abū al-Dardā' ﷺ asked, "So you have not come for trade?" He replied, "No." Abū al-Dardā' ﷺ then asked, "And you have not come for anything else?"

He again replied, "No." He ﷺ then said, "I heard the Messenger of Allah ﷺ say, 'Whoever treads a path in the pursuit of knowledge, Allah will make the path to Paradise easy for him. The Angels do lower their wings in approval of the seeker of knowledge, and everyone in the Heavens and on the Earth prays for his forgiveness – even the fish in the sea. The superiority of the scholar over the worshipper is like the superiority of the Moon above all other heavenly bodies. The scholars are the heirs of the Prophets, for the Prophets neither bequeathed dinars nor dirhams. Instead, they only bequeathed knowledge. Consequently, whoever takes it has indeed taken a great share.'"[83]

THE PURSUIT AND DISTRIBUTION OF KNOWLEDGE

ٱقْرَأْ بِٱسْمِ رَبِّكَ ٱلَّذِى خَلَقَ. خَلَقَ ٱلْإِنسَـٰنَ مِنْ عَلَقٍ. ٱقْرَأْ وَرَبُّكَ ٱلْأَكْرَمُ. ٱلَّذِى عَلَّمَ بِٱلْقَلَمِ. عَلَّمَ ٱلْإِنسَـٰنَ مَا لَمْ يَعْلَمْ.

Read with the name of your Lord Who created [everything], He created man from a clot of blood. Read, and your Lord is Most Gracious, Who imparted knowledge by means of the pen. He taught men what they did not know.[84]

The first revelation of the Qur'an and the Prophethood of Muhammad ﷺ began with the above words, the Divine Command of Allah ﷻ to *read.* Thus, the superiority of the pursuit of knowledge over all other endeavours was established at the very beginning of revelation with the very first command.

This pursuit is the intellectual journey a man undertakes to gain knowledge itself, rather than the trappings of knowledge. At this point, one may ask what the trappings of knowledge are. Such insincere motives include desiring titles, prestige, qualifications, deference, and respect. Though there is nothing wrong with achieving these desirable things per se, knowledge itself should be the goal, to which the title is a secondary achievement. And knowledge of the various sciences of Islam is the highest category of knowledge and the only kind that is beneficial to us beyond the transient world, in which we now reside.

The above Hadith mentions that the scholars are the

---

[83] *Sunan Ibn Mājah* 223.

[84] *Qur'an* 96:1-5.

inheritors of the Prophets 🕮, for the latter did not leave behind material wealth for their followers, nor inheritance for their families. The Prophets 🕮 leave behind their communicated words and knowledge, and those that take the message further and pursue this knowledge thus become their inheritors. The superiority of such people over all others is also described in this hadith in several ways, such as the superiority of the 'light' they reflect, or the deference given to them by the Angels themselves.

This superiority and deference is all due to the connection between the student of knowledge and the Prophet 🕮. Imam al-Rabbānī Rashīd Ahmad Gangohī 🕮 explains that the phrase 'Like the superiority of the Moon above all other heavenly bodies' indicates two fundamental points. Firstly, the knowledge under consideration in this Hadith is the information and reports that are in accordance with the Qur'an and Sunnah. For just as the Moon derives its luminescence from the radiance of the Sun and bears no light of its own, so too the light of knowledge emanating from the scholar is light derived from the Sun of Prophethood. Secondly, no personage within the *ummah*, regardless of how high a state they may reach, can ever be comparable to the Prophet 🕮. For whatever grace or light that person bears, it is merely the derived and reflected light and wisdom of the Prophet 🕮.[85]

The Prophet 🕮 explained that the person who walks the path to pursue this knowledge will find the path to Paradise open for him.

---

[85] *Al-Kawkab al-Durrī*, vol. 6: p. 261.

وَقُل رَّبِّ زِدْنِى عِلْمًا

...and say, 'My Lord, improve me in knowledge.'[86]

Thus, it is imperative that as men we are not complacent in the pursuit of knowledge but actively seek it out and obtain it, praying to Allah ﷻ to increase our knowledge. We should never be content with how far we have come, and instead strive to see how far we can go.

The Prophet ﷺ said, 'Lo! Indeed the world is accursed and what is in it is accursed, except for the remembrance of Allah ﷻ and what is conducive to that, the knowledgeable person, and the student.'[87]

عَلَّمَ ٱلْإِنسَـٰنَ مَا لَمْ يَعْلَمْ.

He taught man what he did not know.[88]

Allah ﷻ described Himself to the Prophet ﷺ in the cave of Ḥirā' in three distinct ways: 1) as his Creator, 2) as the Most Gracious, and 3) as his Teacher. Allah ﷻ describes Himself as the One Who taught Man what he did not know. The distribution of knowledge is an act which Allah ﷻ Himself has brought into motion, so what greater seal of approval for such an action can there be? All worthwhile pursuits in this world are those that bring us closer to Allah ﷻ. And if Allah ﷻ described Himself as the Teacher of Man, then teaching others knowledge which shall benefit them will surely bring us closer to Him.

This is supported by the words of the Prophet ﷺ when he stated, 'Indeed, I have been sent as a teacher.' He ﷺ issued these

---

[86] *Qur'an* 20:114.
[87] *Jāmiʿ al-Tirmidhī* 2322.
[88] *Qur'an* 96:5.

golden words upon entering the *masjid* and seeing his Companions ﷺ engaged in teaching and learning. Following this statement, he ﷺ sat down amongst them.[89]

Abū Hurayrah ﷺ narrated that the Messenger of Allah ﷺ said, 'Whoever is asked about some knowledge which he recognises yet conceals will be bridled with a bridle of fire.'[90] The Prophet ﷺ also said, 'The best among you are those who learn the Qur'an and teach it.'[91]

It is the duty of the Muslim to not only seek out knowledge but to distribute it to others as well. Teaching is something that both Allah ﷻ and His beloved Messenger ﷺ have done, and to be counted amongst the teachers of Islamic knowledge is from the highest of honours. A man should therefore engage himself in both of these pursuits throughout his life.

---

[89] *Sunan Ibn Mājah* 229.
[90] *Jāmiʿ al-Tirmidhī* 2649.
[91] *Ṣaḥīḥ al-Bukhārī* 5027.

7

He Learns from Experience

عَنْ أَبِي سَعِيدٍ رَضِيَ اللَّهُ عَنْهُ، قَالَ: قَالَ رَسُولُ اللَّهِ صَلَّى اللَّهُ عَلَيْهِ وَسَلَّمَ: "لاَ
حَلِيمَ إِلاَّ ذُو عَثْرَةٍ، وَلاَ حَكِيمَ إِلاَّ ذُو تَجْرِبَةٍ."

*Abū Saʿīd 🙵 narrated that the Messenger of Allah 🙵 said,
'There is no forbearing man except he who has stumbled, and
there is no wise man except for he who has experienced.*[92]

WISDOM

وَلَمَّا بَلَغَ أَشُدَّهُ ءَاتَيْنَـٰهُ حُكْمًا وَعِلْمًا ۚ وَكَذَٰلِكَ نَجْزِى ٱلْمُحْسِنِينَ.

*And when he reached the prime of his age, We gave him
wisdom and knowledge, and this is how We reward those who
are good in their deeds.*[93]

Knowledge and wisdom are terms that are often used
interchangeably, and as thus men with knowledge are often
described as being wise men. However, in the above verse Allah
🙵 states that He granted the Prophet Yūsuf 🙵 the reward of
knowledge *and* wisdom when he reached his prime. Knowledge
and wisdom, therefore, are not identical concepts. Knowledge is
the information one attains through study and effort, often
through teachers or books. Wisdom, on the other hand, is the
information that one attains through personal experience and
hardship. In academia, this distinction is often described as that
of *theory* and *practice*, where both aspects must be fully explored
to attain mastery in a field. A man can spend a lifetime studying
a subject in its every detail and intricacy, but he cannot say he has

---

[92] *Jāmiʿ al-Tirmidhī* 2033.
[93] *Qurʾan* 12:22.

mastered it until he has gained experience of it. Studying medicine is required to become a doctor, but *practising* medicine is equally important. Knowledge and wisdom are symbiotic in nature, whereby pursuing one without the context provided by the other will often lead to a deficiency in the seeker.

The Prophet ﷺ once described himself as being 'the house of wisdom,'[94] and who can deny that he ﷺ experienced more hardship than anyone else?

This is not to say that a man should seek out hardship, but that a man should learn from it when it befalls him. Experience is what differentiates a man from the boy he once was as he learns from it and becomes better equipped to face each test when it comes about again.

Likewise, men should learn from their elders or people of experience to gain the advantage of hindsight without being tested themselves. The Messenger of Allah ﷺ said, 'A wise statement is the lost property of the believer. Wherever he finds it, he is more worthy of it [than anyone else].'[95] As Muslims, we should gather wisdom and knowledge from wherever we find it, but not at the expense of giving up on our principles.

Learning from the experiences of others also means learning from those that have departed the temporal world before us, and understanding that there is no entertainment or pleasure that is worth wasting one's lifetime in. The Prophet ﷺ said, 'The wise man is the one who takes account of himself and works for what follows after death. The helpless man is the one who follows his whims, and then engages in wishful thinking about Allah ﷻ.'[96]

---

[94] *Jāmiʿ al-Tirmidhī* 3723.
[95] *Jāmiʿ al-Tirmidhī* 2687.
[96] *Sunan Ibn Mājah* 4260.

قُلْ إِنَّمَا حَرَّمَ رَبِّيَ ٱلْفَوَٰحِشَ مَا ظَهَرَ مِنْهَا وَمَا بَطَنَ وَٱلْإِثْمَ وَٱلْبَغْيَ بِغَيْرِ ٱلْحَقِّ وَأَن تُشْرِكُوا۟ بِٱللَّهِ مَا لَمْ يُنَزِّلْ بِهِۦ سُلْطَـٰنًا وَأَن تَقُولُوا۟ عَلَى ٱللَّهِ مَا لَا تَعْلَمُونَ.

Say, 'My Lord has prohibited only the shameful acts, whether open or secret, and every sinful act, and unjust aggression, and that you associate with Allah anything for which He has not sent any authority, and that you attribute to Allah anything about which you do not have sure knowledge.'[97]

فَسْـَٔلُوٓا۟ أَهْلَ ٱلذِّكْرِ إِن كُنتُمْ لَا تَعْلَمُونَ.

So ask the people of the Message, if you do not know.[98]

One of the greatest failings of the men of our age is their insistence on claiming to have knowledge of things they have neither studied nor experienced. People that make such claims are so deficient in understanding that they cannot admit to themselves or others that they do not have the answer to a question. In fact, they will go out of their way to convince people that their conjecture and deduction is the truth. Imam al-Shaʿbī ﷺ once said, 'The statement "I do not know" is one-half of all knowledge,'[99] and a man would be wise to act upon this advice. When we do not know the answer to a question, we should turn to people of knowledge rather than relying on our own estimations and speculations. The Prophet ﷺ made this clear when he said: 'If anyone is given a legal decision in ignorance, the sin lies with the one who made the decision.'[100]

The Prophet ﷺ warned us by stating: 'Do not tell a lie about me, for the one who tells a lie about me will surely enter the

[97] *Qur'an* 7:33.

[98] *Qur'an* 21:7.

[99] *Sunan al-Dārimī* 186.

[100] *Sunan Abī Dāwūd* 3657.

Hellfire.'[101] Today, we find people referencing the Qur'an and Hadiths without any restrictions, simply because they have read the translation of *Ṣaḥīḥ al-Bukhārī* or feel that their degrees in law or psychology give them the authority to interpret the verses of the Qur'an or derive Islamic rulings. The Prophet's Companions ﷺ were so afraid of misquoting a Hadith that they would begin to turn pale or red and sweat when they recited them, adding, 'He may have said something like this,' or adding as a proviso: 'He said something to this effect.' This was done to ensure that they were not telling an unintentional lie.[102]

A man should know when he is out of his depth, or when a matter or solution is outside of his knowledge and experience. He should use these situations as a reason to learn and seek out the answers, rather than inventing an answer and accordingly making a space for himself in the fires of Hell. May Allah ﷻ protect us all. *Āmīn.*

Know Yourself and Your Limits

وَكَذَٰلِكَ جَعَلْنَٰكُمْ أُمَّةً وَسَطًا لِّتَكُونُوا۟ شُهَدَآءَ عَلَى ٱلنَّاسِ وَيَكُونَ ٱلرَّسُولُ عَلَيْكُمْ شَهِيدًا ۗ

Likewise We made you a moderate ummah, such that you will be witnesses over the people, and the Messenger a witness to you.[103]

The Prophet ﷺ once approached ʿAbdullāh ibn ʿAmr ﷺ and said to him, 'I have been informed that you offer *ṣalāh* all through the night and fast during the day.' When Ibn ʿAmr ﷺ confirmed this, the Prophet ﷺ said, 'If you do so, your eyesight will become weak and you will become weak. No doubt, your

---

[101] *Ṣaḥīḥ al-Bukhārī* 106.
[102] *Sunan Ibn Mājah* 23.
[103] *Qur'an* 2:143.

body has a right over you, and your family have a right over you, so fast on some days and not on others, and stand in prayer for some time, and sleep for some time.'[104]

Islam is often described as 'the middle path', and Allah ﷻ has described the *ummah* of the Prophet ﷺ as a 'moderate community' in the above verse. To clarify, moderation here is in relation to Islam itself being moderate, and should not be confused with liberalist notions of what 'moderation' is. The Prophet ﷺ described this to us in very clear terms. The moderation of Islam is to spend a portion of the night in prayer and to fulfil the rights of your body by sleeping in the night as well; it is to fast on some days and to fulfil the rights of your wife on others. It is not what non-Muslims describe as the 'moderate Islam' that espouses the shaving of the beard, discarding of prayers, drinking of alcohol, and the wanton free-mixing of the opposite genders.

As has been mentioned before, and will no doubt be mentioned again, Islam takes the *fiṭrah* into account; it takes the man as he is and not as he hypothetically 'should' be, and then guides him to reach his most optimal level. Everything in life has its own time and place, and Islam makes allowances for men to enjoy life in a reasonable way, that is, within the limits set by Allah ﷻ and his Prophet ﷺ. It is all too common for the 'modern man' to become so engrossed in a hobby or ideology that he spends his entire day engrossed in this one thing, such that everything he reads or sees is in relation to this pursuit, and every conversation he has devolves into a discussion of it. This is not the behaviour of a man, but that of a child. A child becomes obsessive over that which gives him pleasure, or becomes so enamoured by some

---

[104] *Ṣaḥīḥ al-Bukhārī* 1153; 5299.

new experience or discovery that he cannot avoid it in any conversation. Even those so-called men that pursue the 'Red Pill' ideology or espouse incel views – and by extension their opposition as well – are not immune from this obsessiveness.

'Abdullāh ibn 'Amr 🕮 narrated:

> *The Messenger of Allah 🕮 entered upon me and said, 'Have I heard true that you offer prayer throughout the night and fast the entire day?' I said, 'Yes.' He 🕮 said, 'Do not do so. Pray at night and also sleep, fast for some days and do not fast for some. For your body has a right on you, your eyes have a right on you, your guest has a right on you, and your wife has a right on you. I hope that you will have a long life, and it is sufficient for you to fast for three days a month as the reward of a good deed is multiplied tenfold, which ultimately means it is as if you fasted the entire [month].' I insisted on more, so I was given more. I said, 'I can do more than that.' The Prophet 🕮 said, 'Fast three days every week.' But I insisted on more, so I was given more. I said, 'I can fast more than that.' The Prophet 🕮 said, 'Fast as Allah's Prophet Dāwūd 🕮 used to fast.' I said, 'What was the manner of the Prophet Dāwūd's fasting?' The Prophet 🕮 said, 'One half of the year [alternate days].[105]*

A man should know that everything has its time, and this extends beyond acts of worship. A man should make time for his family and time for his work, and likewise make time for self-improvement and time for worship. During these times, a man should focus on what he is doing and fulfil the associated rights that he has on himself or others have over him. Throughout

---

[105] *Ṣaḥīḥ al-Bukhārī* 6134.

these processes, he should be mindful of Allah ﷻ, for even this moderation is a means to bringing oneself closer to Him.

أَوَلَمْ يَتَفَكَّرُوا۟ فِىٓ أَنفُسِهِم ۗ

Did they not reflect in their own selves?[106]

Self-reflection is the act of looking at one's self, actions, or life, and taking stock of what one finds therein. As Muslims, such a process requires every one of us to be able to recognise and rectify our mistakes and to identify our own short-comings. The Prophet ﷺ said, 'There is no wisdom like reflection, and no honour like good manners.'[107]

The Prophet ﷺ would seek Allah's forgiveness over a hundred times a day,[108] and this continuous self-rectification was a daily practice of his. Seeking Allah's forgiveness requires one to believe that he has taken a misstep in some way, which is only possible through the act of self-reflection. A man should take constant stock of his actions and view them objectively in the light of the Qur'an and Sunnah. Where he finds himself wanting, he should seek forgiveness and make amends.

This is not to be confused with self-doubt and second-guessing oneself. Rather, a man should be prepared for his actions to withstand scrutiny and judgement, and hold himself to account. He should be able to look back at his words and actions and know when he had done right and when he had been in the wrong, and then be wise enough to seek forgiveness or correct his wrongs.

---

106 *Qur'an* 30:8.

107 *Sunan Ibn Mājah* 4218.

108 *Ṣaḥīḥ Muslim* 2702a.

8
He Stands for the Truth

عَنْ أَبِي هُرَيْرَةَ رَضِيَ اللهُ عَنْهُ، قَالَ: قَالَ رَسُولُ اللَّهِ صَلَّى اللَّهُ عَلَيْهِ وَسَلَّمَ: "إِذَا ضُيِّعَتِ الأَمَانَةُ فَانْتَظِرِ السَّاعَةَ." قَالَ: "كَيْفَ إِضَاعَتُهَا، يَا رَسُولَ اللَّهِ؟" قَالَ: "إِذَا أُسْنِدَ الأَمْرُ إِلَى غَيْرِ أَهْلِهِ، فَانْتَظِرِ السَّاعَةَ."

Abū Hurayrah ﷺ narrated that the Messenger of Allah ﷺ said, 'When honesty is lost, wait for the Hour.' A man asked, 'How will honesty be lost, O Messenger of Allah?' He ﷺ said, 'When authority is given to those who do not deserve it, wait for the Hour.'[109]

HONESTY AND INTEGRITY

إِنِّي لَكُمْ رَسُولٌ أَمِينٌ.

'I am an honest Messenger for you.'[110]

The above verse is repeated several times in the Qur'an, with the Prophets Nūḥ (Noah), Ṣāliḥ, Lūṭ (Lot), and Mūsā (Moses) ﷺ describing themselves in this manner. Honesty is one of the most fundamental qualities of a man, and every Prophet of Allah ﷺ stood at the pinnacle of honesty, for they had been created to carry the light of truth to the darkest corners of the world.

One of the names of our noble Prophet ﷺ was al-Ṣādiq (The Truthful), and he had gained this name well before he was made a Prophet of Allah on account of his nature. He ﷺ was renowned for being the most honest man amongst the Quraysh, and even after his Prophethood his staunchest enemies still saw

[109] *Ṣaḥīḥ al-Bukhārī* 59; 6496.
[110] *Qur'an* 26:107, 26:143, 26:162, 26: 178, 44:18.

him as such. When he announced his Prophethood to his friends and family, they believed in him without a moment's hesitation; such was their belief in his truthfulness. The Prophet ﷺ said, 'I do not speak except that I speak the truth.'[111] In fact, he advised the general Muslim population to do the same:

> *Abide by truthfulness. Indeed truthfulness leads to righteousness, and righteousness leads to Paradise. A man continues telling the truth and striving to do so until he is recorded with Allah as a truthful person. Refrain from falsehood. Certainly, falsehood leads to wickedness, and wickedness leads to the Fire. A slave of Allah continues to lie and strives to do so until he is recorded with Allah as a liar.*[112]

Subsequently, a key difference between the dwellers of Heaven and Hell is their commitment to the truth. Interestingly, he ﷺ warned us that a sign of the Day of Judgement is the loss of honesty, and explained that this would be the time when the undeserving would be given authority. It is a sad state of affairs that our leaders and politicians are now known to be the least truthful people among us. We live in a world of 'fake news', both real and imagined, where what we see and hear can be - or be made to appear - false; where each person claims to have his or her 'own truth' and the bizarre belief that multiple truths in direct opposition to each other can exist. We often hear them say, 'I'm speaking my truth', as if the existence of one Truth is no longer the case. This post-modernist idea, the notion of 'The death of truth', has found its way into the rhetoric and vocabularies of Western Muslims. It is a poison, and must be opposed. Allah ﷻ

---

[111] *Jāmiʿ al-Tirmidhī* 1990.
[112] *Jāmiʿ al-Tirmidhī* 1971.

describes our religion as the 'Religion of Truth'[113] on several occasions; as long as there is Islam there will always be *the* Truth.

A man must always be honest, even if his honesty goes against his best interest, and he must stand up for the truth even if the whole world stands against him. He must be upright and principled. His integrity must be unwavering. No amount of seduction, enticement, or worldly benefit can shake his resolve to do right. A man's integrity is to be morally principled and incorruptible.

وَرَٰوَدَتْهُ ٱلَّتِى هُوَ فِى بَيْتِهَا عَن نَّفْسِهِۦ وَغَلَّقَتِ ٱلْأَبْوَٰبَ وَقَالَتْ هَيْتَ لَكَ ۚ قَالَ مَعَاذَ ٱللَّهِ ۖ إِنَّهُۥ رَبِّىٓ أَحْسَنَ مَثْوَاىَ ۖ إِنَّهُۥ لَا يُفْلِحُ ٱلظَّـٰلِمُونَ. وَلَقَدْ هَمَّتْ بِهِۦ ۖ وَهَمَّ بِهَا لَوْلَآ أَن رَّءَا بُرْهَـٰنَ رَبِّهِۦ ۚ كَذَٰلِكَ لِنَصْرِفَ عَنْهُ ٱلسُّوٓءَ وَٱلْفَحْشَآءَ ۚ إِنَّهُۥ مِنْ عِبَادِنَا ٱلْمُخْلَصِينَ.

And she, in whose house he was, seduced him towards herself, and bolted the doors, and said, 'Come on!' He said, 'I seek refuge with Allah. Surely, he your husband is my master. He has given me a good lodging. Indeed, the wrongdoers do not prosper.' She certainly desired him, and he might have desired her, had he not seen the proof from his Lord. Thus We did, to turn evil and lewdness away from him. Surely, he was one of Our chosen servants.[114]

The story of the Prophet Yūsuf (Joseph) ﷺ and Zulaykhah is known to all, and *Sayyidunā* Yūsuf's integrity and honourable nature was immortalised in the above verses of the Qur'an. It is reported that the Prophet of Allah ﷺ would often pray, 'O Allah, I ask You for health, continence, integrity, a good character, and acceptance of what is decreed.'[115] Furthermore, in another tradition he ﷺ advised us by stating: 'Have integrity,

---

[113] *Qur'an* 48:28, 61:9.
[114] *Qur'an* 12:23-24.
[115] *Mishkāt al-Maṣābīḥ* 2500.

since Allah ﷻ has integrity with you.'[116]

One way a man can instil this quality within himself is through the constant remembrance of Allah ﷻ and the alertness that He is constantly observing him. A man under constant surveillance will never do anything wrong; the man that understands that all men are being watched by Allah ﷻ and will be judged accordingly cannot ever waver in his principles.

CONFIDENTIALITY, DISCRETION, AND TRUSTWORTHINESS

سَوَآءٌ مِّنكُم مَّنْ أَسَرَّ ٱلْقَوْلَ وَمَن جَهَرَ بِهِۦ وَمَنْ هُوَ مُسْتَخْفٍۭ بِٱلَّيْلِ وَسَارِبٌۢ بِٱلنَّهَارِ

Alike for Him is he, from among you, who speaks quietly and he who speaks aloud, and he who hides in the night and he who walks out in the day.[117]

وَٱللَّهُ يَعْلَمُ مَا تُسِرُّونَ وَ مَا تُعْلِنُونَ

Allah knows what you conceal and what you reveal.[118]

The Prophet ﷺ said, 'It is enough for a man to prove himself a liar when he goes on narrating everything he hears.'[119] Alongside honesty and integrity, a Muslim man is one who respects confidentiality. All matters discussed in confidence are treated with discretion, and in the presence of a Muslim man a person should be confident that the matter will remain discrete - even if this was never specified. It is not of the qualities of a man to engage in gossip, nor to reveal the secrets of others. The Prophet

---

[116] *Muwaṭṭa' Imam Mālik* 1808.
[117] *Qur'an* 13:10.
[118] *Qur'an* 16:19.
[119] *Ṣaḥīḥ Muslim* 5.

ﷺ said, 'The tale-bearer shall not enter Paradise.'[120] Allah ﷻ Himself describes the believers as individuals that can be taken as confidants, as discretion is a quality of the sincere devotee:

أَمْ حَسِبْتُمْ أَن تُتْرَكُوا۟ وَلَمَّا يَعْلَمِ ٱللَّهُ ٱلَّذِينَ جَٰهَدُوا۟ مِنكُمْ وَلَمْ يَتَّخِذُوا۟ مِن دُونِ ٱللَّهِ وَلَا رَسُولِهِۦ وَلَا ٱلْمُؤْمِنِينَ وَلِيجَةً ۚ وَٱللَّهُ خَبِيرٌۢ بِمَا تَعْمَلُونَ

Do you think that you will be left alone without being tested, while Allah has not yet seen those of you who struggle in jihad and never take anyone as their confidant other than Allah and His Messenger and the believers? Allah is fully aware of what you do.[121]

The Prophet ﷺ said, 'Meetings should be confidential except in three instances: those for the purpose of unlawful bloodshed, for committing fornication, or for acquiring property unjustly.'[122] Thus, unless a crime is being planned in a meeting between individuals, a gathering's proceedings are *always* confidential. He ﷺ also said, 'The one consulted is in a position of trust.'[123] The Hadith master Shaykh Khalīl Aḥmad Sahāranpūrī رحمه الله explains further that the one who is being consulted is being entrusted in that matter, and consequently it is not permissible for him to disclose what was said in confidence; besides it being compulsory on him to advise according to what is most beneficial in both this world and the Hereafter, he should not advise that which will cause harm.[124] Further to this, the Prophet ﷺ also said, 'If anyone is given a legal decision in ignorance, the sin lies with the one who made the decision', whilst in the same narration from the chain of Sulaymān al-Mahrī

[120] *Ṣaḥīḥ Muslim* 105a.
[121] *Qur'an* 9:16.
[122] *Sunan Abī Dāwūd* 4869.
[123] *Sunan Abī Dāwūd* 5128.
[124] *Badhl al-Majhūd,* vol. 13: p. 518.

ﷺ, he added: '...if anyone advises his brother, knowing that guidance lies in another direction, he has deceived them.'[125]

If a presently-occurring sin is revealed to a Muslim in the meeting, one should look at the wider context before revealing this to anyone. The Prophet ﷺ said, '...he who conceals the faults of a Muslim, Allah ﷻ will conceal his faults in the world and in the Hereafter. Allah ﷻ is at the aid of His servant so long as the servant is at the aid of his brother...'[126] Ḥudhayfah رضي الله عنه was known as the Confidant of the Prophet ﷺ and as such he kept secret the names of the hypocrites disclosed to him by the Prophet ﷺ throughout his life; never once did he reveal any of their names.[127] However, if they are sinning openly, then there is no need for confidentiality, and if one has witnessed a crime being committed, one should be prepared to testify to what has been seen.

Just as al-Ṣādiq (the Truthful) was a title of our beloved Prophet ﷺ even before his Prophethood, so too was al-Amīn (the Trustworthy). Even the enemies of the Prophet ﷺ would trust him to look after their property, and his trustworthiness in his business dealings was one of the many reasons for why the Mother of the Believers Khadījah رضي الله عنها sent a marriage proposal to him.

Abū 'Ubaydah ibn al-Jarrāḥ رضي الله عنه, a great general amongst the Companions رضي الله عنهم and one of the Ten Promised with Paradise رضي الله عنهم, was renowned even amongst his noble peers as 'The trustworthy

[125] *Sunan Abī Dāwūd* 3657.
[126] *Ṣaḥīḥ Muslim* 2699.
[127] *Ṣaḥīḥ al-Bukhārī* 3761; *Fatḥ al-Bārī*, vol. 11: p. 177.

man of this nation'[128], and there are multiple Hadiths of the Prophet ﷺ referring to him as such. Being trustworthy is an angelic characteristic, and Allah ﷻ describes *Sayyidunā* Mūsā ﷺ as such in the Qur'an:

قَالَتْ إِحْدَىٰهُمَا يَـٰٓأَبَتِ ٱسْتَـْٔجِرْهُ ۖ إِنَّ خَيْرَ مَنِ ٱسْتَـْٔجَرْتَ ٱلْقَوِىُّ ٱلْأَمِينُ

One of the two women said, 'Dear father, hire him; the best man you can hire is someone who is strong and trustworthy.'[129]

Indeed, it is clear from the Hadith corpus of the Prophet ﷺ that trustworthiness was a universal quality of the Companions ﷺ, as he said, 'There will be some people after you who will be dishonest and will not be trustworthy. They will give evidence without being asked to do so, pronounce vows but will not fulfil them, and obesity will appear among them.'[130]

Trustworthiness in our dealings holds great rewards, as the Prophet ﷺ said, 'The trustworthy, honest Muslim merchant will be with the martyrs on the Day of Resurrection.'[131] That said, the reward of being trustworthy is a bonus, and should not be the reason one is inclined toward honouring someone's trust. It is an inherent quality of a Muslim. Indeed, the strength or weakness of a narration in the Hadith sciences is dependent on the level of trustworthiness found in the narrators. A narrator that is known to have lied even once is not considered trustworthy.[132] Such was the quality of the men about whom the Prophet ﷺ said, 'The best of you are my generation, then those that follow after them, then those that follow after them.'[133]

---

[128] *Ṣaḥīḥ al-Bukhārī* 3744.
[129] *Qur'an* 28:26.
[130] *Ṣaḥīḥ al-Bukhārī* 2651.
[131] *Sunan Ibn Mājah* 2139.
[132] *Nuzhat al-Naẓar fī Tawḍīḥ Nukhbat al-Fikar*, p. 58.
[133] *Ṣaḥīḥ al-Bukhārī* 2651.

Finally, trustworthiness for a Muslim goes beyond being able to be relied upon, as it also includes being trustworthy with people's wealth and wellbeing. The Prophet ﷺ stated: 'The believer is the one from whom people's blood and wealth are safe.'[134] As Muslims, it should not be the case that we abuse our privileges if we are left in a position of power over someone else. A Muslim does not rob or steal, nor does he assault the weak man because he is mightier. Furthermore, he does not sully a woman who is haram on him, regardless of whether she allows him to or not.

[134] *Sunan al-Nasāʾī* 4995.

9
'His Manliness is his Good Character'[135]

عَنْ مَالِكٍ رَضِيَ اللَّهُ عَنْهُ، أَنَّهُ قَدْ بَلَغَهُ أَنَّ رَسُولَ اللَّهِ صَلَّى اللَّهُ عَلَيْهِ وَسَلَّمَ قَالَ:
"بُعِثْتُ لِأُتَمِّمَ حُسْنَ الأَخْلَاقِ."

Imam Mālik ﷺ narrated that it had reached him that the Messenger of Allah ﷺ said, 'I was sent to perfect good character.'[136]

GOOD CHARACTER

Our noble and dear Prophet ﷺ himself stated that he was sent to perfect good character (*akhlāq*). But what is 'good' character? The qualities listed in this text are part of good character. When explaining good character, ʿAbdullāh ibn al-Mubārak ﷺ described it as being '...a smiling face, doing one's best in good deeds, and refraining from harm.'[137]

قَدْ أَفْلَحَ ٱلْمُؤْمِنُونَ. ٱلَّذِينَ هُمْ فِى صَلَاتِهِمْ خَـٰشِعُونَ. وَٱلَّذِينَ هُمْ عَنِ ٱللَّغْوِ مُعْرِضُونَ. وَٱلَّذِينَ هُمْ لِلزَّكَوٰةِ فَـٰعِلُونَ. وَٱلَّذِينَ هُمْ لِفُرُوجِهِمْ حَـٰفِظُونَ.

Success is certainly attained by the believers, those who concentrate their attention in humbleness when offering ṣalāh (prayers), and who keep themselves away from vain things, and who are performers of zakāh, and who guard their private parts.[138]

The Mother of the Believers ʿĀ'ishah ﷺ once described the character of the Prophet ﷺ by stating: 'His character was the

---

135 *Muwaṭṭa' Imam Mālik* 996.
136 *Muwaṭṭa' Imam Mālik* 1643.
137 *Jāmiʿ al-Tirmidhī* 2005.
138 *Qur'an* 23:1-5.

Qur'an.' She then recited the above verses and stated, 'That was the character of the Prophet ﷺ.'[139]

The Prophet ﷺ said, 'The most complete of the believers in faith is the one with the best character among them. And the best of you are those who are the best of you towards their womenfolk.'[140]

Good character involves temperance, passion, and compassion; it is in showing kindness to others, especially those you are responsible for. The Prophet ﷺ said, 'The strong man is not the one who wrestles, but rather the strong man is the one who controls himself while in anger.'[141]

Good character is one's drive to be as good as one can be and refraining from anything that could cause others harm; more so, it is doing something good for others for no other reason than it being the right thing to do. The following narration cited by Umm al-Dardā' ﷺ is a perfect example of this:

> *Umm al-Dardā' ﷺ said, 'Abū al-Dardā' ﷺ stood up in the night to pray. He was weeping and said, "O Allah! You made my physical form good, so make my character good!" until morning. I said, "Abū al-Dardā', your only supplication for the entire night was for good character!" He replied, "Umm al-Dardā', a Muslim perfects his character such that its goodness enters him into Paradise; and taints his character such that his badness of character enters him into Hellfire. A Muslim is forgiven even while he sleeps!" I asked, "Abū al-Dardā', how can he be forgiven while he is asleep?" He said, "His brother arises*

[139] *Al-Adab al-Mufrad* 308.
[140] *Jāmiʿ al-Tirmidhī* 1162.
[141] *Ṣaḥīḥ al-Bukhārī* 6114.

in the night, performs the night prayer, and supplicates to Allah Almighty and is answered. He supplicates for his Muslim brother and his supplication is answered."[142]

Abū al-Dardā' ﵁ spent the entire night in prayer asking Allah ﷻ to perfect his character, for he knew how important it was to master his moral personality. The end of the Hadith shows the truly noble character of a Muslim man: he is described as the brother that wakes in the night to pray to Allah ﷻ for the sake of his brother. There is no personal benefit obtained through this action, and none is sought. A man of good character is one who wishes the best for others, as he wishes the best for himself. The Prophet ﷺ said, 'Nothing is placed on the Scale that is weightier than good character. Certainly, the person with good character will attain the rank of the person of fasting and prayer.'[143]

HUMILITY AND MODESTY

إِنَّ ٱلْمُسْلِمِينَ وَٱلْمُسْلِمَٰتِ وَٱلْمُؤْمِنِينَ وَٱلْمُؤْمِنَٰتِ وَٱلْقَٰنِتِينَ وَٱلْقَٰنِتَٰتِ وَٱلصَّٰدِقِينَ وَٱلصَّٰدِقَٰتِ وَٱلصَّٰبِرِينَ وَٱلصَّٰبِرَٰتِ وَٱلْخَٰشِعِينَ وَٱلْخَٰشِعَٰتِ وَٱلْمُتَصَدِّقِينَ وَٱلْمُتَصَدِّقَٰتِ وَٱلصَّٰٓئِمِينَ وَٱلصَّٰٓئِمَٰتِ وَٱلْحَٰفِظِينَ فُرُوجَهُمْ وَٱلْحَٰفِظَٰتِ وَٱلذَّٰكِرِينَ ٱللَّهَ كَثِيرًا وَٱلذَّٰكِرَٰتِ أَعَدَّ ٱللَّهُ لَهُم مَّغْفِرَةً وَأَجْرًا عَظِيمًا.

Surely, Muslim men and Muslim women, believing men and believing women, devout men and devout women, truthful men and truthful women, patient men and patient women, humble men and humble women, and the men who give ṣadaqah (voluntary charity) and the women who give ṣadaqah, and the men who fast and the women who fast, and the men who guard their private parts against evil acts and the women who guard theirs and the men who remember Allah much and the women

[142] *Al-Adab al-Mufrad* 290.
[143] *Jāmiʿ al-Tirmidhī* 2003.

who remember Him – for them, Allah has prepared forgiveness and a great reward.[144]

Understanding the above verse and acting upon it alone would lead to the development and perfection of character for Muslim men and women alike. Amongst the many qualities listed in the verse, Allah ﷻ mentions humility as a characteristic which will lead us to forgiveness and a great reward. *Al-Khāshiʿīn* means those possessing serenity, tranquillity, deliberation, dignity, and humility.[145] These qualities are built through the fear of Allah ﷻ and the awareness that He is watching you incessantly; what motivates a person to be like this is the fear of Allah ﷻ and the awareness that He is constantly watching. This essentially operationalises *iḥsān*, which means to 'worship Allah ﷻ as if you can see Him, for if you cannot see Him, He can see you'.[146]

The Prophet ﷺ explained the necessity of humility in a Muslim's personality when he said, 'Indeed, Allah ﷻ has revealed to me that you should adopt humility, so that no one may wrong another and no one may be disdainful and haughty towards another.'[147] Humility is intrinsically tied to the concept of being constantly aware of Allah ﷻ, and the lowering of one's self in response to this mindfulness. How can one be anything but humble when his Creator watches over him? Qaylah bint Makhramah ؓ once saw the Prophet ﷺ in the *masjid* squatting on his heels, a position of humility. She said, 'When I saw the Messenger of Allah ﷺ displaying such humility in the *masjid*, I trembled with fright.'[148] To see the most powerful man – in terms

---

[144] *Qur'an* 33:35.
[145] *Tafsīr Ibn Kathīr* 33:35.
[146] *Ṣaḥīḥ al-Bukhārī* 4777.
[147] *Riyāḍ al-Ṣāliḥīn* 1589.
[148] *Al-Shamāʾil al-Muḥammadiyyah* 126.

of physicality, presence, intellect, beauty, and sheer *power* - sitting in the House of Allah with such humility was enough to make this blessed Companion ﷺ tremble with fear and awe. Who are we then to be boastful and full of pride, when the Messenger of Allah ﷺ, His most beloved creation, made himself small for fear of his Creator?

Likewise, humility should be adopted in all aspects of life, and this is liked by Allah ﷻ. The Prophet ﷺ said, 'Whoever forgoes expensive or extravagant clothing out of humility to Allah ﷻ while he is able to afford it, Allah ﷻ will call him before all creation on the Day of Judgement, so that he may choose whichever *ḥulal* (garments) of faith[149] he wishes to wear.'[150] He ﷺ also stated, 'Whoever drinks from his hand when he is able to drink from a vessel, intending humility, Allah ﷻ will record good deeds equivalent to the number of his fingers. It (the hand) was the vessel of ʿĪsā Jesus ibn Maryam ﷺ, for he threw away the cup and said, "Ugh! That belongs to this world."'[151]

Humility is a quality of greater value when a person has the means to display wealth or pride, but chooses not to due to his awareness of Allah's presence and humbles himself accordingly. This point does not mean that the poor man cannot be humble, but it indicates that such an orientation is more onerous for a person of high social and material standing. It is interesting to see how modern masculine movements not only forgo such virtues in their ideologies, but also go a step further and encourage prideful and boastful behaviour as well as the flaunting of wealth and status as a core quality of being a 'High-Value Man'. Yet,

---

[149] These refer to special articles of clothing in Paradise which are given to the people of faith.

[150] *Jāmiʿ al-Tirmidhī* 2481.

[151] *Sunan Ibn Mājah* 3431.

within the Islamic theological prism such actions evoke the anger of Allah ﷻ, which deprives them of any value.

The Prophet ﷺ said that 'every *dīn* (religious way of life) has an innate character, and the character of Islam is modesty'.[152] Modern men are in a delusional state if they deem humility and modesty to be outside the sphere of 'manly' traits. Modesty is very much the quality of a man, as the Prophet ﷺ was renowned for his modesty, as can be evidenced from the words of his Companions ﷺ. Abū Sa'īd al-Khudrī ﷺ reported that Allah's Messenger ﷺ was 'more modest than a virgin behind a curtain, and when he disliked anything we recognised that from his face'.[153] The Mother of the Believers Umm Salamah ﷺ said, 'The most loved garment to the Messenger of Allah ﷺ was the *qamīṣ*[154].'[155]

قُل لِّلْمُؤْمِنِينَ يَغُضُّوا۟ مِنْ أَبْصَـٰرِهِمْ وَيَحْفَظُوا۟ فُرُوجَهُمْ ۚ ذَٰلِكَ أَزْكَىٰ لَهُمْ ۗ إِنَّ ٱللَّهَ خَبِيرٌۢ بِمَا يَصْنَعُونَ.

Tell the believing men that they must lower their gazes and guard their private parts; it is more decent for them. Surely Allah is All-Aware of what they do.[156]

The word *yaghuḍḍu* is the present tense verbal form of the gerund *ghaḍḍ*, which means bringing down or lowering.[157] A Muslim lowers his gaze and guards his own chastity. This is done not only to avoid engaging in sinful relationships, but also to refrain from looking towards that which is sinful and immodest.

---

[152] *Muwaṭṭa' Imam Mālik* 1644.
[153] *Ṣaḥīḥ Muslim* 2320.
[154] A long shirt, similar to the modern *thobe*.
[155] *Jāmi' al-Tirmidhī* 1764; *Sunan Abī Dāwūd* 4025.
[156] *Qur'an* 24:30.
[157] *Ma'ārif al-Qur'an*, vol. 6: p. 408.

Ibn Ḥibbān explains that to look at a non-*maḥram* (unrelated person) to derive pleasure is prohibited, and to stare even without such a motive is *makrūh* (undesirable).[158]

Modesty is a quality that was always valued amongst the pious predecessors of Islam. In fact, it was the characteristic that the Prophet used to honour Amīr al-Mu'minīn ʿUthmān ibn ʿAffān with, for he once stated: 'The most modest of my nation is ʿUthmān ibn ʿAffān.'[159] In another narration, he said: 'Should I not be modest in front of a man before whom the Angels are modest?'[160]

More than being a Prophetic quality and a quality of the Companions, modesty is also a branch of faith[161] and a quality of Allah Himself, as the Prophet said, 'Allah is forbearing, modest, and concealing, and He loves modesty and concealment.'[162] Taking these previous moral examples into mind, we conclude that we can never call ourselves men if we forgo modesty in favour of satanic behaviour.

وَإِذْ قُلْنَا لِلْمَلَٰٓئِكَةِ ٱسْجُدُوا۟ لِـَٔادَمَ فَسَجَدُوٓا۟ إِلَّآ إِبْلِيسَ أَبَىٰ وَٱسْتَكْبَرَ وَكَانَ مِنَ ٱلْكَٰفِرِينَ.

And when We said to the Angels, 'Prostrate yourselves before Adam!' So they prostrated, all but Iblīs (Satan). He refused, was arrogant, and became one of the infidels.[163]

قَالَ مَا مَنَعَكَ أَلَّا تَسْجُدَ إِذْ أَمَرْتُكَ ۖ قَالَ أَنَا۠ خَيْرٌ مِّنْهُ خَلَقْتَنِى مِن نَّارٍ وَخَلَقْتَهُۥ مِن طِينٍ.
قَالَ فَٱهْبِطْ مِنْهَا فَمَا يَكُونُ لَكَ أَن تَتَكَبَّرَ فِيهَا فَٱخْرُجْ إِنَّكَ مِنَ ٱلصَّٰغِرِينَ.

Allah said, 'What has prevented you from prostrating when I

---

[158] *Maʿārif al-Qur'an*, vol. 6: p. 408.
[159] *Jāmiʿ al-Tirmidhī* 3790, 3791.
[160] *Al-Adab al-Mufrad* 603.
[161] *Sunan Ibn Mājah* 58.
[162] *Sunan al-Nasā'ī* 406.
[163] *Qur'an* 2:34.

ordered you?' He said, 'I am better than him. You have created me of fire, and created him of clay.' He said, 'Then get down from here, for it is not for you to show arrogance here. So get out, you are one of the degraded.'[164]

Arrogance is the defining quality of Iblīs, and it is ultimately the reason for why he was degraded and disgraced. Fire - by its nature - rises up and dances as it burns, whereas the nature of earth is to remain low. The distinction here between Iblīs being made of fire and being degraded and Adam ﷺ being made of clay and exalted is evident. Humility and modesty are the qualities of a man, whereas pride and arrogance are the qualities of a devil. The Prophet ﷺ said that the inmates of Hell will include 'every violent, impertinent, and proud man'.[165]

NOBILITY AND HONOUR

إِنَّهُ لَقَوْلُ رَسُولٍ كَرِيمٍ.

It [the Qur'an] is surely the word of a noble messenger (Jibrīl).[166]

Having listed some of the satanic qualities that should be shunned by men, we return to desirable virtues once more. Nobility, as can be seen from the above verse, is an angelic quality. But what is nobility and what features define it? Nobility can take many meanings: it can refer to someone's high lineage, excellence in character, or general impressiveness. However, for the purpose of our analysis we will adopt the definition of Ibn ʿAbbās: 'What do you reckon to be nobility? Allah ﷻ has made nobility clear. The noblest of you in the sight of Allah ﷻ is the

[164] *Qur'an* 7:12-13.
[165] *Ṣaḥīḥ al-Bukhārī* 6071.
[166] *Qur'an* 81:19.

one with the greatest *taqwā* (God-consciousness). What do you reckon to be the best lineage? The best of you in lineage is the best of you in character.'[167]

Taqwā is the act of being cognisant of Allah. From the definition of Ibn ʿAbbās we can deduce that the worldly understanding of nobility – namely that of being from prestigious lineage or 'high-born' – is, for the most part, of no use to the Muslim.[168] The one who behaves as if Allah is watching him and perfects his character is the one considered noble. Nobility is found in praiseworthy behaviour. The Prophet said, 'Being honourable is wealth and noble character is piety.'[169] Therefore, perfecting one's character is an act of worship and will be rewarded by Allah.

Indeed, one of Allah's names is The Bountiful (al-Karīm). Allah bestows gifts upon people from His infinite bounties, and has no requirement for anything in return. Imam Ibn Kathīr defines the aforementioned divine attribute by stating: 'He is Bountiful in and of Himself, even if no one were to worship Him. His Greatness does not depend on anyone.'[170]

A noble man is a man that worships his Lord as if he is seeing Him or being watched by Him, perfects his character, and is kind to others without the need for anything in return.

يَقُولُونَ لَئِن رَّجَعْنَآ إِلَى ٱلْمَدِينَةِ لَيُخْرِجَنَّ ٱلْأَعَزُّ مِنْهَا ٱلْأَذَلَّ ۚ وَلِلَّهِ ٱلْعِزَّةُ وَلِرَسُولِهِ

[167] *Al-Adab al-Mufrad* 899.

[168] The noble bloodlines of the Prophets are an exception here, which is why as Muslims we should pay the descendants of the Prophet due respect. 'The honourable is the son of the honourable, the son of the honourable, the son of the honourable i.e., Yūsuf, the son of Yaʿqūb, the son of Isḥāq, the son of Ibrāhīm' (*Ṣaḥīḥ al-Bukhārī* 3382).

[169] *Sunan Ibn Mājah* 4219.

[170] *Tafsīr Ibn Kathīr* 27:40.

وَلِلْمُؤْمِنِينَ وَلَـٰكِنَّ ٱلْمُنَـٰفِقِينَ لَا يَعْلَمُونَ.

They say, 'If we return to Medina, the more honourable ones will drive out the meaner ones from there.' And to Allah belongs the honour, and to His Messenger, and to the believers, but the hypocrites do not know.[171]

This verse was revealed in response to a statement of the hypocrite, Ibn Ubayy. He labelled himself and the inhabitants of Medina as superior in honour to the Holy Prophet ﷺ and the Muhājirīn (Emigrants) ﭫ. In response to this, Allah ﷻ used Ibn Ubayy's own boastful statement against him by pointing out that if the 'honourable' were to drive out the 'mean', it would go against the hypocrites like Ibn Ubayy.[172]

The term honour refers to the quality of being regarded with high respect and great esteem, or to be granted a position bestowing such merits. To honour someone is to pay them great respect, and to be honourable is to be someone worthy of respect and esteem. Many cultures have codes of honour and their own understanding of how to maintain them, but the Muslim understands that true honour can only be bestowed by Allah ﷻ:

تَبَـٰرَكَ ٱسْمُ رَبِّكَ ذِى ٱلْجَلَـٰلِ وَٱلْإِكْرَامِ.

Glorious is the name of your Lord, the Lord of Majesty, the Lord of Honour.[173]

The Lord of Majesty and Honour has privileged us by granting us the highest of honours, namely Islam, and by listing the believers as those to whom honour belongs. As Muslims, it should be understood that honour is not something we can gain through force, but something which is earned through

---

[171] *Qur'an* 63:8.
[172] *Ma'ārif al-Qur'an,* vol. 8: pp. 463-469.
[173] *Qur'an* 55:78.

praiseworthy behaviour, action, and experience. Indeed, the Prophet ﷺ said, 'Glorifying Allah ﷻ involves showing honour to a grey-haired Muslim and to one who can expound the Qur'an without acting extravagantly regarding it or turning away from it, and showing honour to a just ruler.'[174] However, as mentioned above, Allah ﷻ has granted us honour by allowing us to be Muslims, and therefore it is imperative that we do not debase our brothers and sisters. The Prophet ﷺ said, 'If anyone eats a meal at the expense of a Muslim's honour, Allah ﷻ will feed him a like amount of the Hellfire. If anyone clothes himself with a garment at the expense of a Muslim's honour, Allah ﷻ will clothe him with a like amount of the Hellfire. If anyone achieves a position of arrogance and hypocrisy at the expense of a Muslim's honour, Allah ﷻ will put him in a position of arrogance and hypocrisy on the Day of Resurrection.'[175] A man must honour those deserving respect, earn the honour of his peers, and uphold the distinction of those whose honour has been slighted.

The hypocrite, on the other hand, sees honour in terms of the worldly respect he believes he deserves due to his so-called 'noble' lineage, the exercising of might, or avenging wounded pride.

ذُقْ إِنَّكَ أَنتَ ٱلْعَزِيزُ ٱلْكَرِيمُ.

'Have a taste! You are the "man of might", the "man of honour".'[176]

The Keepers of Hell will say the above to the inmates as they are punished, ridiculing them to disgrace them further, showing just how dishonourable and dishonoured they truly are. Ibn

---

[174] *Sunan Abī Dāwūd* 4843.
[175] *Al-Adab al-Mufrad* 240.
[176] *Qur'an* 44:49.

ʿAbbās 🕮 said about this verse, 'This ultimately means: "You are neither mighty nor generous."'[177]

10
He is Good Mannered

حَدَّثَنَا أَيُّوبُ بْنُ مُوسَى، عَنْ أَبِيهِ، عَنْ جَدِّهِ رَضِيَ اللَّهُ عَنْهُم، أَنَّ رَسُولَ اللَّهِ صَلَّى اللَّهُ عَلَيْهِ وَسَلَّمَ قَالَ: "مَا نَحَلَ وَالِدٌ وَلَدًا مِنْ نَحْلٍ أَفْضَلَ مِنْ أَدَبٍ حَسَنٍ."

Ayyūb ibn Mūsā narrated via his father, who related from his grandfather ﷺ that the Messenger of Allah ﷺ said, 'There is no gift that a father gives his son more virtuous than good manners.'[178]

GOOD MANNERS

Good manners can be defined as polite, courteous, and 'correct' social behaviour. Oftentimes, these are shaped by cultural norms and sensibilities in the subject's environment, and instilled in the family home from an early age by his parents and elders. Our Prophet ﷺ taught us that the most virtuous gift a father can give to his son is *adab* (manners). This is part of a man's duties towards his children, a crucial point which will be covered later. Yet, it should be noted here that although the education of the child in his early years is the mother's responsibility,[179] it is nevertheless up to the father to instil *adab.*[180] Numayr ibn Aws ﷺ said, 'They used to say, "Correct action is a gift from Allah ﷻ, but *adab* comes from the parents."'[181]

The Prophet ﷺ said, 'He who has a son born to him should give him a good name and a good upbringing (*adab*) and marry

---

[178] *Jāmiʿ al-Tirmidhī* 1952.
[179] A well-known proverb states: 'The mother's lap is the first *madrasah.*'
[180] The term can also alternatively be used for upbringing and discipline, as in the raising, disciplining, and the setting of boundaries for the child.
[181] *Al-Adab al-Mufrad* 92.

him when he reaches puberty. If he does not marry him when he reaches puberty and he commits sin, his fault rests only upon his father.'[182] He ﷺ also said, 'If anyone cares for three daughters, disciplines them, marries them, and does good to them, he will go to Paradise.'[183]

There is an obligation on the father to introduce good manners, provide a good upbringing and education, and instil discipline in his children. Much of the above points will be explored in further detail in the 'Fatherhood' section later, but for our current objective it suffices to say that it is our responsibility to impart these manners, and it is expected that as Muslim men we expound *adab* in all of its meanings in our day-to-day actions. This encompasses being courteous and respectful, as well as being disciplined. It also involves honouring our parents by showing our good upbringing, and ensuring that we do nothing to humiliate them.

وَإِنَّكَ لَعَلَىٰ خُلُقٍ عَظِيمٍ

And you are surely on an excellent standard of character.[184]

Anas ﷺ stated, 'I served the Prophet ﷺ for ten years. He never said "*Uff!*"[185] to me; nor ever blamed me by saying, "Why did you do such [a thing]?" when I should not have done something; nor "Why did you not do such [a thing]?" when I should have done something. And the Messenger of Allah ﷺ had the best character among all people.'[186]

The Mother of the Believers ʿĀ'ishah ﷺ said, 'The

[182] *Mishkāt al-Maṣābīḥ* 3138.
[183] *Sunan Abī Dāwūd* 5147.
[184] *Qur'an* 68:4.
[185] A word denoting displeasure.
[186] *Jāmiʿ al-Tirmidhī* 2015.

Messenger of Allah ﷺ was never vulgar, never uttered obscenities, and he ﷺ never shouted in the marketplaces. He ﷺ never responded to evil by evil, but always pardoned and overlooked.'[187]

فَبِمَا رَحْمَةٍ مِّنَ ٱللَّهِ لِنتَ لَهُمْ ۖ وَلَوْ كُنتَ فَظًّا غَلِيظَ ٱلْقَلْبِ لَٱنفَضُّوا۟ مِنْ حَوْلِكَ ۖ فَٱعْفُ عَنْهُمْ وَٱسْتَغْفِرْ لَهُمْ وَشَاوِرْهُمْ فِى ٱلْأَمْرِ ۖ فَإِذَا عَزَمْتَ فَتَوَكَّلْ عَلَى ٱللَّهِ ۚ إِنَّ ٱللَّهَ يُحِبُّ ٱلْمُتَوَكِّلِينَ.

Thus [O Prophet], it is through mercy from Allah that you are gentle to them. Had you been rough and hard-hearted, they would have dispersed from around you. So pardon them, and seek forgiveness for them. Consult them in the matter and, once you have taken a decision, place your trust in Allah. Surely, Allah loves those who place their trust in Him.[188]

Good manners were not only instilled in the Prophet ﷺ through his upbringing, but also were placed within him as inherent qualities as a mercy from Allah ﷻ to help spread the message of Islam. Qatādah ؓ and Ibn ʿAbbās ؓ both state that his ﷺ level of gentleness could only have been from Allah ﷻ.[189] ʿAbdullāh ibn ʿAmr ؓ read the description of the Prophet ﷺ in previous books of revelation, which described him ﷺ thus:

'He is not severe, harsh, or obscene in the marketplace, nor [involved] in dealing evil for evil. Rather, he forgives and pardons.'[190]

Such were the manners of the Prophet ﷺ. In *daʿwah* (the propagation of Islam), one should always put these points of

[187] *Maʿārif al-Qur'an*, vol. 8: pp. 552-553.
[188] *Qur'an* 3:159.
[189] *Tafsīr Ibn Kathīr* 3:159.
[190] *Tafsīr Ibn Kathīr* 3:159.

etiquette into practice. Allah ﷻ is also teaching us in the above verse that it was the good manners and soft heart He placed in the Prophet ﷺ which brought people closer to him and helped to spread Islam. Confidence and knowledge that you are spreading the Truth is essential in *da'wah* work, but for it to be successful the *akhlāq* and *ādāb* of the Prophet ﷺ should be emulated as closely as possible. This cannot be an act one puts on, but a natural and in-built habit.

Respect and Courtesy

Respect is a concept that has always existed between men. It is often seen as something earned rather than freely given. However, as Muslims a minimum amount of respect is due to all co-religionists. The Prophet ﷺ said, 'He is not one of us who does not have mercy upon our young, nor respect for our elders, and does not command good and forbid evil.'[191] Greater respect is given to those deserving of it, such as one's teachers, superiors, elders, the pious, and the scholars.

يَـٰٓأَيُّهَا ٱلَّذِينَ ءَامَنُوا۟ لَا يَسْخَرْ قَوْمٌ مِّن قَوْمٍ عَسَىٰٓ أَن يَكُونُوا۟ خَيْرًا مِّنْهُمْ وَلَا نِسَآءٌ مِّن
نِّسَآءٍ عَسَىٰٓ أَن يَكُنَّ خَيْرًا مِّنْهُنَّ ۖ وَلَا تَلْمِزُوٓا۟ أَنفُسَكُمْ وَلَا تَنَابَزُوا۟ بِٱلْأَلْقَـٰبِ ۖ بِئْسَ ٱلِٱسْمُ
ٱلْفُسُوقُ بَعْدَ ٱلْإِيمَـٰنِ ۚ وَمَن لَّمْ يَتُبْ فَأُو۟لَـٰٓئِكَ هُمُ ٱلظَّـٰلِمُونَ.

O you who believe, no men should ever scoff at other men, for perhaps the latter are better than the former. Nor should women [ever scoff] at other women, for perhaps the latter women are better than the former. And do not find fault with one another, nor call one another with bad nicknames. Bad is the name of sinfulness after embracing Faith. If anyone does not repent, then such people are the wrongdoers.[192]

---

[191] *Jāmi' al-Tirmidhī* 1921.
[192] *Qur'an* 49:11.

From here it is clear that showing respect to each other as a general rule is a divine command. But how much respect should be given, and can too much respect be given? In short, it is possible, as bowing or prostrating to anyone other than Allah ﷻ is expressly forbidden.

Abū Saʿīd al-Khudrī ؓ narrates, 'When Banū Qurayẓah agreed to accept Saʿd's judgement, the Prophet ﷺ sent a messenger to him. When he came riding on a white ass, the Prophet ﷺ said, "Stand up for your Chief!" Or, he ﷺ said, "...to the best of you." He came and sat beside the Messenger of Allah ﷺ.'[193] However, Abū Umāmah ؓ narrates, 'The Messenger of Allah ﷺ came out to us leaning on a staff. We stood up to show respect to him. He ﷺ said, "Do not stand up as foreigners do to show respect to one another."'[194]

These two seemingly contradictory Hadiths have ignited a fascinating debate amongst scholars over the span of centuries. Regarding the above traditions, Imams al-Bukhārī, Muslim, and Abū Dāwūd ؒ have all used the former as evidence that standing out of respect is permissible in the Shariah. Ibn al-Ḥājj and Tawribishtī ؒ disagreed, stating that the men were simply ordered to stand as the injured Saʿd ibn Muʿādh ؓ needed to be helped off his mount. Conversely, the renowned Hadith master Shāh ʿAbd al-Ḥaqq Dehlavī ؒ states that to stand up for someone is not merely permissible, but actually a Sunnah – even though some have said it is *makrūh* (disliked) due to the latter narration. For the Prophet ﷺ stood for ʿIkrimah ؓ when he accepted Islam and Ibn Ḥātim ؓ also said that whenever he

---

[193] *Sunan Abī Dāwūd* 5215.

[194] *Sunan Abī Dāwūd* 5230.

visited the Prophet ﷺ, he ﷺ would stand for him.

Other scholars, such as Imams al-Nawawī and Ḥāfiẓ Ibn Ḥajar al-Makkī, were more conservative and merely stated that it is preferred to do so, while Qāḍī ʿIyāḍ al-Mālikī added that it is frowned upon if the other party remains seated. Shaykh Khalīl Aḥmad Sahāranpūrī synthesises all these views to conclude that the correct position is that showing deference to the people of virtue, such as the scholars, the pious, and the honourable ones, by standing is permissible. Standing is, however, disliked when the other person grows to like it as a form of pride. The Prophet ﷺ disliked it for himself as he did not wish to discomfort his Companions by their standing up for him ﷺ.[195] For Abū Mijlaz narrated:

> *Muʿāwiyah went out to meet Ibn al-Zubayr and Ibn ʿĀmir. Ibn ʿĀmir stood and Ibn al-Zubayr remained seated. Muʿāwiyah said to Ibn ʿĀmir, 'Sit down, for I heard the Messenger of Allah ﷺ say, "Let him who likes people to stand up before him prepare his place in Hell."'*[196]

Thus, showing respect to others through permissible means is absolutely within the parameters of appropriate behaviour for a Muslim. But care should be given to ensure that we remain within the Shariah, and that over-deference does not become an expectation for the one being shown respect. A man does not need respect, nor should he expect or demand it. A man gives due respect to others.

Courtesy is a form of respect that is often used

[195] *Badhl al-Majhūd,* vol. 13: pp. 601-602.

[196] *Sunan Abī Dāwūd* 5229.

interchangeably with politeness. Allah ﷻ says in the Qur'an:

وَعِبَادُ ٱلرَّحْمَـٰنِ ٱلَّذِينَ يَمْشُونَ عَلَى ٱلْأَرْضِ هَوْنًا وَإِذَا خَاطَبَهُمُ ٱلْجَـٰهِلُونَ قَالُوا۟ سَلَـٰمًا.

The servants of al-Raḥmān (the Possessor of Mercy) are those who walk on the Earth humbly, and when the ignorant people speak to them, they reply peacefully.[197]

Amīr al-Mu'minīn ʿAlī ibn Abī Ṭālib ؓ narrated that the Messenger of Allah ﷺ said, 'Six courtesies are due from one Muslim to another: (1) to salute him with the *salām* (religious greeting) upon meeting him, (2) to accept his invitation when it is given, (3) to respond with a prayer for him when he sneezes, (4) to visit him when he falls ill, (5) to follow his funeral when he dies, (6) and to love for him what he loves for himself.'[198]

This Hadith lists the six core courtesies that a Muslim owes to his brother. The list is not exclusive, however, for these are the bare minimum rights that every believer enjoys. A Muslim who does not fulfil these matters when dealing with his brother is being discourteous and impolite, and these are not the qualities of an upright man.

The Prophet ﷺ himself was advised to treat his neighbour with courtesy, politeness, and respect. He ﷺ said, 'Jibrīl ؑ continued to advise me about treating neighbours kindly and politely to the extent that I thought he would order me to apportion them part of the inheritance.'[199]

The Messenger of Allah ﷺ also said, 'Shall I not tell you whom the Fire is forbidden to touch? It is a man who is always accessible with a polite and tender nature.'[200] Such is the blessing

---

[197] *Qur'an* 25:63.
[198] *Jāmiʿ al-Tirmidhī* 2736.
[199] *Ṣaḥīḥ al-Bukhārī* 6014.
[200] *Jāmiʿ al-Tirmidhī* 2488.

of Islam. We are taught how to be good men and to benefit society at a collective level. Despite this already being in our own best interests, we are rewarded for this with emancipation from Hellfire and a merciful reward.

Another dimension of courtesy is to look after our neighbours, and to be mindful of their state and needs. The Prophet ﷺ advised, 'Whenever you prepare a broth, add water to it, and have in your mind the members of the household of your neighbours and then give them out of this with courtesy.'[201] Though the broth may not be as thick and flavourful as it would have been prior to adding the extra water, the increased volume will help satiate more people, thereby rendering it to be more beneficial and of greater worth. Note that the Prophet ﷺ added that we distribute the food courteously, such that the recipient does not misconstrue our intentions or feel that they are being given a handout rather than an honourable gift.

It is not the quality of a man to make people feel inferior or of a subordinate status. Instead, he should honour them, give them due respect, and treat them with kindness, politeness, and courtesy. This does not mean that a man should show weakness and inferiority to others, but he should treat his peers as equals and not allow his self-pride to cause him to disrespect his fellow co-religionists or forget his own place as a slave of Allah ﷻ.

---

[201] *Ṣaḥīḥ Muslim* 2625c.

2 | THE SELF-SUFFICIENT MAN

11

He can Survive Alone

عَنْ أَبِي سَعِيدٍ الْخُدْرِيِّ رَضِيَ اللَّهُ عَنْهُ، أَنَّهُ قَالَ: قَالَ رَسُولُ اللهِ صَلَّى اللهُ عَلَيْهِ وَسَلَّمَ: "يُوشِكُ أَنْ يَكُونَ خَيْرَ مَالِ الْمُسْلِمِ غَنَمٌ يَتْبَعُ بِهَا شَعَفَ الْجِبَالِ وَمَوَاقِعَ الْقَطْرِ، يَفِرُّ بِدِينِهِ مِنَ الْفِتَنِ."

Abū Sa'īd al-Khudrī ﵁ narrated that the Messenger of Allah ﷺ said, 'In the near future, the best property of a Muslim will be a flock of sheep which he takes to mountain tops and places of rainfall, so as to flee with his religion intact from trials and tribulations.'[202]

SURVIVAL

The word 'survival' evokes various images in the mind, such as building fires, hunting food, finding water, and undertaking all the steps deemed necessary to stay alive in the face of the worst

[202] *Ṣaḥīḥ al-Bukhārī* 19.

circumstances, tribulations, or afflictions. In this section, all of the above are meant.

حُرِّمَتْ عَلَيْكُمُ ٱلْمَيْتَةُ وَٱلدَّمُ وَلَحْمُ ٱلْخِنزِيرِ وَمَآ أُهِلَّ لِغَيْرِ ٱللَّهِ بِهِۦ وَٱلْمُنْخَنِقَةُ وَٱلْمَوْقُوذَةُ
وَٱلْمُتَرَدِّيَةُ وَٱلنَّطِيحَةُ وَمَآ أَكَلَ ٱلسَّبُعُ إِلَّا مَا ذَكَّيْتُمْ وَمَا ذُبِحَ عَلَى ٱلنُّصُبِ وَأَن
تَسْتَقْسِمُوا۟ بِٱلْأَزْلَٰمِ ۚ ذَٰلِكُمْ فِسْقٌ ۗ ٱلْيَوْمَ يَئِسَ ٱلَّذِينَ كَفَرُوا۟ مِن دِينِكُمْ فَلَا تَخْشَوْهُمْ
وَٱخْشَوْنِ ۚ ٱلْيَوْمَ أَكْمَلْتُ لَكُمْ دِينَكُمْ وَأَتْمَمْتُ عَلَيْكُمْ نِعْمَتِى وَرَضِيتُ لَكُمُ ٱلْإِسْلَٰمَ دِينًا ۚ
فَمَنِ ٱضْطُرَّ فِى مَخْمَصَةٍ غَيْرَ مُتَجَانِفٍ لِّإِثْمٍ ۙ فَإِنَّ ٱللَّهَ غَفُورٌ رَّحِيمٌ

Prohibited for you are carrion, blood, the flesh of swine, and those upon which a name other than that of Allah has been invoked at the time of slaughter, animals killed by strangulation, or killed by a blow, or by a fall, or by goring, or that which is eaten by a beast unless you have properly slaughtered it; and that which has been slaughtered before the idols, and that you determine shares through the arrows. All of this is sin. Today those who disbelieve have lost all hope of [damaging] your faith. So, do not fear them, and fear Me. Today, I have perfected your religion for you, and have completed My blessing upon you, and chosen Islam as a dīn (religious way of life). But whoever is compelled by extreme hunger, having no inclination towards sin, then Allah is Most-Forgiving, Very-Merciful.[203]

Imam Ibn Kathīr ﵀ wrote about the above verse and noted that the animal that dies before being properly slaughtered or hunted is forbidden due to the harm caused by the clogging of the blood in its veins, thereby making it religiously and physically harmful.[204] Fish are an exception to this rule, as Imam Mālik ﵁ in his *Muwaṭṭa'*, Imams Abu Dāwūd, al-Tirmidhī, al-Nasā'ī, and Ibn Mājah ﵏ in their individual *Sunan* works, and Ibn Khuzaymah and Ibn Ḥibbān ﵏ in their respective *Ṣaḥīḥs* all

[203] *Qur'an* 5:3.

[204] *Tafsīr Ibn Kathīr* 5:3.

recorded that Abū Hurayrah 🌸 said that the Messenger of Allah 🌸 was asked about seawater, with the latter replying, 'Its water is pure and its dead are permissible.'[205]

The same ruling applies to locusts.[206] Allah 🌸 also provides us with an allowance to break certain divine laws if one's survival is at stake. In this regard, one is allowed to partake in any of the prohibited foods – as listed in the above verse – and means of attaining them, with the caveat that there is no other option and that there is no intention to commit sin. In an authentic narration recorded by Ibn Ḥibbān and Ibn Khuzaymah 🌸, Amīr al-Mu'minīn ʿUmar 🌸 narrated that the Messenger of Allah 🌸 said, 'Allah 🌸 loves that His concessions be practised, just as He dislikes that disobedience to Him be committed.'[207]

Amīr al-Mu'minīn ʿAlī ibn Abī Ṭālib 🌸 said, 'I left the house of the Messenger of Allah 🌸 on a cold day; I took a tanned skin, tore it in the middle, and covered my neck and wrapped my mid-section, fastening it with a palm leave. I was severely hungry, and had there been food in the house of the Messenger of Allah 🌸 I would have eaten some of it. I went in search of something [to eat]. I passed by a Jew on his property, drawing water from a well with a pulley. I watched him from a gap in the fence. He said, "What is wrong, O Arab? Would you like to get a date for every bucket?" I said, "Yes. Open the door, so I can come in." He opened the door, I entered, and he gave me his bucket. Then for every bucket I pulled out, he would give me a date; this continued until it was enough for me. I put his bucket down and said, "I think I have had enough to eat." I then

---

[205] *Sunan Abī Dāwūd* 83.
[206] *Sunan Ibn Mājah* 3314.
[207] *Bulūgh al-Marām* 427.

scooped some water to drink. When I came to the *masjid,* I found the Messenger of Allah ﷺ within.'"[208]

A man must do what is necessary to survive. From the above narration we can see that Amīr al-Mu'minīn ʿAlī ibn Abī Ṭālib رضي الله عنه was willing to work hard to quench his thirst and satiate his extreme hunger, working in the cold with little clothing to protect him, while simply being paid a date per bucket of water drawn. He did not complain or argue the price, but did what was arranged and necessary to ensure he did not starve.

Survival is the act of doing whatever it takes to survive, and a Muslim should be prepared to do what is necessary and proportionate at the time to ensure his survival. Abū Hurayrah رضي الله عنه narrated that a person came to the Messenger of Allah ﷺ and asked, 'O Messenger of Allah, what is your view about a man who comes to me in order to appropriate my possession?' The Prophet ﷺ replied, 'Do not surrender your possession to him.' The man asked, 'And what if he fights me?' He ﷺ said, 'Then fight.' The man further asked, 'What if I am killed?' He ﷺ replied, 'You would be a martyr.' The man then asked, 'What if I kill him?' He ﷺ said, 'He would be in the Fire.'[209]

A man must be able to protect himself from all outside threats in order to survive and equip himself with the tools required to ensure this end. He must know how to protect himself from his environment or outside forces, while also ensuring he has food, water, heat, and shelter. It is a sad fact of our times that the so-called men of today cannot even iron their own clothes or polish their own boots.

---

[208] *Jāmiʿ al-Tirmidhī* 2473.
[209] *Ṣaḥīḥ Muslim* 140.

HUNTING, COOKING, AND TRAVELLING

Learning the ability to stalk, track, kill, and prepare prey for survival is necessary for every man. A man should be proficient in all of the above areas, so that he can provide for himself and his subordinates at all times, and ensure that he does not become reliant on the assistance of others to survive.

أُحِلَّ لَكُمْ صَيْدُ ٱلْبَحْرِ وَطَعَامُهُۥ مَتَـٰعًا لَّكُمْ وَلِلسَّيَّارَةِ ۖ وَحُرِّمَ عَلَيْكُمْ صَيْدُ ٱلْبَرِّ مَا دُمْتُمْ حُرُمًا ۗ وَٱتَّقُوا۟ ٱللَّهَ ٱلَّذِىٓ إِلَيْهِ تُحْشَرُونَ.

Made lawful for you is the game of the sea and eating thereof, as a benefit for you and for travellers. But the game of the land has been made unlawful for you as long as you are in the state of iḥrām. Fear Allah, the One towards Whom you are to be brought together.[210]

Ibn ʿAbbās ﵄ said that the 'game of the sea' refers to what is taken from water while still alive, and 'eating thereof' refers to what the water throws ashore dead. Similar statements were reported from Abū Bakr al-Ṣiddīq, Zayd ibn Thābit, ʿAbdullāh ibn ʿAmr, Abū Ayyūb al-Anṣārī, Ikrimah, Abū Salamah ibn ʿAbd al-Raḥmān ﵃, Ibrāhīm al-Nakhaʿī, and al-Ḥasan al-Baṣrī ﵀.[211] This is supported by the narration of Wahb ibn Kisān ﵀, who heard the following from Jābir ibn ʿAbdullāh ﵄:

> *Jābir ﵄ said, 'The Messenger of Allah ﷺ sent an army towards the east coast and appointed Abū ʿUbaydah ibn al-Jarrāḥ as their Chief; the army consisted of three-hundred men including myself. We marched until we reached a place where our rations were about to finish. Abū ʿUbaydah ordered us to collect all of the food, and*

[210] *Qur'an* 5:96.
[211] *Tafsīr Ibn Kathīr* 5:96.

it was collected. Our journey food consisted of dates. Abū ʿUbaydah kept on giving us a daily ration in small amounts, until it too was exhausted. Each person's share was a single date.'

I asked, 'How could one date benefit you?'

Jābir ﷺ replied, 'We came to know its value when even that too finished.'

Jābir ﷺ continued, 'When we reached the sea-shore we saw a huge fish, like a small mountain. The army ate from it for eighteen nights. Abū ʿUbaydah ordered that two of its ribs be affixed in the ground and they were. Then he ordered that a she-camel be ridden and it passed under the two ribs without touching them.'[212]

Consequently, trawling live fish from the water, and that which has recently arrived on shore is permissible to eat. Fishing with a rod, net, spear, or one's hands is completely permissible, and a man should be comfortable with at least one method of fishing. However, what about hunting on land?

The Messenger of Allah ﷺ said:

When you let your dog loose, recite the name of Allah, and if it catches your game for you and you find it alive, then slaughter it; if you find it killed and observe that your dog has eaten nothing from it, [even then] you may eat it; but if you find along with your dog another dog, and it is dead, then do not eat from it, for you do not know which of the two has killed it. And if you shoot your arrow, recite the name of Allah, but if you lose sight of it for a day and you do not find on that [the game] anything but

[212] *Ṣaḥīḥ al-Bukhārī* 2483.

the mark of your arrow, then eat from it if you wish; but if you find it drowned in water, then do not eat it.[213]

Hunting with a long-ranged weapon, such as a bow, spear, or firearm are all permissible, as are close ranged weapons such as knives, or the use of a hunting beast such as a trained canine or bird of prey. Again, it is imperative for a man to be proficient in some form of hunting.

The argument against the necessity of learning such skills may be made by the so-called 'modern man'. Proponents of this view argue that at least in the 'developed world', we have access to supermarkets, restaurants, and takeaways where food is readily available for purchase without much effort. Though there is no longer a *necessity* to hunt daily, as there may be in other parts of the world, and as has been throughout most of human history, the skill of hunting is a *necessary skill* rather than a *skill of necessity*; it is something that a man should be able to fall back on in an emergency, when his dependents require food and there is no easy way to obtain it. This is as much about preparedness as it is about self-sufficiency.

وَكُلُوا۟ مِمَّا رَزَقَكُمُ ٱللَّهُ حَلَـٰلًا طَيِّبًا ۚ وَٱتَّقُوا۟ ٱللَّهَ ٱلَّذِىٓ أَنتُم بِهِۦ مُؤْمِنُونَ.

Eat from what Allah has provided you as good and lawful, and fear Allah in Whom you believe.[214]

How self-sufficient is a man that cannot prepare the meal he has caught, hunted, or grown? What use is the hunter-gatherer that starves to death due to his incompetency by the cooking fire or kitchen? A man should not be reliant on his mother, sister, daughter, or wife to prepare his food for him. He is not a dependent. He is depended upon.

[213] *Ṣaḥīḥ Muslim* 1929j.

[214] *Qur'an* 5:88.

Salamah ibn al-Akwaʿ ﵁ narrated, 'In the evening of the day of the conquest of Khaybar, the army made fires [for cooking]. The Prophet ﷺ said, "Why have you lit these fires?" They said, "To cook mule meat." He ﷺ said, "Throw away what is in the cooking pots and break them." A man from the people got up and said, "Shall we throw the contents of the cooking pots and then wash the pots [instead]?" The Prophet ﷺ said, "Yes, you can do either."'[215]

Although the Hadith narrated above is primarily about the impermissibility of eating the meat of a domestic donkey, it also serves to illustrate that the Companions ﵃ knew how to cook and prepare their own meals, and the washing of the dishes and utensils afterwards was not beneath them. Far too often the men of today seem to think that these tasks are for their dependents alone to perform, and consequently they do not need to learn to do them.

Again, a man is self-sufficient, and must know how to survive without outside assistance. This should not, however, be taken as support for the wanton 'degenderisation' of traditional domestic roles that has swept the Western hemisphere, but instead a call to men to relearn and apply skills they should never have forgotten.

The concern of Amīr al-Mu'minīn ʿUmar ibn al-Khaṭṭāb ﵁ for his subjects has been well-documented in history works. He would often patrol the city of Medina and beyond in person, sometimes along with his companion, the freed slave Aslam. There are two well-known stories concerning these patrols, one in which he came across a starving family living in the desert. After bringing them food by carrying it on his own back, he lit a

[215] *Ṣaḥīḥ al-Bukhārī* 5497.

fire for them, and cooked them a meal.

The men of those times were confident in their abilities to survive out in the desert at night without supplies of their own, and this clearly shows the skills they had to find food, prepare meals, and light fires. Aslam ؓ states that he saw smoke blowing up through the beard of Amīr al-Mu'minīn as he prepared the fire.[216] On the second occasion, Amīr al-Mu'minīn ʿUmar ؓ came across a Bedouin whose wife was in his tent and in labour without a midwife. ʿUmar ؓ returned home and brought his wife Umm Kulthūm bint ʿAlī ؓ to be the midwife. He asked the Bedouin to light the fire, and then ʿUmar ؓ again cooked for the family and served it until Umm Kulthūm ؓ announced the birth of the man's son.[217]

This was ʿUmar ؓ. Who are we to scoff at such tasks?

سُبْحَـٰنَ ٱلَّذِىٓ أَسْرَىٰ بِعَبْدِهِۦ لَيْلًا مِّنَ ٱلْمَسْجِدِ ٱلْحَرَامِ إِلَى ٱلْمَسْجِدِ ٱلْأَقْصَا ٱلَّذِى بَـٰرَكْنَا
حَوْلَهُۥ لِنُرِيَهُۥ مِنْ ءَايَـٰتِنَآ ۚ إِنَّهُۥ هُوَ ٱلسَّمِيعُ ٱلْبَصِيرُ.

Glorious is He Who made His servant travel by night from al-Masjid al-Ḥarām to al-Masjid al-Aqṣā whose environs We have blessed, so that We let him see some of Our signs. Surely, He is the All-Hearing, the All-Seeing.[218]

With regard to travelling, this is something people have done as a matter of course throughout the ages. Nowadays, we commute to work on a daily basis. Why then has 'travelling' been singled out here? Simply put, it is not the act of travelling that differentiates a man from a child, but the ability to trek confidently, alone, with or without a map, as well as on foot or on a vehicle; it is the mastery of such skills which is of use to a

216 *Tārīkh al-Ṭabari,* vol. 5: p. 200.
217 *Al-Bidāyah wa al-Nihāyah,* vol. 7: p. 140.
218 *Qur'an* 17:1.

man. A lack of mastery in this area is a sign of boyhood, since a youngster is not skilled or wise enough to make a journey without the aid of an adult.

Al-Barā' ﷦ narrated:

> Abū Bakr ﷦ bought a camel saddle from ʿĀzib ﷦ for thirteen dirhams. Abū Bakr ﷦ said to ʿĀzib ﷦, 'Tell al-Barā' to carry the saddle for me.' ʿĀzib ﷦ replied, 'I will only do so if you relate to me what happened to you and the Messenger of Allah ﷺ when you left Mecca while the pagans were searching for you.' Abū Bakr ﷦ said, 'We left Mecca and we travelled continuously for that night and the following day until midday. I looked around, searching for shelter to take shade and suddenly I came across a rock, and found a little shade there. So I cleaned the area and spread a bed for the Prophet ﷺ in the shade, and said to him, "Lie down, O Messenger of Allah."
>
> So the Prophet ﷺ lay down and I went out, looking around to see if there was any person pursuing us. I saw a shepherd driving his sheep towards the rock, seeking what we had already sought from it. I asked him, "To whom do you belong, boy?" He said, "I belong to a man from Quraysh." He named the man and I recognised him. I asked him, "Is there any milk with your sheep?" He said, "Yes." I said, "Will you then milk some for us?" He said, "Yes." Then I asked him to tie the legs of one of the sheep and clean its udder, and ordered him to clean the dust from his hands. Then the shepherd cleaned his hands by striking one against the another.

After doing so, he extracted a small amount of milk. I used to keep a leather water-container for the Messenger of Allah ﷺ, the mouth of which was covered with a piece of cloth. I poured water on the milk container till its lower part was cold. Then I took the milk to the Prophet ﷺ, whom I found to be awake. I said to him, "Drink, O Messenger of Allah." So he drank until I was pleased.

Then I said, "It is time for us to move, O Messenger of Allah!" He said, "Yes." So we set out while the people (the Qurayshī polytheists) were searching for us, but none found us except Surāqah ibn Mālik ibn Jushm, who was riding his horse. I said, "Our pursuers have found us, O Messenger of Allah!" He ﷺ said, "Do not grieve, for Allah is with us."[219]

A man should be able to prepare for a long journey, and set out on their expedition with confidence, knowing how to find food, water, shelter, and heat, as well as looking after those he is tasked to protect.

قُلْ سِيرُوا۟ فِى ٱلْأَرْضِ فَٱنظُرُوا۟ كَيْفَ بَدَأَ ٱلْخَلْقَ ۚ ثُمَّ ٱللَّهُ يُنشِئُ ٱلنَّشْأَةَ ٱلْـَٔاخِرَةَ ۚ إِنَّ ٱللَّهَ عَلَىٰ كُلِّ شَىْءٍ قَدِيرٌ.

Say, 'Go about in the land and look how He has originated the creation. Then Allah will create the subsequent creation. Surely Allah is powerful to do everything.[220]

When travelling, one should also go with the intention of acting upon the above verse in which Allah ﷻ asks us to look upon the world and witness His creations to better comprehend the scale of His Majesty. That said, the modern idea of travelling for travel's sake and 'seeing the world' is not encouraged, as the

[219] *Ṣaḥīḥ al-Bukhārī* 3652.
[220] *Qur'an* 29:20.

Prophet ﷺ said, 'Travelling is a tortuous experience. It deprives a person of his sleep, food, and drink. When one of you has accomplished his purpose, he should hasten his return to his family.'[221]

[221] *Ṣaḥīḥ Muslim* 1927.

12
He is the Better Physician

عَنْ عَمْرِو بْنِ شُعَيْبٍ، عَنْ أَبِيهِ، عَنْ جَدِّهِ رَضِيَ اللَّهُ عَنْهُ، أَنَّ رَسُولَ اللَّهِ
صَلَّى اللَّهُ عَلَيْهِ وَسَلَّمَ قَالَ: "مَنْ تَطَبَّبَ وَلاَ يُعْلَمُ مِنْهُ طِبٌّ فَهُوَ ضَامِنٌ."

ʿAmr ibn Shuʿayb narrated via his father, who related from his grandfather ﷺ that the Messenger of Allah ﷺ said, 'Anyone who practises medicine when he is not known as a practitioner will be held liable.'[222]

MEDICAL KNOWLEDGE, PRACTISING MEDICINE, AND FIRST AID

A man should understand and know the basics of medicine and First Aid at a level which allows them to deal with common ailments and apply immediate assistance when confronted with injury, either for himself or for others around him. The Prophet ﷺ and his Companions ﷺ administered First Aid to each other during the many battles that occurred throughout their respective lifetimes, and various types of medicine were practised.

In the above Hadith, it is made clear that anyone that is unskilled as a physician and does not know the craft should be held accountable for their mistakes. It is also clear from other Hadith texts that a person should seek out a medical practitioner if suffering from an injury or ailment, as the Prophet ﷺ advised Saʿd ﷺ to go to al-Ḥārith ibn Kaladah ﷺ, who was a medical practitioner.[223]

As Muslims, it is important for us to understand that the

[222] *Sunan Abī Dāwūd* 4586.
[223] *Sunan Abī Dāwūd* 3875.

remedies applied by a doctor or *ḥakīm*[224] are not the causes for being cured of illnesses, but merely the means. It is Allah 🕮 Who cures us. Jābir 🕮 reported that the Messenger of Allah 🕮 said, 'There is a remedy for every malady, and when the remedy is applied to the disease it is cured with the permission of Allah 🕮.'[225]

وَإِذَا مَرِضْتُ فَهُوَ يَشْفِينِ.

...and when I become sick, He heals me.[226]

Allah 🕮 is the One Who decrees pestilence and disease, as well as the One Who cures us from them. Put in another way, it is by His divine decree that we are afflicted by or liberated from disease. Imam Ibn Kathīr 🕮 explains that the verse's import is the following: 'When I fall sick, no one is able to heal me but Him, Who heals me via the means that may lead to recovery.'[227]

Zayd ibn Aslam 🕮 narrated:

> *A man received a wound in the time of the Messenger of Allah 🕮. The blood clotted in the wound and the man called two men from the Banū Anmār tribe. They looked at it and the Messenger of Allah 🕮 said to them, 'Which of you is the better physician?' They said, 'Is there any good in medicine, O Messenger of Allah?' The Messenger of Allah 🕮 said, 'The one who sent down the disease sent down the cure.*[228]

On another occasion, the Messenger of Allah 🕮 was asked,

---

[224] A practitioner of traditional, herbal, or alternative medicine.
[225] *Ṣaḥīḥ Muslim* 2204.
[226] *Qur'an* 26:20.
[227] *Tafsīr Ibn Kathīr,* 26:20.
[228] *Muwaṭṭa' Imam Mālik* 1725.

'Do you think that the medicines with which we treat ourselves, the *ruqyah*[229] by which we seek healing, and the means of protection that we seek, change the decree of Allah ﷻ at all?' He ﷺ said, 'They are part of the decree of Allah ﷻ.'[230]

Various routes of medicine are acceptable in Islam, from traditional medicine to modern medicine to homeopathy, from *ruqyah* to herbalism and aromatology. The Prophet ﷺ said, 'If there is any good in your medicines, then it is in a gulp of honey, a cupping operation, or cauterisation, but I do not like to be cauterised.'[231]

He ﷺ also said, 'The best medicines you apply are those sipped at the corners of the mouth, those snuffed up the nose, cupping, and purgatives; the best thing you apply to your eyes is antimony, for it clears the sight and makes the hair grow; and the best days for cupping are the seventeenth, nineteenth and twenty-first.'[232] The Prophet ﷺ also said, 'The best medicines you may treat yourselves with are cupping and sea incense.' He then added, 'You should not torture your children by treating tonsillitis by pressing the tonsils or the palate with the finger[233], but use incense.'[234]

Our beloved Prophet ﷺ was clearly well-versed in traditional medicine. As men, we too should have at least a basic understanding of how to treat common ailments and injuries.

Imam Mālik ؒ was asked whether someone on a pilgrimage - in the state of *iḥrām* - who had an ear complaint could use

[229] A form of spiritual remedy by means of supplication to Allah.
[230] *Sunan Ibn Mājah* 3437.
[231] *Ṣaḥīḥ al-Bukhārī* 5702.
[232] *Mishkāt al-Maṣābīḥ* 4473.
[233] This was a common treatment for tonsillitis at the time.
[234] *Ṣaḥīḥ al-Bukhārī* 5696.

non-perfumed medicinal oil for dropping into his ears, and he said, 'I do not see any harm in that. Even if he were to put it into his mouth, I still would not see any harm in it.'[235] Imam Mālik ﵁ added that there was no harm in someone in *iḥrām* lancing an abscess that he had, or a boil, or cutting a vein, if he needed to do so.[236]

A man should be prepared to deal with simple medical issues he may come across to safeguard his own health and those of his dependents in a confident manner. At the same time, he should understand that all things are from Allah ﷻ, and the healing process itself is only achieved through the permission of Allah ﷻ.

---

[235] *Muwaṭṭa' Imam Mālik* 799.
[236] *Muwaṭṭa' Imam Mālik* 799.

13
He Looks After Himself

عَنْ أَبِي مَالِكٍ الأَشْعَرِيّ رَضِيَ اللَّهُ عَنْهُ، قَالَ: قَالَ رَسُولُ اللَّهِ صَلَّى اللَّهُ عَلَيْهِ
وَسَلَّمَ: الطُّهُورُ شَطْرُ الإِيمَانِ، وَالْحَمْدُ لِلَّهِ تَمْلأُ الْمِيزَانَ، وَسُبْحَانَ اللَّهِ وَالْحَمْدُ لِلَّهِ تَمْلآنِ –
أَوْ تَمْلأُ – مَا بَيْنَ السَّمَوَاتِ وَالأَرْضِ، وَالصَّلاَةُ نُورٌ، وَالصَّدَقَةُ بُرْهَانٌ، وَالصَّبْرُ ضِيَاءٌ،
وَالْقُرْآنُ حُجَّةٌ لَكَ أَوْ عَلَيْكَ، كُلُّ النَّاسِ يَغْدُو فَبَائِعٌ نَفْسَهُ، فَمُعْتِقُهَا أَوْ مُوبِقُهَا."

*Abū Mālik al-Ash'arī narrated that the Messenger of Allah
said, 'Cleanliness is half of faith and [saying] alhamdulillāh
(praise be to Allah) fills the scale, while subhānAllāh (glory be
to Allah) and alhamdulillāh together fill up what is between the
Heavens and the Earth. Prayer is a light, charity is a proof [of
one's faith], patience is a light [for you], and the Holy Qur'an is
either a proof on your behalf or a proof against you. All men go
out early in the morning and sell themselves, thereby setting
themselves free or leading to their own destruction.'[237]*

CLEANLINESS

Cleanliness holds a high status in Islam. In the above Hadith,
it has been called 'half of one's faith'. A Muslim man must
maintain his cleanliness at all times. A man cannot worship his
Lord in an unclean state, and Islam teaches us to maintain a
constant state of physical, mental, and spiritual purity. The first
step toward this is to ensure cleanliness through *ghusl* (bathing),
istinjā' (cleaning the private parts), and *wudū'* (ablution). Sa'īd
ibn al-Musayyib said, 'Indeed Allah is Good and He loves
what is good, He is Clean and He loves cleanliness, He is Kind
and He loves kindness, and He is Generous and He loves

---
[237] *Sahīh Muslim* 223.

generosity.'[238]

فِيهِ رِجَالٌ يُحِبُّونَ أَن يَتَطَهَّرُوا ۚ وَٱللَّهُ يُحِبُّ ٱلْمُطَّهِّرِينَ.

...In it [the masjid] there are people who like to observe purity; and Allah loves those observing purity.[239]

Abū Hurayrah ﷺ narrated that the Messenger of Allah ﷺ said this verse was revealed about the people of Qubā' as 'They used to clean themselves with water after urinating.'[240] The Mother of the Believers 'Ā'ishah ﷺ advised women by stating, 'Encourage your husbands to clean themselves with water, for I am too shy to tell them, and the Messenger of Allah ﷺ would do that.'[241] Here, the Mother of the Believers ﷺ was referring to *istinjā'*. About this, the Messenger of Allah ﷺ said, 'When any of you cleans himself, he should not clean himself with his right hand. Let him clean himself with his left hand.'[242] The Mother of the Believers 'Ā'ishah ﷺ said, 'The Prophet ﷺ used to like to start from the right side when wearing shoes, combing his hair, cleaning or washing himself, and upon doing anything else.[243]

When cleaning, we should do so from right to left, and the contaminated areas should be cleansed with the left hand. We should be thorough in ensuring purity, as it affects the acceptability of our prayers. The Prophet ﷺ would constantly work on his cleanliness to ensure that it was always impeccable.

---

[238] *Jāmi' al-Tirmidhī* 2799.
[239] *Qur'an* 9:108.
[240] *Sunan Ibn Mājah* 357.
[241] *Jāmi' al-Tirmidhī* 19.
[242] *Sunan Ibn Mājah* 312.
[243] *Ṣaḥīḥ al-Bukhārī* 168.

Ḥudhayfah said, 'Whenever the Prophet got up at night, he used a *siwāk*[244] to clean his mouth [and teeth].'[245]

The Prophet was very particular about ensuring he was clean and pure at all times, and a man that wishes to achieve perfection in all aspects of manhood should follow him in this too. Much more can be said about this topic. However, to go into depth on the subject of *ṭahārah* (purification) would not be productive for the purpose of this book, as many detailed treatises on this very subject have been written by far more knowledgeable people. Every major Hadith compilation has a section on cleanliness, and every major work of *fiqh* (Islamic law) has a section on how to obtain it. It is advisable that every reader takes the time to find a reputable basic work in this field and study it.

GROOMING AND SELF-CARE

فَلَمَّا سَمِعَتْ بِمَكْرِهِنَّ أَرْسَلَتْ إِلَيْهِنَّ وَأَعْتَدَتْ لَهُنَّ مُتَّكَـًٔا وَءَاتَتْ كُلَّ وَٰحِدَةٍ مِّنْهُنَّ
سِكِّينًا وَقَالَتِ ٱخْرُجْ عَلَيْهِنَّ ۖ فَلَمَّا رَأَيْنَهُۥٓ أَكْبَرْنَهُۥ وَقَطَّعْنَ أَيْدِيَهُنَّ وَقُلْنَ حَٰشَ لِلَّهِ مَا هَٰذَا بَشَرًا
إِنْ هَٰذَآ إِلَّا مَلَكٌ كَرِيمٌ.

Accordingly, when she heard of their taunting comments, she extended an invitation to them and arranged for them a comfortable place to sit and dine and gave everyone a knife, and said to Yūsuf, 'Come out to them.' So when they saw him, they found him great, and were so stunned that they cut their hands and said, 'Oh God! He is no human being. He is but a noble Angel.[246]

The Prophet Yūsuf was gifted by Allah with one-half

[244] A twig or branch taken from the *arak* tree, which has intrinsic cleaning properties and a favourable scent.

[245] *Ṣaḥīḥ al-Bukhārī* 245.

[246] *Qur'an* 12:31.

of all beauty, and was so handsome that the women of Egypt did not even realise they had cut their hands instead of their food, for they could not understand how a human being could be so beautiful. Qatādah ﷺ said, 'Allah ﷻ has not sent a Prophet ﷺ unless He endowed him with a handsome face and a beautiful voice. Your Prophet ﷺ was endowed with a handsome face and a beautiful voice, and he did not chant in a quavering tone.'[247]

All other men will struggle to achieve a single percent of the beauty of the Prophets ﷺ, let alone that of the beautiful Prophet Yūsuf ﷺ and our beloved Prophet Muhammad ﷺ. However, this is not to say that men should not try to beautify themselves, or fail to present themselves in their most handsome form. Beautifying oneself does not mean to feminise one's outward appearance or apply makeup, as is quickly becoming normalised in today's societies, but to amplify masculine beauty through grooming, self-care, and professional clothing.

Thumāmah ibn ʿAbdullāh ﷺ said that Anas ﷺ would not refuse perfume and would say, 'Indeed the Prophet ﷺ would not refuse perfume.'[248] The Mother of the Believers ʿĀ'ishah ﷺ used to perfume the Prophet ﷺ with the sweetest perfume she could find until she saw the balm shining on his head and beard.[249] Nāfiʿ ﷺ said that when Ibn ʿUmar ﷺ perfumed himself he used unmixed aloeswood, and also used camphor mixed in with the aloeswood, adding that the Messenger of Allah ﷺ had perfumed himself thus.[250]

A man should not smell of body odour. He should wear a

---

[247] *Al-Shamā'il al-Muḥammadiyyah* 319.
[248] *Jāmiʿ al-Tirmidhī* 2789.
[249] *Mishkāt al-Maṣābīḥ* 4435.
[250] *Mishkāt al-Maṣābīḥ* 4436.

masculine scent and ensure that he smells good at all times. This is a right of his partner(s) and the Sunnah of his Prophet ﷺ. Anas ؓ said, 'I never touched any form of silk or velvet softer than the hand of the Messenger of Allah ﷺ, and never smelled musk or incense more pleasant than the smell of the Messenger of Allah ﷺ.'[251]

The Prophet ﷺ said, 'The perfume of males should be fragrant and without colour, while the perfume of females is to be colourful but not fragrant.'[252] That is to say that women can beautify themselves with bright clothing, jewellery, and makeup, but they should not use perfume. Men are visual creatures and the purpose of makeup is to beautify and magnify feminine features, just as jewellery is meant to draw the eyes to where it is being worn. On the other hand, men should beautify themselves with scent, as the application of makeup and the wearing of jewellery are feminine acts and a man should avoid becoming effeminate at all costs. Here, some readers may try to argue that the Prophet ﷺ wore a silver ring, and therefore 'masculine' jewellery, such as the recent trends of wearing bracelets and chains – a term used to make necklaces sound more masculine – should be allowed. This is a false equivalency, as there is a difference between the Prophet ﷺ occasionally wearing a single silver signet ring for the purpose of sealing letters, and the hordes of young 'metrosexuals' with earrings and nose-piercings that wish to wear 'masculine' necklaces and bangles to look attractive.

Abū Qatādah al-Anṣārī ؓ narrated that as he had long, thick hair, he asked the Prophet ﷺ about it, and he ﷺ told him to take care of it and comb it every day.[253] In another narration

---

[251] Ṣaḥīḥ al-Bukhārī 1973.
[252] Al-Shamā'il al-Muḥammadiyyah 218, 219.
[253] Sunan al-Nasā'ī 5237.

reported by Yaḥyā ibn Saʿīd 🙵, Abū Qatādah al-Anṣārī 🙵 said to the Messenger of Allah 🙵, 'I have a lot of hair which comes down to my shoulders, so should I comb it?' The Messenger of Allah 🙵 said, 'Yes, and honour it.' Occasionally Abū Qatādah 🙵 would oil it twice a day, as the Messenger of Allah 🙵 said to 'honour it'.[254]

A man who is blessed with hair should take care of it, making sure it is clean, oiled, and combed. Those who lack copious amounts of hair or are bald-headed should still ensure that they are presentable. Being well-groomed and presentable is from the *fiṭrah*, and as Muslims we should be exemplary in this regard. The Messenger of Allah 🙵 said, 'To shave the pubic hair, clip the nails, and cut the moustache short are characteristics of the *fiṭrah*.'[255] He 🙵 also said, 'Five practices are characteristics of the *fiṭrah*: circumcision, shaving the pubic region, plucking the underarms, clipping the nails, and cutting the moustaches short.'[256] In another narration, ten traits are prescribed: 'Ten are the acts according to the *fiṭrah*: clipping the moustache, letting the beard grow, using the tooth-stick, snuffing water in the nose, cutting the nails, washing the finger joints, plucking the hair under the armpits, shaving the pubic hair, and cleaning one's private parts with water.' A narrator in the chain said, 'I have forgotten the tenth, but it may have been rinsing the mouth.'[257] There is also a narration in *Sunan Ibn Mājah* which lists the rinsing of the mouth among the ten.[258]

Regarding the clearest sign of a Muslim man, namely the

---

[254] *Muwaṭṭaʼ Imam Mālik* 1738.
[255] *Ṣaḥīḥ al-Bukhārī* 5890.
[256] *Ṣaḥīḥ al-Bukhārī* 5899.
[257] *Ṣaḥīḥ Muslim* 261a.
[258] *Sunan Ibn Mājah* 294.

beard, the Prophet ﷺ said, 'Oppose the pagan: lengthen the beard and cut the moustache short.'[259] Whenever Ibn 'Umar ﷺ performed the Hajj or 'Umrah, he used to hold his beard with his hand and cut whatever remained outside his hold.[260] Jābir ﷺ said, 'We used to grow the beard long, except during the Hajj or 'Umrah.'[261] The Prophet ﷺ specifically commanded us to clip the moustache and grow the beard long.[262] Nowadays, Muslims are too quick and eager to cut their beards short, with some going so far as saying that a short stubble is a Sunnah beard, or worse that there is no need to keep one as it is 'just' a Sunnah.

We have fallen so low that we assign no value to the Sunnah of our Prophet ﷺ and we search for loopholes and shortcuts to avoid keeping a proper beard. A man grows his beard long, and clips his moustache short, and gives his beard the due respect it deserves as one of his ﷺ Sunnahs. Ruwayfi' ibn Thābit ﷺ said that the Messenger of Allah ﷺ said to him, 'O Ruwayfi', you may live for a long time after me, so tell the people that whoever ties up his beard, twists it, hangs an amulet, or cleans himself (after relieving himself) with animal dung or bones that Muhammad has nothing to do with him.'[263]

Yazīd ibn Abī Ḥabīb[264] ﷺ reports that the two messengers of Khosrow who arrived in Medina had shaved their beards and had long moustaches. The Messenger of Allah ﷺ at first refused to even look at them. When he did look at them, he ﷺ asked, 'Who instructed you to do this?' They replied, 'Our Lord.' The

[259] *Ṣaḥīḥ al-Bukhārī* 5892.
[260] *Ṣaḥīḥ al-Bukhārī* 5892.
[261] *Sunan Abī Dāwūd* 4201.
[262] *Sunan Abī Dāwūd* 4199.
[263] *Sunan al-Nasā'ī* 5067.
[264] A reliable Tābi'ī (Successor) and Hadith narrator.

Messenger of Allah ﷺ stated, 'But my Lord has commanded me to lengthen the beard and shorten the moustache.'[265]

How can we claim to love our Prophet ﷺ when we emulate those that he did not even like to look at? Nowadays the people that shout the loudest about loving the Prophet ﷺ are also the ones who fight the hardest to avoid his Sunnah. What kind of a man scrapes away his naturally occurring masculine features in order to more closely resemble the effeminate men of the modern age?

Dressing Well and Mending Clothes

يَـٰبَنِىٓ ءَادَمَ قَدْ أَنزَلْنَا عَلَيْكُمْ لِبَاسًا يُوَٰرِى سَوْءَٰتِكُمْ وَرِيشًا ۖ وَلِبَاسُ ٱلتَّقْوَىٰ ذَٰلِكَ خَيْرٌ ۚ ذَٰلِكَ مِنْ ءَايَـٰتِ ٱللَّهِ لَعَلَّهُمْ يَذَّكَّرُونَ.

O children of Adam, We have sent down to you the dress that covers your shame and provides adornment. As for the dress of taqwā (God-consciousness), that is the best. That is one of the signs of Allah, so that they may learn a lesson.[266]

In this verse, Allah ﷻ addresses the entirety of mankind, and highlights the great blessing of clothing which must be recognised by us all. The verse also points to the fact that the act of covering the body and wearing clothes is both a human need and a natural desire felt by all of humanity, regardless of culture or religion. Clothing is one of the things that differentiates us as a species from animals. How disappointing it is to see that we are now regressing in this regard.

The types of physical clothing mentioned in this verse are divided into three distinct groups:

---

[265] *Tārīkh al-Ṭabarī,* vol. 3: p. 248.
[266] *Qur'an* 7:26.

1. '*Libāsan yuwārī saw'ātikum*' (*clothing that covers your shame*). This relates to those body parts which, if uncovered, would be naturally considered shameful by all human beings. To be given the means to cover these areas is a blessing in and of itself.

2. '*Rīshān*' (*clothing that provides adornment*). Merely covering up one's private parts only requires a simple set of clothing. Yet, Allah ﷻ has provided us with much more: He blessed us with clothing to make us look handsome, decent, neat, and civilised.

3. '*Anzalnā*' (*We have sent down*). Just as no human planning or artifice operates as an active agent in what descends from the Heavens, so too is the case of the base materials for making clothes, such as silk, cotton, and wool. This too is a gift from Allah ﷻ.[267]

As Muslims, there is a fine line to walk between dressing well and ensuring we do not dress extravagantly. A Muslim should maintain an air of humbleness, but this need not be taken to the extreme. A man should therefore dress well, but ensure he checks his intention constantly to protect himself from pride and showing off.

In our current times it has become commonplace for men to always dress in big brand clothes and designer wear. This has reached the point where, like women, we do not want to be seen in the same dress twice on an occasion, or we compete with one another to wear the more expensive wardrobe. A man wearing unbranded clothing is looked down upon, and it has become something of a tradition to always wear new clothes on Eid rather than simply the best clothes one already possesses. The Prophet

---

[267] *Ma'ārif al-Qur'an,* vol. 3: pp. 554-555.

ﷺ said, 'Listen! Listen! Wearing old clothes is a part of faith. Wearing old clothes is a part of faith.'[268] He ﷺ also said, 'He who wears grand clothes in this world will be made by Allah ﷻ to wear clothes of humiliation on the Day of Resurrection.'[269] Amīr al-Mu'minīn 'Umar ibn al-Khaṭṭāb رضي الله عنه once saw a silken cloak for sale, and took it to the Prophet ﷺ, saying, 'O Messenger of Allah, buy this and wear it when delegations come to see you.' He ﷺ said, 'Silk is worn by the one who will have no share of it in the Hereafter.'[270] In fact, the Messenger of Allah ﷺ wore clothes made of wool, and his sandals were made from palm-fibre.[271] 'Umar ibn Abī Salamah رضي الله عنه said, 'The Prophet ﷺ prayed in one garment and crossed its ends.'[272]

From the above it is clear that wearing extravagant dresses is frowned upon in Islam. Silk, red clothes, elaborate designs, or overly expensive clothing are not from the attire of the Muslim man. Amīr al-Mu'minīn 'Umar ibn al-Khaṭṭāb رضي الله عنه said, 'Wear *izārs*[273] and *ridā's*[274] and wear shoes, but not boots and pants; throw away your stirrups and mount your steeds. Wear rough clothes and practise archery; keep away from luxury and the dress of the non-Arabs. Beware of silk, for the Messenger of Allah ﷺ forbade it and said, "Do not wear silk, except this much", and the Messenger of Allah ﷺ gestured with two fingers.'[275]

---

[268] *Sunan Abī Dāwūd* 4161.
[269] *Sunan Abī Dāwūd* 4029.
[270] *Ṣaḥīḥ al-Bukhārī* 6081.
[271] *Sunan Ibn Mājah* 3448.
[272] *Ṣaḥīḥ al-Bukhārī* 354.
[273] A cloth wrapped around the lower body.
[274] A cloth wrapped around the upper body.
[275] *Musnad al-Imam Aḥmad* 301.

This does not mean that a man should wear rags either. On one occasion ʿAbd al-Karīm Abū Umayyah ﵀ approached Abū al-ʿĀliyah ﵀ whilst wearing woollen clothes. Abū al-ʿĀliyah ﵀ said to him, 'These are the clothes of monks. When visiting each other, the Muslims would beautify themselves.'[276]

Al-Barā' ﵁ once said, 'I never saw anyone more handsome than the Messenger of Allah ﷺ, with his hair combed, wearing a partly red two-piece suit.'[277] ʿUmar ibn al-Khaṭṭāb ﵁ said, 'Allah ﷻ has been generous to you, so be generous to yourselves. Let a man wear a combination of his garments.'[278]

Dressing well is not only permissible, but it is the Sunnah, just as it is to dress humbly. Taking these points into mind, one may naturally ask: how should a Muslim dress? The Prophet ﷺ said, 'Wear your white garments, for they are among your best garments, and shroud your dead in them.'[279] Thus, a Muslim should wear his best clothes, with the preferred colour being white. The Mother of the Believers Umm Salamah ﵂ said: 'The clothing that the Messenger of Allah ﷺ liked best was the *qamīṣ*.'[280] Furthermore, Anas ibn Mālik ﵁ said: 'The most beloved garment to the Prophet ﷺ was the *ḥibrah* (a striped cloak from Yemen).'[281]

Primarily, if a man wants to dress well, he should look to the garments and style of the Prophet ﷺ, for there is nothing better than this. Some will try to argue that these were the garments of the time, but this is a twisting of the truth. For the fact of the

---

[276] *Al-Adab al-Mufrad* 348a.
[277] *Sunan Ibn Mājah* 3599.
[278] *Muwaṭṭa' Imam Mālik* 1656.
[279] *Sunan Abī Dāwūd* 3878.
[280] *Sunan Abī Dāwūd* 4025.
[281] *Ṣaḥīḥ al-Bukhārī* 5813.

matter is that the people of the Arabian Peninsula wore many different types of clothing, as elucidated in the collections of Hadith, but those favoured by the Prophet ﷺ have been made clear by his Companions ﷺ.

If someone does not wish to dress like the greatest of men ﷺ, then that is his choice. However, this does not mean that those who do are not undertaking something of worth. Secondly, when choosing what to wear, there is no compulsion on anyone to don a *thobe*. In fact, sometimes wearing such attire is not practical, such as at work or in the gym, and as a result a Muslim should wear what is considered best in each situation.

A man should know how to dress himself and how to maintain his own clothing, just as the Companions ﷺ and the Prophet ﷺ himself did. He should not exceedingly rely on the womenfolk of his household to help him if there is a tear that needs mending, or a shoelace that needs replacing. It is wasteful to throw away perfectly serviceable clothes simply because there is a hole in the pocket.

Hishām ﷺ asked the Mother of the Believers ʿĀ'ishah ﷺ, 'What did the Prophet ﷺ do in his house?' She replied, 'He did what one of you would do in his house. He mended sandals, patched garments, and sewed.'[282]

This was the Prophet ﷺ: he mended and sewed his own garments. He did not expect such tasks to be undertaken by anyone else, and he had the skill and ability to be completely self-sufficient. A man only needs the help of Allah ﷻ. The Prophet ﷺ understood this better than anyone.

---

[282] *Al-Adab al-Mufrad* 540.

This was not something exclusive to the Prophet ﷺ, for his Companions ﷺ also emulated these behavioural standards as well. For instance, another narration mentions how a Companion, Abū Qatādah ﷺ, mended his sandals during the sacred Hajj ceremony.[283]

[283] *Ṣaḥīḥ al-Bukhārī* 5407.

14
He Values Solitude

عَنْ أُمِّ الْمُؤْمِنِينَ عَائِشَةَ رَضِيَ اللهُ عَنْهَا، قَالَتْ: "كَانَ رَسُولُ اللَّهِ صَلَّى اللَّهُ عَلَيْهِ وَسَلَّمَ يَعْتَكِفُ الْعَشْرَ الأَوَاخِرَ مِنْ رَمَضَانَ."

The Mother of the Believers ʿĀʾishah ﵂ narrated that the Messenger of Allah ﷺ would observe iʿtikāf (spiritual seclusion) during the last ten days of Ramadan.[284]

Solitude and Seclusion

A man that knows the worth of solitude readily pursues it. A man that is reliant on others can think of nothing worse. Being alone allows one to think, contemplate life's great mysteries and one's place in the world, and build a connection with Allah ﷻ by concentrating on His remembrance without the distractions of this life. Man came into the world alone, lives his life essentially alone, will return to his Lord alone, and will be judged by Him alone.

Allah ﷻ tells us in His noble Book:

وَكُلُّهُمْ ءَاتِيهِ يَوْمَ ٱلْقِيَـٰمَةِ فَرْدًا

...and each of them is bound to come to Him on Judgment Day, all alone.[285]

Man was born alone, without any wealth or children, and will be questioned by Allah ﷻ about the many blessings he was given by Him on the Day of Resurrection.[286]

---

[284] *Ṣaḥīḥ Muslim* 1172a.
[285] *Qur'an* 19:95.
[286] *Tafsīr Ibn Kathīr* 74:11.

The Prophet ﷺ said, 'Allah ﷻ will grant seven types of people the shade of His Throne on the Day when there shall be no shade other than it: a just ruler; a youth who grew up worshipping Allah; a man whose heart is attached to the *masjid*; two persons who love, meet, and depart from each other for the sake of Allah; a man whom an extremely beautiful woman seduces, but he rejects her by saying, "I fear Allah"; a man who gives in charity and conceals it, to such an extent that the left hand does not know what the right has given; and a person who remembers Allah ﷻ in solitude and his eyes well up.'[287]

Among these seven groups of people is the one who remembers Allah ﷻ when he is alone and sheds tears. Why is this? It is because when we are alone with Allah ﷻ, there is no third person whom we could be trying to convince of our sincerity. A person alone with Allah ﷻ is at his most sincere state, for there can be no ulterior motive in his behaviour. If he does not sincerely believe in the truth, he will not pray to Allah ﷻ. If he does not feel the love, awe, and fear of Allah ﷻ in his heart, he will not weep. Allah ﷻ already knows what is in our hearts and who we truly are. In solitude, our truest selves are revealed to us.

Possessing the ability to be alone is itself a sign of one's strong character and determination. When we are alone with our thoughts with no one and nothing to distract us from them, we are forced to face them head on. There are many men that surround themselves with others and convince themselves that they could face any threat, yet in reality they fear the threat of being forced to look at who they really are. A man does not fear his own reflection, nor does he fear the silence that comes with

[287] *Riyāḍ al-Ṣāliḥīn* 376.

loneliness. This life is a test that each of us must undergo while unaided, as we will pass or fail in it alone.

The Mother of the Believers ʿĀ'ishah ﷺ narrated, 'When Allah ﷻ wanted to honour the Messenger of Allah ﷺ and grant His mercy upon His creatures, He conferred upon the former the first form of Prophethood, whereby he would not see anything in a dream except that it would occur like the break of dawn. So he continued upon that state for as long as Allah ﷻ willed for him to continue. And seclusion was made beloved to him, so much so that there was not anything more beloved to him than being alone.'[288]

The Messenger of Allah ﷺ loved to be alone to worship Allah ﷻ, and he would spend many nights in devotion to his Lord. We should not, however, be expected to seek solitude at all times. We know there is benefit in congregational prayer, brotherhood, building ties with our families, honouring the old, showing mercy to the young, as well as other interpersonal and communal actions.

There is much to be said for spending time with others, and there is something to be said for spending time with Allah ﷻ alone as well. Not all situations benefit from loneliness, and it is wise to bear this in mind. The Prophet ﷺ said, 'If the people knew what I know about being alone, then the rider would not travel alone at night.'[289]

With that being said, *iʿtikāf* (spiritual seclusion) is an act of great merit. Men do this by finding a secluded and quiet spot - ideally in the *masjid* - and cutting themselves off from the world

---

[288] *Jāmiʿ al-Tirmidhī* 3632.
[289] *Ṣaḥīḥ al-Bukhārī* 2998.

for a period of time, spending their day(s) and/or night(s) in the worship of Allah. The Mother of the Believers ʿĀ'ishah ﵂ said: 'When the Messenger of Allah ﷺ intended to engage in private devotion in the *masjid*, he prayed the dawn prayer and then entered his place of seclusion.'[290] She also reported: 'The Messenger of Allah ﷺ would observe *iʿtikāf* in the last ten days of Ramadan.'[291]

A man should put aside some time in the day for solitude and some time every year to go into seclusion. That way, he will be largely independent from society and the need for social interaction, though he can and should benefit from both. He should not fear that the world will reject him due to his conviction in his beliefs, and must stand firm and confident of his religious standpoint. By learning to be alone, one can discover to overcome this fear of rejection; through this, a man will attain the mental freedom needed to stand for what he believes in when confronted by a society he is no longer reliant upon to achieve happiness.

MEDITATION

In Islam, meditation is referred to as *murāqabah* (religious mindfulness), which involves the use of *tafakkur* (introspective reflection) to arrive at the reality of something. It is the act of leaving all other things and pouring all of one's concentration and effort into achieving the state of *iḥsān*, which was explored earlier. This is done by pondering upon Allah's greatness and majesty, whilst purifying one's heart, mind, and soul from all worldly distractions. It is essential for a man to spend time in being mindful of Allah ﷻ and trying to understand the

---

[290] *Sunan Abī Dāwūd* 2464.

[291] *Ṣaḥīḥ Muslim* 1172a.

complexities of the universe he exists in. That way, he will be able to achieve and understand his place in it.

ٱلَّذِينَ يَذْكُرُونَ ٱللَّهَ قِيَـٰمًا وَقُعُودًا وَعَلَىٰ جُنُوبِهِمْ وَيَتَفَكَّرُونَ فِى خَلْقِ ٱلسَّمَـٰوَٰتِ وَٱلْأَرْضِ رَبَّنَا مَا خَلَقْتَ هَـٰذَا بَـٰطِلًا سُبْحَـٰنَكَ فَقِنَا عَذَابَ ٱلنَّارِ.

...those who remember Allah standing and sitting, and lying on their sides, and ponder on the creation of the Heavens and the Earth and say, 'Our Lord, You have not created all this in vain. We proclaim Your purity. So, save us from the punishment of the Fire.[292]

Anyone who truly reflects on the creation of Allah ﷻ will come to the understanding that humans are not the prime shapers of their fate. Instead, our purpose in life is to worship the One Who created all the beauty we see. Modern models of understanding humanity's own progress in the fields of science and technology are based on greed, or on the inherent ingenuity of mankind in shaping machinery from raw materials.

But even a cursory glance at such developments would make it abundantly clear that these human accomplishments and advancements were not achieved through humanity itself, but through the Will of the Being that all reality is contingent upon: the Creator.[293]

ٱلَّذِينَ ءَامَنُوا۟ وَتَطْمَئِنُّ قُلُوبُهُم بِذِكْرِ ٱللَّهِ ۗ أَلَا بِذِكْرِ ٱللَّهِ تَطْمَئِنُّ ٱلْقُلُوبُ.

The ones who believe and their hearts are peaceful with the remembrance of Allah. Certainly, the hearts find peace only in the remembrance of Allah.[294]

As members of His creation, our hearts find comfort in His

[292] *Qur'an* 3:191.
[293] *Ma'ārif al-Qur'an*, vol. 2: pp. 272-280.
[294] *Qur'an* 13:28.

remembrance. In an age where depression, anxiety, and other mental ailments are becoming commonplace and men are even more susceptible than women in suffering from poor mental health, it is important that men take the time to remember Allah ﷻ and find inner peace through this. No amount of time taken for 'your self', earning money, or fulfilling desires will help a man achieve inner peace. Allah ﷻ has made it clear that our hearts will become tranquil only when we take the time to be grateful to Him.

Jaʿfar ibn Nāṣir ﵀ was once asked about *murāqabah,* and said, 'It is to be watchful over one's innermost being, due to the awareness of the Almighty Lord, with every thought.'[295]

The Mother of the Believers ʿĀ'ishah ﵂, who was also the wife of the Messenger of Allah ﷺ, reported:

> *The first [form] with which revelation came to the Messenger of Allah ﷺ was the true vision that came in his sleep. He did not see any vision except that it came like the bright gleam of dawn. Thereafter, solitude became dear to him and he used to seclude himself in the Cave of Ḥirā', where he would devote himself to Allah's worship, before returning to his family and getting provisions again for this purpose. He would then return to Khadījah ﵂ and take provisions for a like period, until Truth came upon him while he was in the Cave of Ḥirā'. There came to him the Angel ﵇ and said, 'Read.' He ﷺ replied, 'I am not lettered.'*

> *[The Prophet ﷺ said:] 'He took hold of me and constrained me, till I was hard pressed; thereafter he let me go and said, "Read." I said, "I am not lettered." He then again took hold*

[295] *Al-Risālah al-Qushayriyyah,* vol. 1: p. 331.

of me and constrained me for the second time, until I was hard pressed. He then let me go, saying, "Read." I replied, "I am not lettered." He took hold of me and constrained me for the third time, until I was hard pressed, and then let me go and said, "Read with the name of your Lord Who created (everything), He created man from a clot of blood. Read, and your Lord is the most gracious, Who imparted knowledge by means of the pen. He taught man what he did not know."[296]

Our noble Prophet ﷺ spent many months in seclusion, contemplating the nature of his Lord. This resulted in a deeper understanding of Allah ﷻ than anyone had ever had and would ever have. Through meditation and contemplation, Allah ﷻ prepared the Prophet ﷺ to receive Divine Revelation through Jibrīl ﵇: an experience that even the mountains could not bear:

لَوْ أَنزَلْنَا هَٰذَا ٱلْقُرْءَانَ عَلَىٰ جَبَلٍ لَّرَأَيْتَهُۥ خَٰشِعًا مُّتَصَدِّعًا مِّنْ خَشْيَةِ ٱللَّهِ ۚ وَتِلْكَ ٱلْأَمْثَٰلُ نَضْرِبُهَا لِلنَّاسِ لَعَلَّهُمْ يَتَفَكَّرُونَ.

Had We sent down this Qur'an to a mountain, you would have seen it humbled and burst apart out of awe for Allah. We cite such examples for people so that they may ponder.[297]

Ibn ʿAbbās ﵄ narrated:

I was behind the Prophet ﷺ one day when he said, 'O boy! I will teach you a statement: Be mindful of Allah and He will protect you. Be mindful of Allah and you will find Him before you. When you ask, ask Allah, and when you seek aid, seek Allah's aid. Know that if all of the creation were to gather to do something to benefit you, you would never get any benefit except that which Allah has written for you. And if they were

---

[296] *Ṣaḥīḥ Muslim* 160a.

[297] *Qur'an* 59:21.

to gather to do some harm to you, you would never be harmed except that which Allah has written for you. The pens are lifted and the pages are dried.[298]

Achieving understanding of this is the goal of meditation found in every Muslim. A man that understands this statement cannot comprehend fear or sadness. Our beloved Prophet ﷺ, summed up by his advice to Amīr al-Mu'minīn Abū Bakr ؓ:

لاَ تَحْزَنْ إِنَّ اللَّهَ مَعَنَا

Do not grieve, for Allah is with us.[299]

[298] *Jāmi' al-Tirmidhī* 2516.
[299] *Ṣaḥīḥ al-Bukhārī* 3652.

15
He is Generally Knowledgeable and Widely Read

عَنْ أَبِي هُرَيْرَةَ رَضِيَ اللَّهُ عَنْهُ، قَالَ: قَالَ رَسُولُ اللَّهِ صَلَّى اللَّهُ عَلَيْهِ وَسَلَّمَ:
"تَعَلَّمُوا الْقُرْآنَ وَالْفَرَائِضَ وَعَلِّمُوا النَّاسَ، فَإِنِّي مَقْبُوضٌ."

Abū Hurayrah ﷺ narrated that the Messenger of Allah ﷺ said, 'Learn the Qur'an and the farā'iḍ (legal rulings of inheritance), and teach the people, for I am mortal.'[300]

ACCESS TO A GENERAL KNOWLEDGE OF USEFUL FIELDS

Men need to be widely read, and must understand more than merely the basic tenets of their faith. A man is the leader of his household, and oftentimes has a leadership role outside the domestic sphere as well. It is not enough for him to know the basics in one field - he must be knowledgeable enough in a variety of arenas to undertake his worldly and religious needs. That way, he will be freed of the constant necessity of asking others for help, and can also be at the service of others when they need him. Amīr al-Mu'minīn ʿUmar ibn al-Khaṭṭāb ﷺ once said, 'Learn the rules of inheritance'. Ibn Masʿūd ﷺ issued a similar statement in this regard, but added, '...as well as the rules of divorce and of the pilgrimage'. Both concluded their respective statements by mentioning, '...for it pertains to your religion.'[301]

فَتَعَٰلَى ٱللَّهُ ٱلْمَلِكُ ٱلْحَقُّ ۗ وَلَا تَعْجَلْ بِٱلْقُرْءَانِ مِن قَبْلِ أَن يُقْضَىٰٓ إِلَيْكَ وَحْيُهُۥ ۖ وَقُل رَّبِّ

[300] *Jāmiʿ al-Tirmidhī* 2091.
[301] *Mishkāt al-Maṣābīḥ* 3069.

زِدْنِى عِلْمًا.

So High above all is Allah, the True King! And do not hasten with reciting the Qur'an before its revelation to you is concluded, and say, 'My Lord, improve me in knowledge.'[302]

Ibn ʿUyaynah ﵀ said, 'The Prophet ﷺ did not cease increasing in knowledge until Allah ﷻ took him.'[303] The prayer 'My Lord, improve me in knowledge' is a comprehensive supplication, and includes within it a plea for memorisation and for the ability to understand the true meaning of what is being learned.[304]

Jundub ibn ʿAbdullāh ﵁ said, 'We were with the Prophet ﷺ, and we were strong youths, so we learned faith before we learned the Qur'an. Then we learned the Qur'an, and our faith increased as a result.'[305] On another occasion, the Messenger of Allah ﷺ said, 'Indeed the world is accursed and what it contains is accursed, except the remembrance of Allah ﷻ and those who associate themselves with Allah ﷻ, the learned man, and the student.'[306]

A Muslim man is always learning and reading widely, and as followers of the true faith we are encouraged to do so. In other words, we are inspired to learn many expedient and practical fields, such as religious knowledge, medicine, law, martial skills, strategy, and language. Zayd ibn Thābit ﵁ learned Hebrew in a fortnight when the Prophet ﷺ asked him to do so.[307] Ḥudhayfah ﵁ once said, 'My companions learned something good (by

---

[302] *Qur'an* 20:114.
[303] *Tafsīr Ibn Kathīr* 20:114.
[304] *Maʿārif al-Qur'an*, vol. 6: p. 157.
[305] *Sunan Ibn Mājah* 16.
[306] *Riyāḍ al-Ṣāliḥīn* 477.
[307] *Mishkāt al-Maṣābīḥ* 279.

asking the Prophet 🌸) while I learned something evil.'[308] He would always ask the Prophet 🌸 about the signs of Judgement Day, Dajjāl, and what to do if one lives in those times, as he understood that this would be useful knowledge for those of us that came after the age of the Companions 🌸.

Once knowledge is gained, a man will still be considered a fool if he does not act on the information he has accumulated through his studies. Abū al-Dardā' 🌸 once said: 'The one who will have the worst position in Allah's sight on the Day of Resurrection is the learned man who did not profit from his learning.'[309] Profiting from one's knowledge means to benefit from what has been learned, rather than monetary gain. For example, a man that knows the increased reward of praying in congregation and still prays alone is not benefitting from this knowledge.

Many of the signs of Judgement Day are already becoming commonplace, but each one of us has the ability to keep one of the signs from occurring. The Messenger of Allah 🌸 once said, 'From among the portents of the Hour are the following: Religious knowledge will be taken away; general ignorance [in religious matters] will increase; illegal sexual intercourse will be widespread; the drinking of alcohol will be prevalent; men will decrease in number, and women will increase in number, so much so that fifty women will be looked after by one man.'[310]

The removal of religious knowledge from the people is a sign of the Hour, and we can see today that ignorance is becoming widespread. People have more access to information than any

---

[308] *Ṣaḥīḥ al-Bukhārī* 3607.
[309] *Mishkāt al-Maṣābīḥ* 268.
[310] *Ṣaḥīḥ al-Bukhārī* 5231.

other time in human history, and yet our minds are becoming more idle and docile. The Messenger of Allah ﷺ said, 'Allah ﷻ does not take away knowledge by removing it from men, but rather He takes it away by removing the learned, so that when He leaves no learned man, men will take the ignorant as their leaders. Causes will be presented to them and they will pass judgement without knowledge, erring and leading others into error.'[311] Is this not already occurring? Are the ignorant not already leading us at a local, regional, and national level? Almost every day we are hearing of pious scholars passing away, and with them knowledge is being lifted from us. Meanwhile, people with no knowledge of the faith continue to make claims about what is best for their communities without consulting the few people of comprehension we have left. Is this not a clear indication of the prevalence of ignorance?

Amīr al-Mu'minīn ʿUmar ibn al-Khaṭṭāb رضي الله عنه once asked Kaʿb رضي الله عنه, 'Who are the lords of knowledge?' He replied, 'They are those who act in accordance with what they know.' ʿUmar رضي الله عنه then asked, 'What takes knowledge from the hearts of the learned?' He was told, 'It is covetousness.'[312] As stated previously, what is learned must be passed on; to withhold spreading it is to guarantee its loss.

Once knowledge is gained, acting upon it allows us to benefit the most from what we have learned. The greatest detriment is caused by the person that knows better and still does wrong. The Prophet ﷺ said, 'The worst evil comprises learned men who are evil, and the best good is found in learned men who are good.'[313]

With regard to possessing general knowledge that is

---

[311] *Ṣaḥīḥ al-Bukhārī* 100.
[312] *Mishkāt al-Maṣābīḥ* 266.
[313] *Mishkāt al-Maṣābīḥ* 267.

beneficial, we can find many golden examples from the Companions ﷺ and Successors ﷺ. These past models demonstrate that the true men of worth are those who learn enough about these fields to benefit themselves and their respective communities. Some take a cursory look at these examples of true manhood and believe they were exclusively scholarly men, but this is not the case. Besides being scholars and students, they were also the warriors that conquered half of the known world; under them, the Muslim lands spread from Spain to China in less than 100 years. They were family men who would marry more than once and maintain several large households simultaneously. Moreover, while some of them were judges, teachers, and business men, others among them presided as craftsmen, statesmen, and travellers. The Prophet ﷺ said, 'The best of you are my generation, then those that follow after them, then those that follow after them.'[314] They were the best in every way, and by emulating them we can hope to achieve some small degree of spiritual connection with them.

The Messenger of Allah ﷺ said, 'Learn enough about your lineage to facilitate the maintenance of your ties of kinship. For indeed the maintenance of ties of kinship encourages affection among relatives, increases wealth, and increases one's lifespan.'[315] Abū Hurayrah ﷺ narrated that the Messenger of Allah ﷺ said, 'O Abū Hurayrah, learn inheritance law and teach it, for it is half of knowledge, but it will be forgotten. This is the first thing that will be taken away from my nation.'[316]

Ibn Masʿūd ﷺ reported that the Messenger of Allah ﷺ said to him, 'Acquire knowledge and teach it to the people, learn the

[314] *Ṣaḥīḥ al-Bukhārī* 2651.
[315] *Jāmiʿ al-Tirmidhī* 1979.
[316] *Sunan Ibn Mājah* 2719.

obligatory duties and teach them to the people, learn the Qur'an and teach it to the people; for I am a man who will be taken away, knowledge will be taken away, and dissensions will appear, such that two men will disagree about an obligatory duty and find no one to decide between them.'[317]

Lastly, regardless of what we learn, whether it is religious knowledge, or knowledge in the lesser but still beneficial worldly fields, our intention as always needs to be checked at the onset, during the learning process, and continually thereafter. The Prophet ﷺ warned us thus: 'Do not seek knowledge in order to show off in front of the scholars, or to argue with the foolish, and do not choose the best seat in a gathering due to it (knowledge). For whoever does that will have the Fire, the Fire!'[318]

A man should be knowledgeable enough to be able to start again from nothing. In the worst possible situation, whether forced to move due to unforeseen or unfavourable circumstances, or having lost everything due to debt, oppression, or natural disaster, a man should have the skills, knowledge, and fortitude to arrive at an unknown land with nothing, and begin anew, building himself back up to where he once was. This was the way of the Companions ﷺ on more than one occasion, where people who were once rich ended up without two cloths to cover themselves due to their adoption of Islam. And it was the approach of the migrant generations in many of our own families following World War II who moved from Asia or Africa to Europe or the Americas and started a new life in a foreign land. In essence, they pioneered the way so their womenfolk and children could follow. There is, however, a difference between those who carried out a *hijrah* (emigrating from one land to

[317] *Mishkāt al-Maṣābīḥ* 279.
[318] *Sunan Ibn Mājah* 254.

another for the sake of one's religion) and emigrating for financial reasons.[319]

وَمَن يُهَاجِرْ فِى سَبِيلِ ٱللَّهِ يَجِدْ فِى ٱلْأَرْضِ مُرَٰغَمًا كَثِيرًا وَسَعَةً ۚ وَمَن يَخْرُجْ مِنۢ بَيْتِهِۦ مُهَاجِرًا إِلَى ٱللَّهِ وَرَسُولِهِۦ ثُمَّ يُدْرِكْهُ ٱلْمَوْتُ فَقَدْ وَقَعَ أَجْرُهُۥ عَلَى ٱللَّهِ ۗ وَكَانَ ٱللَّهُ غَفُورًا رَّحِيمًا.

Whoever migrates in the way of Allah shall find on the Earth many a place to settle, and a wide dimension of resources. Whoever leaves his home migrating for the sake of Allah and His Messenger, and death overtakes him, then, his reward is established with Allah. Allah is Most-Forgiving, Very-Merciful.[320]

The above verse was revealed in relation to Khālid ibn Ḥizām ﷺ, who was part of the first group of migrants from Mecca to Abyssinia,[321] but died of a snakebite *en route*.[322] Allah ﷻ promises a safe haven for anyone that emigrates for His sake alone.[323] It is faith in Allah ﷻ that is the key to success, and it should be remembered that no amount of personal skill, knowledge, determination, or ingenuity can be successful without faith in Allah ﷻ and His divine help. Mujāhid ﷺ said that 'many a place to settle' means he will find a way out of what he dislikes.[324] Qatādah ﷺ also said that it means Allah ﷻ will take him from misguidance to guidance and from poverty to richness.[325]

During the lifetime of the Prophet ﷺ, the Muslims were made to migrate three times in order to safeguard their faith and

---

319 *Ma'ārif al-Qur'an*, vol. 2: p. 558.
320 *Qur'an* 4:100.
321 Modern day Ethiopia and Somalia. Even today, there are the ruins of a Masjid Qiblatayn built there by the early Companions.
322 *Ma'ārif al-Qur'an*, vol. 2: pp. 556-557.
323 *Tafsīr Ibn Kathīr* 4:100.
324 *Tafsīr Ibn Kathīr* 4:100.
325 *Tafsīr Ibn Kathīr* 4:100.

their lives. In the first two episodes, groups from the early Muslims migrated to the Christian Kingdom of Abyssinia and were forced to build a life for themselves in a foreign land that they did not fit in.[326] Fortunately, the Negus was a good and just ruler, and he provided safety for them there, ultimately becoming a Muslim himself. The third occasion was when the Muslims migrated from Mecca to Medina, and this was the occasion when the Prophet ﷺ himself also migrated.[327] The Prophet ﷺ said, 'I was ordered to migrate to a town which will swallow other towns, and it is called Yathrib; that is Medina, and it turns out persons as a furnace removes the impurities of iron.'[328] The Prophet Ibrāhīm ﷺ also migrated himself on more than one occasion,[329] and again had to rebuild his life each time.

Abū Mūsā ﷺ narrates:

> *The news of the migration of the Prophet ﷺ reached us while we were in Yemen. So we - namely my two brothers and I - set out as emigrants towards him ﷺ. I was younger than Abū Burdah ﷺ and Abū Ruhm ﷺ, and our total number was either 53 or 52 men from my people. We boarded a ship and it took us to the Negus in Ethiopia. There we met Jaʿfar ibn Abī Ṭālib ﷺ, and stayed with him. Then we all came [to Medina] and met the Prophet ﷺ at the time of the conquest of Khaybar. Some of the people used to say to us, i.e., to the people of the ship, 'We migrated before you.' Asmāʾ bint ʿUmays ﷺ, who was one of those who had come with us, came as a visitor to the Mother of the Believers, Ḥafṣah*

[326] *Sunan Abī Dāwūd* 2086.
[327] *Ṣaḥīḥ al-Bukhārī* 3652.
[328] *Ṣaḥīḥ al-Bukhārī* 1871.
[329] *Ṣaḥīḥ al-Bukhārī* 2635.

, the wife of the Prophet ﷺ. She had migrated along with those other Muslims who migrated to the Negus. ʿUmar came to Ḥafṣah while Asmāʾ bint ʿUmays was with her. Upon seeing Asmāʾ, ʿUmar asked, 'Who is this?' She said, 'Asmāʾ bint ʿUmays.' ʿUmar asked, 'Is she the Ethiopian, sea-faring lady?' Asmāʾ replied, 'Yes.'[330]

As men, the responsibility falls on us to be ready and competent to lead the way if and when the time comes where we have to restart again. A man is someone who can do this with patience and faith in Allah. The modern notion of the man is someone who has money and high social status, that is, the so-called 'High-Value Man' that lives a life of luxury. This does not define a man. A man is he who can strive through hardship with patience and fortitude, who is prepared for any eventuality, and has the skills and knowledge to re-establish himself in any location if he so requires, whether there is help available or not. Abū Saʿīd narrates:

Once a Bedouin came to the Prophet ﷺ and asked him about the migration. The Prophet ﷺ said, 'May the mercy of Allah be on you! The migration is quite a difficult matter. Have you got some camels?' He replied in the affirmative. Then the Prophet ﷺ said, 'Do you give their zakāh?' He replied in the affirmative. The Prophet ﷺ said, 'Do you let others benefit from their milk?' He replied in the affirmative. Then the Prophet ﷺ asked, 'Do you milk them on their watering days and give their milk to the poor and needy?' He replied in the

[330] *Ṣaḥīḥ al-Bukhārī* 4230.

affirmative. The Prophet ﷺ said, 'Go on doing the same beyond the seas. There is no doubt that Allah will not overlook any of your good deeds.'[331]

These were indeed true men.

[331] *Ṣaḥīḥ al-Bukhārī* 3923.

16
He Values Time

عَنِ ابْنِ عَبَّاسٍ رَضِيَ الله عنهما، قَالَ: قَالَ النَّبِيُّ صَلَّى اللَّهُ عَلَيْهِ وَسَلَّمَ: "نِعْمَتَانِ مَغْبُونٌ فِيهِمَا كَثِيرٌ مِنَ النَّاسِ، الصِّحَّةُ وَالْفَرَاغُ."

Ibn ʿAbbās ﵄ narrated that the Prophet ﷺ said, 'There are two blessings that many people are deceived into losing: health and free time.'[332]

Timekeeping and the Awareness and Value of Time

A man keeps track of time. He is aware of it, he values it, and he does not squander it. Benjamin Franklin once proclaimed that 'time is money', but time is a much more valuable currency. The Greek philosopher Theophrastus said:

'Time is the most valuable thing a man can spend.'

This is much closer to the truth. Just like any currency, time can be wasted, invested, lost, or spent. Unlike any other currency, however, it is perpetually depleting. Time not invested or spent is consequently being wasted or lost. Sitting in front of a screen for entertainment is not time well spent, but time wasted. As men, we should be acutely aware of this and not waste time in idle pursuits and childish play, for if there is one thing we can be certain of about time, it is the reality that it will inevitably end.

وَٱلْعَصْرِ. إِنَّ ٱلْإِنسَـٰنَ لَفِى خُسْرٍ. إِلَّا ٱلَّذِينَ ءَامَنُوا۟ وَعَمِلُوا۟ ٱلصَّـٰلِحَـٰتِ وَتَوَاصَوْا۟ بِٱلْحَقِّ وَتَوَاصَوْا۟ بِٱلصَّبْرِ.

I swear by the Time, man is in a state of loss indeed, except

---

[332] *Ṣaḥīḥ al-Bukhārī* 6412.

those who believed, did righteous deeds, exhorted each other to follow the truth, and exhorted each other to observe patience.[333]

In this *sūrah* (chapter), Allah ﷻ teaches us the most valuable lesson about time. We are all at a loss in relation to it by default, and it is only those who believe, do good works, and drive each other towards truth and patience that will be successful.[334] The first two relate to one's personal betterment, and the latter two relate to the guidance and reform of others.[335] A life subsisted without these actions is a life wasted. Man, his growth, development, and deeds all take place within time, and man will constantly lose this capital, as the 'hours, days, months, and years of life pass quickly; spiritual and material potentialities decline, and abilities fade. Man is like a person who possesses great capital and, without his permission and will, every day, a portion of that capital is taken away. This is the nature of life in this world; the nature of continual loss'.[336] Imam al-Ṭabarānī ؒ recorded that ʿAbdullāh ibn Ḥiṣn Abī Madīnah ؓ said that the Companions ؓ of the Prophet ﷺ would often recite these verses when they met one another, which ultimately served as a reminder to not squander their time. Regarding Sūrah al-ʿAṣr, Imam Shāfiʿī ؒ said, 'If the people were to ponder on this *sūrah*, it would be sufficient for them.'[337]

A poem, often attributed to Amīr al-Mu'minīn ʿAlī ؓ, reads as follows:

---

[333] *Qur'an* 103:1-3.
[334] *Tafsīr Ibn Kathīr* 103:1-3.
[335] *Maʿārif al-Qur'an,* vol. 8: pp. 869-873.
[336] *Maʿārif al-Qur'an,* vol. 8: pp. 869-873.
[337] *Tafsīr Ibn Kathīr* 103:1-3.

حَياتُكَ أنفاسٌ تُعَدُّ فَكُلَّما

مَضىٰ نَفَسٌ مِنهَا انتَقَصْتَ بِه جُزءَا

Every breath of your life has been recorded;

With each one spent your life has been eroded.[338]

One should not, however, complain about time, and how much or little of it has been provided to us. Allah ﷻ has given each of us exactly how much time we need to prove ourselves. Those who live the most fleeting lives are saved from Divine Judgement, and those that live the longest spans have the longest test, but more time to prove themselves worthy. The Prophet ﷺ said, 'Let none of you complain about Time (*al-Dahr*), for Allah ﷻ is Time.'[339]

The Prophet ﷺ was greatly concerned about time, its value, and ensuring we are aware of it. Ibn ʿAbbās ﷺ reported that the Messenger of Allah ﷺ said, 'Take advantage of five before five: your youth before your old age, your health before your illness, your wealth before your poverty, your free time before your busyness, and your life before your death.'[340] This is a warning to each of us to not waste the time we have, as youth, health, wealth, free time, and life in general are all things that are finite.

The Prophet ﷺ also said, 'Hasten to do good before you are taken by one of the seven afflictions. Are you waiting for overwhelming poverty, distracting richness, debilitating illness, babbling senility, sudden death, the Dajjāl (Antichrist), who is the worst of the awaited, or the Hour? The Hour will be the most

---

[338] *Maʿārif al-Qur'an*, vol. 8: pp. 869-873.

[339] *Muwaṭṭa' Imam Mālik* 1816.

[340] *Shuʿab al-Īmān* 9767.

grievous and bitter.'[341]

When our time is over and we are resurrected on the Day of Judgement, we will have to account for the time we have spent. The Prophet ﷺ said, 'The feet of the slave of Allah ﷻ shall not move (on the Day of Judgement) until he is asked about five things: his life and how he spent it; his knowledge and what he did with it; his wealth, and how he earned it and where he spent it; and his body and why he wore it out.'[342]

Farīd al-Dīn ʿAṭṭār ؒ of Nishapur famously related the story of a Persian king who had asked his wise men to create him something that would make him happy when he was sad and appreciative when he was happy. They forged a ring for him, upon which was the inscription:

This too shall pass.

TIMELINESS AND PUNCTUALITY

Timeliness and punctuality are qualities that are essential for every man, compulsory for every Muslim, and lacking in the majority of people. Islam is a religion that harnesses time to ensure that obligations are completed and, as already discussed, not a single valuable breath is wasted. Every prayer has a set time in which it must be performed, and failure to do so is sinful. Every fast is set within an allotted time, from sunrise to sunset, and failure to comply with the rules of fasting during this time invalidates it. *Zakāh* is to be collected from accumulated wealth within a year, and failure to pay it on time is sinful.

The Hajj can only be performed during a handful of days in the year, and is not accepted at any other time. Every action in the Hajj ritual must be performed at the correct time and place.

---

[341] *Jāmiʿ al-Tirmidhī* 2306.
[342] *Jāmiʿ al-Tirmidhī* 2417.

Punctuality is built into every waking moment of the Muslim; his day is structured around his obligations and the set times they must be carried out in.

Shakespeare wrote, 'Better three hours too soon than a minute too late.'[343] This is generally true, as being early to complete one's obligations ensures that they will be done on time. If you plan to arrive early, you will arrive on time; if you plan to arrive on time, you will arrive late.[344] The Messenger of Allah ﷺ said that the person who waits for *ṣalāh* in the *masjid* is counted as one who is in *ṣalāh*.[345] Thus, in worship - and by extension in all matters of life - there is benefit in punctuality.

The Prophet ﷺ also said, 'The beginning of the time for *ṣalāh* is pleasing to Allah ﷻ, and the end of its time is pardoned by Allah ﷻ.'[346] Even within the set times we have been given, being timely is what is most pleasing to Allah. Delaying it, despite it being carried out within the set time, is *pardoned* by Allah ﷻ. This indicates that just because praying at the end of the set time is acceptable, it does not mean that one should be lax in this regard.

يَٰٓأَيُّهَا ٱلَّذِينَ ءَامَنُوٓاْ أَوۡفُواْ بِٱلۡعُقُودِۚ

O you who believe, fulfil the contracts.[347]

The opening words of this verse specify that this is a requirement in faith, and to 'fulfil the contracts' is a divine command.[348] The general meaning of the verse is that we must 'take the fulfilling of mutual contracts to be binding and

[343] *The Merry Wives of Windsor*, William Shakespeare.
[344] An English proverb.
[345] *Riyāḍ al-Ṣāliḥīn* 1061.
[346] *Jāmiʿ al-Tirmidhī* 172.
[347] *Qur'an* 5:1.
[348] *Maʿārif al-Qur'an*, vol. 3: p. 22.

necessary'.[349] We have discussed the fulfilment of contracts earlier, and therefore will not delve into detail with regard to this. However, the commentators of the Qur'an have said that contracts here refers to every commitment and 'strict adherence to all permissible provisions and conditions which have been mutually agreed upon is mandatory and all parties must observe and fulfil these'.[350] Therefore, if a time has been established by the parties, it is compulsory for a Muslim to be present within the set period. At the very least, it is considered improper and unbecoming of a Muslim to miss such a meeting.

ʿUqbah ﵁ reports, 'I offered the ʿAṣr prayer behind the Prophet ﷺ at Medina. When he had finished the prayer, he stood up hurriedly and left by crossing the rows of the people to one of the dwellings of his wives. The people became worried due to his speed. The Prophet ﷺ returned to find the people surprised at his haste and said to them, "I remember a piece of gold lying in my house and I did not like it to divert my attention from Allah's worship, so I have ordered it to be distributed (in charity)."'[351] The Prophet ﷺ did not want any wealth in his home to distract him from the worship of Allah ﷻ. As soon as he made the intention to give it away, he did so rapidly to ensure he did not delay in doing so.

This is how a man should be: punctual in his actions, timely in his commitments, and swift in undertaking acts of good.

---

[349] *Maʿārif al-Qur'an*, vol. 3: p. 22.
[350] *Maʿārif al-Qur'an*, vol. 3: p. 22.
[351] *Ṣaḥīḥ al-Bukhārī* 851.

17
He Adapts

عَنْ أَنَسِ بْنِ مَالِكٍ رضيَ الله عنه، قَالَ: قَالَ النَّبِيُّ صَلَّى اللَّهُ عَلَيْهِ وَسَلَّمَ: "أَخَذَ الرَّايَةَ زَيْدٌ فَأُصِيبَ، ثُمَّ أَخَذَهَا جَعْفَرٌ فَأُصِيبَ، ثُمَّ أَخَذَهَا عَبْدُ اللهِ بْنُ رَوَاحَةَ فَأُصِيبَ - وَإِنَّ عَيْنَيْ رَسُولِ اللهِ صَلَّى اللَّهُ عَلَيْهِ وَسَلَّمَ لَتَذْرِفَانِ - ثُمَّ أَخَذَهَا خَالِدُ بْنُ الْوَلِيدِ مِنْ غَيْرِ إِمْرَةٍ، فَفُتِحَ لَهُ."

Anas ibn Mālik ﷺ narrated that the Prophet ﷺ said, 'Zayd took the flag and was martyred, then it was taken by Jaʿfar who was martyred as well, and then ʿAbdullāh ibn Rawāḥah took the flag, but he too was martyred.' At that moment, the eyes of the Messenger of Allah ﷺ were full of tears. 'Then', he ﷺ continued, 'Khālid ibn al-Walīd took the flag without being a nominated commander and was blessed with victory.'[352]

Adaptability, Versatility, and Flexibility

Situations change, and the best laid plans can fall by the wayside. A man can adapt to any circumstances, and the complete fall-through of an intricate idea, be it at home, in the workplace, or in the field of war, should not cause him distress. A man needs to be adaptable and versatile; in other words, he should be able to change with the situation presented to him and make it work for his goals and needs. The Prophet ﷺ and his Companions ﷺ showed many examples of this in their lifetimes, and even the most monumental changes were taken in their strides as they displayed an ability to be flexible in times of upheaval and change.

قَدْ نَرَىٰ تَقَلُّبَ وَجْهِكَ فِي السَّمَاءِ ۖ فَلَنُوَلِّيَنَّكَ قِبْلَةً تَرْضَاهَا ۚ فَوَلِّ وَجْهَكَ شَطْرَ الْمَسْجِدِ الْحَرَامِ ۚ وَحَيْثُ مَا كُنتُمْ فَوَلُّوا وُجُوهَكُمْ شَطْرَهُ ۗ وَإِنَّ الَّذِينَ أُوتُوا الْكِتَابَ لَيَعْلَمُونَ أَنَّهُ

[352] *Ṣaḥīḥ Muslim* 526a.

الْحَقُّ مِن رَّبِّهِمْ ۗ وَمَا اللَّهُ بِغَافِلٍ عَمَّا يَعْمَلُونَ

We have been seeing you turning your face to the Heavens. Thus, We will certainly assign to you a qiblah that you would like. You may now turn your face in the direction of the Sacred Mosque (al-Masjid al-Ḥarām), and wherever you are, turn your faces in its direction. Even those who have been given the Book know well that it is the truth from their Lord, and Allah is not unaware of what they do.[353]

Anas ﷺ reported:

> *The Messenger of Allah ﷺ used to pray towards Bayt al-Maqdis until it was revealed to him: 'We have been seeing you turning your face to the Heavens. Thus, We will certainly assign to you a qiblah that you would like. You may now turn your face in the direction of the Sacred Mosque (al-Masjid al-Ḥarām).' A person from Banū Salamah was walking by when he found people performing rukūʿ (bowing) while praying the dawn prayer, and they had already completed one rakʿah (unit of prayer). He said in a loud voice, 'Listen! The qiblah has been changed!' As a result, they turned towards the new qiblah, Mecca, in that very state.*[354]

Al-Barā' ﷺ said, 'We prayed toward Bayt al-Maqdis with the Messenger of Allah ﷺ for 16 or 17 months (the narrator, Ṣafwān ﷺ, was unsure of the correct number), and then it was changed to the new *qiblah*.'[355] Allah ﷻ is free from the confines of physical form or direction, and the appointment of a *qiblah* was done as a means to create unity amongst the Muslims, wherever they are

[353] *Qur'an* 2:144.
[354] *Ṣaḥīḥ Muslim* 527.
[355] *Sunan al-Nasā'ī* 488.

in the world.[356]

Even with something as monumental as the change of the *qiblah,* the Companions ﷺ adapted to this new ordinance immediately, so much so that the people who were in mid-prayer changed the direction of their prayer *whilst* praying. The same was true when alcohol and intoxicants were banned.[357] In the latter case, the Muslims again adapted to the new ruling straightaway.

In the Battle of the Confederates, also known as the Battle of the Trench, a confederation of idolaters united with the Quraysh in an attempt to wipe out the Muslims, and marched to Medina in the year 5 AH. The Prophet ﷺ arranged a war council, and among the people present was Salmān al-Fārisī ؓ, a Persian Companion. He opined that due to the excessive numbers of the enemy - who were approximately 10,000 men - it would not be advisable to engage in hostilities with them in the open, since there were less than 3000 Muslims. Furthermore, if all the Muslim troops were deployed outside Medina, no one would be left behind to defend the city.

He therefore advised the Prophet ﷺ to use the Persian tactic of trench warfare.[358] The Prophet ﷺ approved of this proposed course of action and personally arranged the dimensions and positions of the trench lines. The Prophet ﷺ took part in the digging process as well, breaking great boulders and carrying dirt out alongside his men, all the while praying for his Companions ؓ. He also recited the poetry composed by ʿAbdullāh ibn Rawāḥah ؓ in a tune, thus lifting the spirits of all around him,

[356] *Maʿārif al-Qur'an,* vol. 1: p. 383.
[357] *Sunan al-Nasāʾī* 5699.
[358] *Sīrat al-Muṣṭafā:* vol. 2, p. 343.

saying:[359]

اللَّهُمَّ لَوْلاَ أَنْتَ مَا اهْتَدَيْنَا | وَلاَ تَصَدَّقْنَا وَلاَ صَلَّيْنَا

فَأَنْزِلَنْ سَكِينَةً عَلَيْنَا | وَثَبِّتِ الأَقْدَامَ إِنْ لاَقَيْنَا

إِنَّ الأُلَى قَدْ بَغَوْا عَلَيْنَا | وَإِنْ أَرَادُوا فِتْنَةً أَبَيْنَا

O Lord, if not for You we'd be unguided,

We would not pray or give our wealth in alms.

So Lord we beg Thee send upon us calm,

Make firm our feet if we should meet our foes,

In truth they have opposed us and rebelled,

If war they want, then they will be repelled.[360]

This strategy was one that had never been seen before in the history of the Arabs. But when confronted with overwhelming odds and no way to fight the enemy in a bottleneck fashion to even the numbers, the Muslims created the bottlenecks themselves by using a Persian war strategy.

The Hadith cited at the start of this section is a narration in which the Prophet ﷺ – whilst still in Medina – described the epic events of the Battle of Mu'tah as they were occurring in Jordan. The Battle of Mu'tah was waged against the Byzantine Empire, where a Muslim army of 3000 men faced more than 10,000 Byzantine soldiers (some historical sources estimate that the Byzantines actually comprised of approximately 100,000 troops). During the encounter, the Muslim commanders Zayd ibn Ḥārithah, Jaʿfar ibn Abī Ṭālib, and ʿAbdullāh ibn Rawāḥah

---

[359] *Ṣaḥīḥ al-Bukhārī* 4106.

[360] This is a poetic translation of ʿAbdullāh ibn Rawāḥah's poetry. The Arabic script has been included to ensure that the unworthy words of the author do not sully or misconstrue the rendition of our beloved Prophet ﷺ or his blessed Companions ﵃.

were all martyred in the field and the Muslims were left leaderless. The Muslims quickly selected a new general from amongst their ranks, Khālid ibn al-Walīd ﷺ, and he reluctantly took up the banner of leadership.[361]

On that day, Khālid ﷺ himself narrates that he broke nine swords during the warfare, and only his Yemeni sword remained intact.[362] On the following day, Khālid ﷺ rearranged his troops so that his vanguard switched positions with his rear-guard, and his left flank switched with his right. To the Byzantines it appeared as though the Muslims had received reinforcements in the night, and they became unconfident of their capabilities and prospects. Khālid ﷺ pressed this advantage and secured a tactical advantage against the numerically superior enemy.[363] On that day onward, Khālid ibn al-Walīd ﷺ received the title 'Sword of Allah'[364], and he never sustained a defeat in the battlefield.

COMPETENCE

Competence is the ability to do something efficiently and well. Just as a man can adapt to any eventual outcome, he must also be proficient in what he does in response and how he does it. The example given above of Khālid ibn al-Walīd ﷺ being thrust into the commanding role during a losing battle perfectly exemplifies the concept of competence.[365] When the original three commanders of the Muslims were slain in the Battle of Mu'tah, it was originally Thābit ibn Arqam ﷺ who took up the white banner and rallied the Muslims. He exhorted them to fight

---

[361] *Ṣaḥīḥ al-Bukhārī* 1246.
[362] *Ṣaḥīḥ al-Bukhārī* 4266.
[363] *Sīrat al-Muṣṭafā*, vol. 2: pp. 507-511.
[364] *Ṣaḥīḥ al-Bukhārī* 4262.
[365] *Ṣaḥīḥ al-Bukhārī* 1246.

and they rallied to him. Thābit 🙢 then gave the banner to Khālid 🙢, stating, 'You are well acquainted with the art of war.'[366] Khālid 🙢 was extremely competent in everything he did, and was an expert in strategy, tactics, and warfare, not to mention a great warrior and inspiring commander. Within moments of being handed authority, he turned the tide of the battle around. That is true competence.

Shaykh al-Islam Ibn Taymiyyah 🙢 states, 'Anyone who delegates a position to someone whilst knowing someone else is more competent has certainly cheated Allah 🙢, His Apostle 🙢, and all Muslims.'[367] Giving positions of leadership to incompetent people is rife in the modern world. From the supermarket manager to the elected leaders of nation states, we find the wrong person is consistently put in place, often simply for the sake of familial ties, friendship, or malleability.

Abū Rāfi' was a war criminal who had financed a campaign of aggression against the Prophet 🙢. As a result, 'Abdullāh ibn 'Atīk 🙢 and four other Companions 🙢 were dispatched to conduct a night raid on his fortress and neutralise him. 'Abdullāh ibn 'Atīk 🙢 took the lead on the operation and, during a reconnaissance round, observed that the men in the fortress had lost a donkey and had left the fortress after dark to find it. Pretending to relieve himself near the gate, he was ushered into the fortress when the guards at the gate thought he was one of their own men. Inside, he waited until everyone had fallen asleep, noting where the fortress keys were kept. At night, he unlocked the gate to clear his escape route, and proceeded to lock every door he came across, as well as every door on the way

[366] *Sīrat al-Muṣṭafā*, vol. 2: p. 507.
[367] *Al-Siyāsah al-Shar'iyyah.*

up to the quarters of Abū Rāfiʿ. Finding the room pitch black, and acutely aware of the orders of the Prophet ﷺ of not harming any women, children, or non-combatants, he called out to Abū Rāfiʿ, who answered. He assassinated the man and left in the darkness, unseen.[368]

This episode highlights clear skill and competence in the task he was given. The Companions رضي الله عنهم were not assassins by trade, but when ʿAbdullāh رضي الله عنه and his counterparts were requested to neutralise the threat of Abū Rāfiʿ and were ordered not to harm any non-combatants, they responded in a prompt and effective manner. ʿAbdullāh ibn ʿAtīk رضي الله عنه showed courage, skill, and competence, single-handedly infiltrating an enemy fort, armed with only his sword, and carrying out his task surgically and efficiently, with no collateral damage sustained in the process.

Trust in Allah

Ultimately, no amount of adaptability or competence can ensure success. A man should always undertake all tasks by placing his trust in Allah ﷻ first and foremost, as without His permission, nothing can be completed.

The concept of having trust in Allah ﷻ is called *tawakkul* (reliance on Allah's divine plan). A Muslim should hold to this trust at all times, and take comfort in it, even as he reminds himself that nothing he has achieved was done by his own might, skill, or wit, for these were just the means by which Allah ﷻ caused events to occur.

وَمَا لَنَآ أَلَّا نَتَوَكَّلَ عَلَى ٱللَّهِ وَقَدْ هَدَىٰنَا سُبُلَنَا ۚ وَلَنَصْبِرَنَّ عَلَىٰ مَآ ءَاذَيْتُمُونَا ۚ وَعَلَى ٱللَّهِ فَلْيَتَوَكَّلِ ٱلْمُتَوَكِّلُونَ.

[368] *Ṣaḥīḥ al-Bukhārī* 4039, 4040.

'What is wrong with us that we should not put our trust in Allah when He has guided us to our paths? We shall, of course, endure with patience all your persecutions; and all those who have to trust should trust only in Allah.'[369]

Because it is Allah ﷻ Who guides us, He is the One worthy of complete trust. Whatever hardships are placed in our way are assigned for a reason. Whatever blessings we are given are prearranged through his Divine Mercy and Grace. If we need to place our trust in anyone or anything, we should be putting that trust in Allah ﷻ alone. No one else is worthy of this trust, and it is this trust in Allah ﷻ which allowed our Prophets ﷺ to accomplish miracles and wonders, despite the greatest of tribulations.

Amīr al-Mu'minīn 'Umar ibn al-Khaṭṭāb ﷺ heard the Messenger of Allah ﷺ say, 'If you were to put your trust in Allah ﷻ as you should, you would be given sustenance like the birds; they leave hungry in the morning and come back with full bellies in the evening.'[370]

This is the level of trust in Allah ﷻ that a man should strive to exercise in his daily life routine. He should be so content with Allah's plan that he wakes in the morning with the sole purpose of worshipping Him, without worrying about where his food or income will come from. This is exactly how the Prophet ﷺ lived his life. For example, he once took a man who had leprosy by the hand, and put it in the same dish he was eating from, saying, 'Eat with confidence in Allah ﷻ and place your trust in Him.'[371]

This is the ideal level of trust, but many of us do and will fall

[369] *Qur'an* 14:12.
[370] *Musnad al-Imam Aḥmad* 205.
[371] *Sunan Abī Dāwūd* 3925.

short of this eminent plane; it is not for everyone. For the rest of us, the following advice of the Prophet ﷺ should be a template for how we live our lives. When a man came to the Prophet ﷺ to ask about how he should look after his camel, he asked, 'O Messenger of Allah, shall I tie it [and rely upon Allah ﷻ], or leave it loose [and rely upon Allah ﷻ]?' He ﷺ said, "Tie it."[372]

The message here is crystal-clear. Whether it is security or something else that is sought, we should exert our utmost efforts to achieve our ambition, and then leave the result to Allah ﷻ. Whatever Allah ﷻ wills to happen will be the outcome, but this does not mean that we do nothing to achieve our goals and simply sit idly at home and expect miracles to occur. Such a passive attitude rails against the Islamic ethos. For us, hard work and *tawakkul* go hand in hand.

It was narrated from Abū Hurayrah ؓ that whenever the Prophet ﷺ left his house, he ﷺ would say:

بِسْمِ اللَّهِ لاَ حَوْلَ وَلاَ قُوَّةَ إِلاَّ بِاللَّهِ التُّكْلاَنُ عَلَى اللَّهِ

'In the Name of Allah, there is no power and strength except with Allah, and trust is placed in Allah.'[373]

Abū al-Dardā' ؓ advised that if anyone repeats the following litany seven times in the morning and evening, Allah ﷻ will be sufficient for him against anything which grieves him:

حَسْبِيَ اللَّهُ لاَ إِلَهَ إِلاَّ هُوَ عَلَيْهِ تَوَكَّلْتُ وَهُوَ رَبُّ الْعَرْشِ الْعَظِيمِ

Allah suffices me; there is no god but He. I trust in Him, and He is the Lord of the Supreme Throne.[374]

---

[372] *Sunan al-Tirmidhī* 2517.
[373] *Sunan Ibn Mājah* 3885.
[374] *Sunan Abī Dāwūd* 5081.

18
He Lives Simply

عَنِ ابْنِ أَبِي لَيْلَى رحمه الله، قَالَ خَرَجْنَا مَعَ حُذَيْفَةَ رَضِيَ اللَّهُ عَنْهُ وَذَكَرَ النَّبِيَّ صَلَّى اللهُ عَلَيْهِ وَسَلَّمَ قَالَ: "لاَ تَشْرَبُوا فِي آنِيَةِ الذَّهَبِ وَالْفِضَّةِ، وَلاَ تَلْبَسُوا الْحَرِيرَ وَالدِّيبَاجَ، فَإِنَّهَا لَهُمْ فِي الدُّنْيَا وَلَكُمْ فِي الآخِرَةِ."

Ibn Abī Laylā ﵀ said: 'We once set off with Ḥudhayfah ﵁, who mentioned that the Prophet ﷺ said, "Do not drink in gold or silver utensils, nor wear clothes of silk or brocade, for these things are for them (the unbelievers) in this world and for you in the Hereafter."'[375]

SIMPLICITY

Islam is often described as a simple religion. Its tenets are easy to understand, its rules are easy to follow, and its laws correspond with the natural intuitions of mankind. The followers of Islam are also modest people, as simplicity is encouraged in Islam. When Islam tells us to believe in the One God, Allah ﷻ, our monotheism is pure; there can be no confusion as to Whom we mean. When we are told to pray daily, we are told exactly how, when, and the number of times to pray.

In the above Hadith, the Prophet ﷺ has told the Muslims to steer clear of a life of extravagance. This is to the extent that eating and drinking from expensive utensils or wearing clothing made from expensive materials is not permissible for a Muslim. A Muslim lives a simple life, and does not value the trappings of this world. His goal is the pleasure of Allah ﷻ, not his own; he values the Hereafter, not the world. The Prophet ﷺ said, 'The world is a prison for the believer and a paradise for the

[375] *Ṣaḥīḥ al-Bukhārī* 5633.

disbeliever.'[376]

وَأَصْبَحَ ٱلَّذِينَ تَمَنَّوْاْ مَكَانَهُۥ بِٱلْأَمْسِ يَقُولُونَ وَيْكَأَنَّ ٱللَّهَ يَبْسُطُ ٱلرِّزْقَ لِمَن يَشَآءُ مِنْ عِبَادِهِۦ وَيَقْدِرُ ۖ لَوْلَآ أَن مَّنَّ ٱللَّهُ عَلَيْنَا لَخَسَفَ بِنَا ۖ وَيْكَأَنَّهُۥ لَا يُفْلِحُ ٱلْكَٰفِرُونَ.

And those who wished to be in his position the day before, started saying, 'Oh, it seems that Allah extends provision to whom He wills and straightens [for whom He wills]. Had Allah not favoured us, He would have made us sink [too]. Oh, it seems that the infidels do not succeed.'[377]

This verse quotes the people who looked up to Qārūn, an extremely rich tyrant during the time of the Prophet Mūsā ﷺ. He walked upon the Earth with pride and flaunted his wealth through jewellery, adornments, and expensive clothing, while also claiming that his wealth was the result of his own intellect rather than a blessing from Allah ﷻ. When he was punished by Allah ﷻ for his transgressions by being swallowed up by the Earth, the people that had once wanted to be like him quickly changed their opinion of him. They finally understood that wealth is not an indication of Allah's love for someone.[378] Allah ﷻ grants wealth to persons that He loves and those He does not; however, it is *faith* that is given to those He loves alone.[379]

The Prophet ﷺ constantly linked a life of simplicity to a life of faith. He ﷺ said, 'Listen, listen! Wearing old clothes is a part of faith, wearing old clothes is a part of faith.'[380] On another occasion, the Prophet ﷺ said, 'The believer is simple and

[376] *Jāmiʿ al-Tirmidhī* 2324.
[377] *Qur'an* 28:12.
[378] *Tafsīr Ibn Kathīr* 28:12.
[379] *Al-Adab al-Mufrad* 275.
[380] *Sunan Abī Dāwūd* 4161.

generous, but the evil-doer is deceitful and ignoble.'[381]

A Muslim is simple in dress and manners; he rejects worldliness and materialism and adopts an open and honest demeanour. The Mother of the Believers ʿĀ'ishah ﷺ said, 'The Messenger of Allah ﷺ once prayed wearing a garment that had patterns. He ﷺ looked at its patterns and, upon invoking salutations (to complete the prayer), said, "Take this garment of mine to Abū Jahm, for it distracted me in my prayer. Bring a simple garment without patterns."'[382]

Such was the desire of the Prophet ﷺ for simplicity in all things. He did not even like to wear clothing that had patterns on it, lest it distract him from his worship. Likewise, Muslim men should avoid such articles of clothing. Unfortunately, the Muslims of today are taken by the same pomposity that affects everyone else. Our youth desire big brands, designer clothing, fancy haircuts, and the latest footwear. A man dressed in plain clothes is scoffed at; a brother following the Sunnah dress code is looked down upon. When did we fall so low, such that the things our beloved Prophet ﷺ preferred are now the things we shun, and the things he ﷺ abhorred are the things we love? Is this who we truly are? If so, it is not who we are supposed to be.

The Prophet ﷺ said, 'May the slave of dinars, dirhams, and fine cloaks perish! He is pleased if these things are given to him, and becomes upset if not. Let such a person perish and become wretched, and if he is pierced with even a thorn, let him find no one to remove it. Paradise is for him who holds the reins of his horse to strive in Allah's cause, with his hair unkempt and feet covered with dust. If he is appointed in the vanguard, he is

---

[381] *Sunan Abī Dāwūd* 4790.
[382] *Sunan Abī Dāwūd* 4052.

perfectly satisfied with his post, and if he is appointed in the rear guard, he accepts his orders with satisfaction; his worldly reputation is so lowly that his requests and words of intercession would not receive any positive response (from the rulers).'[383]

The difference between the people of Paradise and the people of the world are laid bare in the above Hadith. Those who worship money and find happiness only in the accumulation of wealth are enslaved by the temporal world and there is nothing for them in the Hereafter. Those who shun the materialistic world, strive in the path of Allah ﷻ, and do not complain about their lot in life are the people of Paradise. Though they may be looked down upon by their hollow-hearted peers, kingliness is not found in monetary wealth but in the capital of one's character. The Prophet ﷺ advised ʿAbdullāh ibn ʿUmar رضي الله عنه, 'Be in this world as if you were a stranger or a traveller.'[384]

In the words of JRR Tolkien:

All that is gold does not glitter,

Not all those who wander are lost;

The old that is strong does not wither,

Deep roots are not reached by the frost.[385]

ASCETICISM

Asceticism (*zuhd*) is man's ability to suffice with less, choosing self-discipline and the avoidance of self-indulgence over a life of worldly luxury. To be materialistic is to love the decorations and trappings of the temporal world to the extent that one only finds happiness in the delights of this material

---

[383] *Ṣaḥīḥ al-Bukhārī* 2887.
[384] *Ṣaḥīḥ al-Bukhārī* 6416.
[385] *All That is Gold does not Glitter,* JRR Tolkien.

plane. If these delights were to be taken away, such a person would be so upset that he could not survive.[386] This is not the way of a Muslim. A Muslim is happy with what he has; he makes do. A man bears the hardships placed upon him without any complaint. Allah ﷻ says in the Qur'an:

لَا يُكَلِّفُ ٱللَّهُ نَفْسًا إِلَّا وُسْعَهَا ۚ

Allah does not obligate anyone beyond his capacity.[387]

Allah ﷻ does not test us with anything that is beyond our ability to bear. A Muslim understands this, and is therefore content with what he has been given - from both the blessings and the trials - and perseveres without complaint. This separates the man from his former childish self. However, men also have weaknesses in their hearts that must be overcome. These include cravings for wealth, fame, and the base sensual pleasures. Allah ﷻ says:

وَإِنَّهُۥ لِحُبِّ ٱلْخَيْرِ لَشَدِيدٌ

...and in his love for wealth, he is very intense.[388]

The word *khayr* literally means any good thing, but idiomatically it refers to wealth.[389] Man's love for wealth is intense and makes him miserly.[390] He covets it and craves it. The Muslim recognises this base desire within himself, and he curbs it and controls it. Wealth is a means by which a man's needs can be met, and consequently the Shariah not only permits earning wealth, but makes it obligatory to the point where one can fulfil his needs.[391]

---

[386] *Ṣaḥīḥ al-Bukhārī* 2887.
[387] *Qur'an* 2:286.
[388] *Qur'an* 100:8.
[389] *Maʿārif al-Qur'an*, vol. 8: p. 860.
[390] *Tafsīr Ibn Kathīr* 100:8.
[391] *Maʿārif al-Qur'an*, vol. 8: p. 861.

Excessive love for wealth is what is being condemned in this verse, as is ungratefulness for what one has been given. A man who has poor vision should still be thankful that he has been granted a minimum degree of eyesight; a man with a small home should be grateful that he has shelter and warmth for his family. The earning of wealth is a necessity of life, just as answering the call of nature is, or taking medication when one is unwell. One does not begin to love such things, but instead simply does them out of necessity. A believer should treat wealth in the same way.[392]

آب اندر زیر کشتی پشتی است

آب در کشتی هلاک کشتی است

As long as water stays below, we float.

But once it seeps within, it sinks the boat.[393]

Wealth and the love of the material world cannot be allowed to enter and poison our hearts and distract us from our purpose in life. We were made to worship Allah ﷻ and act as responsible stewards of this world. We are caretaker slaves, not covetous kings. The Prophet ﷺ said, 'A little that suffices is better than an abundance that distracts.'[394] He ﷺ also said, 'Food for one suffices two, food for two suffices four, and food for four suffices eight.'[395]

The men of today seem intent on consuming everything that is put in front of them, and often speak with conceit when discussing how much they can consume. Just like the other 'deadly sins', gluttony is not only acceptable in today's day and age, but encouraged. As Muslims, we should not be eating to

---

[392] *Ma'ārif al-Qur'an*, vol. 8: p. 861.

[393] Shaykh Jalāl al-Dīn Muhammad Rūmī ؒ.

[394] *Ṣaḥīḥ Muslim* 2059a.

[395] *Ṣaḥīḥ Muslim* 2059d.

excess, but instead restrict ourselves to merely consuming the amount required for our daily needs. A Muslim not only suffices himself with what he has, but he shares it with others and is grateful for it. The Prophet ﷺ said, 'Glad tidings to whoever was guided to Islam, his livelihood was sufficient, and he was satisfied.'[396]

ʿUqbah ibn ʿĀmir رضي الله عنه once asked the Prophet ﷺ, 'O Messenger of Allah ﷺ, what is the means to salvation?' He ﷺ replied, 'That you control your tongue, suffice yourself with your house, and cry over your sins.'[397]

Wealth is not the goal in life, but a mere means to get through it. A man should appreciate this fact and act accordingly.

[396] *Jāmiʿ al-Tirmidhī* 2349.
[397] *Jāmiʿ al-Tirmidhī* 2406.

19
He is Dependable, not Dependent

عَنْ أَبِي هُرَيْرَةَ رَضِيَ اللَّهُ عَنْهُ، قَالَ: سَمِعْتُ رَسُولَ اللَّهِ صَلَّى اللَّهُ عَلَيْهِ وَسَلَّمَ يَقُولُ: "لأَنْ يَغْدُوَ أَحَدُكُمْ، فَيَحْتَطِبَ عَلَى ظَهْرِهِ، فَيَتَصَدَّقَ مِنْهُ، فَيَسْتَغْنِيَ بِهِ عَنِ النَّاسِ، خَيْرٌ لَهُ مِنْ أَنْ يَسْأَلَ رَجُلاً أَعْطَاهُ أَوْ مَنَعَهُ ذَلِكَ، فَإِنَّ الْيَدَ الْعُلْيَا أَفْضَلُ مِنَ الْيَدِ السُّفْلَى، وَابْدَأْ بِمَنْ تَعُولُ."

Abū Hurayrah ﷺ narrated that he heard the Messenger of Allah ﷺ saying, 'For one of you to go out early to gather firewood and carry it on his back, so that he can give charity from it and be free of being dependant on others, is better for him than having to ask a man who may give to him or refuse. Certainly, the upper (giving) hand is more virtuous than the lower (receiving) hand, and begin with your dependents.'[398]

GENEROSITY

A man relies on the One alone: Allah ﷻ. He is not reliant on other people to look after him, and he is not a dependent in his household. He provides for himself and his family. If someone has a need, he helps them to fulfil it. If *he* has a need, he asks for Allah's help and then goes out and realises it. A man is dependable, not dependent.

إِنَّ ٱلْمُصَّدِّقِينَ وَٱلْمُصَّدِّقَـٰتِ وَأَقْرَضُوا۟ ٱللَّهَ قَرْضًا حَسَنًا يُضَـٰعَفُ لَهُمْ وَلَهُمْ أَجْرٌ كَرِيمٌ.

Surely those men who give ṣadaqah (voluntary charity) and those women who give ṣadaqah and have advanced a good loan to Allah, for them it will be multiplied, and for them there is a noble reward.[399]

Those that give 'a good loan to Allah' are those people who

[398] *Jāmi' al-Tirmidhī* 680.
[399] *Qur'an* 57:18.

spend in His path or give alms to the poor, for He will reward any good deed in this life with a manifold recompense in the Hereafter.[400]

This quality of the dependable Muslim – which is none other than generosity – is what Allah ﷻ loves so much and wants to reward him for. For it is one of His own qualities, and to find it in one of His slaves is endearing to Him. The Prophet ﷺ said, 'They talk about "generosity", while in fact generosity is the heart of a believer.'[401] Being generous is who we are. It is no wonder that even today Muslims are demonstrably the most charitable group of people in the world. In Ramadan, when we find ourselves at our spiritual zenith, we become even more generous. Ibn ʿAbbās ؓ said, 'The Prophet ﷺ was the most generous of all people, and he would become more generous in Ramadan when Jibrīl ؑ met him. Jibrīl ؑ would meet him every night during Ramadan to revise the Qur'an with him. The Messenger of Allah ﷺ then used to be more generous than the fastest wind.'[402]

The Prophet ﷺ described the believer as a generous person; this is how intrinsic generosity is to the Muslim. He ﷺ said, 'The believer is simple and generous, but the evil-doer is deceitful and ignoble.'[403] A Muslim man gives freely and supports those less fortunate than him, or at the very least those that depend upon him. At the same time, he does not rely on anyone except Allah ﷻ. The Messenger of Allah ﷺ said, 'Whoever can promise me one thing, Paradise will be his.' One of the narrators of this Hadith, Yaḥyā ؒ, says, 'Here he made a statement which means,

[400] *Tafsīr Ibn Kathīr* 57:18.
[401] *Ṣaḥīḥ al-Bukhārī* 6183.
[402] *Ṣaḥīḥ al-Bukhārī* 3554.
[403] *Sunan Abī Dāwūd* 4790.

"That he will not ask the people for anything.'"[404]

A man must avoid depending on the material support of others unless there is no other way to survive. If he is eligible for charity, is in poverty, or unable to earn a living due to some disability or other issue, there is no harm in taking what charity he needs. But it would still be better for him to not become dependent on the good will of others.

In which ways is a Muslim dependable though? The Prophet ﷺ said, 'Your smiling at your brother is a form of charity; commanding good and forbidding evil is a form of charity; your giving directions to a man lost in the land is a form of charity; using your sight to help a man with poor vision is a form of charity; your removal of a rock, thorn, or a bone from the road is a form of charity; and your pouring what remains from your bucket into the bucket of your brother is a form of charity for you.'[405]

These acts of kindness and generosity make a man dependable, and bring him closer to Allah ﷻ. The Prophet ﷺ said, 'The generous one is near to Allah ﷻ, near to Paradise, near to the people, and far from the Hellfire. The miserly one is far from Allah ﷻ, far from Paradise, far from the people, and near to the Hellfire. An ignorant and generous person is more beloved to Allah Almighty than the stingy scholar.'[406]

The examples of the Muhājirūn ﵃[407] and Anṣār ﵃[408] perfectly encapsulate this virtue. When the Muhājirūn ﵃ first

---

[404] *Sunan al-Nasāʾī* 2590.

[405] *Jāmiʿ al-Tirmidhī* 1956.

[406] *Jāmiʿ al-Tirmidhī* 1961.

[407] The immigrant Companions ﵃ from Mecca.

[408] The Companions ﵃ who were the helpers of the immigrants and the original residents of Medina.

arrived in Medina following the *hijrah*[409], they disembarked with no material possessions. They were unable to bring anything with them save the clothes on their backs, and many a wealthy man arrived in the city of the Prophet ﷺ with no wealth or shelter. The Anṣār responded to this situation in a display of generosity that is still unmatched to this very day; they split everything that they possessed in half, and then conferred this divided part of their wealth to the Muhājir brothers they had been paired with.[410] One such example is that of ʿAbd al-Raḥmān ibn ʿAwf ؓ, who was paired with Saʿd ibn al-Rabīʿ ؓ. Saʿd ؓ was one of the richest members of the Anṣār ؓ, and he offered to split half of everything he had to give to ʿAbd al-Raḥmān ؓ. But the latter replied, 'I am not in need of that. Is there any marketplace where trade is practised?' He was directed to the market of Qaynuqāʿ, and he spent the following days trading in the market, beginning with the buying and selling of yoghurt and butter. After a few days, ʿAbd al-Raḥmān ؓ had earned enough wealth to marry a woman from the Anṣār.[411]

Those men knew their worth, and they understood that even if the easier path of dependence on others was offered, self-reliance and the ability to provide for oneself and one's family is worth every drop of blood and sweat spent, regardless of how much more difficult the latter course of action was.

ALTRUISM

Altruism is a fundamental component of what the Prophet ﷺ brought when he began to propagate Islam. It is the notion of

---

[409] The great migration of the Muslims from Mecca to Medina, and the event that started the *hijrī* calendar.

[410] The Prophet ﷺ paired each Anṣārī with a Muhājir in a pact of brotherhood, so one could support the other.

[411] *Ṣaḥīḥ al-Bukhārī* 2048.

putting the welfare of others before yourself, and a move away from the egocentrism that permeates most societies. In Islamic parlance, this is referred to as *īthār* (altruism). Putting the interests and welfare of others first improves the quality of life for every member of society, and it is important to understand that the modern concept of 'looking out for number one' and 'dog eat dog' mentality – all of which encapsulate the idea of individualistic thinking and selfishness – is detrimental to society. When the focus is on yourself alone, the natural by-product of such thinking is ignorance with regard to the plight of others. This is not utilitarianism[412], but the concept of a Muslim putting someone else's needs before his own, which should be reiterated by every individual. It is the individual doing what is best for other persons, with the overall goal of creating a society that looks out for every one of its members.

وَٱلَّذِينَ تَبَوَّءُو ٱلدَّارَ وَٱلْإِيمَـٰنَ مِن قَبْلِهِمْ يُحِبُّونَ مَنْ هَاجَرَ إِلَيْهِمْ وَلَا يَجِدُونَ فِى صُدُورِهِمْ حَاجَةً مِّمَّآ أُوتُوا۟ وَيُؤْثِرُونَ عَلَىٰٓ أَنفُسِهِمْ وَلَوْ كَانَ بِهِمْ خَصَاصَةٌ ۚ وَمَن يُوقَ شُحَّ نَفْسِهِۦ فَأُو۟لَـٰٓئِكَ هُمُ ٱلْمُفْلِحُونَ

And (fay')[413] *is also for those who established themselves in the homeland [of Medina] and in faith before the former ones (arrived in Medina), who have love for those who emigrated to them, and do not feel in their hearts any ambition for what is given to the former ones (from fay'), and give preference [to them] over themselves, even though they are in poverty. And those who are saved from the greed of their hearts are the successful.*[414]

Abū Hurayrah ﷺ reported that a man from the Anṣār was

[412] The ideology of putting the needs of the many over the needs of the few or the individual, or doing what is best for society as a whole, even if it is detrimental to a minority of society.
[413] Left over property.
[414] *Qur'an* 59:9.

hosting a guest and he had nothing with him, except a minimal amount to feed himself and his family. He said to his wife, 'Put the children to sleep, put out the lamp, and serve our guest with what we have.' Then Allah ﷻ revealed the verse, '*And give preference [to them] over themselves, even though they are in poverty.*'[415] Allah ﷻ loved this action so much that He revealed this verse at that time to honour the sacrifice made by Abū Ṭalḥah al-Anṣārī and his wife ﷺ.[416]

Abū Hurayrah ﷺ once asked the Messenger of Allah ﷺ, 'What kind of *ṣadaqah* is most excellent?' He ﷺ replied, 'That which is given by a man with little property; and begin with those for whom you are responsible.'[417] Even when a man finds himself in a state of dire need, he still puts the welfare of others first. This is the true meaning of altruism, and it is the form of *ṣadaqah* most loved by Allah ﷻ and His Messenger ﷺ.

ʿUmar ibn al-Khaṭṭāb ﷺ once passed by a group of people eating while their servants stood nearby. ʿUmar ﷺ asked, 'Why do I not see your servants eating with you? Do you not like them?' One of the men said, 'No, by Allah, O Leader of the Faithful. Rather, we have preference over them.' ʿUmar ﷺ was greatly angered by this and said, 'What is the matter with people who prefer themselves over their servants? Allah ﷻ will deal with them and it is done!' Then ʿUmar ﷺ said to the servants, 'Sit down and eat.' The servants sat to eat, whilst the Amīr al-Mu'minīn did not.[418]

Abū Hurayrah ﷺ reported that the Prophet ﷺ once

---

[415] *Ṣaḥīḥ al-Bukhārī* 3587; *Ṣaḥīḥ Muslim* 2054.
[416] *Tafsīr Ibn Kathīr* 59:9.
[417] *Sunan Abī Dāwūd* 1677.
[418] *Musnad al-Fārūq li Ibn Kathīr* 582.

informed him of the following event, 'A prostitute was once forgiven. She passed by a dog panting near a well; thirst had nearly killed him. She took off her sock, tied it to her veil, and drew up some water (from the well). Allah ﷻ forgave her for that.'[419]

Putting the less fortunate before ourselves is the truest form of *īthār*. Whether it is a slave or a servant, a child or a woman, a poor person or a guest, or even an animal, a Muslim gives preference to others before himself. When a prostitute did this out of her own natural compassion for a dog, she earned forgiveness. How is it then that we, being males, literate, intelligent, comparatively wealthy, and living lives of ease, struggle to do the same? How is it that obesity and related illnesses are commonplace now, whilst hundreds of millions whom we can help feed via modern technology starve? The Prophet ﷺ once saw a man with a large belly. The Prophet ﷺ pointed to his belly and said, 'If this had been placed elsewhere, it would have been better for you.'[420] He ﷺ referred to himself as 'the nearest to the believers out of all mankind', and then said, 'Thus, those among you who die in debt or leave behind destitute children should call me for help, for I am his guardian...'[421]

In another Hadith, the Mother of the Believers ʿĀ'ishah رضي الله عنها said, 'A poor woman came to me along with her daughters. I gave her three dates. She gave a date to each of them and afterwards, proceeded to take up one date and brought it to her mouth to eat it. But at this point, her daughters expressed their desire to eat it. She divided the date that she intended to eat between them. This kind treatment of her impressed me, and I mentioned it to

[419] *Ṣaḥīḥ al-Bukhārī* 3321; *Ṣaḥīḥ Muslim* 2245.
[420] *Al-Muʿjam al-Kabīr* 2140.
[421] *Ṣaḥīḥ Muslim* 1619.

the Messenger of Allah ﷺ. Subsequently, he ﷺ said, "Indeed Allah ﷻ has assured Paradise for her because of her [actions], and He has rescued her from the Hellfire."'[422]

The Mother of the Believers ؓ had only a few dates with which to open her own fast on this occasion but proceeded to give it to the woman, as she would never refuse someone that came asking for help. Such was the love of the mother for her children, for she chose to starve to give them each half a date more. Women tend to be naturally inclined towards caring for others, and this is a gift bestowed on them by Allah ﷻ. As men, however, we should be willing and ever-prepared to put others before ourselves, and epitomise altruistic behaviour. A day, a week, or even years of hardship cannot compare to the eternal ease of the Hereafter, and hence we must put aside the consumerist concept of instant gratification and focus instead on the welfare of others and the long-term benefits of the Hereafter.

All men are ready to invest their money

But most expect dividends.

I say to you: Make perfect your will.

I say: take no thought of the harvest,

But only of proper sowing.[423]

---

[422] *Ṣaḥīḥ Muslim* 2630.
[423] *Choruses from 'The Rock'*, T.S. Eliot.

20
He Has a Trade

عَنِ الْمِقْدَامِ رضيَ الله عنه، عَنْ رَسُولِ اللَّهِ صَلَّى اللَّهُ عَلَيْهِ وَسَلَّمَ، قَالَ: "مَا أَكَلَ أَحَدٌ طَعَامًا قَطُّ خَيْرًا مِنْ أَنْ يَأْكُلَ مِنْ عَمَلِ يَدِهِ، وَإِنَّ نَبِيَّ اللَّهِ دَاوُدَ عَلَيْهِ السَّلاَمُ كَانَ يَأْكُلُ مِنْ عَمَلِ يَدِهِ."

Al-Miqdām ﷺ narrated that the Prophet ﷺ said, 'Nobody has ever eaten a better meal than that which was earned by the labour of his own hands. Indeed, Allah's Prophet Dāwūd ﷺ would eat from the earnings of his own manual labour.'[424]

Earning a Halal Living and Providing for Dependents

A man provides for himself and his dependents, and does so by earning a living through legal means, for this was the Sunnah of the Prophet ﷺ and his Companions ﷺ. He does not lie, cheat, or swindle; he does not accrue material gains through theft or usury; and he does not threaten or rob others. A man earns a living through hard work and effort, and the best way that one can earn a living is through manual labour and working with one's own hands. The blacksmith, the carpenter, the trader, the farmer, and the shepherd are all titles of honest, hardworking men. It is very much a part of manliness and masculinity for a man to have a trade, craft, or skill of some sort. When asked what type of earning was best, the Prophet ﷺ said, 'A man's work with his hand and every business transaction which is approved.'[425]

When the first Caliph Abū Bakr al-Ṣiddīq ﷺ was chosen to

[424] *Ṣaḥīḥ al-Bukhārī* 2072.
[425] *Mishkāt al-Maṣābīḥ* 2783.

lead the Muslims, he originally attempted to continue trading in the marketplace to earn his living with his own hands, despite becoming the head of state for the entire Muslim nation. When this proved too difficult to accomplish, his daughter, the Mother of the Believers, ʿĀ'ishah ﷺ narrated that he said, 'My people know that my profession was not incapable of providing subsistence for my family. As I will be busy serving the Muslim nation, my family will eat from the national treasury of the Muslims, and I will practise the profession of serving the Muslims.'[426]

وَجَعَلْنَا ٱلنَّهَارَ مَعَاشًا.

...and We made the day a source of livelihood.[427]

Allah ﷻ created the night as a time of rest for us, and the day as a time for us to earn our livelihoods.[428] As men, it is our duty to earn a living for ourselves as well as those that depend upon us, and great care should be taken to ensure these duties are fulfilled correctly. The Prophet ﷺ said, 'A time will certainly come when people will no longer be concerned whether they earn their money by lawful means or unlawful means.'[429] He ﷺ also said, 'There will come a time when there will be no one left who does not consume usury, and whoever does not consume it will nevertheless be affected by it.'[430]

We are already living in the times we were warned about. People do not care if their income is permissible according to Islam's ethical framework. The amount they are earning has become far more important to them than how they are earning

---

426 *Ṣaḥīḥ al-Bukhārī* 2070.
427 *Qur'an* 78:11.
428 *Tafsīr Ibn Kathīr* 78:11.
429 *Ṣaḥīḥ al-Bukhārī* 2083.
430 *Sunan Ibn Mājah* 2278.

it. It is becoming extremely difficult to buy a house without paying interest in some way, or even place one's money in a bank account without being involved in the standard interest system. If one is not *taking* interest, one is *paying* it. The methods that the Prophet ﷺ taught us with regard to earning a living, however, protect us from such issues. A man should work towards becoming financially free of the constraints of modern society and its reliance on haram economics. Jābir ؓ said, 'The Messenger of Allah ﷺ cursed the acceptor of interest, its payer, the one who records it, and the two who witness the transaction, and he ﷺ said, "They are all equal."'[431] Thus, *any* involvement in haram transactions - whether that is involvement in usury or stacking alcohol on the shelves of a supermarket - becomes equally as sinful as the person directly committing the action. There are many kinds of illegal methods of earning, and a man should avoid these at all costs. Transactions involving non-existent 'services' such as stud fees for a stallion when horse-breeding[432] are prohibited, as well as haram services such as soothsaying.[433] Charging people for medical aid, such as cupping[434], and haram acts such as prostitution are also illegal.[435]

Amīr al-Mu'minīn 'Uthmān ibn 'Affān ؓ said, 'Do not oblige the slave-girl to earn money unless she has a skill. When you oblige her to do that, she will earn money by prostitution. Do not oblige the child to earn money. If he does not find it, he will steal. Have integrity since Allah ﷻ has integrity with you, and

---

[431] *Ṣaḥīḥ Muslim* 1598.
[432] *Sunan al-Nasā'ī* 4673.
[433] *Ṣaḥīḥ al-Bukhārī* 5346.
[434] *Sunan al-Nasā'ī* 4673.
[435] *Ṣaḥīḥ al-Bukhārī* 5346.

you must nourish them with wholesome food.'[436]

A man should not push his dependents into earning for him, for it is exclusively his duty to provide for them. Just as Allah ﷻ has provided for him, he should extend the same courtesy for those that he is materially entrusted with. The Prophet ﷺ said, 'The most virtuous of the dinars is the dinar spent by a man on his dependants.'[437] On another occasion, he ﷺ said, 'A man is the guardian of his family and he is responsible for them.'[438] He ﷺ also said, 'Seeking to earn a lawful livelihood is an obligatory duty...'[439]

That said, this duty is not exclusive to the patriarch of a household, but to all men belonging to the family unit. A man does not have to be 'the man of the house' to fulfil this responsibility; the prerequisite for this duty is simply being a man. ʿĀ'ishah ؓ narrated that the Prophet ﷺ said, 'Your children are the best of your earnings, so eat from what your children earn.'[440] Thus, a son's earnings are lawful for a father to use for the household. And as a man, the son should assist his father by partially assuming the responsibility of upholding the financial maintenance of the household.

The Companions ؓ would work to earn their own living, no matter how dire their straits would be. Qays ibn Muslim ؓ narrated that Abū Jaʿfar ؓ said:

> *There was not a family of the Muhājirīn who did not farm for a third or a quarter of the produce, and ʿAlī, Saʿd ibn*

---

[436] *Muwaṭṭa' Imam Mālik* 1808.
[437] *Jāmiʿ al-Tirmidhī* 1966.
[438] *Ṣaḥīḥ al-Bukhārī* 7138; *Ṣaḥīḥ Muslim* 1829.
[439] *Mishkāt al-Maṣābīḥ* 2781.
[440] *Sunan al-Nasā'ī* 4450.

Mālik, ʿAbdullāh ibn Masʿūd, ʿUmar ibn ʿAbd al-Azīz, al-Qāsim, ʿUrwah, the family of Abū Bakr, the family of ʿUmar, the family of ʿAlī, and Ibn Sīrīn made contracts for part of the produce in return for working the land. ʿAbd al-Raḥmān ibn al-Aswad said that he partnered with ʿAbd al-Raḥmān ibn Yazīd in the area of cultivation, and ʿUmar employed people on the condition that if he provided the seed, he should have half the crop, and if they provided the seed then they should [have likewise].[441]

Rather than relying on the welfare provisions of others, a man should earn his living through his own means if he can. If this means doing manual labour, then he should do what he has to to earn an independent living. The directive of ʿUmar ﷺ sharing in the resulting crop - regardless if one works the field or provides the seed - exemplifies the saying of the Prophet ﷺ, 'With risk comes reward.'[442]

[441] *Mishkāt al-Maṣābīḥ* 2980.

[442] *Sunan Abī Dāwūd* 3509.

3 | THE INTERPERSONAL MAN

21
He Leads his Household

عَنْ عَبْدِ اللَّهِ بْنِ عُمَرَ رَضِيَ اللَّهُ عَنْهُمَا، أَنَّ رَسُولَ اللَّهِ صَلَّى اللَّهُ عَلَيْهِ وَسَلَّمَ قَالَ: "أَلَا كُلُّكُمْ رَاعٍ وَكُلُّكُمْ مَسْئُولٌ عَنْ رَعِيَّتِهِ، فَالْإِمَامُ الَّذِي عَلَى النَّاسِ رَاعٍ، وَهُوَ مَسْئُولٌ عَنْ رَعِيَّتِهِ، وَالرَّجُلُ رَاعٍ عَلَى أَهْلِ بَيْتِهِ، وَهُوَ مَسْئُولٌ عَنْ رَعِيَّتِهِ، وَالْمَرْأَةُ رَاعِيَةٌ عَلَى أَهْلِ بَيْتِ زَوْجِهَا وَوَلَدِهِ، وَهِيَ مَسْئُولَةٌ عَنْهُمْ، وَعَبْدُ الرَّجُلِ رَاعٍ عَلَى مَالِ سَيِّدِهِ، وَهُوَ مَسْئُولٌ عَنْهُ. أَلَا فَكُلُّكُمْ رَاعٍ وَكُلُّكُمْ مَسْئُولٌ عَنْ رَعِيَّتِهِ."

ʿAbdullāh ibn ʿUmar ﵄ reported that the Messenger of Allah ﷺ said, 'Every one of you is a shepherd and is responsible for his flock. The leader of the people is a guardian and is responsible for his subjects. A man is the guardian of his family and is responsible for them. A woman is the guardian of her husband's home and children, and she is responsible for them. The servant of a man is a guardian of his property and is responsible for it. Undoubtedly, every one of you is a shepherd and every one of you is responsible for his flock.'[443]

[443] *Ṣaḥīḥ al-Bukhārī* 7138; *Ṣaḥīḥ Muslim* 1829.

THE GUARDIAN OF HIS FAMILY

Guardianship involves the protection, supervision, leadership, and responsibility of someone or something. In this narration, the Prophet ﷺ used the term *rāʿ*, which can mean both 'guardian' and 'shepherd'. The usage of this term points to the patriarchal nature of man's responsibility towards his family. A man is the guardian of his family, which means he must watch over every single household member, steer them from pitfalls, and divert others that would seek to do them harm, and if required, defend them. A man's family includes everyone he is responsible for in his household.[444] Thus, if he is wealthy enough to have servants or workers, he is their guardian as well. It is evident from this Hadith that the idea of 'gender roles' is supported by the Islamic way of life. Every person is given his or her own role in the family; everybody is a guardian of someone or something, and thus has a responsibility for those they watch over.

The Prophet ﷺ said, 'Whoever is killed while protecting his wealth is a martyr. Whoever is killed while protecting his family is a martyr. Whoever is killed while protecting his religion is a martyr. Whoever is killed protecting himself is a martyr.'[445]

The protection of one's household is the duty and responsibility of every man. He must be prepared to do so at all times, even if it means the ultimate sacrifice. The Prophet ﷺ has guaranteed the martyrdom of such a person, and what greater incentive can there be than that? As a guardian, it is your duty to protect your household and keep its members safe. A man should be prepared to do whatever is necessary to ensure the

[444] *Maʿārif al-Qur'an,* vol. 8: p. 523.
[445] *Sunan al-Nasāʾī* 4095.

safety and security of his home. When the sanctity of the home is broken and it no longer feels like a safe haven for those that live within its walls, every day becomes an ordeal.

As a side point, it is important to note here the employee's responsibility towards the property of his employer. He is a guardian of this property while it is in his possession and he must defend it as his own. This is because the Messenger of Allah ﷺ said, 'The hand that takes is responsible for what it has taken until it returns it.'[446]

يَـٰٓأَيُّهَا ٱلَّذِينَ ءَامَنُوا۟ قُوٓا۟ أَنفُسَكُمْ وَأَهْلِيكُمْ نَارًا وَقُودُهَا ٱلنَّاسُ وَٱلْحِجَارَةُ عَلَيْهَا مَلَـٰٓئِكَةٌ غِلَاظٌ شِدَادٌ لَّا يَعْصُونَ ٱللَّهَ مَآ أَمَرَهُمْ وَيَفْعَلُونَ مَا يُؤْمَرُونَ.

O you who believe, save yourselves and your families from a Fire, the fuel of which is human beings and stones, appointed on which are Angels, stern and severe, who do not disobey Allah in what He orders them, and do whatever they are ordered to do.[447]

Ibn ʿAbbās ﵄ commented on the passage '*Save yourselves and your families from a Fire*' by stating, 'Work in the obedience of Allah ﷻ, avoid disobedience of Allah ﷻ, and order your families to remember Allah ﷻ. Then Allah ﷻ will save you from the Fire.' Mujāhid ﵀ said it means to 'have *taqwā* of Allah ﷻ and order your family to have *taqwā* of Him.' In his discussion of this verse, Qatādah ﵀ said that a man 'commands obedience to Allah ﷻ, to not disobey Him, and he orders his family to obey His orders and helps them to act upon His directives. When one sees disobedience, he stops them and forbids them from doing it.' Al-Ḍaḥḥāk and Muqātil ﵀ state that it is an obligation for the Muslim to teach his close family members and those he is

[446] *Sunan Ibn Mājah* 2400.
[447] *Qur'an* 66:6.

responsible for about what Allah ﷻ has made obligatory for them and what He has forbidden.[448]

When this verse was revealed, Amīr al-Mu'minīn ʿUmar ؓ inquired, 'O Messenger of Allah, we understand how to save ourselves from Hell, that is, we guard ourselves against sins and carry out the divine injunctions. But how do we safeguard our families from Hell?' The Messenger of Allah ﷺ replied, 'Instruct them to refrain from deeds that Allah ﷻ has prohibited, and ask them to carry out deeds that Allah ﷻ has enjoined. This will rescue them from the Hellfire.'[449]

It is the responsibility of a man to educate his family regarding their religious obligations, provide sufficient elucidation of the halal and haram realms, and to train them diligently to act upon them.[450] To do otherwise is the ultimate failure of one's responsibilities as a husband, father, brother, or son to protect one's loved ones from the Fires of Hell. Too often men fear 'upsetting' family members by enjoining them to fulfil their responsibilities as the slaves of Allah ﷻ. This is not compassion, but weakness, and to cause long-term harm to one's flock for the sake of avoiding minor personal discomfort is the height of selfishness.

The man of the house has the responsibility of financially supporting them, for this is part of his guardianship. In this regard, he ensures that they are fed, clothed, and housed within the means he has at his disposal. Ibn ʿUmar ؓ said, 'Nothing that a man spends on himself and his family – while anticipating a reward from Allah ﷻ – will fail to be rewarded by Allah ﷻ. He

---

[448] *Tafsīr Ibn Kathīr* 66:6.

[449] *Maʿārif al-Qur'an*, vol. 8: p. 523.

[450] *Maʿārif al-Qur'an*, vol. 8: p. 523.

should begin with those whose support is his responsibility. If there is something left over, he should spend it on his nearest relative and then the closest one that follows. If there is still something left over, he can give it away.'[451] The Prophet ﷺ said, 'The best of charity is that which is given when you are self-sufficient, and start with those for whom you are responsible.'[452]

Being wealthy is contemporarily considered to be one of the qualities of a so-called 'High-Value Man'. Yet, in Islam no such constraint on masculinity exists. The Prophet ﷺ said, 'The family of Muhammad hardly has a *mudd*[453] of food.'[454] And Ibn ʿAbbās said, 'A man would give his family food that was abundant and another would give his family food that was barely sufficient. As a result, the verse "*at an average of what you feed your family with*"[455] was revealed.'[456]

A man must provide for his family, but this requirement is in accordance with his means. Therefore, there is no responsibility on a man to ensure he is considered wealthy in order to fulfil the criteria of being a patriarch and providing for his family. The Prophet ﷺ constantly lived in a state where he did not have wealth sufficient to 'eat wheat bread with meat or soup to their satisfaction for three successive days'.[457]

GOOD TREATMENT OF FAMILY

Besides assuming the responsibility of looking after his dependents as their guardian, and ensuring that they follow the rules and laws of Islam, a man is also required to treat his family

---

[451] *Al-Adab al-Mufrad* 62.
[452] *Sunan al-Nasāʾī* 2544.
[453] An amount of weight equal to around half a kilogram.
[454] *Sunan Ibn Mājah* 4148.
[455] *Qur'an* 5:89.
[456] *Sunan Ibn Mājah* 2113.
[457] *Ṣaḥīḥ al-Bukhārī* 5438.

members well. A man should not be a tyrant in his home, but rather he should be the loving patriarch of his family. His good treatment of them, and his displaying of love for them, should be sufficient in helping to guide them on the path of righteousness. The Prophet ﷺ said, 'The best of you is the best to his family, and I am the best of you to my family.'[458]

Bahz ibn Ḥakīm relates from his father that his grandfather ﷺ asked the Prophet ﷺ, 'O Messenger of Allah, to whom should I show dutiful kindness?' He ﷺ replied, 'Your mother, then your mother, then your mother, then your father, and then your relatives in order of relationship.'[459] Kulayb ibn Manfaʿah reported that his grandfather ﷺ asked a similar question: 'O Messenger of Allah, towards whom should I be dutiful?' He ﷺ replied, 'Your mother, your father, your sister, and your brother...'[460]

The mother has a unique place in Islam, and consequently was mentioned three times before anyone else in many traditions. Dutiful kindness (*birr*) is a form of loving respect, and we have been told by the Prophet ﷺ to show it to our close family members, including our children and grandchildren, as well as our nephews and nieces.

ʿUmar ibn Abī Salamah ﷺ, the step-son of the Prophet ﷺ, narrated: 'When these verses "*Allah only intends to keep [all sorts of] filth away from you, O members of the family [of the Prophet], and to make you pure through a perfect purification*"[461] were revealed to the Prophet ﷺ in the home of the Mother of

[458] *Jāmiʿ al-Tirmidhī* 3895.
[459] *Sunan Abī Dāwūd* 5139.
[460] *Al-Adab al-Mufrad* 47.
[461] *Qur'an* 33:33.

the Believers Umm Salamah 🌸, he called for Fāṭimah 🌸, al-Ḥasan, and al-Ḥusayn 🌸, and then wrapped them in a cloak. ʿAlī 🌸 was behind him, so he wrapped him in the cloak too, and said, "O Allah! These are the people of my house, so remove all impurity from them, and purify them with a thorough purification." So the Mother of the Believers, Umm Salamah 🌸 said, "And am I with them, O Messenger of Allah?" He 🌸 said, "You are in your place, and you are more virtuous to me."[462]

This was often the way of our beloved Prophet 🌸. He showed love and kindness to his family at all times, embracing them and praying for them often. He 🌸 would not allow any one of them to feel unloved, and ensured that each of them knew how dear they were to him 🌸. This is the type of manhood that should be sought within the Muslim ethos: a complete, holistic manhood, not one stunted by cultural influences or modern sensibilities. The Prophet 🌸 said, 'If a man spends on his family sincerely for Allah's sake, then it will be considered an episode of alms-giving in terms of reward.'[463]

Thawbān 🌸 narrated that the Messenger of Allah 🌸 said, 'The most virtuous dinar is the dinar spent by a man on his dependants, which is followed by the dinar spent on his beast in the cause of Allah 🌸, and then the dinar spent on his companions in the cause of Allah 🌸.' Abū Qilābah 🌸 states that the Prophet 🌸 began with the dependents, while also observing: 'And which man is greater in reward than a man who spends upon his dependents, having little ones by which Allah 🌸 causes him to abstain (from the unlawful) and by which Allah 🌸

---

[462] *Jāmiʿ al-Tirmidhī* 3787.
[463] *Ṣaḥīḥ al-Bukhārī* 55.

enriches him?'[464]

HONOURING TIES OF KINSHIP

In essence, maintaining and honouring kinship ties (*ṣilat al-raḥim)* is an act of great reward in Islam, and the man that strives to preserve these bonds is worthy of boundless virtues. The Prophet ﷺ said, 'The most quickly rewarded of good deeds are kindness and upholding the ties of kinship, and the most quickly punished evil deeds are injustice and severing the ties of kinship.'[465]

وَهُوَ ٱلَّذِى خَلَقَ مِنَ ٱلْمَآءِ بَشَرًا فَجَعَلَهُۥ نَسَبًا وَصِهْرًا ۗ وَكَانَ رَبُّكَ قَدِيرًا.

And He is the One Who created man from water, then made of him relations created by lineage and relations created by marriage. Your Lord is All-Powerful.[466]

Nasab relates to the kinship formed through lineage or one's ancestry and bloodline, whereas *ṣihr* relates to relationships formed through legal means or one's in-laws. These are blessings from Allah ﷻ and should be treated as such, and the maintenance of such bonds leads to a tranquil and pleasant life.[467] Too often these ties are disrespected or seen as an inconvenience, and the result is always a chaotic, unpleasant life.

Therefore, it is of benefit for a man to learn about his relatives and build ties with them. We live in a culture where the modern man has no ties but to those he works with or those he spends recreational time with, and our connection to those with whom we share a common line of descent and blood ties has been all but severed. It is important for each of us to learn who

---

[464] *Jāmiʿ al-Tirmidhī* 1966.
[465] *Sunan Ibn Mājah* 4212.
[466] *Qur'an* 25:54.
[467] *Maʿārif al-Qur'an,* vol. 6: p. 497.

we are, what our origins are, and rebuild these bonds. The Prophet ﷺ advised us, 'Learn enough about your lineage to facilitate the observance of your ties of kinship. For keeping the ties of kinship encourages affection among relatives, increases wealth, and increases lifespan.'[468]

Furthermore, the maintenance of these kinship ties is not enough to fulfil this duty; one must find the ties that were severed and reconnect them, or failing this to treat well those relatives who have broken their ties with you. The Prophet ﷺ said, 'Merely maintaining the ties of kinship is inadequate. For connecting the ties of kinship is when his relations to the womb are severed and he connects them.'[469]

He ﷺ also said, 'The one who honours his ties of kinship is not the one who recompenses the good done to him by his relatives, but the one who keeps good relations with those relatives who had severed the bond of kinship with him.'[470]

---

[468] *Jāmiʿ al-Tirmidhī* 1979.
[469] *Jāmiʿ al-Tirmidhī* 1908.
[470] *Ṣaḥīḥ al-Bukhārī* 5991.

22
He Has *Ghayrah*

عَنْ أُمِّ الْمُؤْمِنِينَ عَائِشَةَ رضي الله عنها، أَنَّ رَسُولَ اللَّهِ صَلَّى اللَّهُ عَلَيْهِ وَسَلَّمَ قَالَ: "يَا أُمَّةَ مُحَمَّدٍ، مَا أَحَدٌ أَغْيَرَ مِنَ اللَّهِ أَنْ يَرَى عَبْدَهُ أَوْ أَمَتَهُ تَزْنِي، يَا أُمَّةَ مُحَمَّدٍ، لَوْ تَعْلَمُونَ مَا أَعْلَمُ لَضَحِكْتُمْ قَلِيلاً وَلَبَكَيْتُمْ كَثِيرًا."

The Mother of the Believers ʿĀʾishah ﵂ narrated that Allah's Messenger ﷺ said, 'O followers of Muhammad! There is no one who has more ghayrah than Allah, so He has forbidden that His slave or slave girl ever fornicate. O followers of Muhammad! If you only knew what I know, you would laugh little and weep much.'[471]

Ghayrah

Ghayrah is a word that does not have a direct translation in the English language, which is telling in itself. Oftentimes, it is defined as a type of 'protective jealousy', or a sense of affronted honour and respect in relation to someone partaking in a right which is explicitly yours. Whilst this is true to an extent, the concept of *ghayrah* is much more than this. It is an earnest concern in relation to something dear to you, a sense of honour and self-respect, and a feeling of vigilant protectiveness. It is that sentiment in the heart which propels one to protect their loved ones from indecency and sin. The man of *ghayrah* has such high morals and modesty that the idea of these virtues being challenged by the behaviour of someone related to them is intolerable. *Ghayrah* is an inability to bear immodesty, and the need to set things right if they are ever put in doubt.

Ghayrah can be in relation to oneself, one's loved ones, or one's property, but it also can be in relation to Allah ﷻ, our

[471] *Ṣaḥīḥ al-Bukhārī* 5221.

Prophet ﷺ, Islam, and the rulings of the last religion. In the Western world, there appears to be no equivalent to this concept, and thus it appears alien to those steeped in liberal cultures and ideologies. In the East, however, it is a simple concept and has many equivalents, such as the renowned traditional honour and shame systems of China and Japan, where 'losing face' means more than merely a loss of station or damaged pride. In the case of the Samurai, the latter upshot could ultimately result in *seppuku*[472] as a means of retaining nobility after bringing shame on one's self or one's household.

ٱلرِّجَالُ قَوَّٰمُونَ عَلَى ٱلنِّسَآءِ بِمَا فَضَّلَ ٱللَّهُ بَعْضَهُمْ عَلَىٰ بَعْضٍ وَبِمَآ أَنفَقُوا۟ مِنْ أَمْوَٰلِهِمْ

Men are caretakers of women, since Allah has made some of them excel the others, and because of the wealth they have spent.[473]

A classic form of *ghayrah* is that which is experienced in relation to one's spouse. The idea of someone tarnishing their modesty in any way is not tolerable for a man of self-worth, and if someone truly loves his spouse, he would not allow her to be placed in a position or situation where such a thing could ever be brought into doubt. Saʿd ibn ʿUbādah ؓ once said, 'If I found a man with my wife, I would kill him with the sharp edge of my blade.' When the Prophet ﷺ heard this, he said, 'Do you marvel at Saʿd's sense of *ghayrah*? Indeed, I have more *ghayrah* than Saʿd, and Allah has more *ghayrah* than I.'[474]

In Homer's *Odyssey*, what is it that drives Odysseus and his son to slay the Suitors of Penelope if not their strong sense of *ghayrah*? They eat his food, drink his wine, abuse their guest rights, mistreat his servants, plot to kill his son, and seek to wed

[472] Ritual suicide by disembowelment.
[473] *Qur'an* 4:34.
[474] *Ṣaḥīḥ al-Bukhārī* 6846.

his wife – all while he still lives! As the King of Ithaca, what kind of man would he be if he allowed this to go on?

Asmā' bint Abī Bakr ❁ narrated an incident which shows the *ghayrah* and modesty of the women of the first blessed generation:

> *When al-Zubayr married me, he had no real property, slave, or anything else except a camel – which drew water from the well – and his horse. I used to feed his horse with fodder, draw water and sew the bucket for drawing it, and prepare the dough, though I did not know how to bake bread. So our Anṣārī neighbours used to bake bread for me, and they were honourable ladies. I used to carry the date stones on my head from al-Zubayr's land, which was given to him by the Messenger of Allah ﷺ; this land was two thirds of a farsakh[475] from my house. One day, while I was returning and carrying date stones on my head, I met the Messenger of Allah ﷺ along with some Anṣārī people. He ﷺ called me and then (directing his camel to kneel) said, 'Ikh! Ikh!' so as to offer me to ride behind him (on the camel). I felt shy to travel with men and remembered al-Zubayr and his ghayrah, as he was from amongst those with the greatest sense of it. The Messenger of Allah ﷺ noticed that I felt shy, and so he proceeded. I came to al-Zubayr and said, 'I met the Messenger of Allah ﷺ while I was carrying date stones on my head, and he had some Companions with him. He ﷺ made his camel kneel down so that I might ride (instead of walk), but I felt shy in his presence and remembered your ghayrah. Upon hearing that, al-Zubayr*

---

[475] A *farsakh* is equal to roughly 3 miles.

🌸 said, 'By Allah, your carrying the date stones is more shameful to me than your riding with him 🌸.' [I continued in this way] until Abū Bakr sent me a servant to look after the horse. I felt as if he had set me free.[476]

The women had such *ghayrah* and modesty that travelling with the Prophet 🌸 himself was not possible for them. We can see from this that al-Zubayr 🌸 felt shame at his wife having to work so hard to make ends meet, which also affected his *ghayrah*.

There are also examples of *ghayrah* in relation to one's property, such as when the Prophet 🌸 said, 'Whilst sleeping, I saw myself in Paradise and witnessed a woman performing ablution beside a palace. I asked, "For whom is this palace?" She replied, "It is for ʿUmar." Then I remembered ʿUmar's *ghayrah* and left quickly.' ʿUmar 🌸 wept [upon hearing this] and said, 'O Messenger of Allah! How dare I think of my *ghayrah* being offended by you?'[477]

From the above we can see that a man should also be aware of the *ghayrah* of others, be mindful of it, and ensure it is given due respect. After all, there are always consequences for offending another person's *ghayrah*. Our noble Prophet 🌸 exemplified the best of behaviour in this regard; he was an example for how a man should act, and thus through his actions we can learn how the *ghayrah* of others should be respected.

One notes from the above Hadiths that the *ghayrah* of the Companions would never be affronted by the pure personage of the Prophet 🌸; on the contrary, the mere *idea* that it *ever could* have an effect on their sense of *ghayrah* is used as a way to show

---

[476] *Ṣaḥīḥ al-Bukhārī* 5224.
[477] *Ṣaḥīḥ al-Bukhārī* 3680.

how much *ghayrah* they had.

From the first Hadith of this section, we deduce that Allah ﷻ Himself has the greatest level of *ghayrah.* The Messenger of Allah ﷺ said, 'Allah ﷻ has *ghayrah,* and the believer has *ghayrah.* The *ghayrah* of Allah ﷻ is affected when a believer does what He has forbidden him to do.'[478] We are the property of Allah ﷻ due to our status as His creation, and we are loved by Him for the same reason. Consequently, it stands to reason that His infinite *ghayrah,* which is of the highest calibre, would be affronted by our disobedience to His commands.

The Prophet ﷺ also explained to us that *ghayrah* being triggered without grounds for suspicion is disliked by Allah ﷻ. For he ﷺ says: 'There is a kind of *ghayrah* that Allah ﷻ loves and a kind that Allah ﷻ hates. As for that which Allah ﷻ loves, it is the *ghayrah* when there are grounds for suspicion. As for that which He hates, it is the *ghayrah* when there are no grounds for suspicion.'[479] Therefore, a man must always keep his emotions in check, lest he forget himself and react in a way which would have unnecessarily ill effects on everyone involved.

The wretched man without *ghayrah* is referred to as a *dayyūth,* which in the English language would likely correspond to the term 'cuckold'[480]. But once more the lesser language does not fully cover the malignant nature of such a man. The *dayyūth* does not care if his wife is loyal or adulterous, whether his children are on the correct path or have fallen to deviancy, or even whether the name and honour of the Prophet ﷺ are being

---

[478] *Ṣaḥīḥ Muslim* 2761a.

[479] *Sunan Ibn Mājah* 1996.

[480] A man who is indifferent as to whether his spouse commits adultery with someone else.

disrespected for the purpose of so-called 'freedom of speech'. He is devoid of morals, lacking in modesty, and signifies the nadir of honour and respect. The Messenger of Allah ﷺ said, 'There are three parties who Allah ﷻ will not look at on the Day of Resurrection: The one who disobeys his parents, the woman who imitates men in her outward appearance, and the *dayyūth*. There are three who will not enter Paradise: The one who disobeys his parents, the drunkard, and the one who reminds people of what he has given them.'[481]

Thus, fear Allah ﷻ with regard to your *ghayrah*. Preserve it when it needs to be defended, but do not act rashly.

[481] *Sunan al-Nasā'ī* 2562.

23
He Treats Women Well

عَنْ أُمِّ الْمُؤْمِنِينَ عَائِشَةَ رَضِيَ اللَّهُ عَنْهَا، قَالَتْ: قَالَ رَسُولُ اللَّهِ صَلَّى اللَّهُ عَلَيْهِ وَسَلَّمَ:
"النِّكَاحُ مِنْ سُنَّتِي، فَمَنْ لَمْ يَعْمَلْ بِسُنَّتِي فَلَيْسَ مِنِّي، وَتَزَوَّجُوا فَإِنِّي مُكَاثِرٌ بِكُمُ الأُمَمَ، وَمَنْ
كَانَ ذَا طَوْلٍ فَلْيَنْكِحْ، وَمَنْ لَمْ يَجِدْ فَعَلَيْهِ بِالصِّيَامِ، فَإِنَّ الصَّوْمَ لَهُ وِجَاءٌ."

The Mother of the Believers ʿĀʾishah ﷺ narrates that the Messenger of Allah ﷺ said, 'Marriage is from my Sunnah, and whoever does not follow my Sunnah has nothing to do with me. Get married, for I will boast of your great numbers before the nations. Whoever has the means, then let him marry; whoever does not, then he should fast for it will diminish his desire.'[482]

MARRIAGE

A marriage (*nikāḥ*) is a legal contract between a man and a woman, where both parties agree to fulfil each other's spousal rights. The Prophet ﷺ said, 'Publicise this marriage rite, hold it in the *masjids*, and beat the drum (or sieve) for it.'[483] Thus, a wedding should be a public event to ensure that members of the wider community are aware that both parties are not fraternising with one another outside of the bonds of marriage.

Those that refuse to get married are in essence repudiating the Sunnah of the Prophet ﷺ, and thus have nothing to do with him ﷺ. The Messenger of Allah ﷺ said, 'Four things are from the Sunnahs of the Messengers: modesty, using perfume, the *siwāk*, and marriage.'[484] He ﷺ also stated, 'When a man marries he has fulfilled half of the religion; so let him fear Allah ﷻ

[482] *Sunan Ibn Mājah* 1846.
[483] *Jāmiʿ al-Tirmidhī* 1089; *Sunan Ibn Mājah* 1970.
[484] *Jāmiʿ al-Tirmidhī* 1080.

regarding the remaining half.'[485] Such is the status of marriage. It is from the Sunnahs of the Messengers and completes one half of a person's faith; it protects one from falling into lust and sin; it continues one's bloodline, which is a duty one's ancestors performed for him, and thus a responsibility on a man to do the same for the next generation; and it increases the *ummah* of the Prophet ﷺ. He ﷺ advised that we should 'marry women who are loving and very prolific [in childbearing], for I shall outnumber the peoples [of the other nations] by you'.[486] Further to this, he ﷺ also said: 'A man will be raised in status in Paradise and will say, "Where did this come from?" And it will be said (to him), "From your son's praying for forgiveness for you."'[487] Each child born and raised well will be a means of forgiveness for his parents. However, having children outside of wedlock is a great disservice to them and the woman who birthed them.

Any sexual relationship that falls outside of the definition of a *nikāḥ* is illegal, immoral, and dishonourable. In recent years, a new culture has developed which encourages young men to engage in illegal sexual relationships, dishonouring themselves and the other party. Historically, across all cultures, including the Western world until the late 20th century, someone that engaged in immoral behaviour became an outcast. It was universally considered a crime against morality, as well as a crime against the unborn child, as his or her parentage came into dispute. Ever since social and familial norms have broken down in the West, the entire region has been stricken with rampant immorality.

The modern man is now in a position where it is no longer considered socially or morally reprehensible to have multiple sexual partners outside of wedlock, and in some movements and

---

[485] *Mishkāt al-Maṣābīḥ* 3096.
[486] *Sunan Abī Dāwūd* 2050.
[487] *Sunan Ibn Mājah* 3660; *Musnad al-Imam Aḥmad* 10618.

ideologies (such as the 'Red Pill' ideology) it is considered the ideal toward which one should strive. Somehow, at a certain point in Western society, the idea of having multiple sexual partners became problematic only when the female parties were given the legal rights of a spouse. Polygamy is considered iniquitous, but being a 'stud'[488] is considered to be commendable. The break away from the historically universally accepted idea of polygamy to strict monogamy has the direct impact of the aforementioned adulterous society,[489] as a legal outlet for this aspect of human nature is no longer provided.

Men differ from women in many aspects. One facet is that men naturally have the desire in them to seek more than one sexual partner, and can build new loving relationships without diminishing those that they already have. Islam recognises this as part of the *fiṭrah* and thus allows a polygamous lifestyle within certain limits, such as the number of spouses one can have. These unions are regulated with a number of legal prescriptions, for the husband is required to provide for each of them in accordance with the Shariah, as well as providing an income, separate living quarters, and so on. Additionally, Islamic polygamy does not allow for immoral sexual acts to take place behind closed doors, such as those carried out in view of another spouse.

فَٱنكِحُوا۟ مَا طَابَ لَكُم مِّنَ ٱلنِّسَآءِ مَثْنَىٰ وَثُلَـٰثَ وَرُبَـٰعَ ۖ فَإِنْ خِفْتُمْ أَلَّا تَعْدِلُوا۟ فَوَٰحِدَةً.

...marry the women that please you, in twos, in threes and in fours. However, if you fear that you will not maintain equity, then [keep to] one woman...[490]

Ibn Jubayr, Ibn Mālik, and Ḥasan al-Baṣrī ﷺ clarify that

[488] Interestingly, this term was previously reserved for male animals used for breeding.
[489] *Ma'ārif al-Qur'an*, vol. 2: p. 301.
[490] *Qur'an* 4:3.

'*marry the women that please you*' means from amongst those who it is legal to marry.[491]

There are some important stipulations placed here, however. Firstly, the maximum number of women a man can marry is four. When Ghaylān ibn Salamah ﵁ accepted Islam, he had ten wives and was ordered by the Prophet ﷺ to 'choose four of them'.[492] Similarly, al-Ḥārithah ibn Qays ﵁ had eight wives, and was again told to keep only four.[493] The only exception to this rule was that of the Prophet ﷺ himself, due to the necessity of providing teachings with regard to his private life inside the marital home. Whereas all other aspects of his life could easily be documented, there was a need to record his life behind closed doors.[494] The majority of the Hadith texts mentioned in this section were only transmitted to us as a result of this concession. For example, we only know the Hadith relating to the raising of one's step-children through reports related from such private channels. In this regard, one may cite the report of ʿUmar ibn Abī Salamah ﵁, who stated, 'I was a boy under the care of the Messenger of Allah ﷺ and my hand used to go around the dish while I was eating. So the Messenger of Allah ﷺ said to me, "Dear son, mention the name of Allah ﷻ, eat with your right hand, and eat what is nearer to you from the dish." Since then I have applied those instructions when eating.'

Secondly, if equity cannot be maintained, then polygamy becomes impermissible.[495] It is incumbent upon us to consider the legal requirements around maintaining this equality, and

---

[491] *Qur'an* 4:3.
[492] *Sunan Ibn Mājah* 1953.
[493] *Sunan Abī Dāwūd* 2241.
[494] *Maʿārif al-Qur'an*, vol. 2: pp. 303-304.
[495] *Maʿārif al-Qur'an*, vol. 2: pp. 310-311.

one's own ability to manage the financial constraints, related stress, and family politics of such an arrangement before committing to polygamy. The Messenger of Allah ﷺ said, 'When a man has two wives and he is not just between them, he will come on the Day of Judgement with one side drooping.'[496] This will be a sign of dishonour upon him during that Day.

It is also important to note that between the ages of 25 and 50 the Prophet ﷺ remained in a monogamous marriage with the Mother of the Believers Khadījah ﵂, a woman his elder by 15 years.[497] Monogamy is therefore considered to be the default and better position for anyone that does not have the means or ability to treat multiple spouses equitably.

With the above provisions established, it is imperative to recognise that one should not worry too deeply about the financial constraints of espousing someone if they have the ability to get married. Indeed, it is unanimously agreed that it is obligatory upon a man to get married if he has the means, for the man that does not do so in such a situation will find it extremely difficult not to fall into sin.[498] The Prophet ﷺ advised young men by saying, 'O young people! Whoever among you is able to marry should do so, for it is most effective in lowering his gaze and guarding his chastity. And whoever is unable to marry should fast, as fasting is a means of restraint.'[499]

Fasting allows a person to build spiritual strength at the expense of physical stamina, and therefore is a remedy for sexual desires when a man cannot marry. That said, marriage should be sought for someone as soon as he is able to fulfil the rights of a

---

[496] *Jāmiʿ al-Tirmidhī* 1141.
[497] *Maʿārif al-Qur'an*, vol. 2: p. 306.
[498] *Maʿārif al-Qur'an*, vol. 6: pp. 420-421.
[499] *Ṣaḥīḥ al-Bukhārī* 5065, 5066; *Ṣaḥīḥ Muslim* 1440a, 1400c.

woman, and he should be supported to do so. Allah ﷻ says:

وَأَنكِحُوا۟ ٱلْأَيَـٰمَىٰ مِنكُمْ وَٱلصَّـٰلِحِينَ مِنْ عِبَادِكُمْ وَإِمَآئِكُمْ ۚ إِن يَكُونُوا۟ فُقَرَآءَ يُغْنِهِمُ ٱللَّهُ مِن فَضْلِهِۦ ۗ وَٱللَّهُ وَٰسِعٌ عَلِيمٌ.

Arrange the marriage of the spouseless among you, and the capable from among your bondmen and bondwomen. If they are poor, Allah will enrich them out of His grace. Allah is All-Encompassing, All-Knowing.[500]

The guardians or representatives of single men and women - whether they have never been married, are divorced, or were widowed - have been directed to arrange a marriage for them.[501] This is a moral and religious duty, and therefore is not a matter that a man with guardianship over another can defer or forgo.

Finally, when it comes to arranging such a marriage,[502] there are particular characteristics one should pursue. The Messenger of Allah ﷺ said, 'When someone whose religion and character you are pleased with proposes to someone under your care, then marry to him. If you do not do so, then there will be turmoil in the land and abounding discord.'[503]

For a man, faith and good character are the key attributes for being the 'High-Value Man' that we have heard so much about. When we receive proposals for our daughters, faith and character are the essential prerequisites, not money, appearances, and lineage. Faith and good character are the high-value attributes that should be sought and refined in the case of those looking for spouses, rather than attempting to perfect one's

500 *Qur'an* 24:32.

501 *Maʿārif al-Qur'an*, vol. 6: p. 420.

502 It should be noted that the proper etiquette for getting married involves deputising a guardian or representative to arrange it, rather than being so forward or immodest as to arrange it oneself. When there is no other choice, this is of course permissible.

503 *Jāmiʿ al-Tirmidhī* 1084, 1085; *Sunan Ibn Mājah* 2043.

'game'. The *complete* man is the high-value man.

In terms of what constitutes a 'High Value Woman', the Prophet ﷺ told us to 'marry women who are loving and prolific in childbearing'.[504] In another pertinent report, he ﷺ said: 'A woman is married for four reasons: her wealth, her family status, her beauty, and her religion. So you should marry the religious woman, or else you will be ruined.'[505] He also described the women we should marry, saying, 'They are the kindest women to their children in their childhood and the most vigilant of women with regard to the property of their husbands.'[506]

The woman you should seek to marry is thus the one who is loving in character, willing and able to have children, loving towards her offspring, fulfils her duties as a wife, and above all is strong in her faith. The other qualities listed are sought after by men, and there is no harm in factoring them into marriage decisions. At the same time, however, they are not nearly as valuable. Beauty is a blessing from Allah ﷻ and if it is halal for you, it is to be enjoyed. In fact, a Hadith cites looking at a potential spouse as a means of building love and affection.[507] But an undeniable fact is that beauty fades. Wealth is also a blessing of Allah ﷻ, yet it is also a test from Him. Family status and prestige is often sought, but for the Muslim, it has little worth. The only exception here is the bloodline of the Prophet ﷺ, for there is true virtue and nobility in his blood that cannot be found in all the kings and queens of the world. Even then, such familial status also comes with its own tests and responsibilities that not every man can live up to.

---

[504] *Sunan Abī Dāwūd* 2050.
[505] *Ṣaḥīḥ al-Bukhārī* 5090; *Ṣaḥīḥ Muslim* 1466.
[506] *Ṣaḥīḥ al-Bukhārī* 5082.
[507] *Jāmiʿ al-Tirmidhī* 1087.

QIWĀMAH

The concept of *qiwāmah* is extremely important in understanding the role of a man in his household, specifically his function with regard to the womenfolk in his household, such as his wives, daughters, and sisters.

ٱلرِّجَالُ قَوَّٰمُونَ عَلَى ٱلنِّسَآءِ بِمَا فَضَّلَ ٱللَّهُ بَعْضَهُمْ عَلَىٰ بَعْضٍ وَبِمَآ أَنفَقُوا۟ مِنْ أَمْوَٰلِهِمْ ۚ

Men are caretakers of women, since Allah has made some of them excel the others, and because of the wealth they have spent.[508]

In light of the aforementioned verse, one deduces that *qiwāmah* refers to our responsibility towards both the women in our households specifically, as well as women in general. *Qiwāmah* denotes responsibility and guardianship, firm and persistent commitment, as well as calm, restrained, and correct use of the natural physical power that men have over women. Allah ﷻ gave men strength, and thus increased the burden upon them to use this strength wisely, as '*Allah does not obligate anyone beyond his capacity*.'[509] As a result, one's burden is assigned according to his ability to bear it.[510] *Qiwāmah* relates to Allah's name al-Qayyūm (the Sustainer), and accordingly it is our responsibility to help sustain the women we are responsible for. This form of liability includes financial maintenance and support, with some schools of Islamic law considering a lack thereof to be legitimate grounds for a divorce.

The man in the relationship needs to be calm, thoughtful, and capable of managing the emotions of his spouse delicately.

---

[508] *Qur'an* 4:34.
[509] *Qur'an* 2:286.
[510] *Tafsīr al-Qushayrī*, vol. 1: p. 205.

In one report, Anas ﷺ narrated: 'It reached Ṣafiyyah that Ḥafṣah labelled her as "the daughter of a Jew", so she wept. The Prophet ﷺ entered upon her while she was weeping, and asked her, "What makes you cry?" She said, "Ḥafṣah called me the daughter of a Jew." So the Prophet ﷺ said, "You are the daughter of a Prophet, your uncle is a Prophet[511], and you are married to a Prophet, so what is she boasting to you about?" Then he said to Ḥafṣah, "Fear Allah, O Ḥafṣah."'[512]

He addressed the comment made about her cultural background with tact, diplomacy, and great care to ensure his spouses were not hurt by his balanced rejoinder. That said, he ﷺ also admonished the Mother of the Believers Ḥafṣah ﷺ, whilst he ensured he was not unnecessarily harsh with her. A man should always bear in mind the words of the Messenger of Allah ﷺ in such matters: 'Treat women nicely, for a woman is created from a rib,[513] and the most curved portion of the rib is its upper portion. If you try to straighten it, it will break, but if you leave it as it is, it will remain crooked. Thus, treat women nicely.'[514] A man cannot be harsh with a woman, as that will hurt her and potentially break her. But if he is too soft and never puts his foot down on crucial matters, then this can only cause him pain in the long term. The middle path must be chosen here: the man should guide her kindly, lovingly, and help her to understand his views, rather than forcing her to adopt them or allowing her to control everything herself. The Prophet ﷺ said, 'The best of you is the best to his wives (or family), and I am the best of you to my

---

[511] Ṣafiyyah's ancestor was the Prophet Hārūn, brother of Mūsā ﷺ.

[512] *Jāmiʿ al-Tirmidhī* 3894.

[513] The mother of mankind, Ḥawwā', was created from the rib of our father, Adam ﷺ.

[514] *Ṣaḥīḥ al-Bukhārī* 3331.

wives (or family).'[515] In another report, he ﷺ said: 'Do not raise a stick against your wife.'[516]

A man oversees his household with love, kindness, and mercy. A man that uses abuse and tyranny to control his family members is no real man at all. The Prophet ﷺ lived the most documented life in all of history. Despite this, there is not a single occasion of him ever being abusive, violent, or unkind to any of his family members. This is how a man should be.

ROMANCE

It is often the case that people try to place romance and classical ideas of masculinity at odds with each other, as if the idea of a romantic man is only compatible within the modern context of the 'metrosexual', who is 'in touch with his feminine side'. This could not be further from the truth. A man knows how to treat a woman, and understands that she needs attention, surprise, and playfulness in a relationship in order to maintain it. At the beginning of a relationship, everything is new and consequently these effects emanate naturally to both parties, as each unfolding moment is one of discovery. However, a man knows the importance of maintaining this when the relationship is no longer new, as it is beneficial to both parties and the relationship as a whole. The Prophet ﷺ said, 'There is nothing like marriage for two people who love each other.'[517]

وَمِنْ ءَايَـٰتِهِۦٓ أَنْ خَلَقَ لَكُم مِّنْ أَنفُسِكُمْ أَزْوَٰجًا لِّتَسْكُنُوٓا۟ إِلَيْهَا وَجَعَلَ بَيْنَكُم مَّوَدَّةً وَرَحْمَةً ۚ
إِنَّ فِى ذَٰلِكَ لَـَٔايَـٰتٍ لِّقَوْمٍ يَتَفَكَّرُونَ.

And it is among His signs that He has created for you wives from among yourselves, so that you may find tranquillity in

[515] *Jāmi' al-Tirmidhī* 3895; *Sunan Ibn Mājah* 1977.
[516] *Al-Adab al-Mufrad* 18.
[517] *Sunan Ibn Mājah* 1920.

them, and He has created love and kindness between you. Surely in this there are signs for a people who reflect.[518]

The purpose of creating two genders is described beautifully here in a single word, namely *taskunū*, which translates to 'you find tranquillity'. We were created from the same genus, the same species, and yet are marked with a number of substantial differences; despite these disparities, our partners provide us with peace of mind, tranquillity, and comfort.[519] This is clearly the case when one enters into a halal marriage contract, where both parties understand and fulfil their roles and responsibilities properly.

The Mother of the Believers ʿĀ'ishah ﷺ narrated many incidents that describe the romantic relationship she had with the Prophet ﷺ. She said, 'I would eat meat from a bone when I was menstruating, then hand it over to the Prophet ﷺ. He would then put his mouth where I had put my mouth; I would drink, then hand it over to him, and he would put his mouth where I had drank.'[520] This is an act of love between a husband and his wife, and also a lesson for the people of that time; prior to the advent of Islam, they would see the food touched by a menstruating woman as unclean. On another occasion, he ﷺ stated, 'You will be rewarded for whatever you spend for Allah's sake, even if it were a morsel which you put in your wife's mouth.'[521] Thus, eating and drinking from the same place as one's spouse and feeding her with one's own hands is encouraged as these actions demonstrate the husband's love for her and strengthen the bond between them.

---

[518] *Qur'an* 30:21.
[519] *Maʿārif al-Qur'an*, vol. 6: p. 732.
[520] *Sunan Abī Dāwūd* 259.
[521] *Ṣaḥīḥ al-Bukhārī* 56.

Similarly, expressing one's love through other means is also encouraged. In this context, one may cite the following report narrated by the Mother of the Believers ʿĀ'ishah ﵂: 'The Prophet ﷺ used to recline on my lap and recite the Qur'an while I was in my menses.'[522] In another report, she stated: 'The Messenger of Allah ﷺ and I took a bath from one vessel[523] which was placed between us. And he would often get ahead of me, such that I would say, "Spare some for me, spare some for me!"'[524]

Likewise, expressing your love for your spouse publicly is also permissible. When ʿAmr ibn al-ʿĀṣ ﵁ asked the Prophet ﷺ, 'Which person do you love most?' He ﷺ replied, 'ʿĀ'ishah.'[525] In fact, the Prophet ﷺ would use a loving nickname for her, often calling her Ḥumayrā'[526] (lit. 'little red-cheeked one'), on account of her rosy red cheeks.

Romance assumes many forms, and as long as it is expressed within the confines of the Shariah it is a good action that is worthy of reward. Taking one's spouse somewhere to enjoy herself is therefore permissible. The Mother of the Believers ʿĀ'ishah ﵂ relates how the Prophet ﷺ graced her with kind treatment during the day of Eid: 'He was screening me with his *ridā'*[527] while I watched the Ethiopians playing in the courtyard of the *mosque*. [I kept watching] until I was satisfied.' One ultimately deduces

---

[522] *Ṣaḥīḥ al-Bukhārī* 297.

[523] This is the Islamic style of *ghusl* (ritual bath) where a vessel is filled with water, and the person bathing would not be in a state of complete undress and water wastage is kept to a minimum. This narration should not be used to justify bathing or showering together with one's spouse while being completely undressed. In Islam, there is still an element of modesty to be observed, even between spouses.

[524] *Ṣaḥīḥ Muslim* 321d.

[525] *Ṣaḥīḥ al-Bukhārī* 4358.

[526] *Sunan Ibn Mājah* 2474.

[527] An upper cloak-like garment, such as the upper half of the *iḥrām*.

from this event how a young lady who wishes to enjoy amusement should be treated in this respect.[528]

The Prophet ﷺ would often remember his first wife, that is, the Mother of the Believers Khadījah ◈, even long after she had passed away. Regarding this matter, the Mother of the Believers 'Ā'ishah ◈ said, 'I did not feel jealous of any of the wives of the Prophet ﷺ as much as I did of Khadījah ◈, though I never met her. The Prophet ﷺ used to mention her very often, and whenever he slaughtered a sheep, he would cut [some of] its parts and send them to the women [who had been] friends of Khadījah. Sometimes I would say to him, "It is as if there is no other woman on Earth except Khadījah," and he ﷺ would reply, "Khadījah was such-and-such, and from her I had children."'[529]

What greater expression of love for one's spouse can there be than to continue to remember them long after their passing?

SEXUALITY

When discussing masculinity in a contemporary context, the discussion often turns to one of three things: financial and social status, physical and martial prowess, or sexuality and sexual dominance. These are the elements which men seem to value the most, and what the modern man associates with masculinity. Indeed, the modern woman sees men through these features as well, as these are often seen as desirable qualities in men. Feminism attacks these ideas and considers them to be the basis for the concept of the so-called 'toxic man'. The Muslim man is far more than these things, though he is likely to have one or more of them in his repertoire.

---

[528] *Ṣaḥīḥ al-Bukhārī* 5236.
[529] *Ṣaḥīḥ al-Bukhārī* 56.

On the subject of sexuality, the Muslim man has been given clear guidelines, as with all things, around which he should base his sex life. Islam is not prudish about this subject, nor is it animalistic and base. Instead, the true religion adopts the middle path, taking our *fiṭrah* as it is, and introducing legal boundaries within which a man is free to explore.

Legal sexual intercourse is not only permissible or encouraged, but it is also considered a *ṣadaqah* and thus worthy of reward. When the Prophet ﷺ told the Companions ﷺ this, they asked how it was possible that fulfilling one's sexual desires could be considered worthy of reward. He replied, 'Then tell me: if he were to devote it to something forbidden, would it not be a sin on his part? Similarly, if he were to devote it to something lawful, he should have a reward.'[530]

That said, a Muslim is always modest and in control. While many others may give into the throes of passion during sexual intercourse, it is incumbent upon the Muslim man to maintain his sense of self and decency. The Prophet ﷺ said, 'When one of you has intercourse with his wife, let him cover himself and not be naked like donkeys.'[531] The Mother of the Believers ʿĀ'ishah ﷺ said that she never once saw the private parts of the Prophet ﷺ.[532] The Shariah gives guidance for all aspects of life, and sex is no exception to this overarching principle. The Prophet ﷺ said, 'If a man likes he may have intercourse on his back or in front of her, but it should be through one opening (the vagina).'[533]

---

[530] *Ṣaḥīḥ Muslim* 1006.
[531] *Sunan Ibn Mājah* 1921.
[532] *Sunan Ibn Mājah* 1922.
[533] *Ṣaḥīḥ Muslim* 1435c.

Allah ﷻ says:

نِسَآؤُكُمْ حَرْثٌ لَّكُمْ فَأْتُوا۟ حَرْثَكُمْ أَنَّىٰ شِئْتُمْ ۖ وَقَدِّمُوا۟ لِأَنفُسِكُمْ ۚ وَٱتَّقُوا۟ ٱللَّهَ وَٱعْلَمُوٓا۟ أَنَّكُم مُّلَـٰقُوهُ ۗ وَبَشِّرِ ٱلْمُؤْمِنِينَ.

Your women are tillage for you to cultivate. Consequently, come to your tillage from where you wish, and advance something for yourselves. Fear Allah, and know that you are to meet Him, and give good news to the believers."[534]

This makes it clear that a man can adopt any and all sexual positions with his wife, so long as it is legal sex.[535] Anal sex is prohibited and is a major sin. The Prophet ﷺ said three times, 'Allah ﷻ is not shy to tell the truth,' and then said, 'Do not have intercourse with women in their rears.'[536] Likewise, as discussed previously, other forms of illegal sexual intercourse are also prohibited, such as any form of forced sex, sex with more than one partner, or having marital relations in view of anyone else. All such acts are considered sexual deviancy and should be avoided at all costs.

A man should not behave like an animal when having sex with his wife; instead, he should be soft and gentle with her. Every narration or verse that covers the subject of sex uses meticulous terminology to make this matter clear to us. A man should engage in foreplay and become proficient in understanding what his wife prefers, as women are not like men in how they achieve gratification through sex. The Prophet ﷺ said, 'One should not fulfil their need from their wife like an animal, rather there should be a messenger between them.' Someone asked, 'What messenger?'

---

[534] *Qur'an* 2:223.

[535] *Ma'ārif al-Qur'an*, vol. 1: p. 561.

[536] *Sunan Ibn Mājah* 1924.

He ﷺ replied, 'Talking and kissing.'[537] The Mother of the Believers 'Ā'ishah ﵂ narrated that the Prophet ﷺ used to kiss her and suck her tongue.[538] Being gentle does not mean passionless. There is no such thing as a passionless man, as people without any sensual appetite are mere automatons, not human beings. Imam Ibn al-Qayyim ﵀ said, 'If sexual intercourse takes place with gentleness, much passion, complete desire, and with the intention of obtaining reward, there will not be any enjoyment equal to it.'[539]

Regarding sexual prowess, one fundamental question remains: how often *should* a man fulfil his wife's right in the bedroom, and how often *can* he fulfil his own?

A woman once came to Amīr al-Mu'minīn 'Umar ibn al-Khaṭṭāb ﵁ to relate that her husband spent the nights standing in prayer and the days fasting. He believed that she was praising him, until Ka'b ibn Sawwar ﵁ pointed out that this was actually a complaint, as he was not fulfilling her marital rights; the woman was too modest to express this point openly.

Ka'b ﵁ was asked to give the ruling on this matter, and he stated, 'O Amīr al-Mu'minīn, Allah ﷻ has permitted him four wives, so she has one day in every four days and one night in every four nights.'[540] Thus a man should (and by extension should be *able* to) give his wife at least one day in four for her needs, and one night in four for her marital rights.

With regard to how often one can fulfil their own needs, there is no upper limit *per se*, as there are narrations whereby

---

[537] *Musnad al-Firdaws li al-Daylamī* 2:55.
[538] *Sunan Abī Dāwūd* 2386.
[539] *Rawḍah al-Muḥibbīn*, p. 187.
[540] *Muṣannaf 'Abd al-Razzāq* 12586, 12587.

the Prophet ﷺ visited all of his wives in a single night.[541] However, one should not lose oneself in such pursuits, as this is not the way of the Muslim man. The Sunnah demonstrates that a husband can enjoy his wife and vice versa, whilst maintaining self-control and discipline, and ensuring one's worship and other duties are given their due time and attention.

Within this context it is also important to note that a man is responsible for ensuring that his wife's physical and mental concerns are properly met. This point is crucial, since just because a man *can* fulfil his needs nightly, it does not mean that he *should*. It may be that his wife is not as capable as he is in this regard.

Sexuality is definitely a fundamental part of being a man, but it is neither his goal nor his focus. It is an allowance for him to fulfil his needs, and should be seen as such.

[541] *Ṣaḥīḥ al-Bukhārī* 284.

24
He is a Father and a Son

عَنْ عَبْدِ اللَّهِ بْنِ عَمْرٍو رَضِيَ اللَّهُ عَنْهُما، عَنِ النَّبِيِّ صَلَّى اللَّهُ عَلَيْهِ وَسَلَّمَ، قَالَ: "رِضَا الرَّبِّ فِي رِضَا الْوَالِدِ، وَسَخَطُ الرَّبِّ فِي سَخَطِ الْوَالِدِ."

ʿAbdullāh ibn ʿAmr ﷺ narrated that the Prophet ﷺ said, 'The Lord's pleasure is in the father's pleasure, and the Lord's anger is in the father's anger.'[542]

FATHERHOOD

One of the greatest duties a man can fulfil in his life is fatherhood. Fathers are the yardstick by which men are measured in the eyes of their children. They are their rule-setters and their disciplinarians, their advisors and their teachers, their friends and their mentors; they provide for them, protect them, and lead them. A man plays many roles in a child's life, but all of these functions can be summarised in a single but powerful word: *father*. He is the moral leader in the home, and by his successes and failures his household will either be a prosperous stronghold of Islam or a wasteland in which nothing of worth grows. Therefore, fatherhood is a *responsibility* more than anything else. Allah ﷻ has gifted this duty to those fortunate enough to be given it, and thus it should not be taken for granted.

The Prophet ﷺ referred to himself as a father figure to his followers, stating, 'I am like a father to you. When any one of you goes to the outhouse, he should not face or turn his back towards the *qiblah*. He should not cleanse himself with his right hand...'[543] He ﷺ taught his followers exactly how a father should

[542] *Jāmiʿ al-Tirmidhī* 1899.
[543] *Sunan Abī Dāwūd* 8.

teach his children, by noting that words of instruction should be issued with love and care, and without being shy with regard to the subject matter at hand.

يَـٰٓأَيُّهَا ٱلنَّاسُ ٱتَّقُوا۟ رَبَّكُمْ وَٱخْشَوْا۟ يَوْمًا لَّا يَجْزِى وَالِدٌ عَن وَلَدِهِۦ وَلَا مَوْلُودٌ هُوَ جَازٍ
عَن وَالِدِهِۦ شَيْـًٔا ۚ إِنَّ وَعْدَ ٱللَّهِ حَقٌّ ۖ فَلَا تَغُرَّنَّكُمُ ٱلْحَيَوٰةُ ٱلدُّنْيَا وَلَا يَغُرَّنَّكُم بِٱللَّهِ ٱلْغَرُورُ.

O people, fear your Lord and fear a day when no father will help his son, nor will a son be helpful to his father at all. Surely, the promise of Allah is true. Consequently, the worldly life must not deceive you, nor should you ever be deceived about Allah by the Deceiver.[544]

In his work of *tafsīr*, Imam Ibn Kathīr ﵀ explains this verse by stating that even if the father wanted to sacrifice himself in place of his son, he would not be able to do so, and vice versa.[545] Such is the level of love the father should have for his child and, in this temporal world, this is the expectation of what the father should be prepared and willing to do. The 'fear' mentioned in this verse is not the fear one has when confronted with an enemy, oppressor, or a predator, but the fear one has regarding his father or teacher; it is the awe a child has for them that makes them want to please and obey them.[546] The verse warns of the Day of Resurrection by showing us two examples of what is (or should be) the norm, thereby conveying how grave a day the Last Day will be.

A father *helps* his son; a son is *helpful* to his father. Thus, the father's function is to help his child succeed in life, whereas the child's role is to be of use to the father. Ultimately, a father's core role is the moral and spiritual guidance of his child, and true success is achieved when entry to Paradise is gained. The

[544] *Qur'an* 31:33.

[545] *Tafsīr Ibn Kathīr* 31:33.

[546] *Ma'ārif al-Qur'an*, vol. 7: p. 54.

Prophet ﷺ said, 'There is no gift that a father gives his son more virtuous than good manners.'[547]

Ibn Faḍlān, an envoy of the Caliph al-Muqtadir in the early 900s CE, was a famous traveller and chronicler who is recognised for writing accurate and detailed descriptions of the Bulgar people and the Norsemen, as well as having documented the only witness account of a so-called Viking Chieftain's funeral. During his time with the Bulgars, he wrote about how when a man's son had a child, the grandfather would raise the boy, stating, 'I have more of a right than his father to raise him until he becomes a man.'[548] The implication was that the grandfather was better placed to teach the child about manhood, for he had more experience in being a man. The teaching of *ādāb* (rules of etiquette) was considered a *right* of the man as well as a responsibility, and it was a matter of pride to teach one's son manners. ʿAbd al-Malik ibn Marwān entrusted the teaching of his children to al-Shaʿbī and said, 'Teach them poetry so that they will possess dignity and vigour. Feed them meat so that their hearts will be strong. Cut off their hair so that their necks will be strong. Make them sit with men of distinction, who will contradict them in words.'[549]

The Prophet ﷺ said, 'He who has a son born to him should give him a good name, provide him a good upbringing, and marry him to someone when he reaches puberty. If he does not marry him to someone when he reaches puberty and he commits sin, its guilt rests only upon his father.'[550]

There are several matters to further explore in this

---

[547] *Jāmiʿ al-Tirmidhī* 1952.
[548] *Ibn Fadlan and the Land of Darkness*, p. 36.
[549] *Al-Adab al-Mufrad* 873.
[550] *Mishkāt al-Maṣābīḥ* 3138.

aforementioned Hadith. Firstly, the giving of a good name is a duty, and it should be taken as such. A child should not be given a name because you want them to have a 'unique' designation, or a label that sounds 'Western'. It is equally incorrect to confer them a name that you find given to a television actor or character. Instead, it should be a name that contains a good meaning and is likely to exert a positive influence on the child. Accordingly, the names of the Prophets ﷺ or Companions ﷺ are often chosen to fulfil this duty. On the Day of Judgement, we will be called by our given names and the names of our fathers, and consequently a respectable name is extremely important.[551] The Prophet ﷺ would often change bad names to good names, as such a designation has an effect on the person:

> *Saʿīd ibn al-Musayyib ﷺ narrated that his father ﷺ said on the authority of his grandfather ﷺ that the Prophet ﷺ asked him: 'What is your name?' He replied, 'Hazn (Rugged).' He ﷺ said, 'You are Sahl (Smooth).' He said, 'No, smooth is trodden upon and disgraced.' Saʿīd ﷺ said about this, 'I then thought that ruggedness would remain among us after this.'*
>
> *Imam Abū Dāwūd further comments on this by stating, 'The Prophet ﷺ changed the names al-ʿĀṣ, ʿAzīz, ʿAtalah, Shayṭān, al-Ḥakam, Ghurāb, Ḥubāb, and also Shihāb – calling him Hishām. He changed the name Ḥarb (War) to Salm (Peace), al-Munbaʿith (The One Who Lies) to al-Muḍtajiʿ (The One Who Stands Up), as well as the name of the land known as ʿAfirah (Barren) to Khaḍirah (Green) instead. He changed the name of a*

[551] *Sunan Abī Dāwūd* 4948.

> *mountain path originally known as Shiʿb al-Ḍalālah (The Mountain Path of Strays) to Shiʿb al-Hudā (The Mountain Path of Guidance). He changed the name Banū al-Zinyah (The Children of Fornication) and Banū Mughwiyah (Children of a Woman who Allures and Leads Astray) to Banū al-Rishdah (Rightly Guided Children).*[552]

Secondly, a father has the duty of disciplining his child. The Prophet ﷺ said, 'That a man should discipline his son is better for him than to have given a *ṣāʿ*[553] in charity.'[554] If the child steps beyond the boundaries of Allah ﷻ, or those set by his father, it is the father's duty to ensure he is taught the error of his ways. This is not to say that the father should physically punish the child as a rule, but rather the child should be educated with love and kindness. Although Islam allows for corrective disciplining, the Prophet ﷺ never used anything other than compassion and tenderness to teach the children around him.

Anas ibn Mālik رضي الله عنه said, 'The Messenger of Allah ﷺ used to come to visit us. I had a younger brother who was called Abū ʿUmayr as a *kunyah*.[555] He had a sparrow with which he used to play, but it died. So one day the Prophet ﷺ came to see him and saw him grieving. He ﷺ asked, "What is the matter with him?" The people replied, "His sparrow has died." He then said, "Abū ʿUmayr! What has happened to the little sparrow (*al-nughayr*)?"'[556] He showed the child kindness when he was greatly saddened by a relatively trivial matter, and cheered him up by

---

552 *Sunan Abī Dāwūd* 4956.
553 A unit of measure which roughly approximates 3 kilograms in weight.
554 *Jāmiʿ al-Tirmidhī* 1951.
555 A name by which someone is known.
556 *Sunan Abī Dāwūd* 4969.

employing a rhyme. The Messenger of Allah ﷺ also said, 'There is no one who has three daughters or three sisters and he treats them well except that he will enter Paradise.'[557]

Thirdly, when a child comes of age, we should not delay their marriage. Frequently we are influenced by societal norms and delay their marriage until their late 20s or even early 30s and beyond, using the pretext of the young man being unable to run his household in his late teens and early 20s. We are then somehow shocked when they go down the haram route to fulfil their needs. Society is not the yardstick by which we decide what is right or wrong; Islam is the objective moral standard that must be employed to evaluate all problems. Modern society deals with the issue of teenage pregnancy by handing out contraceptives to 13-year-olds, and it is deemed as normal to encourage abortions in cases where birth control methods fail. The superior situation where the male party has to give her rights and has a legal responsibility to support both the mother and the child is somehow considered offensive to modern society, whereas premarital sex between teenagers is completely legal and reasonable.

A father should not play favourites with his children, be they his sons or his daughters. Instead, he must be kind and loving to each of them in an equitable manner. Al-Nuʿmān ibn Bashīr ؓ said, 'My father took me to the Prophet ﷺ to ask him to bear witness to something that he had given to me. He ﷺ said, "Do you have any other children?" He said, "Yes." He ﷺ gestured with his hand held horizontally, saying, "Why do you not treat them all equally?"'[558] Ibn ʿUmar ؓ said, 'Allah ﷻ has called

[557] *Jāmiʿ al-Tirmidhī* 1912.
[558] *Sunan al-Nasāʾī* 3685.

them the "dutiful" because they are dutiful to their parents and children. Just as you have a duty which you owe to your parents, so too do you have a duty which you owe to your child.'[559] Love, kindness, support, protection, fair treatment, and mercy are all part of this duty to our children. Al-Aqraʿ ibn Ḥābis ﷺ once saw the Prophet ﷺ kissing al-Ḥasan ﷺ and in response said, 'I have ten children and I do not kiss any of them.' So the Messenger of Allah ﷺ said, 'Whoever shows no mercy is shown no mercy.'[560]

Children are a blessing and a means of raising the status of their parents in the Hereafter. The Prophet ﷺ said, 'Allah ﷻ will certainly raise the status of His righteous servants in Paradise and they will say, "O Lord, what is this?" Allah ﷻ will say, "This is due to your child seeking forgiveness for you."'[561] As for those parents who raised children and placed all of their hopes and dreams into them only to then tragically become the buriers and not the buried, comfort can be taken in the words of our beloved Prophet ﷺ: 'There are no two Muslims who have three children who die before reaching puberty except that Allah ﷻ will admit them to Paradise by virtue of His mercy toward them. It will be said to them, "Enter Paradise." They will say, "Not until our parents enter." So it will be said, "Let both you and your parents enter Paradise."'[562] Those children will be admitted to Paradise without any reckoning, and they will likewise ensure that their parents are granted entry as well, *in shā' Allāh.*

A man should be able to be kind and playful with his children, but ready to adjust and become their protector at the drop of a hat. Amīr al-Mu'minīn ʿUmar ﷺ said, 'I am amazed

---

[559] *Al-Adab al-Mufrad* 94.
[560] *Jāmiʿ al-Tirmidhī* 1911.
[561] *Musnad Imam Aḥmad* 10232.
[562] *Sunan al-Nasā'ī* 1876.

that a man can be with his family like a child, but if he is called forth he is found to be a true man.'[563]

Ya'lā ibn Murrah ✿ said, 'We went out with the Prophet ✿ and we were invited to eat. Al-Ḥusayn ✿ was playing in the road and the Prophet ✿ raced to him in front of the people and then spread out his arms. The boy began to run this way and that, and the Prophet ✿ made him laugh until he caught hold of him. He ✿ put one of his hands under his chin and the other on his head and then embraced him. Then the Prophet ✿ said, "Al-Ḥusayn is from me and I am from al-Ḥusayn. Allah ✿ loves anyone who loves al-Ḥasan and al-Ḥusayn. They are two of my distinguished descendants."'[564]

A famous saying that is oftentimes attributed to Amīr al-Mu'minīn 'Alī ibn Abī Ṭālib ✿ encapsulates the role of the father:

Play with them for the first seven years; teach them for the next seven years; and befriend them for the seven years after that.

SONSHIP AND FILIAL PIETY

Filial piety (*birr al-wālidayn*) refers to being good to one's parents. It involves kindness, love, respect, dutifulness towards them, taking care of them, good conduct both in and out of the home to honour and respect them, and awareness of their *ghayrah*. It entails supporting them, offering them wise, moral counsel when required, and praying for them after they depart from this world.

Respecting one's elders is a common sentiment across the

---

[563] *Shu'ab al-Īmān* 7851.
[564] *Al-Adab al-Mufrad* 364.

globe, and there are no societies or cultures that do not have an understanding that elders should be respected. However, we are losing or have already lost the sense of duty that filial piety comes with. Parents that spent their lives and livelihoods raising and supporting us are shipped away to care homes to live out their days among other discarded elders, a lifetime of wisdom wasted as they wait for visits from their preoccupied children that come fewer and further between. In the West, filial piety is either non-existent as an idea, or completely forgotten, and the term has been coined as a way of translating the concept into the English language. Its only Western equivalents are found in antique Mediterranean cultures. For instance, the ancient Greeks championed the concept of *eusebeia*, which refers to traditional pious reverence to relationships and deities. Failure to comply with this was a punishable crime (*asebeia*). The term was possibly brought to Ancient Rome by its founder Aeneas as *pietas*, which involved carrying out one's duty to his country (in this case Rome), his parents, and his other blood relations. In the East it is still commonplace, with China calling it *xiao* and Japan calling it *kō*, or *oyakōkō*. The word *xiao* is an amalgamation of the character for 'old' being held up by the character for 'son', signifying that it is imperative for the youth to look after and support their elders. In Korea it is *hyo*, and in Vietnam it is *hiếu*. In Filipino society it is '*utang na loob'*, which can be rendered 'inner debt of gratitude'. Filial piety is now waning in the East too, with some regions in China making legal contracts for newlyweds to look after parents in their sixties, which is a complete shift from the Confucian preference of inherent morality over state law-making.

وَٱعْبُدُوا۟ ٱللَّهَ وَلَا تُشْرِكُوا۟ بِهِۦ شَيْـًۭٔا ۖ وَبِٱلْوَٰلِدَيْنِ إِحْسَـٰنًۭا

Worship Allah, and do not associate with Him anything, and be

good to parents...[565]

After the command to worship Allah ﷻ alone, the rights of the parents are immediately mentioned. This is because while all blessings come from Allah ﷻ, the favours one receives in life are often given by means of his parents, who are with him from birth and throughout his youth for every trial, taking care of him and doing whatever is within their means to make him comfortable and successful.[566] We are told to be good to them, which is far more than merely fulfilling their rights: it includes supporting them financially, providing them physical assistance, being respectful when talking to them at all times, and being mindful of never breaking their hearts. In fact, even if the parents have fallen short in fulfilling his rights, he should never take it as an excuse for their ill-treatment.[567] Ibn ʿAbbās ؓ said, 'If any Muslim obeys Allah ﷻ regarding his parents, Allah ﷻ will open two gates of Paradise for him. If there is only one parent, then one gate will be opened. If one of them is angry, then Allah ﷻ will not be pleased with him until that parent is pleased with him.' He was asked, 'Even if they wrong him?' 'Even if they wrong him', he replied.[568]

To deny one's parents is to invite calamity upon oneself. Perhaps your father was abusive, perchance your mother never looked after you, or maybe their lack of care resulted in you being taken into the care of another, whether adopted or in the foster care system. Even in these circumstances, we are not exonerated from our duty towards them. One such form of denial is to change one's surname, or to claim another man as

---

565 *Qur'an* 4:36.
566 *Maʿārif al-Qur'an*, vol. 2: p. 432.
567 *Maʿārif al-Qur'an*, vol. 2: p. 432.
568 *Al-Adab al-Mufrad* 7.

your 'only real father'. Allah ﷻ says:

ٱدْعُوهُمْ لِءَابَآئِهِمْ هُوَ أَقْسَطُ عِندَ ٱللَّهِ ۚ فَإِن لَّمْ تَعْلَمُوٓا۟ ءَابَآءَهُمْ فَإِخْوَٰنُكُمْ فِى ٱلدِّينِ وَمَوَٰلِيكُمْ ۚ وَلَيْسَ عَلَيْكُمْ جُنَاحٌ فِيمَآ أَخْطَأْتُم بِهِۦ وَلَٰكِن مَّا تَعَمَّدَتْ قُلُوبُكُمْ ۚ وَكَانَ ٱللَّهُ غَفُورًا رَّحِيمًا

Call them by [the name of] their fathers; it is more equitable in the sight of Allah. And if you do not know their fathers, then they are your brothers in faith and your friends. There is no sin on you in the mistake you make, but in that which you do with the intention of your heart; and Allah is Most-Forgiving, Very-Merciful.[569]

And His Prophet ﷺ said, 'Do not deny your fathers (i.e., claim to be the sons of persons other than your fathers), and whoever denies his father, is charged with disbelief.'[570]

Your name is more than letters on a page, or a connection to your father. Rather, your name is a link to all of your ancestors who came before you, and the love, duty, and hardship that led to your existing in this world. Therefore, it should not merely be cast aside due to the mistakes of one man in that chain of people linking you to the Father of Mankind, *Sayyidunā* Adam ﷺ.

وَوَصَّيْنَا ٱلْإِنسَٰنَ بِوَٰلِدَيْهِ حَمَلَتْهُ أُمُّهُۥ وَهْنًا عَلَىٰ وَهْنٍ وَفِصَٰلُهُۥ فِى عَامَيْنِ أَنِ ٱشْكُرْ لِى وَلِوَٰلِدَيْكَ إِلَىَّ ٱلْمَصِيرُ

We commanded man to be good in respect of his parents. His mother carried him (in her womb) despite weakness upon weakness, and his weaning is in two years. We said to man, 'Be grateful to Me, and to your parents. To Me is the ultimate return.'[571]

---

[569] *Qur'an* 33:5.

[570] *Ṣaḥīḥ al-Bukhārī* 6768.

[571] *Qur'an* 31:14.

Abū Usayd 🌸 said, 'We were with the Messenger of Allah 🌸 when a man asked, "Messenger of Allah, is there any act of dutifulness which I can do for my parents after their death?" He 🌸 replied, "Yes. There are four things: Supplication for them, asking forgiveness for them, fulfilling their pledges, and being generous to their friends. You only have ties of kinship through your parents."'[572] The Prophet 🌸 said, 'Among the most dutiful of deeds is that a man nurture relations with the people his father was friends with.'[573] The Prophet 🌸 also said, 'Allah, Most Blessed and Most High, said, "I am Allah, and I am al-Raḥmān (the Possessor of Mercy). I created the *raḥim* (womb), and named it after My Name. So whoever keeps good relations with it, I keep good relations with him, and whoever severs it, I am finished with him."'[574] The word for womb in Arabic is derived from the name of Allah 🌸 Himself, and therefore the position of the mother in whose womb you were developed is above even that of your father.

Muʿāwiyah ibn Jāhimah al-Sulamī 🌸 narrates that Jāhimah 🌸 came to the Prophet 🌸 and said, 'O Messenger of Allah! I want to go out and fight in jihad, and I have come to ask for your advice.' He 🌸 said, 'Do you have a mother?' He said, 'Yes.' He 🌸 said, 'Then stay with her, for Paradise is beneath her feet.'[575] The Prophet 🌸 also said, 'The father is in the middle of the gates of Paradise, so keep this gate or lose it.'[576] We must serve and protect these people, namely our mothers and fathers, as just as our children will be a means of entering Paradise for us, so too

---

[572] *Al-Adab al-Mufrad* 35.
[573] *Jāmiʿ al-Tirmidhī* 1903.
[574] *Jāmiʿ al-Tirmidhī* 1907.
[575] *Sunan al-Nasāʾī* 3104.
[576] *Sunan Ibn Mājah* 3663.

will our parents so long as we fulfil our duties towards them. The Prophet ﷺ said, 'Let him be humbled into dust; let him be humbled into dust.' A Companion ؓ asked, 'O Messenger of Allah, who is he?' He ﷺ said, 'He who sees either of his parents during their old age or both of them, but he does not enter Paradise.'[577]

ʿAbdullāh ibn Masʿūd ؓ asked the Messenger of Allah ﷺ which deed was the best of all actions. He ﷺ replied, 'Prayer at its appointed hour.' He again said, 'Then what [is best]?' He ﷺ replied, 'Kindness to parents.' He again asked, 'Then what [is best]?' He replied, 'Jihad in the cause of Allah ﷻ.'[578]

They are our keys to Paradise, and service to them is considered a higher calling than even fighting in the path of Allah ﷻ.

رَّبِّ ارْحَمْهُمَا كَمَا رَبَّيَانِي صَغِيرًا

O Lord, have mercy on them as they raised me when I was small!

[577] *Ṣaḥīḥ Muslim* 2551a.
[578] *Ṣaḥīḥ Muslim* 85a.

25
He is a Loyal Brother

عَنْ أَنَسٍ رَضِيَ اللَّهُ عَنْهُ، عَنِ النَّبِيِّ صَلَّى اللَّهُ عَلَيْهِ وَسَلَّمَ، قَالَ: "لاَ يُؤْمِنُ أَحَدُكُمْ حَتَّى يُحِبَّ لأَخِيهِ مَا يُحِبُّ لِنَفْسِهِ."

Anas ﵁ narrated that the Prophet ﷺ said, 'None of you believes until he loves for his brother what he loves for himself.'[579]

BROTHERHOOD, FRATERNITY, AND DUTY

Brotherhood is a bond between men. It connects them through mutual interest, belief, or cause. It is a fraternity bound together by brotherly love, and built through shared duty, hardship, pain, and sincere belief. Your fellow Muslims are your brothers. Just as you would be willing to give up everything for the sake of your siblings, so too should you be willing to make the same sacrifice for your fellow Muslim.

Abū Jahm ibn Ḥudhayfah ﵁ narrated: 'During the Battle of Yarmūk, I went out in search of my cousin (who had been at the forefront of the fighting), and took along some water for him. When I found him he was in his final throes of death, and I sought to quench his thirst or wash his face with the water. I asked him, "Would you like some water?" He indicated in the affirmative. As he did so, a man moaned in pain. My cousin motioned for me to go to that man first. I did so and found that it was Hāshim ibn al-ʿĀṣ, the brother of ʿAmr. I asked him, "Would you like some water?" As I did so, another man cried

579 *Jāmiʿ al-Tirmidhī* 2515.

out in pain. Hāshim indicated for me to help the other man first. When I approached him, I found that he had just passed away. I returned to Hāshim, only to find he had also died. I went back to my cousin, but alas he had also passed away.'[580]

Even in the field of battle, in their last throes of death, when every breath is a desperate gasp for life, they thought of their brothers first and died in that same condition, worrying about their fellow man as their own life ebbed away. What greater example of brotherhood could there be in the annals of history?

The Prophet ﷺ perfectly described the concept of brotherhood when he ﷺ said, 'The Muslim is the brother of a Muslim. He does not wrong him, nor surrender him. Whoever fulfils the needs of his brother, Allah ﷻ will fulfil his needs. Whoever relieves a Muslim's distress, Allah ﷻ will relieve his distress on the Day of Resurrection. Whoever covers the faults of a Muslim, Allah ﷻ will cover his faults on the Day of Resurrection.'[581] He ﷺ also said, 'It is sufficient evil for a man to look down on his Muslim brother.'[582] In another narration, he ﷺ said: 'Whoever protects his brother's honour, Allah ﷻ will protect his face from the Fire on the Day of Resurrection.'[583]

A man should understand brotherhood, be part of it, and practise its tenets. Brotherhood is a fundamental aspect of Islam, and is often referenced even by the enemies of Islam. It is one of the great strengths of the *ummah*. The Prophet ﷺ said: 'The Muslims are like one man; if his eye is in pain his whole body aches, and if the head is in pain his whole body aches.'[584] This is

---

[580] *Shuʿab al-Īmān* 3483.
[581] *Ṣaḥīḥ al-Bukhārī* 2422, *Ṣaḥīḥ Muslim* 2580.
[582] *Sunan Ibn Mājah* 4213.
[583] *Jāmiʿ al-Tirmidhī* 1931.
[584] *Ṣaḥīḥ Muslim* 2586d.

our strength: we feel what our brothers feel, and are hurt when our sisters go through physical and spiritual pain. This mutual empathy in the *ummah* is ebbing slowly away, and it is for men such as us to reignite the flames of brotherhood and become united once more.

وَٱلْمُؤْمِنُونَ وَٱلْمُؤْمِنَـٰتُ بَعْضُهُمْ أَوْلِيَآءُ بَعْضٍۢ ۚ يَأْمُرُونَ بِٱلْمَعْرُوفِ وَيَنْهَوْنَ عَنِ ٱلْمُنكَرِ وَيُقِيمُونَ ٱلصَّلَوٰةَ وَيُؤْتُونَ ٱلزَّكَوٰةَ وَيُطِيعُونَ ٱللَّهَ وَرَسُولَهُۥٓ ۚ أُو۟لَـٰٓئِكَ سَيَرْحَمُهُمُ ٱللَّهُ ۗ إِنَّ ٱللَّهَ عَزِيزٌ حَكِيمٌ.

The believers, male and female, are friends to each other. They bid virtue and forbid vice and establish ṣalāh and pay zakāh and obey Allah and His Messenger. Those are the ones whom Allah will bless with mercy. Surely, Allah is Powerful, Wise.[585]

Earlier in the same *sūrah*, Allah ﷻ pronounces the expression '*they are all alike*'[586] in relation to the hypocrites. But He employs a subtle literary variation when describing the true believers by saying, '...[they] *are friends to each other*'. This illuminates a key difference between the two groups. Hypocrites base their bonds on building functional cooperation between kinsfolk or mutual self-interest; these bonds are short-lived and built on sand, with no spiritual connection between the parties involved. The bonds between true believers, however, are sincere, free of self-interest, and for Allah ﷻ alone. They are long-lasting and constant under all conditions, open or secret, present or absent.[587] This sincere spiritual bond is described again when Allah ﷻ says:

إِنَّ ٱلَّذِينَ ءَامَنُوا۟ وَعَمِلُوا۟ ٱلصَّـٰلِحَـٰتِ سَيَجْعَلُ لَهُمُ ٱلرَّحْمَـٰنُ وُدًّا.

Surely, those who believe and do righteous deeds, for them the

585 *Qur'an* 9:71.
586 *Qur'an* 9:67.
587 *Ma'ārif al-Qur'an*, vol. 4: p. 426.

All-Merciful will create love.[588]

Belief in Allah ﷻ and righteous actions result in mutual love between the believers. The Prophet ﷺ said, 'You shall not enter Paradise until you believe, and you have not believed until you love one another. Shall I tell you of something you can do to make you love one another? Spread *Salām* (the greeting of peace) amongst yourselves.'[589] Reciprocated love from one Muslim to another is fundamental; the bonds of Islam tie us together and make billions of us as one man. Thus, if a brother is in need, he should be helped, be it through physical or financial means, or simply through prayer. The First Caliph, Abū Bakr al-Ṣiddīq ؓ said, 'The supplication of a brother in Allah ﷻ is answered.'[590]

Umm al-Dardā' ؓ said, 'Abū al-Dardā' stood up in the night to pray. He was weeping and said, "O Allah, You made my physical form good, so make my character good!" until morning. I said, "Abū al-Dardā', your only supplication for the entire night was for good character!" He replied, "Umm al-Dardā', a Muslim perfects his character until good character enters him into Paradise; and taints his character until his bad character enters him into Hellfire. A Muslim can be forgiven while he is asleep." I asked, "Abū al-Dardā', how can he be forgiven while he is asleep?" He said, "His brother arises in the night, performs the night prayer, and supplicates to Allah ﷻ and is answered. He supplicates for his Muslim brother and his supplication is answered."'[591]

The Prophet ﷺ said, 'If I were to take a friend I would have

---

588 *Qur'an* 19:96.
589 *Ṣaḥīḥ Muslim* 54a.
590 *Al-Adab al-Mufrad* 624.
591 *Al-Adab al-Mufrad* 290.

taken him (Abū Bakr) as a friend, but the Islamic brotherhood is better.'[592] The friendship of the noble Prophet ﷺ and Abū Bakr ؓ is legendary. Yet, it is important to note that the Prophet ﷺ did not use the term friendship to describe their link, but rather the phrase 'Islamic brotherhood'. Upon the Prophet's arrival in Medina, he created bonds of brotherhood between the Muhājirūn ؓ, who had emigrated to Medina with nothing, and the Anṣār ؓ, who were the indigenous populace of Medina. This brotherhood, as mentioned earlier, created ties of kinship between both parties that were stronger than even blood relations. Anas ؓ said, 'The Prophet ﷺ formed a pact of brotherhood between Ibn Masʿūd and al-Zubayr.'[593] Another report of a similar nature states: 'ʿAbd al-Raḥmān ibn ʿAwf came to us and the Messenger of Allah ﷺ established a bond of brotherhood between him and Saʿd ibn Rabīʿah.'[594]

Ibn ʿUmar ؓ narrated that when the Messenger of Allah ﷺ established the bonds of brotherhood among his Companions ؓ, ʿAlī approached him with tears in his eyes, saying, 'O Messenger of Allah, you have made bonds of brotherhood among your Companions, but you have not made a bond of brotherhood for me with anyone.' The Messenger of Allah ﷺ said to him, 'I am your brother both in this life and the next.'[595]

Those men that fight for you, bleed for you, go through hardship with you, and are ready to give their very lives for you are as much your brothers as your own flesh and blood. This

---

592 *Ṣaḥīḥ al-Bukhārī* 3657.
593 *Al-Adab al-Mufrad* 568.
594 *Ṣaḥīḥ al-Bukhārī* 2293
595 *Jāmiʿ al-Tirmidhī* 3720.

point has been eloquently expressed in the Bard's words:

We few, we happy few, we band of brothers;

For he to-day that sheds his blood with me

Shall be my brother; be he ne'er so vile,

This day shall gentle his condition.[596]

LOYALTY AND DISAVOWAL

This leads us on to the concepts of *al-walā'* (loyalty) and *al-barā'* (disavowal). Essentially, these two concepts prescribe demonstrating loyalty to the *ummah* and the teachings of Islam, as well as disavowing the actions of all those who persecute the *ummah* or oppose orthodox Islamic teachings. Oftentimes, they are misconstrued as entailing a type of blind loyalty to all Muslims, whether they are in the right or the wrong, but this is far from the truth. A Muslim that propagates teachings that are against those of Islam should be opposed. The Prophet ﷺ said, 'Help your brother, whether he is the oppressor or the oppressed.' It was said, 'O Messenger of Allah, we can understand helping the one being oppressed, but how can we help an oppressor?' The Prophet ﷺ said, 'By seizing his hand.'[597]

The Companions ﷺ could not conceive the notion of helping someone who was oppressing another, and this is why they sought clarification from the Prophet ﷺ. When one's brother is suffering at the hands of another person, it is the duty of a Muslim to oppose the oppressor and stand against him. When one's brother is the oppressor, it is the duty of a Muslim to seize his hand and stop him from what he is doing. Likewise, if one's brother is performing an immoral act, he should correct

---

596 *Henry V*, William Shakespeare.

597 *Ṣaḥīḥ al-Bukhārī* 2312.

him. Abū Hurayrah ﷺ said, 'A believer is the mirror of his brother. When he sees a fault in him, he should correct it.'[598] The Prophet ﷺ said, 'Whosoever of you sees an evil, let him change it with his hand; and if he is not able to do so, then with his tongue; and if he is not able to do so, then with his heart - and that is the weakest of faith.'[599]

Our allegiances and loyalties are more often than not fragmented along tribal or cultural lines. The white man will stand with his fellow white men, the black man with his fellow black men; and the Indian Muslims and Pakistani Muslims will argue and fight over a cricket match. Racism, nationalism, and xenophobia are not sound reasons for expressing allegiance to one party or disavowal of another. The Prophet ﷺ said, 'The one who calls toward tribalism is not of us. The one who fights for the sake of tribalism is not of us. The one who dies following the way of tribalism is not of us.'[600] He ﷺ also said openly, 'Indeed, the relatives of my father are not my allies. Indeed, only Allah ﷻ and the righteous believers are my allies. Yet, they have the bonds of kinship and I will uphold their family ties.'[601]

The Prophet ﷺ famously made this unifying concept clear when he addressed the people by saying, 'O people, indeed your Lord is One and your father is one. Indeed, there is no superiority of an Arab over a non-Arab, or of a non-Arab over an Arab; or of a red man over a black man, or of a black man over a red man, except in terms of *taqwā*. Have I conveyed the message?' They (the people) said, 'The Messenger of Allah

[598] *Al-Adab al-Mufrad* 238.
[599] *Ṣaḥīḥ Muslim* 49a.
[600] *Sunan Abī Dāwūd* 5102.
[601] *Ṣaḥīḥ al-Bukhārī* 5644.

ﷺ has conveyed the message.'[602]

Only piety and virtuous acts can make someone better than his peers in humanity. The Prophet ﷺ said, 'O people, indeed Allah ﷻ has taken away from you the arrogance of *jāhiliyyah*[603] and its expression of pride in one's forefathers. People are of two types: the righteous and pious who are dear to Allah ﷻ, and the doomed evildoers who are insignificant before Allah ﷻ. All people are the descendants of Adam, and Allah ﷻ created Adam from dust.'[604]

إِنَّمَا ٱلْمُؤْمِنُونَ إِخْوَةٌ فَأَصْلِحُوا۟ بَيْنَ أَخَوَيْكُمْ ۚ وَٱتَّقُوا۟ ٱللَّهَ لَعَلَّكُمْ تُرْحَمُونَ.

All believers are but brothers, so seek reconciliation between your two brothers, and fear Allah, so that you may be blessed with mercy.[605]

The Prophet ﷺ said, 'If anyone removes his brother's anxiety in this world, Allah ﷻ will remove for him one of the anxieties found on the Day of Resurrection; if anyone gives ease to an impoverished man, Allah ﷻ will provide ease for him in this world and on the Day of Resurrection; if anyone conceals a Muslim's secrets, Allah ﷻ will conceal his secrets in this world and on the Day of Resurrection; Allah ﷻ will provide aid to a servant so long as the servant gives aid to his brother.'[606]

Abū Mūsā ؓ related the following tradition: 'The Prophet ﷺ said, "A faithful believer to a faithful believer is like the bricks of a wall, with every one of them enforcing the other." While

---

[602] *Musnad al-Imam Aḥmad* 22978.
[603] The Days of Ignorance, a term used to refer to pre-Islamic Arabia and its society.
[604] *Jāmiʿ al-Tirmidhī* 3270.
[605] *Qur'an* 49:10.
[606] *Sunan Abī Dāwūd* 4946.

stating this the Prophet ﷺ clasped his hands by interlacing his fingers.'[607]

The brotherhood of Islam is such: every one of us is a source of reliance for the other, and our bounds are made stronger if our cooperative ties increase. A lone brick can be tossed aside and ignored; but a wall, cemented by our shared *īmān,* cannot be so easily cast aside or mistreated. As Muslims, we cannot fight our brothers for unjust causes, nor can we abuse one another physically, verbally, or financially. The Messenger of Allah ﷺ said, 'A Muslim fighting his brother is disbelief, and verbally abusing him is disobedience.'[608] He ﷺ also counselled his nation by stating: 'Neither nurse mutual hatred, nor jealousy, nor enmity; become as fellow brothers and servants of Allah ﷻ. It is not lawful for a Muslim to continuously break his relations with his brother beyond three days.'[609] He ﷺ also said, 'A believer is the brother of a believer, so it is not lawful for a believer to outbid his brother, and he should not propose an engagement when his brother has thus proposed until he gives it up.'[610]

A man is loyal to his brothers to the last breath and the last drop of blood, loves them for the sake of Allah ﷻ, helps them in their times of need, and remains faithful and true. He also disavows those that stand against the commandments of Allah ﷻ and opposes them, be they Muslim or otherwise.

[607] *Ṣaḥīḥ al-Bukhārī* 481.
[608] *Jāmiʿ al-Tirmidhī* 2634.
[609] *Ṣaḥīḥ Muslim* 2558b.
[610] *Ṣaḥīḥ Muslim* 1414.

26

He is a Leader

عَنْ أَبِي سَعِيدٍ الْخُدْرِيِّ رَضِيَ اللَّهُ عَنْهُ، أَنَّ رَسُولَ اللَّهِ صَلَّى اللَّهُ عَلَيْهِ وَسَلَّم قَالَ: "إِذَا
خَرَجَ ثَلَاثَةٌ فِي سَفَرٍ فَلْيُؤَمِّرُوا أَحَدَهُمْ."

Abū Saʿīd al-Khudrī 🌸 *narrated that the Prophet* 🌸 *said, 'When three men leave on a journey, they should appoint one among them as their leader.*[611]

LEADERSHIP AND LEADING BY EXAMPLE

Leadership (*qiyādah*) is a quality which every man must utilise at some point in his life. The Prophet 🌸 said, 'Every one of you is a shepherd and is responsible for his flock. The leader of the people is a guardian and is responsible for his subjects. A man is the guardian of his family and he is responsible for them. A woman is the guardian of her husband's home and his children, and she is responsible for them. The servant of a man is a guardian of his property and is responsible for it. Undoubtedly, every one of you is a shepherd and is responsible for his flock.'[612]

The qualities of good leadership are carefully enumerated in this book, for the best of leaders is the best of men, and the Prophet 🌸 was the best of us all.

لَّقَدْ كَانَ لَكُمْ فِى رَسُولِ ٱللَّهِ أُسْوَةٌ حَسَنَةٌ لِّمَن كَانَ يَرْجُواْ ٱللَّهَ وَٱلْيَوْمَ ٱلْءَاخِرَ وَذَكَرَ ٱللَّهَ
كَثِيرًا.

Indeed, in the Messenger of Allah you have an excellent example for whoever has hope in Allah and the Last Day, and

---

[611] *Sunan Abī Dāwūd* 2608.
[612] *Ṣaḥīḥ al-Bukhārī* 7138; *Ṣaḥīḥ Muslim* 1829.

remembers Allah often.[613]

A leader exemplifies all of the expected, required, and admired qualities of his followers. He is the best example of everything they hold in high esteem. He is the epitome of humane qualities, such as kindness, humanity, compassion, and humility; he is the yardstick by which his followers are measured. He exhibits enthusiasm, integrity, firmness, fairness, and resilience. He embodies all the qualities of *murū'ah* (masculine behaviour), such as bravery, generosity, honour, and practical wisdom, with the latter quality being forged through personal aptitude, experience, practice, and reflection. He is competent and benevolent.

The Prophet ﷺ said, 'The office of a Chief is necessary, for people must have superiors. Yet, the Chiefs are in the Fire.'[614] This Hadith is a warning against being an unjust leader and falling into the temptation of committing injustice when one is in a position of power. Being 'in the Fire' is a term used to explain in no uncertain terms that this is their starting position: a leader must work to keep himself out of the Fire, and can never become lax or complacent in such matters. That being said, he ﷺ also stressed that the role was necessary. Anarchy has no place in Islam, for Islam is guidance through and through. Jābir ibn ʿAbdullāh ﷺ reported: 'The Messenger of Allah ﷺ sent an expedition to the lands of the tribe of Juhaynah, and appointed a person as a Chief over them.'[615] There are many such Hadiths that are reported in this regard, with all of them pointing to the same conclusion: a leader was always appointed, though it came with grave responsibility.

---

[613] *Qur'an* 33:21.
[614] *Sunan Abī Dāwūd* 2934.
[615] *Ṣaḥīḥ Muslim* 1935g.

Indeed, delegation is an essential part of leadership, and the Prophet ﷺ would often delegate people to take command of tasks, be they expeditions, the teaching of others, or collection of charity. Anas ؓ said: 'Qays ibn Saʿd was to the Prophet ﷺ like a Chief of Police is to a leader.'[616] The Prophet ﷺ said, 'Indeed the most beloved to Allah ﷻ from amongst the people on the Day of Judgement, and the nearest to Him, is the just leader; and the most hated of people to Allah ﷻ, and the furthest from Him, is the oppressive leader.'[617]

A leader must accomplish three goals to be deemed a competent head: he must successfully achieve the tasks he sets out on, he must create and maintain his group's unity and coherence, and he must care for each individual in the group. People follow leaders because they have confidence in them as individuals, in their ability to lead, in their knowledge and wisdom, and in the fact that they matter to the authorities. A good leader is thus a just leader, as he has a real interest in the welfare of his followers, and does not feign interest to exploit them for personal gain.

Reciprocity is an essential component of human interaction, and a leader can only expect to gain from his followers what he offers them himself. The incapable leader will not be followed; the divisive leader will lose half his manpower; the immoral leader is despised; the uncaring leader will not be cared for. The Prophet ﷺ said, 'The leader of a people is their servant.'[618] When the Prophet ﷺ appointed ʿUthmān ibn Abī al-ʿĀṣ ؓ as the Imam of his people, he ﷺ told him, 'You are their Imam, but only execute that which the weakest of them is capable of,

---

[616] *Ṣaḥīḥ al-Bukhārī* 7155.
[617] *Jāmiʿ al-Tirmidhī* 1329.
[618] *Arbaʿīn Shāh Walī Allāh* 34.

and employ a *mu'adhdhin* who does not accept any payments for his *adhān*.'[619]

The Prophet ﷺ exemplified the qualities he instilled in others, and through this they were filled with love and awe for him ﷺ. Despite this, he ﷺ remained humble and made every man feel welcome and cared for. Abū Masʿūd ؓ said, 'A man came to the Prophet ﷺ and his voice trembled out of awe as he spoke to him. The Prophet ﷺ said to him, "Be calm, for I am not a king. I am only the son of a woman who ate dried meat."'[620]

A man has authority over others in three distinct ways: through his position, his knowledge, and his moral conduct. The last of these qualities – namely moral authority – is the hardest to come by in the modern age. The leader of a people is not merely the leader of their practical or political affairs, but also their moral example. Men of poor morals were historically never *chosen* as leaders, and only ever came into power through accession, revolution, or by the force of arms. The leaders of today seem to exemplify the worst qualities of mankind; they are adulterers, xenophobes, cheats, misers, free of compassion and humility, while also being devoid of integrity, honour and decency. How can they be anything but, when we find ourselves in the same condition? As the saying goes:

As you are, so will be the men that rule you.[621]

Likewise, the moral corruption of a leader will result in the moral corruption of his followers; the connection is bicausal, as the relationship between the leader and those being led is symbiotic. We have arrived where we are today, in part, due to

---

[619] *Sunan Abī Dāwūd* 531.
[620] *Sunan Ibn Mājah* 3312.
[621] An Arab proverb.

our own moral bankruptcy, which led to the election of those who were equally bankrupt. When they were conferred unlimited political powers, they could not do anything but sow further corruption and give in to their every whim and desire. And when the people saw them doing so, they said, 'Why should we restrain ourselves, when our moral leaders do no such thing?' Accordingly, the cycle has continued, with each generation more depraved than the last, and each successive leader less fit to rule. The people of the Maghreb often say:

When the shepherd is corrupt, so is his flock.[622]

The shepherd is to his flock what the leader is to his group. The three goals of leadership are wholly encompassed in this function. He has a goal to successfully achieve in ensuring they are protected, fed, and returned; he must keep the group together at all costs, lest they fall victim to a wolf or hazard; and he cares for every one of them individually. The good shepherd fulfils all three goals, and the poor shepherd falls short in every one of them. This is why Allah ﷻ ensured that every Prophet He sent first learned to lead as a shepherd. The Prophet ﷺ said, 'Allah ﷻ did not send any Prophet who did not shepherd sheep.' His Companions ﷺ asked him, 'Did you do the same?' The Prophet ﷺ replied, 'Yes, I used to shepherd the sheep of the people of Mecca for some *qīrāṭs*.'[623][624]

The best leaders provide guidance by example and lead from the front, just as the Prophet ﷺ himself always did. The shepherd does the same. Even when the shepherd is at the rear of his herd, he remains their leader by guiding them and protecting them as their spiritual head. When wolves attack, he

---

[622] A Moorish proverb.
[623] A form of currency which was less than a dirham.
[624] *Ṣaḥīḥ al-Bukhārī* 2262.

is the first entity they will meet; when the safety of home beckons, he is the last to enter.

Jābir ﷺ narrates:

> *We were digging the trench on the day of al-Khandaq (the Trench) and we came across a large, solid rock. We went to the Prophet ﷺ and said, 'There is a rock blocking the trench.' He ﷺ said, 'I am coming down.' As he stood up, I noticed a stone was tied to his stomach*[625] *as we had not eaten anything for three days. So the Prophet ﷺ took up a spade and struck the boulder, and it became like sand...*[626]

Authority and Assertiveness

Men who make the best leaders have a presence or aura that exudes authority. A leader inspires awe in his followers and those that come into his presence, and fear and dread in those who seek to oppose them. For some individuals, this property is attained naturally, as was the case with the Prophet ﷺ, but for most it is something that must be developed. This aura is a by-product of all the leadership qualities listed above: a person's nobility of character, his ability as a leader, and his prowess in the fields of conflict and diplomacy. Some men build for themselves a facade of this authoritative presence, but it leaves them the moment the trappings of rule are taken away from them. Men of true authority are kingly in their character, even when dressed in rags.

---

[625] This was a tactic used to curb the pangs of extreme hunger. Every man among the Companions ﷺ was doing the same. In another narration, it is said that the Prophet ﷺ had two stones tied to his stomach, for he ﷺ had eaten less than his followers.

[626] *Ṣaḥīḥ al-Bukhārī* 4101.

Qaylah bint Makhramah 🙵 once saw the Prophet 🙵 sitting with his arms around his legs. She said, 'When I saw the Messenger of Allah 🙵 seated in such a humble condition, I trembled with awe.'[627] Abū Mas'ūd 🙵 said, 'A man came to the Prophet 🙵 and his voice trembled out of awe as he spoke to him. The Prophet 🙵 said to him, "Be calm, for I am not a king. I am only the son of a woman who ate dried meat."'[628] The Prophet 🙵 himself said, 'I have been supported against the enemy by dread, and have been given concise, meaningful words. While I was sleeping, the keys of the treasures of the Earth were brought to me and placed in my hand.'[629]

Oftentimes, assertiveness is valued in the leadership of others. More often, it is misconstrued as being aggressive in one's actions and speech, or dominating others by overbearing will. This is not the case, and in reality such behaviour only displays a weakness of character. An assertive man should be able to express his thoughts confidently and considerately, and stand up for what he believes to be correct, regardless of the number or stature of his opposition. He does not meekly accept what is wrong out of fear or awe, but instead puts forth his view and commands attention.

Ibn 'Abbās 🙵 narrated, 'I was behind the Prophet 🙵 one day, when he 🙵 said, "Dear boy, I will teach you a statement: Be mindful of Allah 🙵 and He will protect you. Be mindful of Allah 🙵 and you will find Him. When you ask, ask Allah 🙵, and when you seek aid, seek Allah's aid. Know that if the entire creation were to gather together to do something to benefit you, you

---

[627] *Sunan Abī Dāwūd* 4847.
[628] *Sunan Ibn Mājah* 3312.
[629] *Ṣaḥīḥ al-Bukhārī* 2977; *Ṣaḥīḥ Muslim* 523.

would never get any benefit except that which Allah ﷻ had written for you. And if they were to gather together to harm you, you would never be harmed except if Allah ﷻ had written it for you. The pens have been lifted and the pages are dried.'"[630] The Prophet ﷺ also said, 'The best jihad is [to speak] a word of justice to a tyrant.'[631]

This is how a leader should be. The assertive leader knows that there is nothing to fear in this world, as nothing happens outside of the Will of Allah ﷻ. Consequently, no man or army can do anything through their own will or initiative. The assertive leader remains true to himself and to his cause; he ensures that all actors who interact with him, be they his opposition, subordinates, or anyone else, faithfully receive from him his exact views, without any need of diluting them to make them more palatable.

THE BURDEN OF RESPONSIBILITY AND BEING CALM UNDER PRESSURE

A virtuous leader assumes responsibility for his actions and bears the risk that is attached to the decisions he undertakes. Leadership is a burdensome endeavour, and those that do not feel the weight of leadership will feel its burden soon on the Day of Judgement, when all our decisions–great or small–will be weighed and all our deeds are reckoned accordingly. As the Prophet ﷺ said, 'Whoever takes the responsibility of a judge, or is appointed as a judge between the people, he has been slaughtered without a knife.'[632]

---

[630] *Jāmiʿ al-Tirmidhī* 2516.
[631] *Sunan Abī Dāwūd* 4344.
[632] *Jāmiʿ al-Tirmidhī* 1325.

Al-Miqdām ibn Maʿdīkarib ⸙ narrated that the Messenger of Allah ⸙ struck him on his shoulders and said, 'You will attain success, Qudaym, if you die without having been a ruler, secretary, or Chief.'[633]

The story of the Sword of Damocles is an anecdote that has survived for thousands of years, due to the lessons it imparts concerning the burden of leadership. Damocles sought to curry favour with his king, Dionysius, by praising the life of ease he was living. In response, the king offered to switch places with him for a day, and Damocles eagerly agreed. He was placed on the throne and surrounded by every luxury imaginable. But then a sword was placed above his head, hung from the pommel by a single horse hair. This measure was undertaken to signify the danger, constant stress, and apprehension that a leader always faces. Suffice it to say that Damocles did not enjoy the food, gold, entertainment, concubines, and status that he had previously lusted after.

William Shakespeare succinctly captured the weight of responsibility when he compared the slumber of a cabin boy at sea on a stormy night with the insomnia suffered by a king on the eve of war:

> And in the visitation of the winds,
>
> Who take the ruffian billows by the top,
>
> Curling their monstrous heads and hanging them
>
> With deafening clamour in the slippery clouds,
>
> That, with the hurly, death itself awakes?
>
> Canst thou, O partial sleep, give thy repose

---

[633] *Sunan Abī Dāwūd* 2933.

To the wet sea-boy in an hour so rude,

And in the calmest and most stillest night,

With all appliances and means to boot,

Deny it to a king? Then happy low, lie down!

Uneasy lies the head that wears a crown.[634]

ʿAbdullāh ibn al-Mubārak ﵀ advised, 'If you are afflicted with the responsibility of judgeship, you must follow the Hadith!'[635] Following the standards of the prophetic leadership model is indeed the only correct way of taking command or choosing a leader. The Prophet ﷺ said, 'You will find that the best people are those who hate the responsibility of ruling most of all, until they are chosen to be the rulers. People are of different natures: The best in the pre-Islamic period are the best in Islam.'[636]

Ibn ʿUmar ﵄ astutely observed: 'When the Messenger of Allah ﷺ would dispatch troops, he would say to their commander, "I leave to Allah's keeping your religious commitments, your responsibility, and the end of your deeds."'[637]

A leader is responsible for his own actions and decisions, as well as those in his care. A man that is put in charge of any level of decision-making, be it in a small group, at an organisational level, or at the strategic level, must be aware of the power he wields over those affected by his decisions, and ultimately appreciate the weightiness of his role. The predicament can be summed up by the powerful dictum:

---

[634] *King Richard IV*, William Shakespeare.

[635] *Al-Shamaʾil al-Muḥammadiyyah* 416.

[636] *Ṣaḥīḥ al-Bukhārī* 3587, 3588, 3589.

[637] *Sunan Ibn Mājah* 2826.

With great power comes great responsibility.[638]

A leader is also able to remain steadfast and strong, despite the burden of responsibility and the threats to his leadership and his people from outside or from within. He is calm under pressure, and even thrives in it; he does not baulk at the challenges he faces, but meets them head on.

لَّقَدْ كَانَ لَكُمْ فِى رَسُولِ ٱللَّهِ أُسْوَةٌ حَسَنَةٌ لِّمَن كَانَ يَرْجُوا۟ ٱللَّهَ وَٱلْيَوْمَ ٱلْـَٔاخِرَ وَذَكَرَ ٱللَّهَ كَثِيرًا.

Indeed, in the Messenger of Allah you have an excellent example for whoever has hope in Allah and the Last Day, and remembers Allah often.[639]

The above verse was revealed in relation to the Battle of the Trench, in which the Muslim force of less than 3000 men had to face the Confederate army of 10,000, which had come to Medina to wipe them out once and for all. Allah ﷻ commanded the Companions ﵃ to take the Prophet ﷺ as an example with regard to his patience, sense of duty, striving through hardship, and anticipation of victory from Allah ﷻ.[640]

At times of great stress, the Prophet ﷺ advised us to recite the following:

حَسْبُنَا اللَّهُ وَنِعْمَ الْوَكِيلُ عَلَى اللَّهِ تَوَكَّلْنَا

Allah is sufficient for us and what a good protector He is! And upon Allah we rely.[641]

It is this trust and belief in Allah ﷻ that makes a Muslim ready and able to hand any tribulation, and to remain steadfast

---

[638] This famous axiom concerning the burden of power was coined by Stan Lee.
[639] *Qur'an* 33:21.
[640] *Tafsīr Ibn Kathīr* 33:21.
[641] *Jāmi' al-Tirmidhī* 2431.

under the greatest pressure.

Following Orders, Taking Advice, and Accepting Criticism

It is a fact of life that every man cannot be a leader in every situation. Too often in modernist articulations of manhood, there is a temptation to teach young men that manhood requires them to fight for rights of leadership by dominating others. This model cannot stand up to even the slightest bit of scrutiny, for if all men were to follow this principle there would be no order. Anarchy would be king and all men his subjects.

A man's spirit is indomitable and he should not give this up for any living thing. At the same time, however, he must also acknowledge that leadership is required to maintain order and when he is presented with someone better suited to lead, he should accept their governance. The five daily *ṣalāhs* are prayed by men in congregation, and the Imam (lit. leader*)*, selected due to his being best placed to fill the role, leads them in prayer. As thus, we practise this act of electing or accepting leadership and following orders on a daily basis via our *ṣalāh*. By extension, society can only function when this is extrapolated to life as a whole. In an important report, Tamīm al-Dārī ﷺ narrated: 'The Prophet ﷺ said, "The fundamental basis of religion is sincerity." We said, "To whom?" He ﷺ said, "To Allah, to His Book, to His Messenger, and to the leaders of the Muslims and their masses."'[642]

He ﷺ also said, 'We are the last but will be the foremost [to enter Paradise]. He who obeys me, obeys Allah, and he who disobeys me, disobeys Allah. He who obeys the Chief, obeys me,

[642] *Ṣaḥīḥ Muslim* 55a.

and he who disobeys the Chief, disobeys me. The leader is like a shelter for whose safety the Muslims should fight and where they should seek protection. If the leader orders people with righteousness and rules justly, then he will be rewarded for that, and if he does the opposite, he will be responsible for it.'[643]

However, blindly following someone is not what Islam promotes. A man must only follow lawful orders, and they must be consistent with the moral code of Islam. To do otherwise is folly, and to commit unlawful or immoral acts on the orders of others makes one just as culpable as the man giving the orders. The man that attempts to use 'I was just following orders' as an excuse for immoral actions will not get a free pass. The Prophet ﷺ said, 'Listening to and obeying the leader is an obligation upon a Muslim, whether he likes it or dislikes it, as long as he is not commanded to disobey Allah ﷻ. If he is commanded to disobey, then there is no listening or obedience.'[644]

يَـٰٓأَيُّهَا ٱلَّذِينَ ءَامَنُوٓا۟ أَطِيعُوا۟ ٱللَّهَ وَأَطِيعُوا۟ ٱلرَّسُولَ وَأُو۟لِى ٱلْأَمْرِ مِنكُمْ ۖ فَإِن تَنَـٰزَعْتُمْ فِى شَىْءٍ فَرُدُّوهُ إِلَى ٱللَّهِ وَٱلرَّسُولِ إِن كُنتُمْ تُؤْمِنُونَ بِٱللَّهِ وَٱلْيَوْمِ ٱلْـَٔاخِرِ ۚ ذَٰلِكَ خَيْرٌ وَأَحْسَنُ تَأْوِيلًا.

O believers! Obey Allah and obey the Messenger and those in authority among you. Should you disagree on anything, then refer it to Allah and His Messenger, if you believe in Allah and the Last Day. This is the best and fairest resolution.[645]

This verse was revealed in relation to ʿAbdullāh ibn Ḥudhāfah ibn Qays ibn ʿAdī ؓ,[646] immediately after he issued an unlawful order to the Companions ؓ. In this regard, Amīr al-Mu'minīn ʿAlī ؓ narrates: 'The Prophet ﷺ sent a unit [on a

---

[643] *Ṣaḥīḥ al-Bukhārī* 2956, 2957.
[644] *Ṣaḥīḥ al-Bukhārī* 2796.
[645] *Qur'an* 4:59.
[646] *Tafsīr Ibn Kathīr* 4:59.

military campaign] and appointed a man from the Anṣār as its commander, thereby ordering others to obey him. During the campaign he became angry with some of them and said, "Did the Prophet ﷺ not order you to obey me?" They said, "Yes." He said, "I order you to collect wood, make a fire, and then throw yourselves into it." So they collected wood and made the fire, but when they were about to enter the flames they looked at each other and some of them said, "We follow the Prophet ﷺ to escape from the Fire. How should we enter it now?" While they were in that state, the fire extinguished, and their commander's anger abated. The event was mentioned to the Prophet ﷺ, and he said, "If they had entered it (the fire), they would never have come out of it, for obedience is required only in what is good."[647]

The Companions ﷺ were such staunch followers of the Prophet ﷺ that they followed the orders of the man they were told to obey by him ﷺ without question up to the death. But because they were also intelligent men of the most morally upright character, they recognised the unlawful order and thus refused to follow it.

Equally, a leader should be able to accept constructive criticism and sincere advice, and even correct his decision-making model or strategies if—upon reflection—he deems himself to be in the wrong. Muhammad ibn Jubayr ibn Muṭʿim ﷺ narrated that his father ﷺ said:

> *The Messenger of Allah ﷺ stood up in Khayf - which is situated in Mina - and said, 'May Allah make the face shine of the man who hears my words and conveys them. It may be that the bearer of knowledge does not*

---

[647] *Ṣaḥīḥ al-Bukhārī* 7145.

> *understand it, but it is he who takes it to one who will understand it more than he does. There are three things which the heart of the believer does not betray: sincerity of action for the sake of Allah, offering sincere advice to the rulers of the Muslims, and adhering to the jamāʿah.*[648] *Their supplications are answered.'*[649]

Abū Saʿīd al-Khudrī ﷺ narrated that the Prophet ﷺ said, 'Allah ﷻ never sends a Prophet or appoints a Caliph except that they have two groups of advisors: a group advising and exhorting him to do good, and a group advising and exhorting him to do evil. But the protected person is the one protected by Allah ﷻ.'[650]

Ibn ʿAbbās ﷺ narrates:

> *ʿUyaynah ibn Ḥiṣn ibn Ḥudhayfah came to stay with his nephew al-Ḥurr ibn Qays, who was one of those whom ʿUmar used to keep near him; the qurrā*[651] *were present in ʿUmar's meetings and were his advisors, whether they were old or young.*[652] *ʿUyaynah said to his nephew, 'O nephew, you have access to this Chief, so obtain permission for me to see him.' Al-Ḥurr said, 'I will obtain permission for you to see him.' So al-Ḥurr sought permission for ʿUyaynah and ʿUmar admitted him. When ʿUyaynah entered his court, he said, 'Beware, O son of al-Khaṭṭāb! By Allah, you neither give us sufficient provision, nor judge among us with justice!' ʿUmar was so furious that he intended to harm him, but al-Ḥurr said,*

---

[648] The main body of Muslims, or the consensus of the Muslim *ummah*.

[649] *Sunan Ibn Mājah* 3056.

[650] *Ṣaḥīḥ al-Bukhārī* 7198.

[651] The learned scholarly class who had memorised the Qur'an and understood it.

[652] Ibn ʿAbbās ﷺ himself had a place of honour within the court of Amīr al-Mu'minīn ʿUmar ﷺ whilst still an adolescent.

'O Chief of the Believers, Allah said to His Prophet ﷺ:

خُذِ ٱلْعَفْوَ وَأْمُرْ بِٱلْعُرْفِ وَأَعْرِضْ عَنِ ٱلْجَـٰهِلِينَ

Be gracious, enjoin what is right, and turn away from those who act ignorantly.[653]

And this man is one of the foolish.' By Allah, 'Umar did not overlook that verse when al-Ḥurr recited it before him; he observed [the orders of] Allah's Book exactingly.[654]

In short, a leader must be able to take advice, assess its merits, and apply it within its context. Similarly, a follower must follow lawful and moral orders, and ignore commands when they are illegal or immoral.

653 *Qur'an* 7:199.
654 *Ṣaḥīḥ al-Bukhārī* 4642.

27
He is a Problem-Solver

عَنْ أَبِي مُوسَى رَضِيَ اللَّهُ عَنْهُ، قَالَ: كَانَ رَسُولُ اللهِ صَلَّى اللَّهُ عَلَيْهِ وَسَلَّمَ، إِذَا بَعَثَ أَحَدًا مِنْ أَصْحَابِهِ فِي بَعْضِ أَمْرِهِ، قَالَ: "بَشِّرُوا وَلاَ تُنَفِّرُوا، وَيَسِّرُوا وَلاَ تُعَسِّرُوا."

Abū Mūsā ﷺ reported that whenever the Messenger of Allah ﷺ would send one of his Companions on a mission, he would say, 'Gladden people and do not scare them; make things easy and do not make them difficult.'[655]

RECONCILIATION, NEGOTIATION, AND MEDIATION

One of the inherent qualities of a man is that he is a problem solver. He cannot be presented with an issue and not try to resolve it. If there is an issue, he will try to find the solution; if there is a dispute, he will try to settle it. This again is part of our *fiṭrah*, and Islam embraces it once more. The Prophet ﷺ said, 'If anyone removes his brother's anxiety of this world, Allah ﷻ will remove for him one of the anxieties of the Day of Resurrection.'[656]

As a leader, a man will regularly have to deal with disputes between followers, or pockets of dissent. In these situations, a man's ability to resolve the conflict will make or break his position as a respected leader. In such contexts, the skills of reconciliation, negotiation, and mediation are invaluable. This is because that which can be accomplished through goodwill, compromise, and diplomacy cannot be attained through the

[655] *Sunan Abī Dāwūd* 4835.
[656] *Sunan Abī Dāwūd* 4946.

strength of arms and violence.

The Prophet ﷺ ordered all the individuals he deployed on missions to solve people's worries, and not to add to them. Creating problems is an act of Shayṭān, and thus solving them is an angelic act that is worthy of reward. Sahl ibn Saʿd ؓ narrated that the Messenger of Allah ﷺ heard that there was a dispute among Banū ʿAmr ibn ʿAwf, so he went to them with some other people to reconcile between them.[657]

Abū al-Dardā' reported that the Messenger of Allah ﷺ said, 'Shall I not tell you regarding that which is more virtuous than voluntary fasting, prayer, and charity?' The Companions ؓ replied, 'Of course!' The Prophet ﷺ said, 'Reconciliation between people. Indeed, corrupted relations between people are the razor.'[658]

إِنَّمَا ٱلْمُؤْمِنُونَ إِخْوَةٌ فَأَصْلِحُوا۟ بَيْنَ أَخَوَيْكُمْ ۚ وَٱتَّقُوا۟ ٱللَّهَ لَعَلَّكُمْ تُرْحَمُونَ.

All believers are but brothers, therefore seek reconciliation between your two brothers, and fear Allah, so that you may be blessed with mercy.[659]

To make peace between Muslims is a divine injunction and therefore must be implemented whenever possible. When there are two parties of Muslims at odds with each other, a Muslim man should take it as his moral and religious duty to bring both sides to the negotiating table and make peace with them.

The Prophet ﷺ famously negotiated a peace treaty with the polytheists of Mecca during the ʿUmrah of al-Ḥudaybiyyah, choosing to compromise and use terminology that was agreed

---

[657] *Sunan al-Nasāʾī* 784.
[658] *Jāmiʿ al-Tirmidhī* 2509.
[659] *Qur'an* 49:10.

upon by all parties, rather than making a point of matters that would suit one side over another. Many of the terms of the treaty appeared on the surface to go against the Muslims, and yet were agreed upon for the sake of avoiding bloodshed and the farsighted vision of the noble Prophet ﷺ. Ibn ʿUmar ‎ narrated that the Messenger of Allah ﷺ set out with the intention of performing ʿUmrah, but the infidels of the Quraysh intervened between him and the Kaʿbah.

Consequently, the Prophet ﷺ slaughtered his sacrificial animals, shaved his head at al-Ḥudaybiyyah, and concluded a peace treaty with them (i.e., the infidels) on condition that he would perform the ʿUmrah the following year, that he would not carry arms against them except swords, and would not stay (in Mecca) beyond the duration they would allow. So the Prophet ﷺ performed the ʿUmrah in the following year and, in accordance with the peace treaty, entered Mecca. When he had stayed there for three days, the infidels told him to leave, and he left.[660] There are many narrations from multiple Companions that cover these events and the treaty itself, but for the sake of brevity we will not list them here.

Another great example of peace-making and negotiation was that which took place between Muʿāwiyah and al-Ḥasan ibn ʿAlī. Al-Ḥasan al-Baṣrī reported:

> *By Allah, al-Ḥasan ibn ʿAlī led battalions as large as mountains against Muʿāwiyah. ʿAmr ibn al-ʿĀṣ said to Muʿāwiyah, 'Surely, I see battalions which will not turn back before slaying their opponents.' Muʿāwiyah, who*

[660] *Ṣaḥīḥ al-Bukhārī* 4252.

was really the better of the two men,[661] *said, 'O 'Amr, if these men kill those and those men killed these, who will be left with me for the service of the public, who would be left with me [to look after] their women, and who would be left with me [to look after] their children?'* Then Mu'āwiyah sent two Qurayshī men from the tribe of 'Abd Shams, namely 'Abd al-Raḥmān ibn Samurah and 'Abdullāh ibn 'Āmir ibn Kurayz, to al-Ḥasan, with the orders, 'Go to this man (al-Ḥasan) and negotiate peace with him; talk to him and appeal to him.' Consequently, they went to al-Ḥasan and appealed to him to accept peace. Al-Ḥasan said, 'We, the offspring of 'Abd al-Muṭṭalib, have wealth, and some people have indulged in killing and corruption, and only money will appease them.' They said to al-Ḥasan, 'Mu'āwiyah offers you such and such, and appeals to you and entreats you to accept peace.' Al-Ḥasan said to them, 'But who will take responsibility for what you have said?' They said, 'We will be responsible for it.' So, whatever al-Ḥasan asked for in the negotiation they said, 'We will take responsibility for it for you.' So, al-Ḥasan accepted the peace treaty with Mu'āwiyah.*[662]

Al-Ḥasan al-Baṣrī 🌸 continued:

I heard Abū Bakrah saying, 'I saw the Messenger of Allah 🌼 on the pulpit and al-Ḥasan ibn 'Alī was by his side.

---

[661] This judgement was issued by al-Ḥasan al-Baṣrī 🌸 after he comparatively assessed the respective responses of Mu'āwiyah and 'Amr ibn al-'Āṣ 🌸. For while 'Amr ibn al-'Āṣ believed that an organised military counter-attack was needed against al-Ḥasan ibn 'Alī, Mu'āwiyah determined that a peaceful resolution could be reached without any need for further hostilities.

[662] *Ṣaḥīḥ al-Bukhārī* 2704.

> *The Prophet ﷺ would look once at the people and once at al-Ḥasan ibn ʿAlī, declaring, 'This son of mine is a sayyid[663] and may Allah make peace between two big groups of Muslims through him.'[664]*

Being the solution to a problem is always the right choice, and making peace between rival parties is always the best option. Such was the practice of the Prophet ﷺ and his Companions رضي الله عنهم.

[663] A nobleman, a term which became synonymous with the descendants of the Prophet ﷺ.

[664] *Ṣaḥīḥ al-Bukhārī* 2704.

28
He is Just and Merciful

عَنْ أَبِي هُرَيْرَةَ رضيَ الله عنه، قَالَ: قَالَ رَسُولُ اللهِ صَلَّى اللَّهُ عَلَيْهِ وَسَلَّمَ "لَمَّا قَضَى اللَّهُ الْخَلْقَ، كَتَبَ فِي كِتَابِهِ، فَهْوَ عِنْدَهُ فَوْقَ الْعَرْشِ 'إِنَّ رَحْمَتِي غَلَبَتْ غَضَبِي.'"

Abū Hurayrah ﵁ narrated that the Messenger of Allah ﷺ said, 'When Allah decreed the creation, He wrote in His Book which is with Him above the Throne, "My Mercy prevails over My Wrath."'[665]

FAIRNESS AND JUSTICE

A leader deals with those he supervises justly and fairly - he does not abuse his position to judge in favour of those he prefers, nor does he engage in nepotism or favouritism. As leaders, we cannot fall into such traps, as these are not the qualities of true men. The tyrant rules over others with injustice and fear, but the just ruler does so with love and compassion. The Prophet ﷺ reported that 'Allah the Exalted said, "O My servants, I have forbidden oppression for Myself and have made it forbidden among you, so do not oppress one another."'[666]

يَـٰٓأَيُّهَا ٱلَّذِينَ ءَامَنُوا۟ كُونُوا۟ قَوَّٰمِينَ لِلَّهِ شُهَدَآءَ بِٱلْقِسْطِ ۖ وَلَا يَجْرِمَنَّكُمْ شَنَـَٔانُ قَوْمٍ عَلَىٰٓ أَلَّا تَعْدِلُوا۟ ۚ ٱعْدِلُوا۟ هُوَ أَقْرَبُ لِلتَّقْوَىٰ ۖ وَٱتَّقُوا۟ ٱللَّهَ ۚ إِنَّ ٱللَّهَ خَبِيرٌۢ بِمَا تَعْمَلُونَ.

O you who believe, be steadfast for [obeying the commands of] Allah, [and] be witnesses for justice. Malice against a people should not prompt you to avoid doing justice. Do justice, for that is nearer to taqwā. Fear Allah. Surely, Allah is All-Aware of what you do.[667]

---

[665] *Ṣaḥīḥ al-Bukhārī* 3194.
[666] *Ṣaḥīḥ Muslim* 2577.
[667] *Qur'an* 5:8.

Justice is not a quality one reserves for his brothers and sisters, but instead it is a right of all. Allah ﷻ clarifies in this verse that disbelief does not disqualify a person from their right to justice.[668] There are two main reasons for committing injustice or oppression: to benefit oneself and those close to you, or to cause harm to those one dislikes or has enmity with.[669] A man's enmity or friendship with someone should not sway his judgement in a matter[670] – he must be just at all times. Amīr al-Mu'minīn ʿUmar ibn al-Khaṭṭāb ؓ was once presented with a dispute between a Muslim and a Jew, and he ruled in favour of the Jewish man.[671] Wāthilah ibn al-Asqaʿ ؓ asked the Prophet ﷺ, 'What is tribalism?' He ﷺ replied, 'That you should help your people in wrongdoing.'[672]

Likewise, our treatment of people should not be based on their treatment of us. A person who has been wronged should not use a turn of circumstances in their favour to seek retaliation or retribution. The Prophet ﷺ said, 'Do not be a people without a will of your own, saying, "If people treat us well, we will treat them well; and if they do wrong, we will do wrong," but accustom yourselves to undertaking good if people do good, and not behaving unjustly if they do evil.'[673]

The following incident will illustrate this concept far better than any written explanation that can be provided here. Jaʿfar ibn ʿAmr ibn Umayyah and ʿUbaydullāh ibn ʿAdī al-Khiyār ؓ asked Waḥshī ibn Ḥarb ؓ, about the incident where he had martyred – years before accepting Islam – the Prophet's uncle

---

[668] *Tafsīr al-Qurṭubī* 5:8.
[669] *Maʿārif al-Qur'an*, vol. 3: p. 84.
[670] *Tafsīr Ibn Kathīr* 5:8.
[671] *Muwaṭṭa' Imam Mālik* 1403.
[672] *Sunan Abī Dāwūd* 5119.
[673] *Jāmiʿ al-Tirmidhī* 2007.

Ḥamzah 🕮, the Lion of Allah, during the Battle of Uḥud. Waḥshī 🕮 replied:

> Yes, Ḥamzah killed Ṭuʿaymah ibn ʿAdī ibn al-Khiyār at Badr, so my master, Jubayr ibn Muṭʿim, said to me, 'If you kill Ḥamzah in revenge for my uncle, then you will be set free.' When the people set out for battle in the year of ʿAynayn – a mountain near the mountain of Uḥud, and between it and Uḥud there is a valley – I went out with the people for the encounter. When the army aligned for the fight, Sibāʿ came out and said, 'Is there any [Muslim] to accept my challenge to a duel?' Ḥamzah ibn ʿAbd al-Muṭṭalib came out and said, 'O Sibāʿ! O Ibn Umm Anmār, the one who circumcises other ladies! Do you challenge Allah and His Apostle?' Then Ḥamzah overcame him and he became like a bygone yesterday. I hid myself behind a rock, and when he came near me, I hurled my spear at him, driving it into his stomach so that it came out (of his back, killing him). When the people returned to Mecca, I returned with them. I stayed there until Islam spread within it and then I left for Ṭāʾif. When the people of Ṭāʾif sent their envoys to the Messenger of Allah 🕮, I was told that the Prophet 🕮 did not harm the envoys. Thus, I too went out with them until I reached the Messenger of Allah. When he saw me, he 🕮 said, 'Are you Waḥshī?' I said, 'Yes.' He 🕮 asked, 'Was it you who killed Ḥamzah?' I replied, 'What happened is what you have been told of.' He 🕮 said, 'Can you hide your face from me?' So I left. When the Messenger of

Allah ﷺ died, and Musaylamah al-Kadhdhāb[674] *appeared (claiming Prophethood), I said to myself, 'I will go out to Musaylamah and slay him to make amends for the killing of Ḥamzah. So I went out with the people [to fight] and the famous events of that battle took place. During the battle I sighted a man (Musaylamah) standing near a gap in a wall. He looked like an ash-coloured camel and his hair was dishevelled. I hurled my spear at him, driving it into his chest in between his breasts until it passed through his shoulders. And then an Anṣārī*[675] *attacked him and struck his head with a sword.'*[676]

At the Conquest of Mecca, when the Prophet ﷺ became the ruler over all the people who had tormented and slain his followers, he had the man that he had seen slay his uncle in his control. In such a situation, there is not a man reading this book nor writing it, who would not take revenge. In this situation, where revenge was but a word away, the Prophet ﷺ forgave Waḥshī ؓ, and the man would go on to slay the *dajjāl* of his time, Musaylamah the Liar. Waḥshī ؓ had accepted Islam, and though the Prophet ﷺ could not bear to look at the man for the pain it brought him, he ruled in favour of Waḥshī ؓ being spared, and even forgave him.

The Prophet ﷺ said, 'Whoever seeks the office of judge among the Muslims, achieves this position, and then causes his justice to prevail over his tyranny, he will go to Paradise. But the

---

674 Literally, 'Musaylamah the Liar', a man who falsely claimed Prophethood after the Prophet ﷺ passed away.

675 This was Abū Dujānah ؓ, a famed warrior amongst the Companions ؓ, of whom we will hear more about in a later section.

676 *Ṣaḥīḥ al-Bukhārī* 4072.

man whose tyranny prevails over his justice will go to Hell.'[677] The Prophet of Allah ﷺ also said, 'A commander of the Muslims is a shield for them. They fight behind him and they are protected by him. If he enjoins the fear of Allah, the Exalted and Glorious, and dispenses justice, there will be a great reward for him; and if he enjoins otherwise, he will be treated in kind.'[678]

Fairness and justice do not look at the person, his previous deeds, or his position in life, but simply at what is right at the given moment. A king must be held to the same standards as the homeless man, or there can be no true justice in a land. Equality in judging disputes between people is paramount. This concept is not reserved for those in positions of leadership alone, but presides as a universal quality for each of us. Whenever we are in a position of power above others, we must be aware of our duty and responsibility to judge justly and treat others fairly. Al-Nuʿmān ibn Bashīr ﵁ reported, 'My father took me to the Prophet ﷺ to ask him to bear witness to something that he had given to me. The Prophet ﷺ asked, "Do you have any other children?" He said, "Yes." He ﷺ gestured with his hand held horizontally like this, saying, "Why do you not treat them all equally?"'[679]

Justice, equality, and fairness are all Prophetic qualities, and should be sought and strived for. Amīr al-Mu'minīn ʿAlī ibn Abī Ṭālib ﵁ narrated that the Prophet ﷺ said, 'If only one day of this [world] remained, Allah ﷻ would raise up a man from my family who would fill this Earth with justice as it has been filled with oppression.'[680] A man must work to build these virtuous

[677] *Sunan Abī Dāwūd* 3575.
[678] *Ṣaḥīḥ Muslim* 1841.
[679] *Sunan al-Nasā'ī* 3685.
[680] *Sunan Abī Dāwūd* 4283.

qualities in himself, and be mindful that this is a constant effort: being deemed unjust is only ever a poor decision away. The Prophet ﷺ warned, 'Guard yourself from oppression, for oppression will be darkness on the Day of Resurrection. Guard yourself from greed, for greed destroyed those who came before you. It caused them to shed blood and to make lawful what was unlawful.'[681]

He ﷺ also warned, 'Beware of the supplication of the oppressed, even if he is an unbeliever, for there is no screen between it and Allah ﷻ.'[682]

The Prophet ﷺ said, 'The most quickly rewarded of good deeds are kindness and upholding the ties of kinship, and the most quickly punished evil deeds are injustice and severing the ties of kinship.'[683]

MERCY AND COMPASSION

As men, we live in constant hope of the mercy of Allah ﷻ and constant fear of His justice. It is, or indeed *should* be, the sincere wish of every believer that Allah ﷻ deals with us with mercy, and does not subject us to true justice, as we will all be found wanting on such a day. As mentioned previously, one should earnestly hold his Creator in good regard and hope fervently for His Mercy.[684] As men, we should exercise compassion and mercy at every opportunity, as this is the means by which Allah ﷻ will grant us His mercy in recompense. The Prophet ﷺ said, 'Allah ﷻ is compassionate and loves compassion. He gives for compassion what He does not give for

---

681 *Ṣaḥīḥ Muslim* 2578.
682 *Musnad al-Imam Aḥmad* 12140.
683 *Sunan Ibn Mājah* 4212.
684 *Sunan Ibn Mājah* 4212.

harshness.'[685]

The mercy and compassion of Allah ﷻ should be sought after with every fibre of our being, and the mercy that He has put in us is a drop in the ocean of His mercy. How can we ask for His mercy on the Day of Judgement and show none ourselves? A man that has the capability of doing harm to someone and chooses mercy is a man that truly follows the Sunnah of the Prophet ﷺ, as we saw in the incident with Waḥshī ibn Ḥarb ؓ.[686] The Prophet ﷺ said, 'Allah ﷻ will not be merciful to those who are not merciful to mankind.'[687]

Regarding the mercy of Allah ﷻ, Abū Hurayrah ؓ narrated that the Prophet ﷺ said, 'Allah ﷻ has one hundred degrees of mercy, of which He has shared one between all of creation. It is by virtue of this that you show mercy and compassion towards one another and the wild animals show compassion towards their young. And He has kept back ninety-nine degrees of mercy, by virtue of which He will show mercy to His slaves on the Day of Resurrection.'[688] In a similar narration Abū Saʿīd ؓ related, '...by virtue of which mothers show compassion to their children and animals as well as the birds show compassion to one another.'[689] The number mentioned here is a rhetorical device to show the difference between the mercy of Allah ﷻ in comparison to the combined mercy of His creation. In actual truth, the mercy of Allah ﷻ is infinite.

The Prophet ﷺ also said, 'Allah ﷻ said, "I am Allah, and I

---

685 *Al-Adab al-Mufrad* 472.
686 *Ṣaḥīḥ al-Bukhārī* 4072.
687 *Ṣaḥīḥ al-Bukhārī* 7376.
688 *Sunan Ibn Mājah* 4293.
689 *Sunan Ibn Mājah* 4294.

am al-Raḥmān. I created the *raḥim* (womb), and named it after My Name. So whoever maintains good relations with it, I maintain good relations with him, and whoever severs it, I am finished with him."'[690]

Indeed, a lack of compassion towards our fellow man constitutes a betrayal of their rights as the creation of Allah ﷻ. Each of us is deserving of some portion of compassion and mercy, even the worst of us. The lowest and basest of all men, such as the rapists and the murders, deserve their own degree of compassion, whether it be in upholding their rights as people or the granting of a swift death.

The Prophet ﷺ said, 'Whoever has been given his portion of compassion has been given his portion of good. Whoever is denied his portion of compassion has been denied his portion of good...'[691] Furthermore, he ﷺ said in another narration: 'If there is roughness in anything it is bound to disgrace it. Allah ﷻ is compassionate and loves compassion.'[692]

Mercy is a quality best expressed from a position of power. A man who is in a position of weakness cannot express mercy to someone above him. This ultimately entails that the follower cannot show mercy to his leader, and the child cannot be expected to show mercy to his father; quite intuitively, the natural expectation is that the father and the leader will show mercy to those in their care. The Prophet ﷺ said, 'He is not one of us who does not have mercy upon our young, respect our elders, and command good and forbid evil.'[693] When al-Aqraʿ ibn Ḥābis ﷺ told the Prophet ﷺ, 'I have ten children and I do not kiss any

---

[690] *Jāmiʿ al-Tirmidhī* 1907.
[691] *Al-Adab al-Mufrad* 464.
[692] *Al-Adab al-Mufrad* 466.
[693] *Jāmiʿ al-Tirmidhī* 1921.

of them', the Messenger of Allah ﷺ replied, 'Whoever shows no mercy is shown no mercy.'[694]

Al-Ḥasan said, 'I remember a time among the Muslims when their men would shout, "O family, O family: your orphan, your orphan! O family, O family: your poor, your poor! O family, O family: your neighbour, your neighbour!" Time has been swift in taking the best of you, while every day you become baser.'[695]

Abū Hurayrah narrated, 'While some Ethiopians were playing in the presence of the Prophet ﷺ, ʿUmar came in, picked up a pebble, and hit them with it. After that occurred, the Prophet ﷺ said, 'O ʿUmar, allow them to continue.' One of the narrators, Maʿmar, added that they were playing inside the *masjid*.[696]

Care is not reserved for our children alone, nor is it a thing that only the leaders of society present to their followers. It is for the orphan and the homeless; it is for the neighbour and the stranger. The Messenger of Allah ﷺ said, 'Feed the hungry, visit the sick, and free the captive.'[697] The entirety of worldly creation deserves a portion of the mercy of Allah, and it is of great benefit to us to be blessed enough to be the means of delivering that mercy, and of great harm to withhold it when it is within our power to give.

The Mother of the Believers ʿĀ'ishah said, 'I was on a camel which was somewhat intractable, and the Prophet ﷺ advised, "Be compassionate. Whenever there is compassion

[694] *Jāmiʿ al-Tirmidhī* 1911.
[695] *Al-Adab al-Mufrad* 139.
[696] *Ṣaḥīḥ al-Bukhārī* 2901.
[697] *Sunan Abī Dāwūd* 3105.

in something, it adorns it, and when it is removed from something, it disgraces it.'"[698]

As mentioned previously, in one Hadith the Prophet ﷺ said, 'A prostitute was once forgiven. She passed by a dog panting near a well; thirst had nearly killed him. She took off her sock, tied it to her veil, and drew up some water (from the well). Allah ﷻ forgave her for that.'[699] In contrast, the Prophet ﷺ also said, 'A lady was punished due to a cat which she had imprisoned until it died. She entered the Fire because of it, for she neither gave it food nor water as she had held it. Nor did she ever set it free to eat from the vermin of the Earth.'[700] He ﷺ also said, 'Anyone who shows mercy, even to an animal intended for slaughtering, will be shown mercy by Allah ﷻ on the Day of Resurrection.'[701]

The mistreatment of animals is an act deserving of punishment from Allah ﷻ, whereas their good treatment, even if they are meant for slaughter by one's own hand, is an act that is loved by Allah ﷻ and will be rewarded by Him, *in shā' Allāh.*

وَمَآ أَرْسَلْنَـٰكَ إِلَّا رَحْمَةً لِّلْعَـٰلَمِينَ.

And We have not sent you but as a mercy for all the worlds.[702]

The reference to 'worlds' includes all creatures and various realms of the creation, thereby incorporating humans, animals, plants, jinn, and so on.[703]

When the Prophet ﷺ went to Ṭā'if to invite its people to Islam, he was at the receiving end of mockery, abuse, and assault.

---

698 *Al-Adab al-Mufrad* 469.
699 *Ṣaḥīḥ al-Bukhārī* 3321; *Ṣaḥīḥ Muslim* 2245.
700 *Ṣaḥīḥ al-Bukhārī* 3482.
701 *Al-Adab al-Mufrad* 381.
702 *Qur'an* 21:107.
703 *Ma'ārif al-Qur'an*, vol. 6: p. 236.

Bleeding profusely from wounds inflicted on him by being pelted with stones, he reached a nearby field, and himself reported:

> *I did not recover until I reached Qarn al-Tha'ālib. When I raised my head, I saw a nearby cloud which had cast its shadow on me. Lo and behold, in the cloud there was the Angel Jibrīl, who called out to me and said, 'Allah, the Honoured and Glorious, knows what your people have said to you, and how they reacted to your call. He has sent to you the Angel of the Mountains so that you may order him to do as you wish to them.' The Angel of the Mountains then called out a greeting to me and said, 'O Muhammad, Allah has listened to what your people have said to you. I am the Angel of the Mountains, and your Lord has sent me to you, so that you may order me as you see fit. If you wish, I will bring together the two mountains that stand either side of them and crush them in between.'*[704]

The Prophet's reply was one that only the Mercy to the Worlds ﷺ could give:

> *Rather, I hope that Allah will produce from their descendants persons of the kind who will worship Allah, the One, and will not ascribe partners to Him.*[705]

Such was the Messenger of Allah ﷺ. Such a man we can only ever aspire to be.

---

704 *Ṣaḥīḥ Muslim* 1795.
705 *Ṣaḥīḥ Muslim* 1795.

29

He is a Generous Host

عَنْ أَبِي شُرَيْحٍ الْعَدَوِيِّ رَضِيَ اللَّهُ عَنْهُ، أَنَّهُ قَالَ: سَمِعَتْ أُذُنَايَ وَأَبْصَرَتْ عَيْنَايَ حِينَ تَكَلَّمَ رَسُولُ اللَّهِ صَلَّى اللَّهُ عَلَيْهِ وَسَلَّمَ، فَقَالَ: "مَنْ كَانَ يُؤْمِنُ بِاللَّهِ وَالْيَوْمِ الآخِرِ فَلْيُكْرِمْ ضَيْفَهُ جَائِزَتَهُ." قَالُوا: "وَمَا جَائِزَتُهُ، يَا رَسُولَ اللَّهِ؟" قَالَ: "يَوْمُهُ وَلَيْلَتُهُ، وَالضِّيَافَةُ ثَلاَثَةُ أَيَّامٍ، فَمَا كَانَ وَرَاءَ ذَلِكَ فَهُوَ صَدَقَةٌ عَلَيْهِ – وَقَالَ – مَنْ كَانَ يُؤْمِنُ بِاللَّهِ وَالْيَوْمِ الآخِرِ فَلْيَقُلْ خَيْرًا أَوْ لِيَصْمُتْ."

Abū Shurayḥ al-ʿAdawī ﵁ narrated that, 'My ears heard and my eyes witnessed when the Messenger of Allah ﷺ spoke and said, "Whoever believes in Allah and the Hereafter should show respect to the guest with the utmost kindness and courtesy." The Companions asked, "Messenger of Allah, what is this utmost kindness and courtesy being referred to?" He ﷺ replied, "It is for a day and a night. Hospitality extends for three days, and what is beyond that is a ṣadaqah for him; and whoever believes in Allah and the Hereafter should say something good or keep quiet."'[706]

HOSPITALITY AND GUEST RIGHTS

As men, it is our responsibility to provide for our guests when they attend our homes. This is their right, as guest privileges have been a part of human society since the time of the Prophet Ibrāhīm ﵇. Saʿīd ibn al-Musayyib ﵀ said, 'Ibrāhīm ﵇ was the first person to give hospitality to a guest, the first to be circumcised, the first to trim the moustache, and the first to see grey hair. He said, "O Lord! What is this [grey hair]?" Allah ﷻ replied, "It is dignity, Ibrāhīm." He said, "Lord, increase me in dignity!"'[707]

---

[706] *Ṣaḥīḥ Muslim* 48b.
[707] *Muwaṭṭa' Imam Mālik* 1677.

It is universally established across all creeds, cultures, and continents that the guest should be afforded rights which should be upheld to the utmost degree possible. This is the reason why messengers were never harmed when they brought ill news to kings, and why it was such a scandalous affair when this rule was broken. For the Muslim, these rights are set in stone, and cannot be cast aside for want or worry. Where other cultures and creeds have fallen at this hurdle, the Muslim man takes it in his stride.

ʿUqbah ibn ʿĀmir 🙵 narrated, 'We said to the Prophet 🙵, "You send us out and it sometimes happens that we have to stay with people who do not entertain us. What do you think about this?" He 🙵 said to us, "If you stay with some people and they entertain you as they should for a guest, accept their hospitality; but if they do not, take the right of the guest from them."'[708]

To reiterate, hospitality is a *right* of the guest, not the *choice* of the host, as it may be seen in other societies. A right can be taken if it is not given, but it should never come to this when members of society are god-fearing and true men still walk on the Earth.

Abū Shurayḥ al-Khuzāʿī 🙵 reported that the Prophet 🙵 said, 'The period of the entertainment of a guest is three days, and utmost kindness and courtesy is for a day and a night. It is not permissible for a Muslim to stay with his brother until he makes him sinful.' The Companions 🙵 asked, 'Messenger of Allah, how would he make him sinful?' He 🙵 said, 'He stays with him [for so long] that nothing is left to entertain him.'[709]

Three points can be derived from this Hadith: 1) a guest has

---

[708] *Ṣaḥīḥ al-Bukhārī* 2461.
[709] *Ṣaḥīḥ Muslim* 48c.

three days of lodging rights at the house he stays in; 2) the host should give the best of what he can offer for the first day and night; and 3) the guest should not remain at the home for so long that the host begins to struggle to provide hospitality. The Prophet ﷺ said, 'Whoever believes in Allah ﷻ and the Last Day should serve his guest generously. To honour the guest is to provide him with superior food for a night and a day, and a guest is to be entertained with food for three days. Whatever is offered beyond that is regarded as a *ṣadaqah.* And it is not lawful for a guest to stay with his host for such a long period so as to put him in a critical position.'[710]

وَيُؤْثِرُونَ عَلَىٰٓ أَنفُسِهِمْ وَلَوْ كَانَ بِهِمْ خَصَاصَةٌ ۚ وَمَن يُوقَ شُحَّ نَفْسِهِۦ فَأُو۟لَـٰٓئِكَ هُمُ ٱلْمُفْلِحُونَ

...and give preference [to them] over themselves, even though they are in poverty. And those who are saved from the greed of their hearts are the successful.[711]

You will recall from earlier that this verse was revealed in relation to Abū Ṭalḥah al-Anṣārī ﷺ[712] and his wife ﷺ,[713] about whom Abū Hurayrah ﷺ reported the following: 'A man from the Anṣār was hosting a guest and he had nothing with him, except a minimal amount to feed himself and his family. He said to his wife, "Put the children to sleep, put out the lamp, and serve our guest with what we have." Then Allah revealed the verse, "*...and give preference [to them] over themselves, even though they are in poverty.*"'[714] Such was the honour afforded to guests

[710] *Ṣaḥīḥ al-Bukhārī* 6135.
[711] *Qur'an* 59:9.
[712] *Tafsīr Ibn Kathīr* 59:9.
[713] There are also similar narrations in relation to other Companions, such as Thābit ibn Qays.
[714] *Ṣaḥīḥ al-Bukhārī* 3587; *Ṣaḥīḥ Muslim* 2054.

by the Companions ⬥: to go hungry so their guest could eat.

The Prophet ⬥ said, 'Putting up a guest for one night is obligatory. If you find a guest at your door in the morning, then this [hospitality] is a debt that you owe him. If he wants, he may request it, and if he wants, he may leave it.'[715] He ⬥ also said, 'If a guest arrives then it is *wājib* (compulsory) on every Muslim to serve him the night's meal. Additionally, if a guest stays at his house until morning, then the morning meal is a debt on him, which the guest may receive or forsake.'[716] The first night is therefore *compulsory*, and the morning meal is *owed*. It is not a choice to forsake when it suits you. A man knows what he owes and pays in full.

It is up to the host whether he entertains a guest that was not invited to be accommodated by simply following the invitees into the house. The same ruling applies for people who 'crash' weddings or celebrations uninvited. Guest rights are not for people to abuse so that they may eat and board for free. Even if the additional person arrives with the best of intentions and is unaware of the invited status of those with him, it is up to the host if he wants to entertain the additional person and grant him guest rights. It is nevertheless best practice to do so. Abū Mas'ūd al-Ansārī ⬥ narrates:

> *There was a man called Abū Shu'ayb, and he had a slave who was a butcher. He said to his slave, 'Prepare a meal to which I may invite the Messenger of Allah ⬥ along with four other men.' So he invited the Messenger of Allah ⬥ and four other men, but another man followed them. As a result, the Prophet ⬥ said to Abū Shu'ayb,*

---

[715] *Sunan Ibn Mājah* 3677.
[716] *Al-Adab al-Mufrad* 744.

'You have invited me as one of five guests, but now another man has followed us. If you wish you can admit him, and if you wish you can refuse him.' In response, the host said, 'I admit him.' [717]

One of the narrators, Muhammad ibn Ismāʿīl 🕮, said:

'If the guests are sitting at a dining table, they do not have the right to carry food from other tables to theirs, but they can pass on food from their own table to each other; otherwise, they should leave it. [718]

Muhammad ibn Ziyād 🕮 shared the following observation: 'The Predecessors (i.e., the Companions 🕮 and the Successors 🕮) lived together with their families. When a guest of one of them arrived and he found the cooking pot of another on the stove, he would take it to serve his guest from it. When the owner of the cooking pot found it missing, he would inquire about it and the man who had taken it would tell him that he took it for his guest. Thereupon the owner would exclaim, "May Allah bless it for you," or something similar.' He further added, 'When bread was baked, the host would take all of it for the guest. Their homes were separated by walls made of canes.' Baqiyyah, another narrator, said, 'I too found Muhammad ibn Ziyād and his peers observing this practice.' [719]

Taking an item when you know or believe that the owner will not mind is not theft, and there was an understanding between these noble generations – who had very little – that it was not always possible for every man to entertain his guest. Yet, their generosity was such that they would forgo their own meals to

---

[717] Ṣaḥīḥ al-Bukhārī 5434.
[718] Ṣaḥīḥ al-Bukhārī 5434.
[719] Al-Adab al-Mufrad 739.

entertain the visitors of another host. The Prophet ﷺ said, 'If any Muslim is the guest of a people and is given nothing, it is the duty of every Muslim to help him to the extent of taking from their crop and property to fulfil the needs of one night.'[720]

Lastly, when a guest decides to leave, the host should follow him to the door as a sign of respect and honour. The Prophet ﷺ said, 'It is the Sunnah for a man to go out with his guest to the door of the house.'[721]

As men, we must be aware of the rights of our guests and consistently uphold them. A man maintains the rights of others, even if they may be detrimental to himself.

---

[720] *Sunan Abī Dāwūd* 3751.

[721] *Sunan Ibn Mājah* 3358.

30
He is a Master Communicator

عَنِ الْحَسَنِ بْنِ عَلِيٍّ رَضِيَ اللَّهُ عَنْهُما، قَالَ: سَأَلْتُ خَالِي هِنْدُ بْنُ أَبِي هَالَةَ رَضِيَ اللَّهُ عَنْهُ، وَكَانَ وَصَّافًا، فَقُلْتُ: صِفْ لِي مَنْطِقَ رَسُولِ اللهِ صَلَّى اللَّهُ عَلَيْهِ وَسَلَّم، قَالَ: "كَانَ رَسُولُ اللهِ صَلَّى اللَّهُ عَلَيْهِ وَسَلَّمَ مُتَوَاصِلَ الأَحْزَانِ، دَائِمَ الْفِكْرَةِ، لَيْسَتْ لَهُ رَاحَةٌ، طَوِيلُ السَّكْتِ، لا يَتَكَلَّمُ فِي غَيْرِ حَاجَةٍ، يَفْتَتِحُ الْكَلامَ وَيَخْتِمُهُ بِاسْمِ اللهِ تَعَالَى، وَيَتَكَلَّمُ بِجَوَامِعِ الْكَلِمِ، كَلامُهُ فَصْلٌ، لا فُضُولَ، وَلا تَقْصِيرَ، لَيْسَ بِالْجَافِي، وَلا الْمُهِينِ، يُعَظِّمُ النِّعْمَةَ وَإِنْ دَقَّتْ لا يَذُمُّ مِنْهَا شَيْئًا، غَيْرَ أَنَّهُ لَمْ يَكُنْ يَذُمُّ ذَوَّاقًا وَلا يَمْدَحُهُ، وَلا تُغْضِبُهُ الدُّنْيَا، وَلا مَا كَانَ لَهَا، فَإِذَا تُعُدِّيَ الْحَقُّ، لَمْ يَقُمْ لِغَضَبِهِ شَيْءٌ، حَتَّى يَنْتَصِرَ لَهُ، وَلا يَغْضَبُ لِنَفْسِهِ، وَلا يَنْتَصِرُ لَهَا، إِذَا أَشَارَ بِكَفِّهِ كُلِّهَا، وَإِذَا تَعَجَّبَ قَلَبَهَا، وَإِذَا تَحَدَّثَ اتَّصَلَ بِهَا، وَضَرَبَ بِرَاحَتِهِ الْيُمْنَى بَطْنَ إِبْهَامِهِ الْيُسْرَى، وَإِذَا غَضِبَ أَعْرَضَ وَأَشَاحَ، وَإِذَا فَرِحَ غَضَّ طَرْفَهُ، جُلُّ ضَحِكِهِ التَّبَسُّمُ، يَفْتَرُّ عَنْ مِثْلِ حَبِّ الْغَمَامِ."

It is narrated from al-Ḥasan ibn ʿAlī ﵁ that he said, 'I asked my maternal uncle, Hind ibn Abī Hālah ﵁, who was skilled at describing people, to explain to me the manner of speech of the Messenger of Allah ﷺ. He said, "The Messenger of Allah ﷺ was constant in his concern [for the Hereafter], persistent in thought [for the betterment of his ummah], without repose, and prolonged in silence. He would not speak without reason. He would begin and conclude his speech with the Name of Allah the Exalted. He used concise and profound words when he spoke. His speech was succinct, neither excessive nor abridged; neither rude nor offensive. He would extol a blessing, however small, and would find no fault with any aspect of it. He neither criticised food nor overly praised it, and he would not be angered by this world nor by any part of it. If the truth were overstepped, nothing could stand before his fury until he had defended it. He ﷺ would not grow angry for his own sake, nor come to his own defence. When he beckoned, he beckoned with [the palm of] his whole hand; when he was astonished, he turned [his hand] over; when he spoke, he articulated with his hands, and would place his right palm over the base of his left thumb. When he was angry, he turned away and averted his face, and when he was happy, he lowered his gaze. His laughter was mostly in the form of a smile that revealed teeth as white as hailstones."[722]

COMMUNICATION, ELOQUENCE, AND RHETORIC

Communication refers to the passing of information through speech, writing, or some other medium. It is how knowledge is passed from one person to another, and how information is being imparted to you as you read this book. Eloquence (*faṣāḥah*) is fluent, persuasive communication, that is, speech that is delivered effectively. Rhetoric (*balāghah*) is the art of employing eloquent communication in a persuasive way. As men, our first line of offence, defence, or general connection with other people is through effective rhetoric and eloquent communication. The Prophet ﷺ was a master communicator, and was often described as being gifted with *jawāmiʿ al-kalim* (someone whose speech is concise yet profound). He ﷺ said, 'I have been given words which are concise but comprehensive in meaning...'[723] and 'I have been given concise, meaningful words.'[724]

In the above Hadith, Hind ibn Abī Hālah ؓ, who clearly had an incredible grasp of the Arabic language, beautifully described the speech and communicative mannerisms of our blessed Prophet ﷺ. He ﷺ felt every word he spoke, and focused on what was needed to be said in a given situation, such that he would never stray from his goal. He ﷺ would not speak to merely fill periods of silence, for he was known to be comfortable in observing reticence in his speech. Too many of us find long

[722] *Al-Shamāʾil al-Muḥammadiyyah* 224.
[723] *Ṣaḥīḥ Muslim* 523a.
[724] *Ṣaḥīḥ al-Bukhārī* 2977.

silences uncomfortable, or believe the quiet person has nothing to say because another man is speaking in the greatest frequency. Words for the sake of words are nothing more than wasted breaths and energy. When he ﷺ did speak, the name of Allah ﷻ was at the beginning and end of everything he ﷺ said. His words were carefully chosen, succinct, profound, and eloquent. They overflowed with meaning, so much so that *one and a half millennia* later, they still surprise and move us. He ﷺ never pointed at anyone with his finger, but used his whole hand; he ﷺ never looked at the man he was listening to with just his eyes, but turned his whole face toward them. He ﷺ was neither brash nor timid in his laughter and his speech. Such was our noble Prophet ﷺ.

The Mother of the Believers ʿĀ'ishah رضي الله عنها said, 'The Messenger of Allah ﷺ did not speak quickly like you do now. Instead, he would speak so clearly and exactly that those sitting with him would memorise it.'[725]

A Greek playwright said:

Wisdom lies in clarity.[726]

Abū Wā'il رحمه الله reported:

> *ʿAmmār delivered a sermon to us that was succinct and eloquent. When he descended from the pulpit we said to him, 'O ʿAmmār, you have delivered a short and eloquent sermon. If only you had lengthened it a bit more!' He said, 'I heard the Messenger of Allah ﷺ saying, "The lengthening of prayer by a man and the shortness of his sermon is the sign of his understanding*

[725] *Jāmiʿ al-Tirmidhī* 3639.
[726] Euripides.

[of faith]. So lengthen the prayer and shorten the sermon, for there is charm [in precise] expression."[727]

When did we move away from his ﷺ perfect example? When did the examples of proud, boastful men, of the arrogant and loud and self-centred fools, sway us to their mannerisms over his ﷺ perfect speech and habits? These habits and modes of discourse were not reserved for his Companions ﷺ alone but everyone he spoke to, even those who saw themselves as his enemies.

فَقُولَا لَهُ قَوْلًا لَّيِّنًا لَّعَلَّهُ يَتَذَكَّرُ أَوْ يَخْشَىٰ.

So speak to him in soft words. Perhaps he will accept the exhortation or fear (Allah).[728]

Those whom we wish to reform and lead to a life of virtue, which should be our sincere wish for even our gravest enemies, should be spoken to gently and amiably, no matter how perverse or despicable they may be.[729] This is not to say that we cannot raise our voices to meet those of others in order to control a situation.

Pharaoh claimed godhood and was a war criminal who massacred thousands of Jews. Yet, when Allah ﷻ sent the two Messengers ﷺ to him, He guided them to speak to him in a gentle and persuasive manner. Allah ﷻ knew that Pharaoh would never give up his evil ways, but the order was still the same.[730] Our intention should be for the betterment of the speaker before the listener, and our conduct should be accurate and truthful for the

727 *Ṣaḥīḥ Muslim* 869.
728 *Qur'an* 20:44.
729 *Ma'ārif al-Qur'an*, vol. 6: p. 124.
730 *Ma'ārif al-Qur'an*, vol. 6: p. 124.

sake of Allah ﷻ, not for those we address.

Being eloquent is a quality that every man should seek to instil in himself, as words have great power: entire nations moved, armies were mobilised, and decades of hostility ended with the turn of a phrase. ʿAbdullāh ibn ʿUmar ﷺ said, 'Two men came from the East and addressed the people, who were amazed by their eloquent speeches. On that, the Messenger of Allah ﷺ said, "Some eloquent speech is as effective as magic."'[731] On another occasion, the Messenger of Allah ﷺ also said, 'In eloquence there is magic and in poetry there is wisdom.'[732]

Indeed, in the right hands the pen can truly be mightier than the sword. It can both wound and heal. It can give men the courage to stand, or drive them into a murderous rage. It can bloom love in the most barren of hearts, and even make tears well from the driest eyes. The Abbasid poet Abū Ḥātim al-Bustī encapsulates this perfectly in his verses:

إذا أقسَمَ الأبطالُ يَوماً بسيفِهِمْ

وعدُّوهُ مِمّا يُكسِبُ المَجدَ والكَرَمْ

كفى قلَمَ الكُتّابِ عِزّاً ورِفعَةً

مدى الدَّهرِ أنَّ اللهَ أقسَمَ بالقَلَمْ

Upon the day that heroes swear

An oath upon their sharpened swords,

And take their blades as noble tools

That glory shall to them afford,

[731] *Ṣaḥīḥ al-Bukhārī* 5767.
[732] *Sunan Abī Dāwūd* 5011.

The pens of scribes shall me suffice

For boon and praise, and ever will

For all of time. Indeed Allah

Did swear an oath upon the quill.

If we are to discuss eloquence and succinctness in communication, poetry is the art of making such communication beautiful. The Mother of the Believers ʿĀ'ishah ﷺ said, 'Poetry is both good and bad. Take the good and leave the bad. I have related some of the poetry of Kaʿb ibn Mālik. That included an ode of forty verses and some less than that.'[733] Khālid ibn Kaysān ﷺ said, 'I was with Ibn ʿUmar when Iyyās ibn Khaythamah got up and said to him, "Shall I recite some poetry, Ibn al-Fārūq?" He replied, "Yes, but only recite good poetry to me." He recited until he came to something which Ibn ʿUmar disliked, whereupon he told him to stop.'[734]

Every man should have enough of a grasp of poetry to appreciate and understand it, though not every man needs to learn to compose it, for 'in poetry there is wisdom'.[735]

Miqdām ibn Shurayḥ narrated from his father that the Mother of the Believers ʿĀ'ishah ﷺ was asked, 'Did the Prophet ﷺ ever recite poetry?' She said, 'He would say parables from the poetry of Ibn Rawāḥah, saying, "News shall come to you from where you did not expect it."'[736] He ﷺ also said, 'The truest word spoken by an [pre-Islamic] Arab in poetry is this verse of Labīd:

[733] *Al-Adab al-Mufrad* 866.
[734] *Al-Adab al-Mufrad* 856.
[735] *Sunan Abī Dāwūd* 5011.
[736] *Jāmiʿ al-Tirmidhī* 2848.

أَلَا كُلُّ شَيْءٍ مَا خَلَا اللهَ بَاطِلُ

[وَكُلُّ نَعِيمٍ لَا مَحَالَةَ زَائِلُ]

"Pay heed! And know that all but God is naught

[While blissful things once made are soon unwrought].""[737]

However, poetry has a way of becoming an obsession for those who begin to understand it, and this is why the Prophet ﷺ said, 'It is better for a man to fill the inside of his body with pus than to fill it with poetry.'[738]

Abū ʿUbayd ﵀ explained the above Hadith by stating: '...his heart is so full of poetry that it makes him neglectful of the Qur'an and the remembrance of Allah ﷻ. If the Qur'an and the knowledge [of religion] are dominant, the belly will not be full of poetry in our opinion. "Some eloquent speech is magic" means that a man expresses his eloquence by praising another man...so much so that he attracts hearts to his speech. He then condemns him...so much so that he attracts the hearts to this other speech, as if he has bewitched the audience by it.'[739]

The poet's words, as Homer describes, can be intoxicating to those who learn to appreciate them:

...But Atreides

Raged still on the other side, and between them Nestor

The fair-spoken rose up, the lucid speaker of Pylos,

From whose lips the streams of words ran sweeter than honey.[740]

---

737 *Ṣaḥīḥ Muslim* 2256a (The second verse of the couplet is not quoted in the Hadith).

738 *Ṣaḥīḥ al-Bukhārī* 6154.

739 *Sunan Abī Dāwūd* 5009.

740 *The Iliad, Book I,* line 249, Homer.

From amongst the ranks of men some must, however, master the art of poetry, as in all fields, to ensure that the Muslim *ummah* is not left undefended in this arena. The Mother of the Believers ʿĀ'ishah 🙏 narrated, 'Once Ḥassān ibn Thābit asked the permission of the Prophet 🙏 to lampoon the infidels (i.e., compose satirical poetry). The Prophet 🙏 said, "What about the fact that I have common ancestry with them?" Ḥassān replied, "I shall take you out of them as a hair is taken out of dough."'[741]

Saʿīd ibn al-Musayyib 🙏 narrates, "ʿUmar passed by Ḥassān ibn Thābit while the latter was reciting poetry in the *masjid* and glared at him. Ḥassān said, "I recited poetry when there was someone better than you in the *masjid*.' He then turned to Abū Hurayrah and said, "Did you not hear the Messenger of Allah 🙏 when he said, 'Answer back on my behalf. O Allah, help him with the Holy Spirit?'" Abū Hurayrah said, "Yes, by Allah."'[742]

Buraydah ibn al-Ḥusayb 🙏 narrated, 'I heard the Messenger of Allah 🙏 say, "In eloquence there is magic, in knowledge ignorance, in poetry wisdom, and in speech heaviness."'[743] Ṣaʿṣaʿah ibn Ṣūḥān said, '"In knowledge there is ignorance" means that a scholar can learn something he does not understand and it can make him ignorant.'[744] For instance, without a teacher a man can *think* he understands something, which is far worse than knowing he does not understand. Ṣaʿṣaʿah further explains, '"In speech is heaviness" means that one can present his speech to a man who is incapable of understanding it, and does not want it.'[745] This kind of speaking is a needless weight to bear for both

---

[741] *Ṣaḥīḥ al-Bukhārī* 3531.
[742] *Sunan al-Nasāʾī* 716.
[743] *Sunan Abī Dāwūd* 5012.
[744] *Sunan Abī Dāwūd* 5012.
[745] *Sunan Abī Dāwūd* 5012.

parties: for the speaker in wasting his breath, and for the listener who is only given trouble due to the frustration of being unable to follow the points being made, or being forced to listen to something he has no interest in. Long-windedness and verbosity can also have such negative effects. Anas ﷺ narrates, 'A man gave a speech in the presence of ʿUmar and spoke at length. ʿUmar said, "Verbosity in oration is from the skills of Shayṭān."'[746]

It is reported on the authority of Ibn ʿAbbās ﷺ:

> *When the verse 'And warn the nearest people of your clan'[747] was revealed, the Messenger of Allah ﷺ left and climbed [mount] Ṣafā and called out loudly, 'Yā ṣabāḥā!'[748] The people of Mecca asked, 'Who is shouting out?' Others from amongst them said, 'Muhammad.' They gathered around him, and he ﷺ said, 'O sons of so and so, O sons of so and so, O sons of ʿAbd Manāf, O sons of ʿAbd al-Muṭṭalib!' And more still gathered around him. He ﷺ said, 'If I were to inform you that there were horsemen emerging out from behind the foot of this mountain, would you believe me?' They said, 'We have never known you to be a liar.' He ﷺ said, 'Well, I am a warner to you before a severe torment [reaches you].'...Abū Lahab then said, 'May you perish! Is it for this that you have gathered us?' He ﷺ then stood up, and the following verse was revealed: 'Perish the two hands of*

[746] *Al-Adab al-Mufrad* 876.
[747] *Qur'an* 26:214.
[748] A warning often used at the time to alert one's clan of an oncoming attack; a call to 'Be on your guard!'

Abū Lahab, and perish he!'[749] [750]

Again, we can see from the above that the public discourse of the Prophet ﷺ followed the same mannerisms and patterns: he ﷺ remained eloquent, succinct, and to the point, neither lengthening his speech or abridging it, and chose his words to deliver the deepest meaning in the most impactful way. As he was speaking publicly, he raised his voice so that everyone could hear him. Although the crowd was hostile to him, he did not shy away from delivering his message. The Prophet ﷺ could never be accused of being timid or scared.

We should not use eloquence in our speeches simply to captivate others, however, but put it to good use. The Prophet ﷺ said, 'On the Day of Resurrection, Allah ﷻ will not accept the repentance or ransom from he who learns excellence of speech simply to captivate the hearts of men.'[751]

From every Hadith we have mentioned in this book, the Prophet ﷺ was never once coarse or vulgar in his speech - he ﷺ never insulted people, nor cursed them, nor swore. He ﷺ was never rude nor obscene. The Prophet ﷺ once said to his wife, 'O ʿĀ'ishah, Allah ﷻ does not love obscenity and immorality.'[752] He ﷺ also said, 'I have not been sent as the invoker of curses, but as a mercy.'[753]

ʿAbdullāh ؓ said, 'The most blameworthy thing in a believer's character is coarseness.'[754]

---

749 *Qur'an* 111:1.
750 *Ṣaḥīḥ Muslim* 208a.
751 *Sunan Abī Dāwūd* 5006.
752 *Ṣaḥīḥ Muslim* 2165d.
753 *Ṣaḥīḥ Muslim* 2599.
754 *Al-Adab al-Mufrad* 314.

Though he was unlettered, the eloquence of the Prophet ﷺ glimmered in his letters. A man should be able to write with skill and eloquence. In writing, this is doubly important, for words put to paper have a way of staying around, unlike those said in the moment. Every word written must be deliberate and clear. The Prophet ﷺ did not have to worry about this as much as we do, for every word of his was concise and profound:

The Letter of the Prophet of Allah ﷺ to Heraclius Caesar, the Byzantine Emperor

بِسْمِ اللَّهِ الرَّحْمَنِ الرَّحِيمِ، مِنْ مُحَمَّدٍ عَبْدِ اللَّهِ وَرَسُولِهِ، إِلَى هِرَقْلَ عَظِيمِ الرُّومِ، سَلاَمٌ عَلَى مَنِ اتَّبَعَ الْهُدَى، أَمَّا بَعْدُ فَإِنِّي أَدْعُوكَ بِدِعَايَةِ الإِسْلاَمِ، أَسْلِمْ تَسْلَمْ، وَأَسْلِمْ يُؤْتِكَ اللَّهُ أَجْرَكَ مَرَّتَيْنِ، فَإِنْ تَوَلَّيْتَ فَعَلَيْكَ إِثْمُ الأَرِيسِيِّينَ وَ {يَٰٓأَهْلَ ٱلْكِتَٰبِ تَعَالَوْا۟ إِلَىٰ كَلِمَةٍ سَوَآءٍۭ بَيْنَنَا وَبَيْنَكُمْ أَلَّا نَعْبُدَ إِلَّا ٱللَّهَ وَلَا نُشْرِكَ بِهِۦ شَيْـًٔا وَلَا يَتَّخِذَ بَعْضُنَا بَعْضًا أَرْبَابًا مِّن دُونِ ٱللَّهِ ۚ فَإِن تَوَلَّوْا۟ فَقُولُوا۟ ٱشْهَدُوا۟ بِأَنَّا مُسْلِمُونَ}.

In the name of Allah, the most Beneficent, the most Merciful. This letter is from Muhammad, the slave of Allah, and His Apostle, to Heraclius, the ruler of Byzantine Rome. Peace be upon the followers of guidance. Now, I invite you to Islam. Embrace Islam and be safe; embrace Islam and Allah will bestow on you twice the reward. But if you reject this invitation, you shall be responsible for misleading the tillers (your nation).

'O people of the Book, come to a word common between us and between you, that we worship none but Allah, that we associate nothing with Him, and that some of us do not take others as Lords instead of Allah.' Then, should they turn back, say, "Bear witness that we are Muslims."'[755]

[755] *Qur'an* 3:64.

Allah's

Prophet

Muhammad'[756]

Abū Sufyān رضي الله عنه, who was present when Heraclius read the letter, and had not embraced Islam at this point, stated:

> *When Heraclius had finished, there was a great hue and cry from the Byzantine royals surrounding him, and there was so much noise that I did not understand what they said. We were turned out of the court. When I went out with my companions and we were alone, I said to them, 'Indeed, Ibn Abī Kabshah's affair has gained power. This is the King of Banī al-Aṣfar fearing him.'*[757]

Guarding the Tongue

The tongue is one of the most devastating tools in one's arsenal. It can raise people up, or tear them down; it can take one to the loftiest gardens of Paradise, or cast him into the deepest pit of Hell. Guarding one's tongue was stressed again and again by our beloved Prophet ﷺ due to the devastating power it holds, and its double-edged nature. He ﷺ said, 'The greatest propensity for good or evil in a man lies between his two lips.'[758]

إِذْ تَلَقَّوْنَهُ بِأَلْسِنَتِكُمْ وَتَقُولُونَ بِأَفْوَاهِكُم مَّا لَيْسَ لَكُم بِهِ عِلْمٌ وَتَحْسَبُونَهُ هَيِّنًا وَهُوَ عِندَ اللَّهِ عَظِيمٌ.

...when you were welcoming it with your tongues, and were saying with your mouths something of which you had no knowledge, and were taking it as a trivial matter, while in the

---

756 *Ṣaḥīḥ al-Bukhārī* 2940, 2941.

757 *Ṣaḥīḥ al-Bukhārī* 2940, 2941.

758 *Ṣaḥīḥ Ibn Ḥibbān* 5717.

sight of Allah it was grave.[759]

In this passage, Allah ﷻ has warned us about repeating hearsay without there being any corroborating evidence or proof.[760] A man cannot be careless with his tongue; it should be kept sheathed behind his lips unless he means to use it for good. There are many such warnings from the Prophet ﷺ in this regard. For instance, he ﷺ said, 'Speak what is good and be rewarded, or refrain from speaking evil and be safe.'[761]

The Prophet ﷺ also said, 'A slave of Allah may utter a word - without giving it much importance - which pleases Allah, and because of that Allah will raise his status; and a slave of Allah may utter a word - without considering its gravity - which displeases Allah, and because of that he will be thrown into the Hellfire.'[762]

Amīr al-Mu'minīn ʿUmar ibn al-Khaṭṭāb ؓ used to proclaim in his sermons, 'There is no good in anything less than truthful speech.'[763]

The Prophet ﷺ also said, 'Every word of the son of Adam is against him, not for him, except for enjoining good, forbidding evil, or the remembrance of Allah.'[764] If there is no good in what one is about to say, it is not worth saying. We should reflect on this: how many times have we said something in jest only to hurt someone we love and then immediately regretted it? How many times have we spoken about something that did not need to be mentioned and caused an argument? That said, it is all too common for people to utter obscenities in everyday discussions,

---

[759] *Qur'an* 24:15.
[760] *Maʿārif al-Qur'an*, vol. 6: pp. 386-387.
[761] *Musnad al-Shihāb al-Quḍāʿī* 666.
[762] *Ṣaḥīḥ al-Bukhārī* 6478.
[763] *Al-Zuhd li Abī Dāwūd* 48.
[764] *Jāmiʿ al-Tirmidhī* 2412.

cursing people or simply swearing for the sake of it. This has become common all over the world. We are in the midst of a pandemic of carelessness, and this inattentiveness will quickly become our downfall if we do not correct ourselves. ʿAbdullāh ibn ʿAmr ﷺ narrated: 'The Prophet ﷺ said, "The best of you are those best in conduct." And the Prophet ﷺ was not one who was obscene, nor one who uttered obscenities.'[765]

Ḥudhayfah ﷺ said, 'A man used to speak a word in the time of the Prophet ﷺ by which he would become a hypocrite. Indeed, I hear one of you say it now in your gatherings ten times a day!'[766]

The Prophet ﷺ said, 'The curse of Allah is upon the one who insults my Companions.'[767] The Companions ﷺ are the people who gave their lives for the sake of Allah ﷻ, His Prophet ﷺ, and the cause of Islam; as a result, their status can never be reached by anyone that followed them. The Prophet ﷺ said, 'The best of you are my generation (the Companions), then those that follow after them, then those that follow after them.'[768] The Companions ﷺ were men and had disputes between themselves, but it is not for us to take sides in their arguments nor prefer one over the other centuries later. The Companions ﷺ tower over our greatest scholars and saints. We who follow are but men, and they are like the stars. We can only gaze upon their examples from lightyears away, and take their light as a source of guidance. The Prophet ﷺ said, 'The stars are a source of security for the sky, and when the stars disappear that which is

---

765 *Jāmiʿ al-Tirmidhī* 1975.
766 *Musnad Imam Aḥmad* 23278.
767 *Al-Muʿjam al-Awsaṭ* 7015.
768 *Ṣaḥīḥ al-Bukhārī* 2651.

promised to the sky will happen; and I am a source of safety and security to my Companions, and when I shall go away it will fall to the lot of my Companions as they have been promised; and my Companions are a source of security for the *ummah*, and when they go away that which is promised to the lot of my *ummah* will befall them.'[769]

Sufyān ibn ʿAbdullāh al-Thaqafī ⚊ said, 'O Messenger of Allah, inform me about a matter that I may hold fast to.' He ⚊ said, 'Say, "My Lord is Allah," and then be steadfast.' Sufyān ⚊ asked, 'O Messenger of Allah, what do you fear most for me?' The Prophet ⚊ took hold of his tongue and said, 'This.'[770]

It is often most difficult for a man to control his tongue when he is angry – he feels he needs to lash out with his hands or his words. This is the time that he must be doubly careful about what he says. Men were given *qiwāmah* (in part) for their ability to control their tempers. There is no man that cannot control his anger; there are only weak men who cave to their base and carnal instincts. The Prophet ⚊ said, 'Whoever restrains his tongue, Allah will cover his faults. Whoever controls his anger, Allah will protect him from His punishment. Whoever apologises to Allah, He will accept his apology.'[771]

As Yeats put it:

> *But I, being poor, have only my dreams;*
>
> *I have spread my dreams under your feet;*
>
> *Tread softly because you tread on my dreams.*[772]

---

[769] *Ṣaḥīḥ Muslim* 2531.
[770] *Jāmiʿ al-Tirmidhī* 2410.
[771] *Al-Ṣamt wa Ādāb al-Lisān li Ibn Abī Dunyā* 21.
[772] *He Wishes for the Cloths of Heaven*, W.B. Yeats.

4 | THE PREPARED MAN

31
He Has a Plan

عَنْ جَابِرَ بْنَ عَبْدِ اللَّهِ رضيَ الله عنهما، قَالَ: قَالَ النَّبِيُّ صَلَّى اللَّهُ عَلَيْهِ وَسَلَّمَ:

"الْحَرْبُ خُدْعَةٌ."

Jābir ibn ʿAbdullāh ﷺ narrated that the Prophet ﷺ said, 'War is deceit.'[773]

PLANNING, TACTICS, AND STRATEGY

Earlier on in this book, we covered adaptability and versatility, both of which are concepts that refer to the ability to change a plan when the factors originally underpinning it change. Here, however, we will discuss the organisational aspects themselves and the importance for a man to have a plan when tackling any issue he is faced with.

---

[773] *Ṣaḥīḥ al-Bukhārī* 3030.

Strategy is the craft of the Warrior. Commanders must enact the craft, and troopers should know this Way.[774]

A plan refers to the advanced preparation and arrangements undertaken to achieve a set goal or objective. Strategy is the term used for setting the routes by which one will achieve the overall plan. Tactics, on the other hand, are the minute, carefully chosen actions that achieve the ends of one's strategy. In general, *strategies* are groups of actions which aim to achieve long-term objectives, and tactics are the actions themselves which aim to achieve short-term goals.

Good planning involves knowing one's self, one's team, and the obstacles one needs to overcome. It also involves the planner having the qualities of headship discussed in the leadership sections earlier. As Sun Tzu states:

If you know the enemy and know yourself, you need not fear the result of a hundred battles.

If you know yourself but not the enemy, for every victory gained you will also suffer a defeat.

If you know neither your enemy nor yourself, you will succumb in every battle.[775]

As men, we should be able to put together plans of action to achieve a set objective. Regardless of whether this is to plan a defence, achieve a goal at work, or simply carry out some do-it-yourself (DIY) initiatives in the home, the ideas and concepts that underpin planning, strategy, and tactics are the same, and it is for each of us to become well acquainted with them.

As we see from the aforementioned Hadith, when making plans there is no need to be open about them with one's

[774] *The Book of Five Rings, the Earth Book,* Miyamoto Musashi.
[775] *The Art of War,* Sun Tzu.

opponent. In the theatre of war, it is acceptable to employ trickery to keep the enemy second-guessing themselves. Likewise, when a person faces an opponent in real life, they should use whatever lawful tactic they have in their disposal to ensure their objective is met.

Al-Barā' ibn 'Āzib ⬥ narrates:

> *The Prophet ⬥ appointed 'Abdullāh ibn Jubayr as the commander of the infantrymen (archers), who numbered fifty on the day of Uḥud. He instructed them, 'Stay in position, and do not leave it, even if you see birds snatching us, until I send for you; and if you see that we have routed the infidels and made them retreat, even then you should not leave your position until I send for you.'*
>
> *Then the infidels were defeated. By Allah, I saw the women [from among them] fleeing, lifting up their clothes and revealing their leg-bangles and legs. The companions of 'Abdullāh ibn Jubayr said, 'The spoils! O people, the spoils! Your companions are victorious, what are we waiting for?' 'Abdullāh ibn Jubayr said, 'Have you forgotten what the Messenger of Allah ⬥ said to you?' They replied, 'By Allah! We will go to the enemy and collect our share from the war booty.' But when they went to them, they were forced to turn back, defeated.*[776]

This was due to a flanking manoeuvre by the polytheist cavalry, led by Khālid ibn al-Walīd ⬥, who was not yet a Muslim, whom the archers had until then prevented by their presence on the hillock where they were positioned. Here we can

---

[776] *Ṣaḥīḥ al-Bukhārī* 3039.

see how, by planning in advance, the Prophet ﷺ had effectively rendered a flanking attack from the enemy cavalry impossible. It was only when this deterrent was removed that the Muslims found themselves flanked and were forced to retreat to Mount Uḥud, where the enemy could only face them from one direction. Moving the army to Uḥud itself was a tactic that the Prophet ﷺ would have had in mind for such a situation.

Another example of this has been mentioned earlier, when in the Battle of the Trench the Muslims faced 10,000 invading troops, with the former having less than a third of the enemy's strength. The Prophet ﷺ set up a war council, and took the advice of his advisors. The famed Persian Companion, Salmān al-Fārisī ؓ, posited the strategy of digging a trench to disrupt cavalry charges, form a defensive barrier, and create bottlenecks through which the Muslims could better defend themselves.[777] Again, by planning ahead and devising a strategy, individual tactics suddenly became viable where a pitched battle without a strategy would result in sure defeat, unless Allah ﷻ granted the Muslims victory notwithstanding such limitations.

Again, earlier in the book, we saw how in the Battle of Mu'tah, the Sword of Allah ﷻ, Khālid ibn al-Walīd ؓ, deployed the tactic of rearranging his army to make the Byzantines believe he had received reinforcements during the night.[778]

The Prophet ﷺ said at the Battle of Badr, 'When they come near you, release arrows at them; and do not draw swords at them until they come near you.'[779]

In a lengthy Hadith that should be read in its entirety (but for

---

[777] *Sīrat al-Muṣṭafā* vol. 2, p. 343.
[778] *Sīrat al-Muṣṭafā* vol. 2, pp. 507-511.
[779] *Sunan Abī Dāwūd* 2664.

the sake of brevity will be mentioned in excerpts throughout this book), Salamah ibn al-Akwaʿ ﷺ narrates an incident that occurred during the return journey from al-Ḥudaybiyyah, whilst he was grazing the camels alongside Rabāḥ ﷺ:

> *...When the day dawned, ʿAbd al-Raḥmān al-Fazārī carried out a raid and drove away all the camels of the Messenger of Allah ﷺ, and killed the man who was looking after them. I said, 'Rabāḥ, ride this horse, take it to Ṭalḥah ibn ʿUbaydullāh, and inform the Messenger of Allah ﷺ that the polytheists have made away with his camels.' Then I stood upon a hillock, turned to Medina, and shouted thrice, 'Yā ṣabāḥā!'*[780]
>
> *Then I set out in pursuit of the raiders, shooting at them with arrows and chanting a eulogy:*
>
> خُذْهَا وَأَنَا ابْنُ الأَكْوَعِ وَالْيَوْمُ يَوْمُ الرُّضَّعِ
>
> *Take this, I am al-Akwaʿ's son,*
>
> *Your day of suckling death has come.*
>
> *I would overtake a man from them, shoot an arrow at him which, piercing through the saddle, would reach his shoulder. Then I would repeat the verse, 'Take this, I am al-Akwaʿ's son, your day of suckling death has come.' By Allah, I continued shooting at them and hamstringing their animals. Whenever a horseman turned upon me, I would take cover at the base of a tree, shoot at him, and hamstring his horse. At last they entered a narrow mountain gorge. I ascended the mountain and held them at bay by throwing stones at them. I pursued them in this*

---

[780] i.e., be on your guard!

> *way until I retrieved every camel of the Messenger of Allah ﷺ and no camel was left with them.*[781]

Here we can see how Salamah ؓ, a lone warrior, pursued a mounted raiding party on foot, using his mastery of archery and the terrain to give himself every advantage possible, and no doubt using the same terrain to keep up with his adversaries. Again, the narration is too lengthy to recount here, but he narrates further on that the raiding party was reinforced by a second group, and they laid siege to him on a hillock. At this point, he kept them at bay through his skills as an archer and with the threat of sure death, said:

> *'Do you recognise me?' They replied, 'No. Who are you?' He announced, 'I am Salamah, son of al-Akwaʿ, and by the One Who has honoured the blessed countenance of Muhammad ﷺ, I will not seek out a man among you except that he will die by my hand, and not a man among you will be able to seek me out.' One of them said, 'I think he is right!' And they retreated.*[782]

As Euripides put it:

Ten soldiers wisely led,

Will beat one hundred without a head.[783]

[781] *Ṣaḥīḥ Muslim* 1807a.
[782] *Ṣaḥīḥ Muslim* 1807a.
[783] Euripides.

32
He is Stoic

عَنْ ثَابِتٍ رحمه الله، قَالَ: سَمِعْتُ أَنَسًا رضي الله عنه، عَنِ النَّبِيِّ صَلَّى اللَّهُ عَلَيْهِ وَسَلَّمَ قَالَ:
"الصَّبْرُ عِنْدَ الصَّدْمَةِ الأُولَى."

*Thābit ؓ narrated that he heard Anas ؓ say that the Prophet
ﷺ said, 'True patience is at the first stroke of calamity.*[784]

PATIENCE, FORBEARANCE, AND STOICISM

In our religious tradition, patience (*ṣabr)* is to bear hardship
without becoming upset or anxious. Forbearance is the act of self-
restraint and control when patience is called for. As for stoicism,
it refers to a school of ancient Greek philosophy that extolled
virtue over all things; however, in its modern usage in English it
means to 'endure patiently'. A man must bear all forms of
hardship in his life, and those that depend on him need him to
be level-headed, stoic, and calm. Hardship is an overbearing
darkness that weighs down on you; patience is a light that fights
it away. The Prophet ﷺ said, 'Patience is an illuminating torch.'[785]

The Roman Emperor Marcus Aurelius wrote:

*You have power over your mind – not outside events. Realise
this, and you will find strength.*[786]

Fasting, an act that every Muslim practises for one month in
the year, is the perfect way to exercise and develop the virtue of

---

[784] *Ṣaḥīḥ al-Bukhārī* 1302.
[785] *Sunan al-Nasāʾī* 2437.
[786] *Meditations*, Marcus Aurelius.

patience. The Prophet ﷺ said, 'Fasting is half of patience.'[787] Fasting teaches self-control, discipline, stoicism, and endurance. By practising this act of worship, a man hones his mind to be able to withstand whatever calamity comes his way.

He ﷺ also said, 'True patience is at the first stroke of calamity,'[788] as this is when the hardship hits the *hardest.* This is the time when people forget themselves and say things that they may later regret, or buckle under the weight of what they have endured. The Prophet ﷺ himself bore many hardships, but always did so with patience and forbearance. Anas ibn Mālik ﷺ narrated:

> *We went with the Messenger of Allah ﷺ to the blacksmith, Abū Sayf, who was the husband of Ibrāhīm's wet-nurse.*[789] *The Messenger of Allah ﷺ took Ibrāhīm, kissed him, and smelled him. Later, we entered Abū Sayf's house and at that time Ibrāhīm was taking his last breaths, and the eyes of the Messenger of Allah ﷺ began to shed tears. ʿAbd al-Raḥmān ibn ʿAwf said, 'O Messenger of Allah, even you are weeping?' He said, 'O Ibn ʿAwf, this is mercy.' Then he ﷺ wept more and said, 'The eyes shed tears and the heart grieves, and we will not say except what pleases our Lord. O Ibrāhīm, indeed we are grieved by your separation.'*[790]

This was the Sunnah of the Messenger of Allah ﷺ. One cannot read the above words without feeling some of the grief he experienced at that time, as his child, still only a baby, died in his

[787] *Sunan Ibn Mājah* 1745.
[788] *Ṣaḥīḥ al-Bukhārī* 1302.
[789] The Prophet's infant son.
[790] *Ṣaḥīḥ al-Bukhārī* 1303.

arms. Even during this time, the Prophet ﷺ showed immense patience. There is a lesson for us in every action he ﷺ did, and every word he ﷺ said.

This was the same Prophet ﷺ who was orphaned as a baby, lost his mother and grandfather in his infancy, lost his wife and uncle whilst enduring a three-year boycott and starvation, watched another uncle be murdered and mutilated before his very eyes, and buried almost all of his ﷺ children. Through all of these calamities, and more, he ﷺ remained steadfast and patient.

لَّقَدْ كَانَ لَكُمْ فِى رَسُولِ ٱللَّهِ أُسْوَةٌ حَسَنَةٌ لِّمَن كَانَ يَرْجُوا۟ ٱللَّهَ وَٱلْيَوْمَ ٱلْـَٔاخِرَ وَذَكَرَ ٱللَّهَ كَثِيرًا.

Indeed, in the Messenger of Allah you have an excellent example for whoever has hope in Allah and the Last Day, and remembers Allah often.[791]

Imam al-Zamakhsharī رحمه الله states that the Prophet ﷺ attained this excellence in character through his great tolerance of the afflictions of his people and his good manners and behaviour towards them.[792] A believer can bear every hardship if he holds true to his belief. Allah ﷻ will reward you for whatever it is you are tested with. Bear it with patience, and He will grant you a greater reward. The Prophet ﷺ said, 'No fatigue, nor disease, nor sorrow, nor sadness, nor pain, nor distress befalls a Muslim – not even the prick of a thorn – except that Allah expiates some of his sins for that.'[793] Anas رضي الله عنه said, 'I heard the Prophet ﷺ say that Allah ﷻ said, "When I test him in his two precious ones (his

[791] *Qur'an* 33:21.
[792] *Al-Jāmiʿ li Akhlāq al-Rāwī wa Ādāb al-Sāmiʿ*, vol. 1: p. 120.
[793] *Ṣaḥīḥ al-Bukhārī* 5641, 5642.

eyes) and he is steadfast, I will repay him with the Garden."'[794] The Prophet ﷺ also said, 'The believer who mixes with people and bears their annoyance with patience will have a greater reward than the believer who does not mix with people and does not put up with their annoyance.'[795]

The Mother of the Believers 'Ā'ishah ؓ said:

> *I asked the Messenger of Allah ﷺ about the plague. He ﷺ said, 'That was a means of punishment which Allah used to send upon whomsoever He willed, but He made it a source of mercy for the believers. For anyone who is residing in a town in which this disease is present, remains there and does not leave that town but has patience and hopes for Allah's reward, and knows that nothing will befall him except what Allah has written for him, then he will attain the same degree of reward conferred to a martyr.'*[796]

This is not to say that we do not stand up to evil when we are faced with it, but that there is merit also in bearing hardship against oneself. Whether patience or confrontation is better depends on the context of the situation. Hamlet mulls over this very question:

> *To be, or not to be, that is the question:*
>
> *Whether 'tis nobler in the mind to suffer*
>
> *The slings and arrows of outrageous fortune,*
>
> *Or to take arms against a sea of troubles*

---

[794] *Al-Adab al-Mufrad* 534.
[795] *Sunan Ibn Mājah* 4032.
[796] *Ṣaḥīḥ al-Bukhārī* 6619.

And by opposing, end them.[797]

MILITARY DISCIPLINE, SELF-CONTROL, AND STEADFASTNESS

Military discipline is when a person attempts to regulate their fears in order to maintain order and execute a task they have determined to fulfil immediately or prospectively. To be steadfast is to control oneself and be unwavering in the face of adversity. It is the captain going down with his ship, the infantryman levelling his spear at an oncoming cavalry charge, or the workers staying at the power plant during a radiation leak to avert nuclear disaster. A man must have these qualities, as it ultimately comes down to men to stand firm and resolute to do what must be done, no matter the odds or the ask. A man must be ready and willing to hold his post, even when fear threatens to unman him.

In the Battle of Yarmūk, 25,000 Muslim warriors - many of whom were Companions - stood against a 140,000 strong Byzantine army, of which 80,000 were Byzantine troops and 60,000 were Ghassānid Arabs.[798] Facing odds of nearly six-to-one, the Muslims would have been awed by the enemy facing them. Over a six-day battle, the Muslims, under the Sword of Allah ﷻ, Khālid ibn al-Walīd ؓ, held back the Byzantines to the point where their lines were reinforced more than once by their womenfolk with tent poles. At last, they broke the Byzantine lines and slew half of the enemy forces in the resulting retreat. Holding against such a superior force was only possible through the steadfastness of their faith in Allah ﷻ and the immense military discipline of the Companions ؓ. For they understood that victory in the field or victory through martyrdom could be the

[797] *Hamlet*, William Shakespeare.

[798] *Chronographia*, Theophanes, pp. 337-8.

result of the battle for the steadfast soldiers of Allah ﷻ.

فَإِن يَكُن مِّنكُم مِّائَةٌ صَابِرَةٌ يَغْلِبُواْ مِائَتَيْنِ ۚ وَإِن يَكُن مِّنكُم أَلْفٌ يَغْلِبُوٓاْ أَلْفَيْنِ بِإِذْنِ ٱللَّهِ ۗ وَٱللَّهُ مَعَ ٱلصَّٰبِرِينَ.

Accordingly, if there are one hundred among you, who are patient, they will overcome two hundred; and if there are one thousand among you, they will overcome two thousand by the will of Allah. Allah is with the patient.[799]

The Prophet ﷺ said, 'Seek closeness and be steadfast, and in all that afflicts the believer there is atonement, even a thorn-prick, and the hardship he suffers.'[800]

Abū al-Dardā' ﷺ said:

The Messenger of Allah ﷺ recommended nine things to me: 'Do not associate anything with Allah, even if you are cut to pieces or burned alive. Do not abandon a prescribed prayer deliberately; anyone who abandons it will forfeit Allah's protection. Do not drink wine, for it is the key to every evil. Obey your parents; if they command you to abandon your worldly possessions, then leave them for their sake. Do not contend with those in power, even if you think that you are in the right. Do not run away from the enemy army when it advances, even if you are killed while your comrades flee. Spend on your wife out of your means. Do not raise a stick against your wife. Cause your family to fear Allah, the Almighty and Exalted.[801]

يُثَبِّتُ ٱللَّهُ ٱلَّذِينَ ءَامَنُواْ بِٱلْقَوْلِ ٱلثَّابِتِ فِى ٱلْحَيَوٰةِ ٱلدُّنْيَا وَفِى ٱلْءَاخِرَةِ ۖ وَيُضِلُّ ٱللَّهُ

---

[799] *Qur'an* 8:66.
[800] *Jāmi' al-Tirmidhī* 3038.
[801] *Al-Adab al-Mufrad* 18.

ٱلظَّـٰلِمِينَ ۚ وَيَفْعَلُ ٱللَّهُ مَا يَشَآءُ.

Allah keeps the believers firm with the stable word in the worldly life and in the Hereafter; and Allah lets the unjust go astray; and Allah does what He wills.[802]

A Muslim man must maintain discipline, even in the thick of battle when the common man casts aside all inhibitions. The Muslim must hold himself to a higher standard. Whether it is on the battlefield or in the street, discipline is paramount. As Tennyson famously wrote about the extremely disciplined, though ultimately doomed, charge of the British light brigade in the Crimean War in 1854:

> *'Forward, the Light Brigade!'*
> *Was there a man dismayed?*
> *Not though the soldier knew*
> *Someone had blundered.*
> *Theirs not to make reply,*
> *Theirs not to reason why,*
> *Theirs but to do and die.*
> *Into the valley of Death*
> *Rode the six hundred.*[803]

In combat, even if you cannot understand why you must be disciplined, it is imperative that you maintain self-restraint. More than simply in the case of following orders, there are rules which must be followed and lines that cannot be crossed. ʿAbdullāh ibn Yazīd ⬥ reported that the Prophet ﷺ prohibited plundering and mutilation.[804] Yaḥyā ibn Saʿīd ⬥ reported that the first Caliph Abū Bakr ⬥ dispatched armies to Syria and said, 'I give

---

[802] *Qurʾan* 14:27.
[803] *The Charge of the Light Brigade*, Alfred, Lord Tennyson.
[804] *Ṣaḥīḥ al-Bukhārī* 5197.

you ten instructions: Do not kill a woman, nor a child, nor an infirm elder. Do not cut down fruit-bearing trees, nor tear down inhabited buildings. Do not slaughter sheep or camels, except for food. Do not burn or drown bee nests. Do not steal from the spoils, and do not be cowardly.'[805] Zayd ibn Wahb ﵁ reported that Amīr al-Mu'minīn ʿUmar ibn al-Khaṭṭāb ﵁ decreed, 'Do not steal the spoils, do not be treacherous with the enemy, do not mutilate the dead, do not kill children, and fear Allah ﷻ regarding the farmers who do not wage war against you.'[806]

A Muslim is patient, steadfast, and disciplined in a fight. He does not transgress, even in battle. He does not run or break the rules of engagement. The non-combatant is safe from his sword, the animals from his bow, and the trees from his torch.

The Prophet ﷺ said, 'O people! Do not wish to face the enemy in battle and ask Allah to keep you safe. But if you should face the enemy, then be patient and let it be known to you that Paradise is under the shades of swords.'[807] He ﷺ also said, 'Do not desire an encounter with the enemy; but when you encounter them, be firm.'[808]

Combat should never be the first course of action, but in international relations it is always an option in consideration. Thus, one should be prepared for it and steadfast should it be deemed necessary. Samurah ibn Jundub ﵁ said, 'The Prophet ﷺ named our cavalry "The Cavalry of Allah". When we were struck with panic or panic overtook us, the Messenger of Allah ﷺ commanded us to be united, to have patience, and

805 *Muwaṭṭa' Imam Mālik* 918.
806 *Sunan Saʿīd ibn Manṣūr* 2466.
807 *Ṣaḥīḥ al-Bukhārī* 2965, 2966.
808 *Ṣaḥīḥ Muslim* 1741.

perseverance, as well as to emulate such values when we fought.'[809]

[809] *Sunan Abī Dāwūd* 2560.

33
He is Physically Fit

عَنْ أَبِي هُرَيْرَةَ رَضِيَ اللَّهُ عَنْهُ، قَالَ: قَالَ رَسُولُ اللَّهِ صَلَّى اللَّهُ عَلَيْهِ وَسَلَّمَ: "الْمُؤْمِنُ الْقَوِيُّ خَيْرٌ وَأَحَبُّ إِلَى اللَّهِ مِنَ الْمُؤْمِنِ الضَّعِيفِ وَفِي كُلٍّ خَيْرٌ..."

Abū Hurayrah ﵁ narrated that the Messenger of Allah ﷺ said, 'A strong believer is better and dearer to Allah than a weak one, while both are good...'[810]

STRENGTH, FITNESS, AND EXERCISE

وَأَعِدُّوا۟ لَهُم مَّا ٱسْتَطَعْتُم مِّن قُوَّةٍ

Prepare against them whatever you can of strength...[811]

A man should be physically fit. He should have enough strength to complete basic tasks, and be fit enough to exert himself without losing composure if forced to do so. The Prophet ﷺ and his Companions ﵃ were warriors who had perfected the craft of war enough to simultaneously attack and defeat the superpowers of their day, and had honed their bodies to be the tools by which they would engage in it.

Kipling's poem 'If-' is an apt summary of some of the virtues of manhood. The composition concludes with the following lines about fitness and perseverance:

If you can fill the unforgiving minute

With sixty seconds' worth of distance run,

Yours is the Earth and everything that's in it,

[810] *Ṣaḥīḥ Muslim* 2664.
[811] *Qur'an* 8:60.

And - which is more - you'll be a Man, my son![812]

Strength is required to keep oneself safe in times of crisis, but it is also necessary to effectively worship Allah ﷻ, fulfil one's duties as a husband and father, and display genuine masculinity. Men have always been differentiated from women by virtue of their superior physical strength. Many of the virtues, qualities, and skills already listed are either enhanced or dependent on the person enacting them from a position of strength. What is the value of 'mercy' from a weak man when he does not have the capability to be cruel and *choose* to be merciful? What good is the guardian of a family who can neither command their respect nor protect them in times of need? The 'leader' who serves his people out of fear of them is no leader at all, but a servant in truth; the leader who serves his people out of compassion for them is no servant, but a leader in truth. Amīr al-Mu'minīn ʿUmar ibn ʿAbd al-ʿAzīz ؒ said, 'The best of asceticism is at a time of abundance, and the best of forgiveness is at a time of power.'[813]

Each of us are thus duty-bound as men to invest in our bodies, in the spirit of preparedness for times of need, but also to fulfil the rights that the body itself has over us. Strength is a gift from Allah ﷻ. Our bodies are not owned by us but loaned to us, and one day they shall be returned. Such blessings must be looked after, improved upon, and developed. Just as a man should train himself spiritually through worship and mentally through study, he should also train himself physically through exercise. ʿAbdullāh ibn ʿAmr ibn al-ʿĀṣ ؓ narrated that the Prophet ﷺ said, 'O ʿAbdullāh...your body has a right over

[812] 'If-', Rudyard Kipling.

[813] *Al-Tawāḍuʿ wa al-Khumūl* 151.

you.'[814]

Of the five core acts of worship that a Muslim must engage in, three of them require a degree of physical strength and fitness. Prayer can only be properly performed when the worshipper can stand, bow, prostrate, and sit correctly; any discomfort when completing these actions can affect concentration and discipline in the prayer. Fasting requires an element of health to be successfully conducted, whether through long winter days or under the sweltering heat of the Sun; a man who is unfit to fast is thus exempted from the requirement to do so. Hajj is a physical feat in and of itself, especially when done in the traditional way: on foot and in sandals, with nothing but two cloths to protect you from the Sun and the remembrance of Allah ﷻ and prayer constantly on your lips. Muslims are thus *required* to be strong and fit, to whatever degree that is in their power.

وَقَالَ لَهُمْ نَبِيُّهُمْ إِنَّ ٱللَّهَ قَدْ بَعَثَ لَكُمْ طَالُوتَ مَلِكًا ۚ قَالُوٓا۟ أَنَّىٰ يَكُونُ لَهُ ٱلْمُلْكُ عَلَيْنَا
وَنَحْنُ أَحَقُّ بِٱلْمُلْكِ مِنْهُ وَلَمْ يُؤْتَ سَعَةً مِّنَ ٱلْمَالِ ۚ قَالَ إِنَّ ٱللَّهَ ٱصْطَفَىٰهُ عَلَيْكُمْ وَزَادَهُۥ
بَسْطَةً فِى ٱلْعِلْمِ وَٱلْجِسْمِ ۖ وَٱللَّهُ يُؤْتِى مُلْكَهُۥ مَن يَشَآءُ ۚ وَٱللَّهُ وَٰسِعٌ عَلِيمٌ.

Their Prophet said to them: 'Allah has appointed Ṭālūt as a king for you.' They said: 'How could he have kingship over us when we are more entitled to the kingship than him? He has not been given affluence in wealth.' He said: 'Allah has chosen him over you and has increased his stature in knowledge and physique, and Allah gives His kingship to whom He wills. Allah is All-Embracing, All-Knowing.'[815]

The above verse was revealed in relation to the appointment of Ṭālūt (Saul) over his people, after they asked for a king to lead them in a military conflict against the Amalekites.[816] He was a

---

[814] *Ṣaḥīḥ al-Bukhārī* 1975, 5199, 6134.
[815] *Qur'an* 2:247.
[816] *Ma'ārif al-Qur'an*, vol. 1: p. 628.

soldier at the time, neither a scion of the rich noble houses nor a descendent of kings. In fact, he was known to bring water to the people and dye skins to earn his living, and they pointed to his lack of wealth as a reason for why he was not fit to lead them.[817] It is worth noting here that to this very day weak men still look to the wealthy for leadership, whereas the above verse reveals that this has nothing to do with leadership, as this was not even considered by Allah ﷻ nor Ṣamū'īl (Samuel) ﷺ, the Prophet of the time.[818] Ṭālūt was chosen as their leader because he was more knowledgeable and honourable overall; he was stronger and more steadfast in combat, and more experienced in the art of war. A leader or king should be distinguished by his knowledge, physique, strength of spirit and body, and leadership qualities.[819] These qualities are also what distinguishes men from one another, and this is why men naturally defer to those from among them who are superior in physicality, knowledge, or spirituality.

Even when we have gained greater knowledge and strength than all of our peers, this is not a reason to sit on our laurels and rest. The Messenger of Allah ﷺ prayed, 'O Allah, strengthen Islam through the one from these two men who is dearer to you: Abū Jahl or ʿUmar ibn al-Khaṭṭāb.' Ibn ʿUmar ﷺ said, 'The more beloved of the two was ʿUmar.'[820] Despite Amīr al-Mu'minīn ʿUmar ibn al-Khaṭṭāb ﷺ being distinguished among the Companions ﷺ for his vast strength and prowess as a ferocious combatant, this mountain of a man would pray, 'O Allah, I am weak, so make me strong. I am harsh, so make me

817 *Tafsīr Ibn Kathīr* 2:247.
818 It is also worth noting that pride withheld them from paying respect to Ṭālūt, which echoes Shayṭān's refusal to bow to Adam ﷺ.
819 *Tafsīr Ibn Kathīr* 2:247.
820 *Jāmiʿ al-Tirmidhī* 3681.

gentle. And I am miserly, so make me generous.'[821]

There is always room for improvement. Always time to become better at being *men.*

It was narrated from Abū Sukaynah 🕮 that a man from the Companions 🕮 of the Prophet 🕮 said:

> *When the Prophet 🕮 commanded the Companions to dig the trench (khandaq), there was a rock in their way preventing them from digging. The Messenger of Allah 🕮 stood, took hold of a pickaxe, put his ridā' (upper garment) at the edge of the ditch, and struck the rock as he recited, 'The Word of your Lord is perfect in truth and justice. None is there to change His words, and He is All-Hearing, All-Knowing.'[822] One-third of the rock broke off while Salmān al-Fārisī was standing there watching, and there was a flash of light when the Messenger of Allah 🕮 struck the rock. Then he struck it again and said, 'The Word of your Lord is perfect in truth and justice. None is there to change His words, and He is All-Hearing, All-Knowing.' And another third of the rock broke off and there was another flash of light, which Salmān saw. Then he struck the rock a third time and said, 'The Word of your Lord is perfect in truth and justice. None is there to change His words, and He is All-Hearing, All-Knowing.' The last third fell, and the Messenger of Allah 🕮 came out, picked up his ridā', and sat down.*[823]

This is but one example of the immense strength of the

---

[821] *Muṣannaf Ibn Abī Shaybah* 5179.

[822] *Qur'an* 6:115.

[823] *Sunan al-Nasā ī* 3176.

Prophet ﷺ, which he never flaunted nor celebrated. It was a quiet strength that was revealed naturally when feats of strength, which only he could achieve, were required. This was the same boulder mentioned earlier in the book, and it was so large that it straddled the trench and the Companions ﷺ had tried and failed to break it. The might of the Prophet ﷺ was so great that each time he struck it with the pickaxe he broke it. Anas ﷺ said, 'We used to say that the Prophet ﷺ was given the strength of thirty men.'[824]

Regarding his ﷺ physique, Amīr al-Mu'minīn ʿAlī ibn Abī Ṭālib ﷺ said:

> *He ﷺ was neither assertively tall, nor reticently short; he ﷺ was of medium height in relation to the people. His ﷺ hair was neither crisply curled nor straight, but wavy. His ﷺ face was neither plump nor chubby-cheeked, but had an element of roundness. He ﷺ was fair with a reddish tinge, and dark-eyed with long eyelashes. He ﷺ was large-boned and broad-shouldered, free of body hair, with only a line of hair from his chest to his navel, and had thickset palms and soles. When he ﷺ walked he walked briskly, leaning forward as if walking on a decline. If he ﷺ turned his head, he turned his body as well. Between his shoulders was the seal of Prophethood, and he ﷺ was the seal of the Prophets. He ﷺ was the best of the people in generosity of hand and heart. He ﷺ was the most truthful in speech, the gentlest in temperament, and the noblest in his relations. Whoever*

[824] *Ṣaḥīḥ al-Bukhārī* 268.

saw him ﷺ for the first time would be awestruck and whoever came to know him, loved him ﷺ. His describer can only say this: "I have never seen his like, before or after him ﷺ."[825]

The physique of the Prophet ﷺ was as perfect as he was himself. It was balanced, functional, and paralleled a warrior's body, not that of a strong man or specifically-adapted athlete. He ﷺ was not overly muscular like the gym-goers we see today who can lift heavy weights and yet cannot scratch an itch on their backs or fight for more than a minute, but strong and firm like a mountain; he ﷺ was able to fight in the battlefield without tiring, or work for days digging a miles-long trench, but was not as the stick-thin distance runners that compete in marathons yet cannot take a blow. Al-Barā' ؓ said, 'He ﷺ had hair that would flow on his shoulders, and his shoulders were broad. He was not too short and not too tall.'[826]

Abū Hurayrah ؓ said, 'I have not seen anything more beautiful than the Messenger of Allah ﷺ; it was as if sunlight flowed upon his face. Nor have I seen anyone quicker in his stride than the Messenger of Allah ﷺ. It was as if the Earth *folded* for him. We would be exerting ourselves while he ﷺ remained cool.'[827]

---

825 *Jāmiʿ al-Tirmidhī* 3638.
826 *Jāmiʿ al-Tirmidhī* 3635.
827 *Jāmiʿ al-Tirmidhī* 3648.

34

He is Competitive

عَنْ أَبِي هُرَيْرَةَ رَضِيَ اللَّهُ عَنْهُ، أَنَّ رَسُولَ اللَّهِ صَلَّى اللَّهُ عَلَيْهِ وَسَلَّمَ قَالَ:

"لاَ سَبَقَ إِلاَّ فِي نَصْلٍ، أَوْ حَافِرٍ، أَوْ خُفٍّ."

*Abū Hurayrah ☙ narrated that the Messenger of Allah ☙ said,
'There should be no prizes for victory except in competitions of
arrows, camels, or horses.'*[828]

HORSEMANSHIP, PRODUCTIVE PASTIMES, AND COMPETITION

As men, we are by our very nature competitive; we are
naturally inclined towards measuring our abilities against those of
other men to see who will emerge as the victor. It is the reason
for why sport was invented: we have vied with one another in
combat throughout history, and looked at our fellow men to
surmise who is the 'better man'. We do not even realise we are
doing it, but we are always in a state of competition. It is in our
fiṭrah and as always Islam takes this into account and provides us
with a better, more productive way to realise this drive and
ambition.

The Companions ☙ abhorred idle play,[829] as there was no
benefit in the playing of games. For the latter are pastimes in the
truest sense, designed to merely pass time; competition in these
games is akin to gambling when money is involved. Indeed, the
Prophet ☙ forbade them from engaging in such.[830] Instead, the

---

[828] *Sunan al-Nasāʾī* 3585.
[829] *Al-Adab al-Mufrad* 1274.
[830] *Sunan Abī Dāwūd* 4938.

Prophet ﷺ taught his Companions ﷺ that there were worthwhile pastimes with which to compete with one another. Each of these was productive in that it provided the person engaging in it with a life skill that was either beneficial for their health, lifecycle, or military prowess. Exercise and training were encouraged by our noble Prophet ﷺ, as a man should be fit, healthy, and prepared for the worst. He ﷺ said, 'Everything in which there is no remembrance of Allah is but idle play, except for four things: a man playing with his wife, a man training his horse, a man moving between two lines, and a man learning how to swim.'[831]

Running, swimming, and horsemanship are religiously-sanctioned stamina and fitness building exercises that a Muslim should engage in, and by doing so with the intention of completing a Sunnah these are acts of worship and worthy of reward. ʿUmar ﷺ wrote to Abū ʿUbaydah ibn al-Jarrāḥ ﷺ with the following piece of advice, 'Teach your children swimming and teach your fighters archery.'[832]

With regard to horsemanship, the Prophet ﷺ clearly had a great love of horses, and encouraged their training, their racing, and the improvement of one's own horsemanship, though even then he warned us not to fall into the trap of idle pastimes and obsession. The Prophet ﷺ said, 'There is always goodness in horses.'[833]

The term *furūsiyyah* is used to describe horse-riding martial exercises, which included being skilled in equestrianism, horse archery, lancing, and the use of a sword on horseback. In fact, the focus on masculine virtues coupled with these martial skills

---

[831] *As-Sunan al-Kubra li al-Nasāʾī* 8889.
[832] *Musnad al-Imam Aḥmad* 323.
[833] *Ṣaḥīḥ al-Bukhārī* 3645.

would evolve into the concept of the Arabian knight, or *fāris*, which would later influence Europe to adopt the same and embrace a parallel chivalric code in its own noble, warrior class.

Shakespeare displayed the value of horses in war when Richard III offers his entire kingdom for a single horse as he seeks out his foe on the battlefield, bellowing:

> *A horse, a horse! My kingdom for a horse!*[834]

The Messenger of Allah ﷺ said:

> *Horses are kept for one of three reasons: a man may keep them to receive a reward in the Hereafter; another may keep them as a means of protection; and a third may keep them to be a burden for him. As for the man for whom the horse is a source of reward, he is the one who ties it for Allah's Cause, and he ties it with a long rope in a pasture or a garden; whatever it grazes from in that pasture will be added to his good deeds; if it breaks its rope and races over one or two hills, then for every footstep and manure it leaves, good deeds will be written for him; and if it passes by a river and drinks of its water, though its owner had no intention to water it from that river, even then he will have good deeds written for him. Thus, that horse will be a source of reward for such a man. If a man ties a horse for earning his livelihood, abstains from asking others for help, and does not forget Allah's right (i.e., pays the zakāh due on the horse), then that horse will be a means of protection for him. But if a man ties it out of pride, to flaunt it, and impress others, then that horse will be a burden of sins for him.*[835]

---

[834] *Richard III*, William Shakespeare.

[835] *Ṣaḥīḥ al-Bukhārī* 4962.

He ﷺ also said, 'Everything with which a man amuses himself is vain except three: a man's training of his horse, his playing with his wife, and his shooting with his bow and arrow.'[836]

وَٱلْعَـٰدِيَـٰتِ ضَبْحًا. فَٱلْمُورِيَـٰتِ قَدْحًا. فَٱلْمُغِيرَٰتِ صُبْحًا. فَأَثَرْنَ بِهِۦ نَقْعًا. فَوَسَطْنَ بِهِۦ جَمْعًا.

I swear by those [horses] that run snorting, then those that create sparks by striking [their hoofs] on the stones, then those that invade at morning, then raise, at the same time, a trail of dust, then enter, at the same time, into the centre of the opposing host.[837]

In the above verses, Allah ﷻ swears by charging horses as a means of elevating their status in the eyes of the reader. Allah ﷻ has nothing to swear on, in the sense that He is Highest and the Greatest and fully self-sufficient. He is the One Who is sworn upon. The Prophet ﷺ said, 'Whoever has to take an oath should swear by Allah ﷻ or remain silent.'[838] Thus, when Allah ﷻ swears on something in the Qur'an, it is a rhetorical device used to highlight the splendour of His Creation.

The Prophet ﷺ encouraged us to race horses. The activity has many benefits, such as improving and maintaining the fitness of the rider and the horse, encouraging good treatment of the animal, fostering good mental health in the carer, and improving the martial skill of all parties, to name a few. The spirit of competition generally is a natural and healthy phenomenon, but it is not one that should be taken to the extreme. A fair race between equal mounts is thus encouraged, even with prize money, but one that will only ever have a clear winner is

---

[836] *Sunan Abī Dāwūd* 2513.
[837] *Qur'an* 100:1-5.
[838] *Ṣaḥīḥ al-Bukhārī* 2679.

considered to be a form of gambling. It should go without saying that betting on horses is forbidden. The Prophet ﷺ said, 'Whoever enters a horse in a race between two other horses – while not knowing whether it will win – will not be considered to be gambling. But whoever enters a horse between two other horses and is certain that it will win is gambling.'[839] A similar narration is recorded in *Sunan Abī Dāwūd.*[840]

The Prophet ﷺ himself arranged races between the Companions to build this spirit of competition in the men and their horses. ʿAbdullāh narrates, 'The Prophet ﷺ arranged a race of the horses which had not been made lean (untrained for racing); the area of the race was from Thaniyyah[841] to the *masjid* of Banī Zurayq.' A narrator of the Hadith added that ʿAbdullāh ibn ʿUmar was amongst the racers.[842]

In a similar Hadith, ʿAbdullāh ibn ʿUmar narrates that 'the Messenger of Allah ﷺ held a race between horses which had been made lean by training, from al-Ḥafyā' to Thaniyyah al-Wadāʿ. He held a race between horses which had not been made lean from Thaniyyah to the *masjid* of Banī Zurayq'.[843] ʿAbdullāh ibn ʿUmar said about that race, 'I came first in the race and my horse jumped into the *masjid* with me.'[844]

ʿIyāḍ al-Ashʿarī narrated that the following episode occurred in the aftermath of the Battle of Yarmūk, 'Abū ʿUbaydah, who had been one of the commanders in the

[839] *Sunan Ibn Mājah* 2876.
[840] *Sunan Abī Dāwūd* 2579.
[841] A mountain pass near Medina.
[842] *Ṣaḥīḥ al-Bukhārī* 2869.
[843] *Muwaṭṭa' Imam Mālik* 1005.
[844] *Ṣaḥīḥ Muslim* 1870b.

battle, challenged his warriors, "Who will compete with me in a horse race?" A young man said, "I will, if it does not upset you." Then he beat him, and I saw the two braids of Abū ʿUbaydah ﵁ flying as he raced behind him on an Arabian horse.'[845]

ʿAbdullāh ibn ʿAmr ibn al-ʿĀṣ ﵁ once said, 'While we were with the Messenger of Allah ﷺ on a journey, we stopped to camp. Some of us were pitching tents, others were competing in shooting arrows, and another group was taking the animals out to race them.'[846]

The Prophet ﷺ himself trained and raced horses and camels. ʿAbdullāh ibn ʿUmar ﵁ narrated, 'The Prophet ﷺ used to make horses lean by training them, which he employed in the races.'[847] Anas ﵁ narrated, 'The Prophet ﷺ had a she-camel called al-ʿAḍbā', which could not be beaten in a race. Once a Bedouin came riding a camel which was younger than six years of age, and it beat al-ʿAḍbā' in the race. The Muslims were upset by this so much that the Prophet ﷺ noticed their distress. He ﷺ said, "It is Allah's law that He brings down whatever rises high in the world."'[848] This is also narrated in *Sunan al-Nasāʾī*.[849]

The Prophet ﷺ himself was not upset for being surpassed in the race, as he understood the winning or losing of the race was arbitrary. What was important was the spirit of competition and the benefits one derived from taking part. The benefit is derived from the struggle, from each party pushing the other to do better, and by pushing oneself to the limit. The Prophet ﷺ said, 'There

---

[845] *Musnad al-Imam Aḥmad* 344.
[846] *Sunan al-Nasāʾī* 4191.
[847] *Sunan Abī Dāwūd* 2576.
[848] *Ṣaḥīḥ al-Bukhārī* 2872.
[849] *Sunan al-Nasāʾī* 3592.

must be no shouting or leading another horse at one's side.'[850] In the narration of Yaḥyā ﷺ he adds, 'When racing for a prize.'[851]

Regarding stakes or prize money, they are not allowed in most occasions. But if done to encourage the spirit of competition in martially viable pastimes, then they are permitted. The Prophet ﷺ said, 'No stake is acceptable except in archery, racing a camel, and racing a horse.'[852]

Racing horses or camels was not the only way that the Companions ﷺ competed with one another. In the long narration from Salamah ibn al-Akwaʿ ﷺ mentioned earlier, he narrates:

> *...Intending to return to Medina, he ﷺ made me mount behind him ﷺ on his she-camel named al-ʿAḍbāʾ. While we were travelling, an Anṣārī man who could not be beaten in a race said, 'Is there anyone who can compete with me in a race to Medina? Is there any competitor?' He repeated this again and again. When I heard him talking, I said, 'Are you not considerate of the dignified? Do you not show awe to the nobleman?' He said, 'No, unless he be the Messenger of Allah.' I said, 'Messenger of Allah, may my father and mother be ransomed for you, allow me to dismount so I may defeat this man.' He ﷺ said, 'If you wish.'*
>
> *I said to the Anṣārī, 'I am coming for you.' I then turned my feet and sprang forward, ran after him, and gasped for a while when I drew near to him, and again followed his*

[850] This was done as it encouraged the horse to run faster. But when there was prize money to be won, the only horses allowed in the race were those competing.
[851] *Sunan Abī Dāwūd* 2581.
[852] *Jāmiʿ al-Tirmidhī* 1700.

> *heel and again gasped for a while when I drew near to him, and again dashed after him until I caught up to him and delivered a blow between his shoulders. I said, 'By Allah, you have been overtaken.' He said, 'I do believe I have.'*[853]

This spirit of competition was a way for the Companions ﷺ to relax and have fun with one another; one can see the playfulness in how these brothers jested with and teased one another. As we read earlier, Salamah ibn al-Akwaʿ ﷺ was a master cross-country runner and had kept up with a cavalry unit prior to this race. His stamina, speed, and self-discipline must have been awe-inspiring to witness.

Once again, the Prophet ﷺ himself also took part in such races in a similarly playful manner. An example of this is the famous narration of the Mother of the Believers, ʿĀ'ishah ﷺ, where she narrated, 'The Prophet ﷺ raced with me and I beat him.'[854] She also narrated in relation to this that while she was on a journey with the Messenger of Allah ﷺ, 'I had a race with him ﷺ and I outstripped him ﷺ on my feet. When I grew, I had another race with him ﷺ and he outstripped me. He ﷺ said, "This is for that defeat."'[855]

Other pastimes of a similar nature were also encouraged in the City of the Prophet ﷺ. The Mother of the Believers ʿĀ'ishah ﷺ narrated, 'Once I saw the Messenger of Allah ﷺ at the door of my house while some Ethiopians were playing in the *masjid,* displaying their skill with spears. Allah's Messenger screened me with his *ridā'* to enable me to see their display.' According to

853 *Ṣaḥīḥ Muslim* 1807a.
854 *Sunan Ibn Mājah* 1979.
855 *Sunan Abī Dāwūd* 2578.

ʿUrwah, the Mother of the Believers ʿĀ'ishah ﵂ said, 'I saw the Prophet ﷺ and the Ethiopians were playing with their spears.'[856]

Such competitive spirit should be encouraged in ourselves and those we are put in charge of. In the modern world, this can take the form of either the classical Sunnahs of horsemanship, archery, and footraces, or their modern equivalents found in the contemporary martial arts, shooting, and motorsports. The activity should be beneficial in terms of one's fitness, have transferable applications, and only be carried out in the spirit of competition and not the desire to dominate one's fellow co-religionists.

We cannot look into the subject of competitiveness and not highlight the strong religious spirit of the Companions ﵃ in their observance of piety and virtuous deeds. The Messenger of Allah ﷺ said, 'If the people knew the reward for pronouncing the *adhān* and standing in the first row, and found no other way to achieve this except by drawing lots, they would draw lots. If they knew the reward of the Ẓuhr prayer they would race for it, and if they knew the reward of the ʿIshā' and Fajr prayers in congregation, they would come, even if they had to crawl.'[857] Ibn ʿAbbās ﵄ narrated that the Messenger of Allah ﷺ:

> *...went to the Zamzam well, and there the people were offering water to others and drawing water from it. The Prophet ﷺ said to them, 'Carry on! You are doing a good deed.' Then he ﷺ added, 'Were I not afraid that others would compete with you [in drawing water from the well], I would have certainly taken the rope and put*

856 *Ṣaḥīḥ al-Bukhārī* 454, 455.
857 *Ṣaḥīḥ al-Bukhārī* 615.

it over this (to draw water).' The Prophet ﷺ pointed to his shoulder as he said it.[858]

Amīr al-Mu'minīn 'Umar ibn al-Khaṭṭāb رضي الله عنه said, 'We never competed in doing good deeds except that Abū Bakr beat us to it.'[859]

[858] *Ṣaḥīḥ al-Bukhārī* 1635.

[859] *Musnad al-Imam Aḥmad* 265.

35
He is a Skilled Warrior

عَنْ أَبِي عَلِيٍّ ثُمَامَةَ بْنِ شُفَيٍّ رحمه الله، أَنَّهُ سَمِعَ عُقْبَةَ بْنَ عَامِرٍ رَضِيَ اللَّهُ عَنْهُ يَقُولُ: سَمِعْتُ رَسُولَ اللَّهِ صَلَّى اللَّهُ عَلَيْهِ وَسَلَّمَ، وَهُوَ عَلَى الْمِنْبَرِ، يَقُولُ: "وَأَعِدُّوا لَهُمْ مَا اسْتَطَعْتُمْ مِنْ قُوَّةٍ؛ أَلاَ إِنَّ الْقُوَّةَ الرَّمْيُ، أَلاَ إِنَّ الْقُوَّةَ الرَّمْيُ، أَلاَ إِنَّ الْقُوَّةَ الرَّمْيُ."

Abū ʿAlī Thumāmah ibn Shufayy ﷺ related that he heard ʿUqbah ibn ʿĀmir al-Juhanī ﷺ narrate that he heard the Messenger of Allah ﷺ say whilst he was standing on the pulpit, 'Prepare against them whatever force you can. Pay heed! Strength is in archery! Pay heed! Strength is in archery! Pay heed! Strength is in archery!'[860]

UNARMED COMBAT, STRIKING, AND GRAPPLING

A man's ability to defend himself, his honour, his family, and his people – through his *martial prowess* – has already been well-documented in this book. And it goes without saying that this ability to defend oneself is one of the fundamental qualities a man should be able to tap into. There are three levels of combat which a warrior should be well-versed in: unarmed combat, armed combat, and ranged combat. The Prophet ﷺ said, 'I am the Followed, the Prophet of Repentance, the Prophet of Mercy, and the Prophet of Fierce Battle.'[861]

يَٰٓأَيُّهَا ٱلَّذِينَ ءَامَنُوا۟ ٱصْبِرُوا۟ وَصَابِرُوا۟ وَرَابِطُوا۟

O you who believe, be steadfast, more steadfast than others, and be vigilant...[862]

With regard to unarmed combat, it can be divided into three basic areas: stand up fighting, clinch fighting, and ground fighting.

---

[860] *Ṣaḥīḥ Muslim* 1917.
[861] *Ibn Ḥibbān* 6314.
[862] Qur'an 3:200.

A man should be comfortable in all three areas, and competent enough to give a good account of himself when pressed to do so. In the world we live in today, learning unarmed combat techniques is incredibly accessible. A man can learn anything from striking styles such as boxing, Muay Thai, kickboxing, Karate, and Tae Kwon Do; grappling styles such as Brazilian Jiu-Jitsu, Judo, Greco-Roman Wrestling, Freestyle Wrestling, and Catch Wrestling; hybrid styles like Mixed Martial Arts, Combat Sambo, or military combatives. However, just as living in the Internet-age has made information incredibly accessible, and knowledge and wisdom incredibly rare, so too has the abundance of access to the martial arts in all of their forms resulted in a world that is infinitely more informed about how to fight, but with little to no real experience. During the time of the Prophet ﷺ, warriors were vastly more experienced in fighting; they practised daily, as their lives would more likely than not depend on how well they fought. The Arabs during this time would show the world in just a few short years that no one was as experienced in fighting as they were.

With regard to fighting on the feet, stand up fighting, and striking in the clinch, a man should avoid striking the face of his opponent unless absolutely necessary. There are numerous Hadiths which explicitly prohibit this. The Prophet ﷺ said, 'When any one of you fights with his brother, he should spare his face'[863]; 'When one of you inflicts a beating, he should avoid striking the face'[864]; as well as the directive, 'If somebody fights, then he should avoid the face.'[865]

This is not to say that a man should not strike at all, but that one should be deliberate and mindful about how he does so. In

---

[863] *Ṣaḥīḥ Muslim* 2612.
[864] *Sunan Abī Dāwūd* 4493.
[865] *Ṣaḥīḥ al-Bukhārī* 2559.

a life-or-death situation, there is no restriction on where one would strike.

Amīr al-Mu'minīn 'Alī ﷺ narrated:

> *'I saw the Quraysh grab hold of the Messenger of Allah ﷺ with one person treating him angrily and another shaking him, while they said to him, "Do you make all the gods into One?" By Allah, none of us dared to go close to the Messenger of Allah ﷺ beside Abū Bakr ﷺ. He would strike one person, wrestle with another, and shake someone else as he said, "Shame on you people! Will you kill a man for saying my Lord is Allah?" Amīr al-Mu'minīn 'Alī ﷺ then lifted the shawl he was wearing and wept until his beard became wet, and then continued, 'I ask you to swear by Allah whether the mu'min (believer) from the court of Pharaoh was better or Abū Bakr?' When everyone remained silent, Amīr al-Mu'minīn 'Alī ﷺ said, 'By Allah, a moment of the life of Abū Bakr ﷺ is better than the Earth being filled with people like the mu'min from the court of Pharaoh. While the mu'min from the court of Pharaoh concealed his īmān, Abū Bakr ﷺ made his īmān public.'*[866]

With regard to grappling, there are two key areas where such combat occurs: in clinching range and on the ground. This form of combat is much preferred over striking, as there is less likelihood of skilled opponents causing unintended long-term damage to one another. A man should be able to wrestle another with confidence and skill, take them to the floor and control them once down. Whenever necessary, he should also be able

[866] *Al-Bidāyah wa al-Nihāyah,* vol. 3, p. 271.

to disable his opponent or incapacitate him.

Amongst the Companions ﷺ, though all were skilled in every form of fighting, there were men of distinction in the realm of grappling. One such man was Rukānah ﷺ, who had made a name for himself as a great wrestler among the Quraysh. There are numerous Hadiths that document significant episodes of grappling that occurred with this Companion. For instance, Abū Jaʿfar ibn Muhammad ibn ʿAlī ibn Rukānah narrates from his father that, 'Rukānah wrestled the Prophet ﷺ, and the Prophet ﷺ wrestled him to the ground.'[867] This happened consistently over several rounds of grappling; while being a champion wrestler, Rukānah could not overcome the Prophet ﷺ even once, notwithstanding his size advantage and experience in the field. Rukānah subsequently accepted Islam.

Even the young men and children among the Companions ﷺ would grapple with one another, and this was encouraged. On the eve of the Battle of Uḥud, the Prophet ﷺ inspected his troops and sent back the Companions ﷺ who were below the minimum age of military service (fifteen years of age), but they hid themselves among the troops to take part in the battle.

Muhammad ibn ʿUmar ﷺ narrated:

> *Samurah ibn Jundub's mother was remarried to Murayy ibn Sinān, the uncle of Abū Saʿīd al-Khudrī, who was then Samurah's stepfather. When the Prophet ﷺ set out towards the battlefield of Uḥud, he inspected his Companions and sent back those who were considered too young. Samurah was among those who were sent back, while the Prophet ﷺ permitted Rāfiʿ ibn Khadīj to*

[867] *Sunan Abī Dāwūd* 2207, 4078; *Jāmiʿ al-Tirmidhī* 1784.

be enlisted.[868] *So Samurah said to his stepfather, 'Father, the Messenger of Allah ﷺ has given permission to Rāfiʿ ibn Khadīj and sent me back, while I am much better at wrestling than him.' Consequently, Murayy ibn Sinān petitioned the Messenger of Allah ﷺ, saying, 'O Messenger of Allah, you turned back my son while permitting Rāfiʿ ibn Khadīj, though my lad can out-wrestle him.' The Prophet ﷺ told Rāfiʿ and Samurah to wrestle, and so they did, and Samurah bested Rāfiʿ. The Prophet ﷺ then gave him permission and he witnessed the battle with the Muslim army.*[869]

A man should be prepared to fight, with or without arms, without a moment's notice. How else can he be the guardian of his family? It is his duty to be ready, and though we often pray that such a situation never befalls us, the following well-known proverb springs to mind:

It is better to be a warrior in a garden than a gardener in a war.

ARMED COMBAT AND SWORDSMANSHIP

A skilled warrior must also have the ability to employ weaponry effectively, to defend himself and, should the need arise, to employ lethal force. A warrior needs to be able to do both: to use the tools and weapons of war, or use whatever advantage he can gain to protect his house or his honour on the streets. Thus, there are two types of weaponry that a man must be acquainted with for the purpose of armed combat: 1) the self-defence sidearm, and 2) the weapon of war.

A sidearm is a weapon used for personal protection, both in

---

868 Rāfiʿ was skilled in archery, and thus was permitted to join the army as an archer.

869 *Tārīkh al-Ṭabarī*, vol. 3: p. 12.

battle and in civilian life. Depending on where a man is from, there are local laws which either cater for or restrict the use of a sidearm. For example, in the United States there are states which have 'open carry' or 'concealed carry' laws with regard to modern sidearms, such as the handgun. In other countries, however, there are rules against what is commonly carried for regular use; in the United Kingdom carrying any sort of weapon is illegal in civilian life, with most police officers only carrying batons and an incapacitant spray.

More potent weapons can only be carried by specially trained, government approved officers. For those who have access to the ability to carry weapons, there is no excuse for not learning how to safely and effectively use all available sidearm options, whether that is a gun, knife, or baton. For those that may not be able to utilise them in most contexts, it is still of benefit to learn their effective usage; after all, there is a Sunnah in becoming proficient in them, and if the need arises to protect one's home or family, being able to use whatever is available to do so could be the key factor in success. The Messenger of Allah ﷺ said, 'Whoever unsheathes his sword and starts to strike the people with it, it is permissible to shed his blood.'[870]

Anas ؓ narrated, 'On the Day of Ḥunayn, Umm Sulaym had drawn a dagger she had in her possession. Abū Ṭalḥah saw her and said, "Messenger of Allah, Umm Sulaym is holding a dagger." The Messenger of Allah ﷺ asked her, "Why are you holding this dagger?" She said, "I have drawn it so I may tear open the belly of the polytheist who comes near me."'[871]

ʿUdaysah bint Uhbān ؓ narrated, 'When ʿAlī ibn Abī Ṭālib

[870] *Sunan al-Nasāʾī* 4097.
[871] *Ṣaḥīḥ Muslim* 1809.

came to Baṣrah, he entered upon my father and said, "O Abū Muslim, will you not aid me against these people?" He said, "Of course." So he summoned a bondswoman and said, "Girl, bring me my sword." So she brought it, and he unsheathed it a span or so; I saw that it was made of wood. He said, "My close friend and your cousin advised me that if *fitnah* (tribulation) arose among the Muslims I should take a sword of wood. If you wish, I will go out with you." He said, "I have no need of you or of your sword."[872]

The dagger, the cudgel, the staff, and the wooden sword all have their modern equivalents in knives, batons, or the walking stick. But the handgun does not fall into any of these categories, for it is a tool designed specifically to maim and kill. Its historical equivalent is the most famed weapon in history and a symbol of manhood and the warrior spirit that transcends space, time, and cultures: the sword. The Messenger of Allah ﷺ said, 'Know that Paradise is under the shades of swords.'[873]

Anas ؓ narrated: 'The Prophet ﷺ met the people while he was riding an unsaddled horse with his sword slung over his shoulder.'[874]

Miyamoto Musashi, the most renowned swordsman in the history of the Samurai, said:

...the training for killing enemies is by way of many contests, fighting for survival, discovering the meaning of life and death, learning the way of the Sword...[875]

No individuals on the face of the Earth were more skilled in

[872] *Sunan Ibn Mājah* 3960.
[873] *Ṣaḥīḥ al-Bukhārī* 2818.
[874] *Ṣaḥīḥ al-Bukhārī* 2866.
[875] *The Book of Five Rings, The Fire Book,* Miyamoto Musashi.

the use of swords than the Companions ﷺ. Their skill was unmatched, honed through generations of training, refinement, and constant tribal warfare. The battles of the Arab people would often begin with bouts of poetry and swordplay, where a warrior would fight their counterpart to gain honour and a morale edge over their opponents. The *mubārizūn* (champions) were the elite class amongst them, having mastered duelling, cavalry combat, swordsmanship, and archery; they also were fully proficient in using the mace, lance, as well as fighting while riding bareback, turning in the saddle to duel while riding backward, or engaging in close-quarter archery within a few feet of their opponents. Abū Isḥāq ﷺ narrated, 'A man asked al-Barā ﷺ[876] while I was listening, "Did 'Alī ﷺ take part in the Battle of Badr?" Al-Barā' ﷺ said, "Yes, he even engaged in a duel and was clad in two pieces of armour."'[877]

Another member of the famed *mubārizūn* was Ḍirār ibn al-Azwar ﷺ. His name was both infamous and feared amongst the enemies of Islam for his incredible skill in combat, especially with the sword. Ḍirār would remove his shirt before a fight, sacrificing the protection of a mail shirt for unhindered movement and speed; he often fought with two swords, again sacrificing the protection of a shield for versatility of offence. Despite what popular culture and fiction tell us, fighting without armour and shields was extremely rare in true combat, especially in war, for a single misstep, slow reaction, or a stray or well-placed arrow could lead to one's death. On one famous occasion at the Battle of Ajnādayn, Ḍirār ﷺ engaged in 30 duels against the Byzantine commanders and champions, and ended up taking 30

[876] Al-Barā' ﷺ himself was a famed champion duellist.
[877] *Ṣaḥīḥ al-Bukhārī* 3970.

lives from the enemy forces.[878]

Despite being a general himself, Khālid ibn al-Walīd ﷺ was also from amongst this group and said: 'On the day of Mu'tah, nine swords were broken in my hand and only a Yemenite sword[879] remained.'[880] He would often begin his battles by challenging the enemy commander. If they accepted, he would slay them, and the enemy forces would be without their most capable commander. If they refused, they would lose face in the eyes of their men; the Muslim morale would increase regardless.

Besides being the cousin of the Prophet ﷺ, Amīr al-Mu'minīn ʿAlī ibn Abī Ṭālib ﷺ was also a champion duellist. Salamah ibn al-Akwaʿ ﷺ narrates:

When we reached Khaybar, its king Marḥab advanced forward, brandishing his sword and chanting:

قَدْ عَلِمَتْ خَيْبَرُ أَنِّي مَرْحَبُ / شَاكِي السِّلَاحِ بَطَلٌ مُجَرَّبُ / إِذَا الْحُرُوبُ أَقْبَلَتْ تَلَهَّبُ

Marḥab am I, and Khaybar knows,

Armed and brave and tried in war,

When flames of battle burn and roar.

My uncle, ʿĀmir ﷺ, strode out to duel with him, saying:

قَدْ عَلِمَتْ خَيْبَرُ أَنِّي عَامِرٌ / شَاكِي السِّلَاحِ بَطَلٌ مُغَامِرٌ

I am ʿĀmir, Khaybar knows,

Armed and reckless, brave and bold.

---

[878] *Islam at War: A History,* p. 27, Nafziger & Walton.
[879] Yemenite swords were made of imported Indian *wootz* steel and were incredibly sought after and durable.
[880] *Ṣaḥīḥ al-Bukhārī* 4266.

They exchanged blows. Marḥab's sword struck the shield of ʿĀmir ﷺ, who leaned forward to attack his opponent from below, but his sword recoiled off Marḥab's armour and cut the artery in his forearm, causing his death. I came out and heard some people among the Companions of the Prophet ﷺ saying, 'ʿĀmir's deed has been wasted; he has killed himself.' So I went to the Prophet ﷺ weeping, and said, 'Messenger of Allah, ʿĀmir's deed has been wasted.' The Messenger of Allah ﷺ said, 'Who passed such a remark?' I said, 'Some of your Companions.' He ﷺ said, 'He who said that told a lie, for ʿĀmir there is a double reward.' Then he sent me to fetch ʿAlī, who had sore eyes, and said, 'I will give the banner of Islam to a man who loves Allah and His Messenger (or whom Allah and His Messenger love).' So I went to ʿAlī, brought him along, and he had sore eyes. I took him to the Messenger of Allah ﷺ, who applied his saliva to ʿAlī's eyes and he was cured. The Messenger of Allah ﷺ gave him the banner, and ʿAlī went out to meet Marḥab in single combat. The latter advanced, chanting:

قَدْ عَلِمَتْ خَيْبَرُ أَنِّي مَرْحَبُ | شَاكِي السِّلاَحِ بَطَلٌ مُجَرَّبُ | إِذَا الْحُرُوبُ
أَقْبَلَتْ تَلَهَّبُ

Marḥab am I, and Khaybar knows,

Armed and brave and tried in war,

When flames of battle burn and roar.

ʿAlī replied:

أَنَا الَّذِي سَمَّتْنِي أُمِّي حَيْدَرَهْ | كَلَيْثِ غَابَاتٍ كَرِيهِ الْمَنْظَرَهْ | أُوفِيهِمُ بِالصَّاعِ
كَيْلَ السَّنْدَرَهْ

She named me Ḥaydar, all men know,

A lion prowling, feared and awed,

I counter foes with hefty blows.

'Alī then struck Marḥab's head and killed him, and so the victory of the conquest of Khaybar was due to him.[881]

While addressing the people, Amīr al-Mu'minīn 'Alī ﷺ once asked, 'O people, who is the most courageous person?'

They replied, 'You are, O Amīr al-Mu'minīn!'

Amīr al-Mu'minīn 'Alī ﷺ then said, 'Although I have defeated every man who stood before me, the most courageous person was Abū Bakr ﷺ. We had constructed a shelter for the Messenger of Allah ﷺ during the Battle of Badr, and then asked for a volunteer who would remain with the Messenger of Allah ﷺ to prevent the polytheists from attacking him ﷺ. By Allah, whenever a polytheist drew close, Abū Bakr ﷺ was there with his sword drawn by the Messenger of Allah's side. He attacked anyone who dared attack the Messenger of Allah ﷺ. He was certainly the bravest of men.'[882]

Anas ﷺ reported: 'The Messenger of Allah ﷺ held aloft his sword on the Day of Uḥud and said, "Who would take it from me?" All the Companions stretched out their hands, saying, "I would do it! I would do it!" He ﷺ said, "Who would take it in order to fulfil its rights?" The Companions withdrew their hands. Simāk ibn Kharashah, Abū Dujānah, said, "I am here to take it and fulfil its rights." He took the sword and struck the heads of

---

[881] *Ṣaḥīḥ Muslim* 1807a.

[882] *Al-Bidāyah wa al-Nihāyah,* vol. 3, p. 271.

the polytheists with it during the battle.'[883]

Oftentimes, when people think of the close-quarter, hand-to-hand weapons that were utilised in the theatre of war, they often visualise the sword and shield combination. However, the primary weapon used by the soldier was the pike or spear. A line of well-disciplined polearm users could stop a fearsome cavalry charge, hold a greater force at bay, or decimate the enemy lines from a safe distance. The spear was easy to learn and use, and even people with little weapons experience could be taught over a day to use spears, or even simple wooden pikes; they would be effective military personnel come the morning, ready for battle.

The Companions ﷺ, however, mastered their use, and this skill with all forms of weaponry, the martial prowess of the men overall, and most importantly the fierceness of their belief in Allah ﷻ were the key components of their success in the fields of battle, which ultimately saw them advance towards both Europe and China within eight decades of the Conquest of Mecca. There were three categories of polearms commonly used: the *ḥarbah,* a short spear or javelin; the *ʿanzah,* a wooden pike; and the *rumḥah,* the iron-tipped spear or lance. The polearm's modern-day counterpart is the rifle. If a man is able to, he should practise and become competent with this weapon also. Amīr al-Mu'minīn ʿAlī ibn Abī Ṭālib ﷺ said, 'When al-Mughīrah ibn Shuʿbah fought alongside the Prophet ﷺ he would carry a spear, and when he would come back he would throw his spear down burying it in the ground until someone picked it up and returned it to him.'[884]

ʿUrwah ﷺ narrated:

---

[883] *Ṣaḥīḥ Muslim* 2470.
[884] *Sunan Ibn Mājah* 2809.

Al-Zubayr ⚜ said, 'I met ʿUbaydah ibn Saʿīd ibn al-ʿĀṣ on the day of Badr and he was encased in armour, so much that only his eyes were visible. He was known as Abū Dhāt al-Karish, and he proudly announced, "I am Abū Dhāt al-Karish." I attacked him with the spear, pierced his eye, and he died. I put my foot on his body to pull it out, but even so I had to exert great force to remove it, as both edges were bent.[885]

During times of peace, the Companions ⚜ would train constantly with these weapons. Anas ibn Mālik ⚜ said, 'When the Messenger of Allah ﷺ came to Medina, the Abyssinians played (or put on a display for his coming) out of joy. They played with spears.'[886] The Mother of the Believers ʿĀ'ishah ⚜ narrated, 'On one occasion I saw the Messenger of Allah ﷺ at the door of my house while some Ethiopians were playing in the *masjid* displaying their skill with spears. Allah's Messenger was screening me with his cloak to enable me to see their display.'[887]

These spears were javelins, which were used both in close-quarters and thrown. They are the same weapons mentioned earlier in the story of Waḥshī ibn Ḥarb ⚜,[888] and would sometimes be paired with shields.[889]

The Muslims were likewise well-trained in the use of the iron-tipped spear, which is alternatively known as the lance. In the long Hadith that we have been referring to throughout the last few sections, Salamah ibn al-Akwaʿ ⚜ narrates that at the time

---

[885] *Ṣaḥīḥ al-Bukhārī* 3998.
[886] *Sunan Abī Dāwūd* 4923.
[887] *Ṣaḥīḥ al-Bukhārī* 454, 455.
[888] *Ṣaḥīḥ Muslim* 1841.
[889] *Ṣaḥīḥ Muslim* 892e.

he was sniping the enemy from the hilltop, he remained in position until reinforcements arrived on horseback, riding through the trees:

> *Lo! Foremost among them was Akhram al-Asadī. Behind him was Abū Qatādah al-Anṣārī and behind him was al-Miqdād ibn al-Aswad al-Kindī. I caught hold of the reins of Akhram's horse as the raiders fled. I said, 'Akhram, guard yourself against them until the Messenger of Allah and his Companions join you.' He said, 'Salamah, if you believe in Allah, the Last Day, and know that Paradise is true and Hell is true, do not stand between me and martyrdom.' So I let him go. Akhram and ʿAbd al-Raḥmān al-Fazārī met in combat. Akhram hamstrung ʿAbd al-Raḥmān's horse and the latter struck him with his lance and killed him. ʿAbd al-Raḥmān turned about on his horse. Abū Qatādah, a knight of the Messenger of Allah, met ʿAbd al-Raḥmān in combat, smote him with his lance, and killed him.*[890]

When there is a choice, a man should try to utilise weapons made by Muslims, as on one occasion Amīr al-Mu'minīn ʿAlī ﷺ narrated, 'The Messenger of Allah ﷺ had an Arabian bow in his hand when he ﷺ saw a man carrying a Persian bow. He ﷺ said, "What is this? Throw it away. You should use this (the Arabian bow), others like it, and the *qanā*.[891] Perhaps Allah ﷻ will thereby support His religion and enable you to conquer lands."'[892]

The Prophet ﷺ always had a spear nearby when travelling or at home. Anas ibn Mālik ﷺ narrated: 'The Messenger of Allah

---

[890] *Ṣaḥīḥ Muslim* 1807a.
[891] Another type of Arabian spear.
[892] *Sunan Ibn Mājah* 2810.

ﷺ prayed Eid at the prayer place in an open field, using a small spear as a *sutrah* (to prevent people from walking in front of him).'[893] Ibn 'Umar also related in this regard: 'The Messenger of Allah ﷺ used to take out an *'anzah* (a short spear) on the days of Eid al-Fitr and Eid al-Adha, plant it in the ground, and pray facing toward it.'[894]

RANGED COMBAT AND ARCHERY

Should he be called to do so, a man should be trained and capable of using ranged combat techniques. All firearms fall into this category, as does traditional archery, axe or javelin throwing, and crossbow usage. As men, it is necessary for each of us to be able to engage with opponents in all three forms of combat, namely the unarmed, armed, and ranged methods. The use of more specific military equipment such as tanks, fighters, and rockets is restricted to military personnel only, and thankfully so, yet the Companions رضي الله عنهم were also trained to use their equivalents (catapults and mangonels) as well, as they were all warriors in the truest sense.

There are many Hadiths which highlight the extent to which the Companions رضي الله عنهم loved archery and the regularity with which they practised the art. 'Uqbah ibn 'Āmir al-Juhanī رضي الله عنه reported that he heard the Messenger of Allah ﷺ saying, 'Lands shall be laid open to you, and Allah ﷻ will suffice you against your enemies, but none of you should neglect practising his skills in archery.'[895] 'Uqbah رضي الله عنه took these words to heart and continued to practise archery throughout his life. Khālid ibn Yazīd al-Juhanī

---

[893] *Sunan Ibn Mājah* 1306.
[894] *Sunan al-Nasā'ī* 1565.
[895] *Ṣaḥīḥ Muslim* 1918.

said, ''Uqbah ibn 'Āmir used to pass by me and say, "O Khālid, let us go out and shoot arrows."'[896] In this context, 'Abd al-Raḥmān ibn Shamāsah also narrated: 'Fuqaym al-Lakhmī said to 'Uqbah ibn 'Āmir, "You frequent the area between these two targets and yet you are an old man. You must be finding it very hard." 'Uqbah said, "But for something I heard from the Prophet, I would not strain myself so."' Ḥārith, one of the narrators, said, 'I asked Ibn Shamāsah, "What was that?" He said that the Prophet had said, "Whoever learnt archery and then gave it up is not from us", or that "He is guilty of disobedience."'[897]

'Umar ibn al-Khaṭṭāb said, 'Wear rough clothes and practise archery.'[898]

In a Hadith about the time of the eclipse, Samurah ibn Jundub narrated, 'When a boy from the Anṣār and I were firing arrows towards two of our targets, the Sun was sighted by the people at the height of two or three lances above the horizon. It became dark like the black herb *tannūmah*.'[899]

Salamah ibn al-Akwa', whose amazing skill with the bow has already been covered in some length in earlier sections, narrated: 'The Prophet passed by a group from the tribe of Aslam practising archery, so the Messenger of Allah said, "O children of Ismā'īl, practice archery, for your father was a great archer! And I am with the sons of So-and-so." Hearing that, one of the two teams stopped and so the Messenger of Allah asked them, "What is the matter? Why do you not loose arrows?"

---

[896] *Sunan al-Nasā'ī* 3578.
[897] *Ṣaḥīḥ Muslim* 1919.
[898] *Musnad al-Imam Aḥmad* 301.
[899] *Sunan Abī Dāwūd* 1184.

They replied, "O Messenger of Allah, how can we do so when you are with the opposite team?" He 🕌 said, "Loose arrows, for I am with you all."'[900]

The Messenger of Allah 🕌 said, 'Allah 🕌 will surely admit three into Paradise by a single arrow: its maker who seeks good by his production of it, the one who shoots it, and the one who holds the arrows for him.' And he 🕌 said, 'Practise archery and practise riding, and that you should practise archery is more beloved to me than that you should ride. All idle pastimes that the Muslim man engages in are falsehood, except for his shooting of his bow, his training of his horse, and his playing with his wife, for they are from the truth.'[901]

Anas 🕌 narrated, 'On the day of the Battle of Uḥud, the people retreated, leaving the Prophet 🕌. But Abū Ṭalḥah 🕌 was shielding the Prophet 🕌 with his shield in front of him. Abū Ṭalḥah 🕌 was a strong, experienced archer who used to keep his bows strong and well-stretched. On that day he broke two or three bows. If any man passed by carrying a quiver full of arrows, the Prophet 🕌 would say to him, "Empty it in front of Abū Ṭalḥah." When the Prophet 🕌 surveyed the enemy by raising his head, Abū Ṭalḥah 🕌 said, "O Messenger of Allah, may my parents be sacrificed for your sake! Please do not raise your head and make it visible, lest an arrow of the enemy should hit you. Let my neck and chest be wounded instead of yours."'[902]

ʿĀmir ibn Saʿd 🕌 narrated, 'Saʿd ibn Abī Waqqāṣ said, "I had seen the Prophet 🕌 laugh at the Battle of the Trench so

---

[900] Ṣaḥīḥ al-Bukhārī 3373.
[901] Jāmiʿ al-Tirmidhī 1637.
[902] Ṣaḥīḥ al-Bukhārī 3811.

hard that his molar teeth became apparent." I said, "How did it come about?" He said, "There was a man holding a shield while Sa'd was shooting, and the man was saying such-and-such with the shield raised and covering his forehead. Sa'd therefore aimed an arrow at him and loosed it when he raised his head, so it did not miss this part of him (his forehead), and the man toppled over and kicked up his feet. The Prophet ﷺ then laughed so much that his molar teeth became apparent." I asked, "What made him laugh?" He replied, "What Sa'd did to the man!""[903]

Gain access to the arms you can legally own, and become skilled with them. While a Muslim man abhors violence, he is always prepared for it.

[903] *Al-Shamā'il al-Muḥammadiyyah* 233.

36
He is Courageous

عَنْ عَلِيٍّ رَضِيَ اللَّهُ عَنْهُ، قَالَ: "لَقَدْ رَأَيْتُنَا يَوْمَ بَدْرٍ ، وَنَحْنُ نَلُوذُ بِرَسُولِ اللَّهِ صَلَّى اللَّهُ عَلَيْهِ وَسَلَّمَ، وَهُوَ أَقْرَبُنَا إِلَى الْعَدُوِّ ، وَكَانَ مِنْ أَشَدِّ النَّاسِ يَوْمَئِذٍ بَأْسًا."

'Alī ﷺ said, 'On the day of Badr, I saw that we all sought recourse with the Messenger of Allah ﷺ. And he was the closest of us all to the enemy lines, and of the bravest of all the people on that day.'[904]

Courage, Bravery, and Volunteering

Courage. Every man aspires to it; each of us knows that it is a fundamental virtue of manliness; many of us believe we do not have it; and some of us believe that we have more of it than we actually do. One's capacity for courage or bravery cannot be known until it is tested. Though courage and bravery are often used interchangeably, there is a subtle difference between the two. Courage entails showing strength in the face of grief or pain, whereas bravery is showing strength in the face of fear. The courageous man is therefore he who bears pain and stands his ground regardless of his circumstances, namely to suffer 'the slings and arrows of outrageous fortune'.[905] The brave man is the one who is faced with something that would scare lesser men into flight or petrify them, yet he stands up to it.

These virtues coursed through the veins of the Companions ﷺ, nourishing every fibre of their being. Nevertheless, as it has no doubt become apparent over the course of this book, even their courage and bravery paled in comparison to the Complete

---

[904] *Musnad al-Imām Aḥmad* 654.
[905] *Hamlet,* William Shakespeare.

Man, our blessed Prophet ﷺ. That is why even the mighty ʿAlī ؓ said that the Companions ؓ sought recourse with the Prophet ﷺ and he was closest to the enemy, and the bravest of them all.[906]

وَمِنَ ٱلنَّاسِ مَن يَشْرِى نَفْسَهُ ٱبْتِغَآءَ مَرْضَاتِ ٱللَّهِ ۗ وَٱللَّهُ رَءُوفٌۢ بِٱلْعِبَادِ.

And among men there is one who sells his very soul to seek the pleasure of Allah, and Allah is ever benignant to His servants.[907]

Ibn ʿAbbās ؓ, Anas ؓ, Saʿīd ibn al-Musayyib, Abū ʿUthmān al-Nahdī, ʿIkrimah ؓ, and several other scholars say that the above verse was revealed in relation to Ṣuhayb ibn Sinān al-Rūmī ؓ.[908] When he left Mecca to emigrate to Medina, a group of Qurayshī disbelievers waylaid him. He dismounted, removed the arrows from his quiver, and took up a position in preparation for a fight. He reasoned with them thus:

> *O Quraysh, you all know that I am the superior archer here. My arrows never miss. I swear by Allah that you shall not reach me until not an arrow remains with me. When they are spent, I shall use my sword as long as I can. After that, you can take your chances. However, if you want to make a deal, I can tell you where my money is in Mecca. You can take all of it and I will go my way.*[909]

During the Battle of Ḥunayn, the Muslims were ambushed by enemy archers who had taken position on higher ground and rained down arrows on them, forcing them to retreat out of range. Regarding this incident, al-Barāʾ ibn ʿĀzib ؓ narrated, 'A man said to us, "Did you flee from the Messenger of Allah ﷺ,

---

906 *Musnad al-Imām Aḥmad* 654.
907 *Qur'an* 2:207.
908 *Tafsīr Ibn Kathīr* 2:207.
909 *Maʿārif al-Qur'an*, vol. 1: p. 513.

O Abū ʿUmārah?" I said, "No! By Allah, I did not flee from the Messenger of Allah ﷺ, but some hasty people fled and the tribe of Hawāzin assaulted them with arrows. The Messenger of Allah ﷺ was mounted on his white mule, and Abū Sufyān ibn al-Ḥārith ibn ʿAbd al-Muṭṭalib was holding its reigns. The Messenger of Allah ﷺ was saying:

أَنَا النَّبِيُّ لاَ كَذِبْ | أَنَا ابْنُ عَبْدِ الْمُطَّلِبْ

I am the Prophet and this is no fib,

I am the son of ʿAbd al-Muṭṭalib.[910]

Even with arrows raining down on him ﷺ, he remained on his mount and recited a terse couplet, announcing who he was to the enemy without fear, and all the while Abū Sufyān ؓ, who had been the leader of the polytheists in the Battle of the Confederates, held the reins of his ﷺ mule and held his nerve; he who was once a great leader of the enemies of Islam, was now a steadfast Companion ؓ, bravely facing death to stand by the Prophet's side. Such was the magnetic power of this man ﷺ, that even his greatest enemies would become willing to give their lives for him when they met him with open hearts and minds.

Thābit ؓ narrated that the Prophet ﷺ was mentioned before Anas ibn Mālik ؓ and he said, 'He ﷺ was the best of people, the most generous of people, and the bravest of people. The people of Medina became alarmed one night, and he ﷺ was the first of them to investigate the noise and din. He ﷺ was riding a horse belonging to Abū Ṭalḥah ؓ bareback, with no saddle. His sword was hanging from his neck and he ﷺ was saying, "O

---

[910] *Jāmiʿ al-Tirmidhī* 1688.

people, do not be afraid," sending them back to their homes. Then he said of the horse, "We found it to be like a sea."'[911] In another narration, Anas ﷺ said, 'One night, the people of Medina were alarmed by a noise and went to its source. The Prophet ﷺ met them on the way, having already reached the source of the noise, and he ﷺ was saying, "Do not be alarmed. Do not be alarmed." He was riding Abū Ṭalḥah's horse without a saddle and had a sword hung from his neck.'[912]

The Prophet ﷺ had armed himself and rushed to face the unknown threat, and was already returning on a borrowed mount when the people came out to investigate. Despite this, he ﷺ always prayed to Allah ﷻ to protect him from cowardliness, saying, 'O Allah! I seek refuge with You from cowardice, being brought back to the poor state of old age, from the afflictions of the world, and the punishments in the grave.'[913]

Yaḥyā ibn Saʿīd ﷺ narrated that ʿUmar ibn al-Khaṭṭāb ﷺ said, 'The nobility of the believer is his *taqwā* (God-consciousness). His *dīn* (religious way of life) is his noble descent. His manliness is his good character. Boldness and cowardice are but instincts which Allah ﷻ places wherever He wills. The coward shrinks from defending even his father and mother, and the bold one fights for the sake of the combat, not the spoils. Being slain is but one way of meeting death, and the martyr is the one who gives himself, expectant of reward from Allah ﷻ.'[914]

---

911 *Sunan Ibn Mājah* 2772.
912 *Al-Adab al-Mufrad* 303.
913 *Ṣaḥīḥ al-Bukhārī* 2822.
914 *Muwaṭṭa' Imam Mālik* 996.

Regarding Bayʿat al-Riḍwān,[915] Yazīd said, 'I said to Salamah, "For what did you give the pledge of allegiance to the Prophet on the Day of al-Ḥudaybiyyah?" He replied, "For death."'[916] Jābir clarified what Salamah meant when he said, 'We did not give our pledge to the Messenger of Allah for death; rather, we pledged not to flee from battle.'[917]

وَأَطِيعُوا۟ ٱللَّهَ وَرَسُولَهُۥ وَلَا تَنَـٰزَعُوا۟ فَتَفْشَلُوا۟ وَتَذْهَبَ رِيحُكُمْ ۖ وَٱصْبِرُوٓا۟ ۚ إِنَّ ٱللَّهَ مَعَ ٱلصَّـٰبِرِينَ

Obey Allah and His Messenger, and do not quarrel with each other, lest you should lose courage, and your prowess should evaporate; and be patient. Surely, Allah is with the patient.[918]

In the above verse, Allah orders the observance of steadfastness upon meeting the enemy. Muslims are *not allowed* to run or shy away, or show cowardice in battle.[919] The strict devotion and obedience that the Companions demonstrated towards the words of Allah and His noble Prophet is the reason that they, though few in number, overcame the various empires of the world in such short order. The Byzantines, Persians, Turks, Slavs, Berbers, Ethiopians, Sudanese tribes, and the Copts were just some of the powers that they decisively defeated; each enemy force was as different from each other as can be, with their own strategies, weaponry, fighting styles, and terrains. Despite never having fought in wars of the scale they would face beyond the sands of Arabia, they continued to

[915] This was the Pledge of Satisfaction, which took place just prior to the Treaty of al-Ḥudaybiyyah when the Muslims believed ʿUthmān ibn ʿAffān, who had been sent as an envoy into Mecca, had been martyred by the Quraysh.

[916] *Ṣaḥīḥ al-Bukhārī* 7206.

[917] *Sunan al-Nasāʾī* 4158.

[918] *Qurʾan* 8:46.

[919] *Tafsīr Ibn Kathīr* 8:46.

conquer their foes.[920] The Companions ﷺ knew the benefit of following the Qur'an and Sunnah, and this understanding allowed them to accomplish wonders. They did not shy away from the fight, regardless of the numbers arrayed against them, nor did they wait for others to step forward when volunteers were requested.

Jābir ibn ʿAbdullāh ﷺ narrated, 'On the day of the Battle of the Trench, the Prophet ﷺ wanted somebody from amongst the people to volunteer for a reconnaissance mission. Al-Zubayr volunteered. He asked again and al-Zubayr volunteered again. Then he repeated the same again thrice and al-Zubayr volunteered once more. The Prophet ﷺ then said, "Every Prophet has a disciple and my disciple is al-Zubayr."'[921]

Following al-Ḥudaybiyyah, Salamah ibn al-Akwaʿ ﷺ narrated, 'Then we moved, returning to Medina, and halted at a place where there was a mountain between us and Banū Laḥyān, who were polytheists. The Messenger of Allah ﷺ requested Allah's forgiveness for the man who ascended the mountain at night to act as a lookout for the Messenger of Allah ﷺ and his Companions. I ascended that mountain twice or thrice that night.'[922]

With regard to courage and exhibiting strength despite pain and hardship, Jābir ibn ʿAbdullāh ﷺ narrated a perfect example from the campaign of Dhāt al-Riqāʿ:

> *One of the unbelievers had taken an oath saying, 'I shall not rest until I kill one of the Companions of*

---

[920] *Tafsīr Ibn Kathīr* 8:46.
[921] *Ṣaḥīḥ al-Bukhārī* 2997.
[922] *Ṣaḥīḥ Muslim* 1807.

Muhammad.'

He set out, following the footsteps of the Prophet ﷺ. The Prophet ﷺ encamped at a certain place, and said, 'Who will keep a watch on us?' A person from the Muhājirīn[923] *and another from the Anṣār*[924] *responded. He ﷺ said, 'Go to the mouth of the mountain pass.' When they went to the mouth of the mountain pass, the Muhājir lay down while the Anṣārī stood praying.*

The man who had sworn the oath came to them. When he saw the person praying he realised that he was the watchman of the Muslims and shot at him with an arrow, hitting his target. But he took the arrow out and threw it away. He - the unbeliever - then shot three more arrows. Then the Anṣārī bowed, prostrated, and awoke his Companion. When he (the enemy) perceived that they had become aware of his presence, he fled. When the Muhājir saw the Anṣārī bleeding, he asked him, 'Glory be to Allah! Why did you not wake me up the first time he shot you?' He replied, 'I was busy reciting a chapter of the Qur'an.[925] *I did not like to leave it.'*[926]

In the above Hadith we have a display of the pinnacle of courage in the face of great pain and a vivid illustration of how the Companions observed complete devotion in prayer. May Allah ﷻ be pleased with each and every one of them. *Āmīn.*

---

[923] This is reported to be ʿAmmār ibn Yāsir.
[924] This is reported to be ʿAbbād ibn Bishr.
[925] It is reported that he was reading Sūrah al-Kahf.
[926] *Sunan Abī Dāwūd* 198.

37
He is Selfless

عَنْ أَنَسٍ رَضِيَ اللهُ عَنْهُ، قَالَ: لَمَّا كَانَ يَوْمُ أُحُدٍ، انْهَزَمَ النَّاسُ عَنِ النَّبِيِّ صَلَّى اللَّهُ عَلَيْهِ وَسَلَّمَ، وَأَبُو طَلْحَةَ رَضِيَ اللهُ عَنْهُ بَيْنَ يَدَيِ النَّبِيِّ صَلَّى اللَّهُ عَلَيْهِ وَسَلَّمَ مُجَوِّبٌ بِهِ عَلَيْهِ بِحَجَفَةٍ لَهُ، وَكَانَ أَبُو طَلْحَةَ رَضِيَ اللهُ عَنْهُ رَجُلاً رَامِيًا شَدِيدَ الْقِدِّ، يَكْسِرُ يَوْمَئِذٍ قَوْسَيْنِ أَوْ ثَلاَثًا، وَكَانَ الرَّجُلُ يَمُرُّ مَعَهُ الْجَعْبَةُ مِنَ النَّبْلِ، فَيَقُولُ: "انْشُرْهَا لأَبِي طَلْحَةَ." فَأَشْرَفَ النَّبِيُّ صَلَّى اللَّهُ عَلَيْهِ وَسَلَّمَ يَنْظُرُ إِلَى الْقَوْمِ، فَيَقُولُ أَبُو طَلْحَةَ: "يَا نَبِيَّ اللَّهِ، بِأَبِي أَنْتَ وَأُمِّي، لاَ تُشْرِفْ يُصِيبُكَ سَهْمٌ مِنْ سِهَامِ الْقَوْمِ، نَحْرِي دُونَ نَحْرِكَ."

Anas ﵁ narrated: 'On the day of the Battle of Uḥud, the people had retreated, leaving the Prophet ﷺ. However, Abū Ṭalḥah ﵁ remained and was shielding the Prophet ﷺ with his shield in front of him. Abū Ṭalḥah ﵁ was a strong, experienced archer who used to keep his bows strong and well-stretched. On that day, he broke two or three bows. If any man passed by carrying a quiver full of arrows, the Prophet ﷺ would say to him, "Empty it in front of Abū Ṭalḥah." When the Prophet ﷺ started surveying the enemy by raising his head, Abū Ṭalḥah ﵁ said, "O Prophet of Allah, let my parents be sacrificed for your sake! Please do not raise your head and make it visible, lest an arrow of the enemy should hit you. Let my neck and chest be wounded instead of yours."'[927]

SELFLESSNESS AND SACRIFICE

A man must be willing and able to make the ultimate sacrifice for the ones he loves. This is a burden which each of us must acutely understand. It is all good and well to list virtues and espouse lofty ideas of manhood and masculinity, but what use are they when they fail at the ultimate test? Your children, your parents, your spouse, and your siblings – can you put them before yourself, even if it means giving up your worldly life for

[927] *Ṣaḥīḥ al-Bukhārī* 3811.

them? This is the peak of manliness that we must struggle to conquer, and a trial of our masculinity that we hope never to be tested by.

The Companions رضي الله عنهم loved the Prophet ﷺ more than life itself. They loved him ﷺ more than their parents, their children, their siblings, their spouses, and even themselves. The Prophet ﷺ said, 'None of you is a believer until I am dearer to him than his child, his father, and the whole of mankind.'[928] Furthermore, they proved this time and again, putting their bodies between the Messenger of Allah ﷺ and his attackers, making shields out of their very lives. This is the truest test of manhood, and the Companions رضي الله عنهم proved themselves worthy of their proximity to the Prophet ﷺ. To walk toward danger while others flee or shy away is no easy thing, but to *know with complete certainty* that you are going to die and still step forward to protect your loved ones is undoubtedly one of the greatest trials. May Allah ﷻ protect us from such a test.

مِّنَ ٱلْمُؤْمِنِينَ رِجَالٌ صَدَقُوا۟ مَا عَـٰهَدُوا۟ ٱللَّهَ عَلَيْهِ ۖ فَمِنْهُم مَّن قَضَىٰ نَحْبَهُۥ وَمِنْهُم مَّن يَنتَظِرُ ۖ وَمَا بَدَّلُوا۟ تَبْدِيلًا.

Among the believers, there are men who came true to the covenant they had with Allah. Accordingly, some of them have fulfilled their vows by sacrificing their lives in the way of Allah, and some of them are still waiting, and they did not change their commitment in the least.[929]

During the Battle of Uḥud there were many such examples of selflessness and sacrifice, and thus the rest of this section will focus on the Companions رضي الله عنهم during this battle. The narration

[928] *Ṣaḥīḥ Muslim* 44b.
[929] *Qur'an* 33:23.

about Abū Ṭalḥah ؓ shows just how much prepared the Companions were to give life and limb for the Prophet ﷺ. Abū Ṭalḥah ؓ would guard the Prophet ﷺ with his own shield and place his body between the Prophet ﷺ and the enemy. Anas ibn Mālik ؓ said, 'Abū Ṭalḥah ؓ and the Prophet ﷺ used to shield themselves with one shield.'[930] During the battle, Abū Ṭalḥah ؓ lost some of his fingers to arrows, and in response he yelled, 'Good!'[931]

When Khālid ibn al-Walīd ؓ – who was not yet a Muslim – flanked the Companions ؓ after the archers on the hill left their position, chaos ensued in the Muslim lines. ʿAbdullāh ibn Jubayr ؓ and the 10 men that remained at their post engaged the cavalry and did not leave their position, giving their lives to defend the exposed rear of the Companions ؓ. Despite the ensuing chaos, 14 Companions ؓ, seven from the Muhājirīn (Abū Bakr ؓ, ʿUmar ibn al-Khaṭṭāb ؓ, ʿAbd al-Raḥmān ibn ʿAwf ؓ, Saʿd ibn Abī Waqqāṣ ؓ, Abū Ṭalḥah ؓ, al-Zubayr ibn al-ʿAwwām ؓ, and Abū ʿUbaydah ؓ) and seven from the Anṣār (Abū Dujānah ؓ, al-Ḥabāb ibn al-Mundhir ؓ, ʿĀṣim ibn Thābit ؓ, al-Ḥārith ibn al-Ṣimmah ؓ, Sahl ibn Ḥunayf ؓ, Saʿd ibn Muʿādh ؓ, and Usayd ibn Ḥuḍayr ؓ) stood by him ﷺ and remained ready to give life and limb for the Beloved of Allah ﷺ. At times they would peel away to engage oncoming attackers or aid their comrades,[932] but this core group – including ʿAlī ؓ, who was also carrying the banner following the martyrdom of Muṣʿab ibn ʿUmayr ؓ – remained around the

---

930 *Ṣaḥīḥ al-Bukhārī* 2902.
931 *Fatḥ al-Bārī,* vol. 7: p. 278.
932 *Ṣaḥīḥ al-Bukhārī* 4561.

Prophet ﷺ.

Abū Dujānah ؓ, the great warrior who had promised to fulfil the rights of the Prophet's sword,[933] had a red ʿimāmah[934] that he would tie prior to engaging in battle, which symbolised that either his enemies would fall or he would, and he tied it on the day of Uḥud after taking up the Prophet's sword. During Uḥud, the Prophet ﷺ came under fire from a barrage of arrows and Abū Dujānah ؓ, seeing the arrows coming and the Prophet ﷺ exposed in the open, placed himself between the Prophet and the danger, with his eyes on his beloved Prophet ﷺ and his broad back towards the enemy like a shield. His back was pierced with many arrows, but he did not move from his position.[935] It is narrated that he survived this battle and took part in many more, and in fact it was he who dealt the final blow to Musaylamah the Liar.[936]

It is reported in Ṣaḥīḥ Muslim that during the Battle of Uḥud seven Anṣārī Companions ؓ died protecting the Prophet ﷺ from a focused onslaught of polytheist attacks.[937]

Even the women amongst the Companions ؓ were able to pass this test. Nusaybah bint Kaʿb ؓ, known as Umm ʿAmmārah, participated as a field medic on that day,[938] providing water to the warriors, carrying away the martyrs, and tending to the wounded. But the biggest test came when she sighted

---

[933] Ṣaḥīḥ Muslim 2470.
[934] The Sunnah style of turban worn by Muslims.
[935] Zurqānī, vol. 2: p. 43.
[936] Ṣaḥīḥ al-Bukhārī 4072.
[937] Ṣaḥīḥ Muslim 1789.
[938] At this time the order to observe the hijab had not been revealed, and thus the women participated in this way. Umm Salīṭ, Umm Sulaym, and Umm al-Muʾminīn ʿĀʾishah ؓ are also cited in Ṣaḥīḥ al-Bukhārī as carrying out this role.

ʿAbdullāh ibn Qumayyah, a polytheist and a famed wrestler of the Quraysh, launching an attack upon the Prophet ﷺ. He ﷺ was already wounded from several stones that had been thrown at him ﷺ, having lost a lower tooth and bleeding from the forehead. ʿAbdullāh ibn Qumayyah struck the Prophet's blessed face with such force that two links from his armour were buried in his cheek. Nusaybah rushed forward and engaged the much larger Ibn Qumayyah and, being a swordswoman of note, defended the Prophet ﷺ from Ibn Qumayyah's attacks. She suffered a deep wound to her shoulder during the fight, yet fought on and even *pressed forward*. She herself says, 'I pressed ahead and attacked Ibn Qumayyah, but the enemy of Allah was clad in two layers of armour.'[939]

The Companions ﷺ are like the stars, and we are but parasites on the Earth. May Allah ﷻ be pleased with each and every one of them, and give us a portion of their sense of duty and self-sacrifice. They truly were the best generation.

[939] *Al-Bidāyah wa al-Nihāyah,* vol. 4, p. 34.

38
He Displays Masculine Qualities

عَنِ ابْنِ عَبَّاسٍ رَضِيَ اللهُ عَنْهُمَا، قَالَ: "إِنَّمَا سَعَى رَسُولُ اللَّهِ صَلَّى اللَّهُ عَلَيْهِ وَسَلَّمَ بِالْبَيْتِ وَبَيْنَ الصَّفَا وَالْمَرْوَةِ لِيُرِيَ الْمُشْرِكِينَ قُوَّتَهُ."

Ibn 'Abbās ﵁ said, 'The Messenger of Allah ﷺ marched as he ﷺ performed ṭawāf[940] *of the House and during the sa'ī*[941] *between Ṣafā and Marwah in order to demonstrate his strength to the polytheists.'*[942]

BRAVADO AND AVOIDING ARROGANCE

Arrogance and pride are not the attributes of men. They are observed in people of poor stock and low minds, namely those who flaunt the gifts they are given and deem themselves to be superior to others because of them. The Prophet ﷺ said, 'He who intentionally lets the people hear of his good deeds to win their praise will have Allah ﷻ let the people know his true intention. And Allah ﷻ will disclose the real intention of the one who does good publicly to show off.'[943]

The Prophet ﷺ also said:

> *The first of men whose matter will be decided on the Day of Resurrection will be a man who apparently died as a martyr. He shall be brought forth. Allah will make him recount His blessings and he will recount them. Allah will*

---

[940] Circumambulation.
[941] Moving between one place and another.
[942] *Ṣaḥīḥ al-Bukhārī* 1649.
[943] *Ṣaḥīḥ al-Bukhārī* 6499.

then say, 'What did you do with these blessings?' The man will say, 'I fought for Your cause until I was martyred.' Allah will say, 'You lie. You fought so that you might be called a courageous warrior, and you were called so.' Allah will pass the order and he will be dragged face-down and cast into the Fire.

Then a man will be brought forward who acquired knowledge, distributed it to others, and recited the Qur'an. Allah will make him recount His blessings and he will recount them. Allah will ask, 'What did you do with these blessings?' The man will say, 'I acquired knowledge and disseminated it to others, and recited the Qur'an, seeking Your pleasure.' Allah will say, 'You lie. You acquired knowledge so that you might be called a scholar, and recited the Qur'an so that you might be called a qārī', and such has been said.' Allah will pass the order and he will be dragged face-down and cast into the Fire.

Then a man will be brought forth whom Allah had made abundantly rich and granted every kind of wealth. Allah will make him recount His blessings and he will recount them. Allah will ask, 'What have you done with these blessings?' The man will say, 'I did not leave a cause You wished for me to support except that I supported it.' Allah will say, 'You lie. You did this to be called a generous man, and so it was said.' Allah will pass the order and he will be dragged face-down and cast into the Fire.[944]

Actions are judged according to their intentions,[945] and thus

[944] *Ṣaḥīḥ Muslim* 1905a.
[945] *Sunan al-Nasā'ī* 3794.

the man that does good deeds to be known as 'good' will be exclusively rewarded with what he desires. Arrogance and pride deserve nothing more. A man should check his intention at every step to ensure he does not fall into the trap of Shayṭān, which can unfortunately convert the greatest deeds into sins by marring them with the mark of pride.

Yet proudness and arrogance should not be confused with bravado, which is the act of showing boldness and strength to impress or intimidate an opponent. It can be used both as an intimidation technique prior to a fight or as a deterrent to avoid a fight altogether. Both are legitimate uses of bravado, and men should have the ability to employ it when they need to.

We can see how the Prophet ﷺ utilised bravado as a deterrent for the polytheists when the Muslims went to Mecca to complete their outstanding ʿUmrah, bearing one arm to show their strength and marching around the Kaʿbah at a fast pace.

In this regard, Ibn ʿAbbās narrated: 'The Prophet ﷺ hastened in circumambulating the Kaʿbah and moving between Ṣafā and Marwah to show the pagans his ﷺ strength.' Ibn ʿAbbās added, 'When the Prophet ﷺ arrived in Mecca in the year of peace,[946] he ordered his Companions to do a fast march to show their strength to the polytheists, who were watching them from Mount Quʿayqʿān.'[947] Ibn ʿAbbās also reported that the Messenger of Allah ﷺ observed *saʿī* and marched rapidly around the House to show his strength to the polytheists.'[948]

---

[946] The year following the Treaty of al-Ḥudaybiyyah, when the Muslims were allowed to return to Mecca as part of the agreement.

[947] *Ṣaḥīḥ al-Bukhārī* 4257.

[948] *Ṣaḥīḥ Muslim* 1266.

Jābir ﷺ also narrated: 'The Prophet ﷺ performed a fast march from the Black Stone to the Black Stone for three circuits, and he walked for four.'[949]

Bravado is a route to winning a conflict before the contest even commences. Sun Tzu said:

To win one hundred victories in one hundred battles is not the pinnacle of skill. To subdue the enemy without fighting is the pinnacle of skill.

Bravado can also be used to intimidate one's opponent. The Hadith mentioned earlier where Amīr al-Mu'minīn ʿAlī ﷺ fought the champion of Khaybar[950] is a classic example of warriors using the technique to intimidate their opponents.

What greater example of this can be found than in the case of Abū Dujānah ﷺ, the Companion who was granted the sword of the Prophet ﷺ before the Battle of Uḥud, and who was renowned for his fearlessness, gallantry, and skill as a swordsman? Before a battle commenced, he would tie his famed red *ʿimāmah*, symbolising an intention to slay or be slain, and then he would prowl in front of the ranks of the Muslims, eyeing his enemies to intimidate them. At Uḥud, as he stalked up and down the ranks and with his eyes fixed on his foes across no man's land, he roared:

أَنَا الَّذِي عَاهَدَنِي خَلِيلِي| وَنَحْنُ بِالسَّفْحِ لَدَى النَّخِيلِ

أَلَّا أَقُومَ الدَّهْرَ فِي الْكَيُّولِ| أَضْرِبْ بِسَيْفِ اللَّهِ وَالرَّسُولِ

My friend did take an oath from me,

At Uḥud's foot beneath the trees,

---

[949] *Jāmiʿ al-Tirmidhī* 857.

[950] *Ṣaḥīḥ Muslim* 1807a.

To tarry not in ranks and stand,

But strike with God and Aḥmad's brand.

When the Prophet ﷺ saw Abū Dujānah's swagger, he ﷺ said, 'Allah ﷻ abhors such a gait, except on such occasions.'[951] Showing strength and courage prior to a battle to intimidate the enemy and show pride for Allah ﷻ and His Prophet ﷺ is a worthy action, whereas the same action in any other context would be abhorred by Allah ﷻ. Abū Dujānah ؓ was also a man who backed up his words, cutting great swathes in the enemy ranks with the sword of the Prophet ﷺ in hand. When he came upon Hind bint ʿUtbah ؓ, the wife of Abū Sufyān ؓ and the mother of Muʿāwiyah ؓ, she screamed for help yet no one came to her aid. Abū Dujānah ؓ spared her. Concerning the incident, Abū Dujānah ؓ later said, 'At that time I felt it was wrong to use the Prophet's blade on a vulnerable and helpless woman.'[952]

Bravado is a display of the outward qualities of manliness and masculinity that have been thus described in this work, and its opposite is the open display of effeminate behaviour.

MASCULINITY IN OPPOSITION TO EFFEMINACY

The inherent masculinity of all men stands in direct opposition to the effeminacy adopted by some sectors of society. Over recent years, Western liberalism has attempted to remove all boundaries and 'liberate' humanity from every possible categorisation, with the idea of humanity itself becoming a question for some. In a godless society, there are no *ḥudūd* (outer limits), just ideas that must be taken to their (un)natural

---

951 *Sīrah al-Muṣṭafā* vol. 2, p. 221.

952 *Al-Bidāyah wa al-Nihāyah,* vol. 4, p. 16.

conclusions. Every idea that is generated in such a society is another Pandora's Box,[953] unleashing upon the world further moral bankruptcy and sin. From amongst these ideas is the claimed toxicity of masculinity and masculine behaviour (*al-murū'ah*), the destruction of patriarchy and - as a natural effect - *qiwāmah* as a whole, and, more recently, the rejection of gender as a fixed binary concept.

Islam is very clear on the need for society to hold fast to the basic communal concepts that shape human civilisation together: heterosexuality, the family unit, defined gender roles, and the Oneness of Allah ﷻ, to name a few. The Prophet ﷺ clearly guided us toward the rejection and avoidance of effeminate behaviour in men, and masculine behaviour in women. In fact, Ibn ʿAbbās ؓ said, 'The Messenger of Allah ﷺ cursed men who behave effeminately and women whose behaviour is masculine',[954] and he also narrated several other Hadiths to the same effect. In one of these narrations touching on the same theme, he ﷺ ordered people to 'Put them out of your homes.'[955] In another, it is related: 'The Prophet ﷺ turned out such-and-such a man, and ʿUmar turned out such-and-such a woman on account of their behaviour.'[956]

In fact, accusing someone of being an effeminate man without proof is in itself abhorrent behaviour, and as such it is a punishable offence in Islamic law. The Prophet ﷺ said, 'If a man says to another, "O effeminate one!" give him 20 lashes; if one man says to another, "O homosexual!", give him 20 lashes.'[957] In

[953] An item from Greek mythology which, once opened, unleashed unexpected troubles and curses upon mankind.
[954] *Jāmiʿ al-Tirmidhī* 2785.
[955] *Sunan Abī Dāwūd* 4930.
[956] *Ṣaḥīḥ al-Bukhārī* 5886.
[957] *Sunan Ibn Mājah* 2568.

another narration, he ﷺ said, 'If a man says, "O effeminate one!", then hit him 20 times.'[958] Abū Hurayrah ؓ reported: 'An effeminate man who had dyed his hands and feet with henna was brought to the Prophet ﷺ. He ﷺ asked, "What is the matter with him?" He ﷺ was told, "Messenger of Allah, he imitates the appearance of women." So he ﷺ issued an order and the effeminate man was banished to al-Naqīʿ.'[959]

In fact, following such a man in prayer, even if he fulfils all requirements of leading the prayer, has the most knowledge, and knows the most Qur'an, should still be avoided. Imam al-Zuhrī ؒ said, 'In our opinion one should not offer prayer behind an effeminate person unless there is no alternative.'[960]

Effeminacy is not merely relevant to the outward trappings of gender and sex, but also to behaviour itself. For such a behavioural disposition in men leads to a society that strives for ease and comfort over all other endeavours, creating an unprepared society without positive ambition. In his definitive book on military strategy entitled *On War*, the renowned 19th century Prussian general Claus von Clausewitz wrote:

> *Now in our days there is not any other means of educating the spirit of a people in this respect, except by War, and that too under bold Generals. By it alone can that effeminacy of feeling be counteracted, that propensity to seek for the enjoyment of comfort, which caused degeneracy in a people rising in prosperity and immersed in an extremely busy commerce. A Nation can*

---

[958] *Jāmiʿ al-Tirmidhī* 1462.
[959] *Sunan Abī Dāwūd* 4928. Abū Usāmah said, 'Al-Naqīʿ is a region near Medina, and not Baqīʿ.'
[960] *Ṣaḥīḥ al-Bukhārī* 695.

> *hope to have a strong position in the political world only if its character and practice in actual War mutually support each other in constant reciprocal action.*[961]

Masculinity encourages preparedness and self-improvement in men. Society cannot function without masculine men who are as virtuous in peace as they are in war, and feminine women to temper their steel and bring them tranquillity. Any deviation from these *fiṭrah*-based societal norms will result in weakness and catastrophe.

[961] *On War*, Claus von Clausewitz, p. 170.

39
He is Confident

عَنْ جَابِرِ بْنِ عَبْدِ اللَّهِ رَضِيَ اللهُ عَنْهُما، قَالَ: غَزَوْنَا مَعَ رَسُولِ اللهِ صَلَّى اللهُ عَلَيْهِ وَسَلَّمَ غَزْوَةَ نَجْدٍ، فَلَمَّا أَدْرَكَتْهُ الْقَائِلَةُ وَهُوَ فِي وَادٍ كَثِيرِ الْعِضَاهِ، فَنَزَلَ تَحْتَ شَجَرَةٍ وَاسْتَظَلَّ بِهَا وَعَلَّقَ سَيْفَهُ، فَتَفَرَّقَ النَّاسُ فِي الشَّجَرِ يَسْتَظِلُّونَ، وَبَيْنَا نَحْنُ كَذَلِكَ إِذْ دَعَانَا رَسُولُ اللَّهِ صَلَّى اللَّهُ عَلَيْهِ وَسَلَّمَ فَجِئْنَا، فَإِذَا أَعْرَابِيٌّ قَاعِدٌ بَيْنَ يَدَيْهِ، فَقَالَ: "إِنَّ هَذَا أَتَانِي وَأَنَا نَائِمٌ، فَاخْتَرَطَ سَيْفِي فَاسْتَيْقَظْتُ، وَهُوَ قَائِمٌ عَلَى رَأْسِي، مُخْتَرِطٌ صَلْتًا، قَالَ 'مَنْ يَمْنَعُكَ مِنِّي؟' قُلْتُ 'اللَّهُ.' فَشَامَهُ، ثُمَّ قَعَدَ، فَهُوَ هَذَا." قَالَ: وَلَمْ يُعَاقِبْهُ رَسُولُ اللَّهِ صَلَّى اللَّهُ عَلَيْهِ وَسَلَّمَ.

Jābir ibn ʿAbdullāh ﷺ narrated, 'We took part in the Battle of Najd along with the Messenger of Allah ﷺ and the time for the afternoon rest approached while he ﷺ was in a valley with plenty of thorny trees. He ﷺ dismounted under a tree and rested in its shade, hanging his sword on it. The people dispersed amongst the trees to benefit from the shade. While we were in this state, the Messenger of Allah ﷺ called us and we went to him. We found a Bedouin sitting in front of him. The Prophet ﷺ said, "This man came to me while I slept and took my sword stealthily. I woke up as he stood by my head, holding my sword unsheathed. He said, 'Who will save you from me?' I replied, 'Allah.' So he sheathed the sword and sat down, and here he is." The Messenger of Allah ﷺ did not punish him.'[962]

Confidence

The abovementioned Hadith highlights two further qualities a man should have: confidence and initiative. The Bedouin who sneaked into the Muslim camp as they slept, and managed to not only reach the Prophet ﷺ, but take his sword and position himself in preparation to assassinate him clearly showed the quality of initiative. However, in response the Prophet

---

[962] *Ṣaḥīḥ al-Bukhārī* 4139.

ﷺ showed pure confidence in his own safety, despite the perilous nature of the situation. We will firstly look at confidence and then initiative.

Confidence is the sentiment of trust and belief in yourself or someone else. A man should have complete confidence in his ability to handle any situation, based upon his trust in Allah ﷻ. Look at how calmly and confidently the Prophet ﷺ reacted to the Bedouin's assassination attempt. How could he ﷺ not be confident, when he ﷺ was provided a guarantee of safety from Allah ﷻ in the Qur'an?

وَٱللَّهُ يَعۡصِمُكَ مِنَ ٱلنَّاسِۗ

Allah shall protect you from the people.[963]

The above verse was revealed whilst the Prophet ﷺ was on a military campaign. Prior to the revelation of this verse, a guard would stand outside his tent as a deterrent against polytheist assassins.[964] When Allah ﷻ revealed the above verse to him, the Mother of the Believers ʿĀ'ishah ﵂ reported: 'The Prophet ﷺ was being guarded until this verse was revealed: "*Allah shall protect you from the people.*" So the Messenger of Allah ﷺ stuck his head out from the tent, and said, "O you guards, leave, for Allah ﷻ will protect me."'[965]

What need did the Prophet ﷺ have for a guard when Allah ﷻ had promised him protection? Even when he was alone with an assassin who held a sword above his neck, the Prophet ﷺ was not perturbed in the least. Allah ﷻ placed awe in the heart of the

[963] *Qur'an* 5:67.
[964] *Tafsīr Ibn Kathīr* 5:67.
[965] *Jāmiʿ al-Tirmidhī* 3046.

Bedouin and all he could do was replace the sword and sit in the Prophet's presence.

A Muslim man should be confident in his actions, his decisions, and in the will of Allah ﷻ. Anas ibn Mālik ؓ said, 'When he ﷺ walked, he used to stride confidently.'[966]

Jābir ibn ʿAbdullāh ؓ said, 'The Messenger of Allah ﷺ took a man who was suffering from tuberculoid leprosy by the hand. He then placed it along with his own hand in the dish and said, "Eat with confidence in Allah ﷻ and trust in Him."'[967]

Every action he ﷺ did, and every word he ﷺ spoke, was with complete confidence and trust in Allah ﷻ, as illustrated in the following verse:

إِلَّا تَنصُرُوهُ فَقَدْ نَصَرَهُ ٱللَّهُ إِذْ أَخْرَجَهُ ٱلَّذِينَ كَفَرُوا۟ ثَانِىَ ٱثْنَيْنِ إِذْ هُمَا فِى ٱلْغَارِ إِذْ يَقُولُ لِصَـٰحِبِهِۦ لَا تَحْزَنْ إِنَّ ٱللَّهَ مَعَنَا ۖ فَأَنزَلَ ٱللَّهُ سَكِينَتَهُۥ عَلَيْهِ وَأَيَّدَهُۥ بِجُنُودٍ لَّمْ تَرَوْهَا وَجَعَلَ كَلِمَةَ ٱلَّذِينَ كَفَرُوا۟ ٱلسُّفْلَىٰ ۗ وَكَلِمَةُ ٱللَّهِ هِىَ ٱلْعُلْيَا ۗ وَٱللَّهُ عَزِيزٌ حَكِيمٌ

If you do not help him, it makes no difference to the Prophet, because Allah has already helped him when the disbelievers expelled him, and he was the second of the two, when they were in the cave, and he was saying to his companion, "Do not grieve. Allah is surely with us." Thus, Allah caused His tranquillity to descend on him, supported him with troops that you did not see, and rendered the word of the disbelievers humiliated. And the word of Allah is the uppermost. Allah is Mighty, Wise.[968]

This verse was revealed in relation to a major incident during the migration to Medina. When the Prophet ﷺ and Abū Bakr

966 *Al-Shamāʾil al-Muḥammadiyyah* 2.

967 *Sunan Abī Dāwūd* 3925.

968 *Qur'an* 9:40.

were seeking refuge in the Cave of Thawr, the Qurayshī patrols came and stood right outside of the cave; all they had to do was look down and they would find them. Abū Bakr himself narrates, 'While I was in the cave, I said to the Prophet ﷺ, "If any of them should look under his feet, he would see us." He ﷺ said, "O Abū Bakr, what do you think of the two, the third of whom is Allah?"'[969]

Such a firm response illustrates complete confidence in Allah ﷻ. Even with the enemy only feet away from them, the Prophet ﷺ had no fear of them.

INITIATIVE

Initiative involves knowing what must be done and doing it without any external stimulus; it is acting and taking charge of a situation before others do. A man should be able to assess a situation and make decisions decisively by weighing the prospective risks, rewards, advantages, and disadvantages of a choice and making a determination before others are prepared to do so. Salamah ibn al-Akwaʿ ﷺ narrates:

> When we and the people of Mecca had concluded a peace treaty and the people of one side began to mix with those of the other, I came to a tree, swept away its thorns, and lay down at its base. As I lay there, four Meccan polytheists came to me and began to talk ill of the Messenger of Allah ﷺ. Enraged by them, I moved to another tree. They hung up their weapons on the tree and lay down. Someone from the lower part of the valley cried out, 'O Muhājirīn! Ibn Zunaym has been murdered!' I drew my sword and approached the four

---

[969] Ṣaḥīḥ al-Bukhārī 3653.

> *polytheists while they slept. I seized their arms, collecting them up in my hand, and said, 'By the One Who has conferred honour upon Muhammad ﷺ, if even one of you raises his head I will smite his face.'*
>
> *I drove them to the Prophet ﷺ. My uncle ʿĀmir also came, bringing a man from ʿAbalāt called Mikraz on a horse with a thick covering on its back, along with seventy polytheists. The Messenger of Allah ﷺ cast a glance at them and said, 'Let them go, for they may prove guilty of breach of trust more than once before we take action.' So the Messenger of Allah ﷺ forgave them. On this occasion, Allah revealed the Quranic verse: "And He is the One Who restrained their hands from you and your hands from them in the valley of Mecca after He had let you prevail over them, and Allah is watchful over what you do."*[970][971]

Salamah ibn al-Akwaʿ ﵁, who would still be considered a child in today's environment, perfectly displayed the ability to assess and act decisively. When the polytheists were speaking ill of the Prophet ﷺ he was enraged, and yet he weighed the situation, realising that they had the advantage and that the peace treaty that had just been signed would be jeopardised by any rash action.

When he heard that Ibn Zunaym ﵁ had been murdered, he made a swift assessment and decided to capture the four men by the tree in case the allegation proved true and there was to be bloodshed. He took the initiative and disarmed them as they

[970] *Qur'an* 48:24.

[971] *Ṣaḥīḥ Muslim* 1807a.

slept, capturing them without incident.

Taking initiative also involves taking advantage of the finite resources you have and benefitting from them. Allah ﷻ says:

أُوْلَـٰٓئِكَ يُسَـٰرِعُونَ فِى ٱلْخَيْرَٰتِ وَهُمْ لَهَا سَـٰبِقُونَ.

Those people are accelerating towards the real good things, and they are the foremost to attain them.[972]

A man should drive himself and those he loves towards good, taking advantage of the blessings of Allah ﷻ while he has access to them. There is no greater example of taking initiative than that of the man who uses the strength he has been given to help others at their times of need, uses the wealth he has been given to feed the needy, or spends the time he has been given in self-improvement and the worship of Allah ﷻ.

Be mindful of the narration where Ibn ʿAbbās ﷺ reported that the Messenger of Allah ﷺ said, 'Take advantage of five before five: your youth before your old age, your health before your illness, your wealth before your poverty, your free time before your busyness, and your life before your death.'[973]

---

[972] *Qur'an* 23:61.

[973] *Shuʿab al-Īmān* 9767.

40

He is Prepared to Die

عَنْ أَبِي هُرَيْرَةَ رَضِيَ اللهُ عَنْهُ، قَالَ: قَالَ رَسُولُ اللَّهِ صَلَّى اللَّهُ عَلَيْهِ وَسَلَّمَ: "أَكْثِرُوا ذِكْرَ هَاذِمِ اللَّذَّاتِ، يَعْنِي الْمَوْتَ."

Abū Hurayrah ﵁ narrated: 'The Messenger of Allah ﷺ said, "Frequently remember the severer of pleasures: death."'[974]

REMEMBERING DEATH AND PREPARING FOR DEATH

It is a word we speak in hushed tones; it instils fear in the hearts of the most courageous men; it is a thought that comes to us unbidden and we desperately push it from our minds as if the thought alone will bring it about, and ignoring it will give us more time. *Death.* We have spoken of courage and confidence, fitness and fighting ability, as well as timekeeping, wisdom, and preparedness. And yet when we come to the end, still we baulk and falter.

كُلُّ نَفْسٍ ذَآئِقَةُ ٱلْمَوْتِ

Every soul has to taste death.[975]

Whether we run from it, hide from it, or pretend it will never come to our door, death will arrive. It will take your closest loved ones and your guardianship of your household will not be able to stop it, and it will challenge you with health issues and close calls, whereby only Allah's will can keep you alive.

Death is the one inevitability of life, the only certainty that all men, Muslim or not, must accept. However, a Muslim man must be ready to meet death when it comes. He must have prepared

---

[974] *Jāmiʿ al-Tirmidhī* 2307; *Sunan Ibn Mājah* 4258.
[975] *Qur'an* 3:185.

for it, be ready to face it, and even embrace it. Every Hadith quoted in this book, every word composed, and every argument formulated has led to this last great Truth: the man who internalises the lessons taught to us by our beloved Prophet ﷺ is ready to die, and the one who has not is spiritually unprepared. For the untrained man, death will always arrive too soon.

Chidiock Tichborne wrote a poem that encapsulates this concept as he sat in his cell in the Tower of London, awaiting execution for the crime of high treason at only 28 years of age:

My tale was heard, and yet it was not told,

My fruit is fallen, and yet my leaves are green,

My youth is spent, and yet I am not old,

I saw the world, and yet I was not seen:

My thread is cut, and yet it is not spun,

And now I live, and now my life is done.[976]

A Muslim is acutely aware of death. He cannot look upon its face and not reflect on his own coming demise. We must be aware of its constant presence. We are in a perpetual state of being given life; each second on this Earth is a gift from Allah ﷻ that we should be grateful for and appreciate. We should not allow ourselves to be distracted from this fact by the hopes we have in this life. *When I get this promotion, I will do such and such. When we get a bigger house, we will have more children. When I am earning this much money, I will be happy.* We allow our hopes to distract us from having an awareness of our coming deaths, but these hopes are only illusions, platonic shadows on the wall that will dance before our eyes until they fade away and we are left with the most terrifying of truths: death was always

[976] *Elegy for Himself*, Chidiock Tichborne.

standing right behind you, and from death there is no escape.

The Prophet ﷺ said, 'The wise man is the one who takes account of himself and strives for what follows after death. The helpless man is the one who follows his whims, and then engages in wishful thinking about Allah ﷻ.'[977]

Furthermore, Anas ibn Mālik رضي الله عنه narrated: 'The Prophet ﷺ drew a few lines and said, "This is man's hope, and this is the instant of his death. And while he is in this state of hope, death comes to him."'[978]

Life is but a handful of moments in time, and time is the most valuable currency we have to spend. The Prophet ﷺ reminded his Companions رضي الله عنهم of this fact constantly. ʿAbdullāh ibn ʿUmar رضي الله عنهما narrated, 'Once the Prophet ﷺ led us in the ʿIshā' prayer during the last days of his life. After finishing it, he ﷺ said, "Do you realise the importance of this night? No one present on the surface of the Earth tonight will be alive one hundred years from now."'[979]

He ﷺ was not only prepared for his own death, but he ﷺ prepared his Companions رضي الله عنهم for it as well. Ibn ʿUmar رضي الله عنهما said, 'I was with the Messenger of Allah ﷺ when a man from the Anṣār came to him and greeted the Prophet ﷺ with *salām*. The Anṣārī asked, "O Messenger of Allah, which of the believers is best?" He ﷺ said, "The one who has the best manners among them." The Anṣārī then asked, "Which of them is wisest?" He ﷺ replied, "The one who most remembers death and is best

---

[977] *Sunan Ibn Mājah* 4260.
[978] *Ṣaḥīḥ al-Bukhārī* 6418.
[979] *Ṣaḥīḥ al-Bukhārī* 116.

prepared for it. Such are the wisest.'"[980] He ﷺ also said, 'O followers of Muhammad! If you knew what I know, you would laugh less and weep more!'[981]

There can be no greater wisdom than this. The man who remembers death frequently and prepares himself for its coming is truly wise, because all the other preparations he makes are futile in the face of it. Death comes like a storm, and all our hopes and dreams are like dust to be blown away by it.

ʿAbdullāh Ibn ʿUmar ﷺ said, 'The Messenger of Allah ﷺ took hold of my shoulder and said, "Be in this world as if you were a stranger or a wayfarer."'[982] Ibn ʿUmar ﷺ himself used to say, 'If you survive until the evening, do not expect to be alive in the morning; if you survive until the morning, do not expect to be alive in the evening. Take from your health for your sickness, and take from your life for your death.'[983]

The Mother of the Believers ʿĀ'ishah ﷺ narrated:

> *When the Prophet ﷺ was healthy, he used to say, 'No Prophet's soul is taken until he is shown his place in Paradise and then he is given the option.' When death approached him while his head was on my lap, he became unconscious and then recovered his consciousness. He then looked at the ceiling of the house and said, 'O Allah, with the Highest Companions!' I said to myself, 'He is not going to choose us', and I realised that this is what he ﷺ had said to us when he was healthy. The last words he spoke were, 'O Allah, with the Highest*

---

[980] *Sunan Ibn Mājah* 4259.
[981] *Ṣaḥīḥ al-Bukhārī* 5221.
[982] *Ṣaḥīḥ al-Bukhārī* 6416.
[983] *Ṣaḥīḥ al-Bukhārī* 6416.

Companions!'[984]

Ṣallallāhu ʿalayhi wa sallam. Who were the Highest Companions he ﷺ spoke of? Allah ﷻ has named them in the Qur'an:

وَمَن يُطِعِ ٱللَّهَ وَٱلرَّسُولَ فَأُو۟لَـٰٓئِكَ مَعَ ٱلَّذِينَ أَنْعَمَ ٱللَّهُ عَلَيْهِم مِّنَ ٱلنَّبِيِّـۧنَ وَٱلصِّدِّيقِينَ وَٱلشُّهَدَآءِ وَٱلصَّـٰلِحِينَ ۚ وَحَسُنَ أُو۟لَـٰٓئِكَ رَفِيقًا

Those who obey Allah and the Messenger are with those whom Allah has blessed, namely, the Prophets, the ṣiddīqīn (paragons of the truth), the shuhadāʾ (martyrs), and the righteous. And how excellent are they as companions!

Such a blessed group includes the Prophets ﷺ, who confirmed the truth of their Prophethood, as well as the martyrs and the righteous. May Allah ﷻ make us from amongst them. *Āmīn.*

Although we should be aware of death, remember it constantly, and be prepared to meet it, we should not long for it nor desire it when going through hard times. The Prophet ﷺ said, 'None of you should wish for death due to a calamity that befalls him; but if he has to wish for death, he should say, "O Allah, keep me alive as long as life is better for me, and let me die if death is better for me."'[985]

Though there are times when death is better than living, life gives us the opportunity to prepare further for our deaths. Thus, we should cherish and appreciate the gift of life and spend it well, for when death comes, there will be no room for excuses. We should not, as those without faith say, live as we wish to be remembered, but instead we should live as we wish to be judged. The Prophet ﷺ said, 'Allah ﷻ will not accept the excuses of

[984] *Ṣaḥīḥ al-Bukhārī* 4463.
[985] *Ṣaḥīḥ al-Bukhārī* 5671.

anyone whose instant of death is delayed until he is sixty years of age.'[986]

Everything we do in life will be weighed and judged accordingly. Our deeds, our words, the food we ate, the wealth we spent, how we made others feel, what we used our blessings for...*everything*. Thus, our aim should be to leave the world with nothing to account for.

Abū Umāmah ﵁ narrated that the Prophet ﷺ said:

> *'Indeed the best of my friends to me is the one of meagre conditions, whose share is in ṣalāh, worshipping his Lord well, and obeying Him even in private. He is unknown among the people, such that the fingers of the people do not point towards him. His provisions merely consist of what is sufficient, and he is patient with that.' Then he ﷺ tapped his fingers and said, 'His death comes quickly, his mourners are few, and his inheritance is little.'*[987]

ʿAmr ibn al-Ḥārith ﵁ said, 'The Prophet ﷺ did not leave anything behind after his death, except his arms, white mule, and a piece of land at Khaybar which he left to be given in charity.'[988]

If we have lived well, death is a gift, and it will bring with it the greatest of rewards: eternal Paradise. ʿAbdullāh ibn ʿAmr ﵄ reported that the Messenger of Allah ﷺ said, 'The gift of a believer is death.'[989]

Death is permanent, and when it takes us our books of deeds will be closed and the pens of the Angels will be put away. The test will be over, the results will be counted, and we will have

---

[986] *Ṣaḥīḥ al-Bukhārī* 6419.
[987] *Jāmiʿ al-Tirmidhī* 2347.
[988] *Ṣaḥīḥ al-Bukhārī* 2912.
[989] *Mishkāt al-Maṣābīḥ* 1609.

either passed or failed. The Messenger of Allah ﷺ said:

> *Death will be brought on the Day of Resurrection and made to stand on the Ṣirāṭ (Bridge). It will be said, 'O people of Paradise!' And they will look up, anxious and afraid, lest they be brought out of the place they reside in. Then it will be said, 'O people of Hell!' And they will look up, hoping that they will be removed from the place they reside in. Then it will be said, 'Do you know what this is?' They will say, 'Yes, this is Death.' Then the Command will be given for it to be slaughtered on the Ṣirāṭ, and it will be said to both groups, 'Your residence is eternal, and there will never be any death.'*[990]

Death itself will die, and our final residence - whether Paradise or Hell - will be everlasting. We possess the agency to either look at our own deeds and decide to improve ourselves, or waste our time in this world and suffer the consequences of our inaction. Those of us who follow the Sunnah will be successful. Those who follow anything else will achieve nothing but ultimate failure.

---

[990] *Sunan Ibn Mājah* 4327.

5 | A FINAL WORD

Over the course of the preceding pages, it has become frighteningly apparent that the masculinity that was commonplace among the Companions ﷺ of the Prophet ﷺ has become regrettably absent in our lives. We waste our time in idle pursuits, we scoff at the Sunnah of our Prophet ﷺ, and we have allowed ourselves to become weak, childish, and effeminate men. We are poor in character, reliant on others, unable to engage with society correctly, and unprepared to deal with the antagonism that our way of life constantly faces. We are shadows of our former selves, looking up to those without shame, honour, or decency to teach us how to live our lives. As modern men, we are lacking in the fundamental masculinity of our ancestors, and so we seek answers from people that claim to have them, the alt-rights and the liberals, the neo-conservatives and the socialists, the secularists, the atheists, and all other forms of ideologies and -*isms.*

But the Perfect Man ﷺ has already laid out a clear path to fulfilment in this world and the Hereafter through the pure example he ﷺ set in his life, which is the most documented in all of history. When he ﷺ has influenced billions over one and a half millennia, who needs to follow the examples of the so-called influencers and rich men of the modern world?

To those who may argue that his Sunnah is a life of perfection which we cannot hope to follow completely, this could not be further from the truth. There are true men alive today that follow the Sunnah completely. We have met them. We have seen them. It is as possible today as it was all those years ago. His Sunnah is a complete, accessible, and simple way of life, with every question answered, and every doubt removed. We hope this short primer on the Sunnah of masculinity has started us all on the path to returning to his way.

Any mistakes in this text were entirely our own, and we pray for forgiveness for the weaknesses and faults we have in ourselves, whether apparent or otherwise. We hope one day to be worthy of the Prophet's Sunnah.

To close, we can only say what the Prophet ﷺ said at the end: the prayer we pray for ourselves, our parents, our wives, our children, our siblings, our relatives, and our friends, and for all of you, our dearest brothers:

O Allah, when all is said and done, join us with the Highest Companions!

اللَّهُمَّ الرَّفِيقَ الأَعْلَى

* * * تمّت * * *